NEVER SUBMIT

Will the Extermination of Christians Get Worse Before it Gets Better?

Lt. Col. Robert Maginnis

U.S. Army, Retired & Adviser to the Pentagon

DEFENDER

CRANE, MO

Defender Publishing Co.
Crane, MO, 65633
© 2015 by Bob Maginnis
All rights reserved. Published 2015.
Printed in the United States of America.

ISBN: 978-0-9904974-9-3

A CIP catalog record of this book is available from the Library of Congress.

Cover illustration and design by Daniel Wright: www.createdwright.com
Unless otherwise indicated, all Scripture quoted is from King James Version.

I gratefully acknowledge...

It is impossible to thank all of those who have been so generous with their time. But I would like to mention: Jan Maginnis, my loving wife of thirty-nine years, for her encouragement and Christian walk. She listens to my wild ideas and dreams, tolerating each inane proposition with a smile. I thank my friend Don Mercer, who constantly provided insights, important information, and skillful assistance in editing. I'm indebted to Terry James, a prolific author and biblical scholar, for his critical counsel and direction regarding biblical and Islamic eschatology. I'm especially indebted to the many Christian brothers and sisters on the front lines exposing and fighting Middle East genocide who shared their stories and insights.

Above all, I acknowledge my Heavenly Father, without whom this book could never have been written.

Robert Lee Maginnis
Woodbridge, Virginia

Dedicated to Jan Maginnis, my loving wife

CONTENTS

FOREWORD

Christians in the Middle East are fleeing their homes or dying at the hand of Islamists, creating the very real possibility of a successful faith-based holocaust. The implications of such an outcome for the region and the world are stark: a very fanatical militarized Islamist region that soon might be armed with nuclear weapons to threaten the world with atomic terrorism—and the same insidious conditions that promote Christian genocide there could spread to America. Reversing this very serious threat must be the top priority for Middle East governments and their populations, the so-called moderate Muslim world, Western governments already frightened by rising Islamist threats, and a genuine global response by Christians to rise up around a doctrine that combines moral, civic, and Christian virtue as the guiding light of future political and Christian social action in the Middle East.

This volume addresses the Islamist threat in five sections that build upon one another, beginning with a sobering view of the genocidal situation facing Christians in the Middle East. The reader will react in disgust and sadness, and perhaps will shed tears when reading about the gripping situation facing modern Christians in the very cradle of Christianity.

The blame for the Christian genocide rests squarely on the shoulders of the region's Islamists—orthodox Muslims who believe their faith gives them license to kill—as well as Islamic governments that refuse to defend innocent Christians, and the so-called moderate Muslim societies that silently stand by because many endorse a truthful, albeit violent, interpretation of Islamic literature. The first section is rounded out with two chapters that provide a glimpse of Islamic teachings with an emphasis on what Muslims are taught to believe about non-Muslims such as Christians. Only an understanding of these teachings helps make the current tragic situation in the Middle East begin to make sense.

Some of the best witnesses regarding the cruelty of Islam are Muslims who converted to Christianity. These people provide heart-wrenching accounts of life under the constant oppression of Islamic fundamentalists and explain the attraction they saw in Christians and their loving message that drew Muslims to Jesus Christ. Unfortunately, these former Muslims—and especially those still in the Middle East—are the most threatened of all Christians today, with many literally living with bounties on their heads (paid by their rejecting Muslim families) because of their Christian conversions.

The second section begins with a sobering rendition of the often-forgotten Christian genocide in the Middle East at the hands of the Ottoman Empire. Early in the twentieth century, millions of Armenian Christians faced a brutal holocaust at the hands of their government: death, exile, persecution, and the destruction of most every artifact associated with their ancient Christian culture.

A review of the circumstances of the Armenian holocaust sets the stage for a walk through eight universal conditions of genocide now facing Christians across the Middle East. Each of these conditions is present in most of the region's countries, and the growing avalanche of disaster facing Middle East Christians becomes all too self-evident; genocide is taking place and unless dramatic action is soon taken, the entire region will be cleansed of the followers of Jesus.

The third section demonstrates that Middle East governments,

Islamist extremist groups in particular, and complicit, "moderate" Muslim societies, along with many outsiders who ignore the inconvenient tragedy, share the blame for the Christian genocide. Specifically, the global Christian community and its governments are not doing enough to stop the genocide. In fact, President Barack Obama and his administration have perhaps the most Christian blood on their hands. Obama's Middle East policies have virtually damned fellow Christians to death, exile, or the most miserable existences under hopelessly oppressive Islamic regimes.

The fourth section explores the implications should the Middle East continue to move to a total Christian cleansing. Middle East Muslims will suffer the most, because the moderating effect of Christian citizenship in those societies will be gone and the fundamentalist Muslim ideology will then have freer opportunity to create an even more draconian life, perhaps one not seen since the seventh century under the Islamic Prophet Muhammad.

There are serious implications of such an outcome for the balance of the world as well. Does anyone really believe that if the Muslim fascists succeed in voiding the Middle East of Christians, the Islamic extremism will stop there? No, Muslim fascists will turn their knives to destroy Israel, and simultaneously infiltrate and incrementally take over the balance of the world (which has already started). The evidence of that strategy and the groundwork already laid is unveiled in this volume for all to see.

Such a frightening scenario will understandably draw snide remarks from naïve, politically correct Western skeptics and Islamic apologists. They will deny the obvious evidence, but for many who are concerned about the rising tide of violence, the undeniable Islamic agendas, and the suspicious avalanche of geopolitical catastrophes across the globe, many will inevitably begin to focus on end-times biblical prophecy for understanding.

There are plenty of clues in God's Word about the geopolitical clashes of culture and religion seen today, and on close examination, there are a host of indicators that suggest, yes, events today are building to an apocalyptic crescendo. It appears that the last days are rapidly approaching.

Those who see a nexus between end-times prophecy and current events will also appreciate that Islamic eschatology has some very interesting parallels with biblical prophecy. You will come to understand from this volume that the Islamic States' terrorists are motivated by an Islamic eschatology that justifies the merciless beheading of Christian children in Iraq and Syria believing that such barbarism will prompt the coming of their messiah and the emergence of Islam as king and their god as the ruler of the earth.

The final section in this volume presents a clarion call for people across the world to launch a campaign that not only saves Middle East Christians from genocide, but also saves the rest of the world from Islamic extremists. That campaign must be called "Never Submit," a response to Islam, defined as "submission," and to Islamists who give Middle East Christians three choices: leave, convert, or die.

The "Never Submit" campaign calls for Christian statesmen across the world, men and women made from the same mold as the late Dr. Martin Luther King Jr., a man who was a giant in his time and the epitome of the type of leader needed today.

Christian leaders like Dr. King are required across the globe to rise up and lead fellow believers and the community of nations in a righteous way to eliminate the threat posed by Islamic extremism and to call all people to include pragmatic Muslims to moral accountability and action. That call requires waging a real war with all the instruments of government and the spiritual participation of godly Christians to defeat the horrific evil posed by radicalized followers of Islam (Islamists).

American Christians must join that fight by first shedding their culturally imposed political correctness, and then answering the righteous call to engage their government—as did our nation's founders in their fight for freedom during the Revolutionary War. Unfortunately, even though America is the most powerful nation in the world in terms of tangible assets, it is evidently a weakling when it comes to the issue of fighting Christian genocide—and the American Christian church is equally feckless.

An effective "Never Submit" campaign against the spreading evil of Islamists requires herculean efforts by government, but also an awakening in the Christian church. Pastors across America and the West must stop myopically focusing on the deacon-like work of running their small businesses—the local church—and begin focusing on their spiritual calling to preach, teach, and lead their people in the fight. They must equip the body of Christ by making it aware of the crisis threatening all Christendom at the hands of Islam and steel their people for what is happening in their local communities.

Finally, the "Never Submit" campaign must go into high gear in American communities if we are to stop the steady drip, drip-like surrender to Islamists. Every aspect of our community life is already being slowly co-opted by Islamists: schools, colleges, our youth, the media, even our prisons—and sharia (Islamic) law is contaminating American law's constitutional supremacy as well. The situation is very serious, and far too few Americans understand the evil threat.

The answer to this threat, as many Muslim converts to Christianity across the world have come to realize, is spiritual rebirth. And as Franklin Graham, the president of the Billy Graham Evangelistic Organization, told this author, "God loves Muslims. Christ died for Muslims." Christ is the only answer to Islam's anger, Christian genocide, and the march of Islamization in the West.

It is past time for Christians, their communities, and God-fearing governments (if there are any left) to stand up against the cesspool of barbarism emerging from the Middle East, as well as the threats by Islamists seeking to drag the balance of the world into seventh-century submission.

Sometimes those who demonstrate the most courage in the face of evil are men and women who have suffered the most. One such "Never Submit" person is an obscure Iraqi Chaldean priest who was kidnapped and tortured by Islamic State terrorists and who now helps hundreds of families in war-torn Erbil, Iraq. In April 2015, that priest explained the challenge facing all Christians and responsible governments today: "It is not about the time to look back and mourn. It is about the time to stand up, continue and do. We are Christians not only for the good days but for the bad days as well. This shows who you really are."[1]

INTRODUCTION

The Islamic State of Iraq and the Syria (ISIS)[2] turned up and
they said to the [Christian] children, "You say the words [the *she-hada*, 'to convert to Islam'], that you will follow Muhammad."
And the children, all under 15, four of them, they said, "No, we
love Jesus [Yesua]. We have always loved Jesus. We have always
followed Jesus. Jesus has always been with us." They [ISIS] said,
"Say the words!" They [the children] said, "No, we can't." They
chopped all their heads off. How do you respond to that? You
just cry. They're my children. That is what we have been going
through. That is what we are going through.[3]

—The Reverend Canon Andrew White, "Vicar of Baghdad"

Christians are the most persecuted religious group on the planet,
and the situation in the Middle East today is especially bad
and will get much worse unless action is soon taken. Governments and military forces certainly have a role in taming Middle East-ern extremism, but just as important is the response of the Christian
world—individuals, local churches, and nongovernment Christian
organizations. That is why we need a kind of "William Wilberforce"
doctrine that combines moral, civic, and Christian virtue as the guiding
light of future political and Christian social action in the Middle East as
well as here in the United States.

William Wilberforce was an English politician and Christian leader of the movement to abolish the slave trade. His conversion to Christianity radically changed his lifestyle, which seeded within him a lifelong concern for reform. Thanks to this one man's tenacity to overcome many obstacles, his campaign led to the Slavery Abolition Act of 1833, which abolished slavery in most of the British Empire.

A Wilberforce-like, dogged determination must be undertaken to help the cradle of Christianity overcome religious extremism that threatens the very existence of Christ followers in that region. That determination must come from the collective effort of Christian communities, regional governments, and their people, as well as outside governments like the United States, if this tragic tide of history is to be reversed.

On average, one hundred thousand Christians are killed annually worldwide for reasons related to their faith, and in the Middle East, followers of Jesus Christ are the most vulnerable, facing the cruelest deaths imaginable: beheading, crucifixion, live burial, and burning alive. This tragic situation is amplified by the fact that virtually every Middle Eastern government and its Muslim-majority societies—from Egypt's Sinai Peninsula in the West to Iran's border with Afghanistan in the East, and from Turkey in the North to the Arabian Sea in the South— have created conditions that are ripe for a modern Christian holocaust, a term taken from the Greek ὁλόκαυστος *holókaustos*: *hólos*, "whole," and *kaustós*, "burnt," and known as the *Shoah*, which is Hebrew for "the catastrophe."[4]

The horrid state of affairs facing Christians in the Middle East isn't new, however. The region's Christian population decreased from 10 percent to 5 percent over the past century, but recently that decline has rapidly accelerated. In Syria, for example, the U.S. Department of State reports the Christian presence is becoming a "shadow of its former self."[5] After years of civil war, hundreds of thousands of Christians fled the country desperate to escape the sectarian violence. In the city of Homs, the number of Christians dwindled to as few as one thousand from approximately 160,000 prior to the conflict.[6]

The real possibility of a Christian holocaust across the Middle East is a view grudgingly shared by many knowledgeable people.

"It seems to me that we cannot ignore the fact that Christians in the Middle East are increasingly being deliberately targeted by fundamentalist Islamist militants," said Charles, Prince of Wales.[7] Fellow Britain, the archbishop of Canterbury, Rowan Williams, said, "The position of Christians in the region [the Middle East] is more vulnerable than it has been for centuries."[8]

A growing number of Islamist attacks exacerbates the already horrendous situation for Middle Eastern Christians who face nothing short of religious cleansing. "Massacres are taking place for no reason and without any justification against Christians. It is only because they are Christians. What is happening to Christians is genocide," said former Lebanese President Amine Gemayal.[9] Yet, Pope Francis I is determined to avoid stating what seems to be inevitable. "We will not resign ourselves to imagining a Middle East without Christians," he optimistically opined.[10] Certainly the pontiff understands that conditions today are very bad for Christians, and are getting worse.

President Barack Obama avoids acknowledging the obvious as well by fingering Islamic extremism for the escalating catastrophic threat to Middle Eastern Christians. "I don't quibble with labels. I think we all recognize that this is a particular problem that has roots in Muslim communities," he told CNN. "But I think we do ourselves a disservice in this fight if we are not taking into account the fact that the overwhelming majority of Muslims reject this ideology."[11]

Mr. President, your view about the Muslim majority is naïve. Based on polling, a significant part of all Muslims do accept the current grave situation, and the balance of that community, with few exceptions, remains deafeningly silent on the issue. If this were otherwise, Mr. President, at least some of the conditions that contribute to the dire situation for Christians and other non-Muslim minorities in Middle East would have been mitigated long ago.

Unfortunately, the stark anti-Christian conditions now pervasive across the Middle East are amplified by the extreme threat posed by a surge in Islamic extremism. Specifically, groups like ISIS (a terrorist group that conquered much of eastern Syria and northern Iraq in 2014), also known as Da'ish (DAESH, the group's Arabic name, is transliterated as *ad-Dawlah al-Islāmīyah fī al-'Irāq wash-Shām*), is only the latest Islamist manifestation to plague the region, and ISIS' radical anti-Christian actions could be around for a long time, thus solidifying a bleak future for the Christian population. That view is shared by U.S. Army General Martin Dempsey, the former chairman of the Joint Chiefs of Staff, who warned in January 2015: "I think this [ISIS] threat is probably a thirty-year issue."[12]

If true, General Dempsey's three-decade forecast could certainly spell the demise of the dwindling Middle East Christian population. It appears that time for Christians and other Middle Eastern religious minorities is running out in the wake of a surge in Islamist fascism complemented by a region chock-full of intolerant Islamic governments and their discriminating societies.

Why are Christians suffering to the point of extinction in the Middle East? Is the crisis really that dire?

A number of competing views may explain the Middle East crisis. One of the more popular views is especially controversial. Harvard professor Samuel Huntington asserts that Islam has "bloody borders" and predicts that the dynamics of civilizational conflict in the post-Cold War era will intensify the phenomenon. His notion of a "clash of civilizations" holds to three points: civilizations are defined by religion; conflicts involving Islamic civilization will be common and violent; and Islamic civilization will be the greatest threat to Western civilization.[13]

Huntington's theory is widely embraced, and as a result, has influenced Western government policies. Advocates of that theory argue that the clash between Islam and Christianity explains the Middle East conflicts that target minority Christian populations.

Another view that might explain the tragedy of anti-Christianism in the Middle East is the nexus of Islam and conflict.

Research suggests that Middle Eastern conflicts should be particularly frequent and intense because of religion's significant influence within those societies. Specifically, Islam tends to exacerbate ethnic conflict, feed discrimination, and dictate political behavior against minority faith groups like Christians. Further, Islam's influence at fostering such outcomes increases when it is married to supportive autocratic regimes, which is the case in every Middle Eastern country.

One such study is the analysis of the Minorities at Risk (MAR) dataset examining the nature of the Middle East's ethno-religious conflicts. MAR research, which considered 267 politically active ethnic minorities throughout the world, discovered that religious factors surface considerably more often in the Middle East than in other world regions. That dataset analysis led researchers to conclude that religion is more important in Middle Eastern conflicts than elsewhere, which means that while Islam, the region's dominant religion, may provide a partial explanation for the conflict, it cannot provide a full explanation.[14]

Perhaps the other ingredient that can explain Middle East conflicts and the associated violence against non-Muslims is the fact that the region is the most autocratic and least democratic in the world. That linkage, the Islamic faith and autocratic governments, may explain the propensity for conflict more because of cultural and historical momentum than anything else.

Proponents of this research conclude that somehow delinking Islam from autocratic governments will lead to a far less oppressive and discriminatory environment. U.S. President Barack Obama appears to be such a proponent, which might explain his attempt to re-engineer the Middle East discriminatory culture beginning with his June 2009 speech at Cairo University.

President Obama began his Cairo speech with "a greeting of peace from Muslim communities in my country: *assalaamu alaykum*" (greeting for Muslims meaning "peace be on you"). But that greeting was an indirect slap in the face to America's mostly (70.6 percent) self-identifying Christians who are left out of the president's vision for the Middle East.[15]

Then Obama used his speech to attack Huntington's theory about the Islamic threat for the West. "I know there are many—Muslim and non-Muslim—who question whether we can forge this new beginning.… Some suggest that it isn't worth the effort—that we are fated to disagree, and civilizations are doomed to clash."[16]

Unfortunately and naïvely, Obama's speech ignored the Middle East's ruinous history and sent a message of appeasement to Islamist objectives: The U.S. will respect and accept conservative forms of Islam, even those who reject Christians and support violence.

President Obama's appeasement message at Cairo and his hands-off policy over the subsequent years encouraged Islamic extremists, who seized the historic opportunity to grab power. Soon the entire region exploded with unrest, and the so-called Arab Spring fueled revolutions that toppled autocratic governments, led to civil war, and put every regional government on edge.

Long before Obama's speech and the emergence of the Arab Spring began to metastasize the cesspool of Islamist fascism across the Middle East, every regional country was already unwelcoming to non-Muslims. But now that Islamic extremists are unfettered, thus threatening to engulf every Middle Eastern state, the problem of Islamist extremism is on steroids, which is the *casus belli* for what is becoming a modern Christian holocaust in the faith's very cradle.

CHRISTIAN GENOCIDE, ISLAMIC TEACHING, & FORMER MUSLIMS

CHAPTER 1

"SQUEEZE" AND "SMASH"
MIDDLE EASTERN CHRISTIANS

Are These the End Times?

Christianity is trending toward extinction in the Middle East, and if that region and its people don't stop the slide soon, there will be no room for Christians in its cradle. Is this evidence of the end times?

Christians were one in four Middle Easterners at the turn of the twentieth century, and today they are less than 3 percent and their numbers are plummeting. Nina Shea, director of the Hudson Institute's Center for Religious Freedom, said Middle Eastern Christians face a "religious cleansing, a type of cultural genocide, which is a crime against humanity."[17]

This "cultural genocide" could well forebode something much worse. The January 2015 beheading of twenty-one Coptic Christians in Libya, one of many atrocities in a line by Islamic extremists, prompted the Reverend Franklin Graham, son of evangelist Reverend Billy Graham, to publish a Facebook post stating, "Can you imagine the outcry if twenty-one Muslims had been beheaded by Christians?… Where is the universal condemnation by Muslim leaders around the world?" Graham knew Muslims would remain silent. Then he soberly wrote: "We'd better take this warning seriously, as these acts of terror will only spread throughout Europe and the United States. If this concerns you like it does me, share this. The storm is coming!"[18]

Graham's "The storm is coming!" warning prompted one of his social media followers to respond that we are "seeing prophecy unfold before our very eyes. God help us!"

Catholic Church leadership is seeing the same horrendous treatment. Archbishop Francis Chullikat came to Capitol Hill on February 10, 2015, to deliver a stark message from Pope Francis to the U.S. Congress. The archbishop said:

> Flagrant and widespread persecution of Christians rages in the Middle East [forced displacement, destruction of their places of worship, rape, abduction of Christian leaders]…no Christian is exempt, whether or not he or she is Arab. Arab Christians…find themselves the target of constant harassment for no reason other than their religious faith.
>
> One of the most graphic illustrations of ongoing brutality confronting Arab Christians is the emergence of a so-called "tradition" of bombings of Catholic and other Christian houses of worship every Christmas eve, which has been going on now for the past several years. Will there be no end in sight for this senseless slaughter for those whom that very night proclaims the Prince of Peace in some of the oldest Christian communities in the world?[19]

The current anti-Christian persecution could be evidence of the end times. That's hard to know, but what is certain is that Jesus warned Christians in the Gospel of John that the world will hate them as it did Him. Christ said in John 15:18–25 (NKJV):

If the world hates you, you know that it hated me before it hated you.

If you were of the world, the world would love its own. Yet because you are not of the world, but I chose you out of the world, therefore the world hates you.

Remember the word that I said to you, "A servant is not greater than his master." If they persecuted me, they will also persecute you. If they kept my word, they will keep yours also.

But all these things they will do to you for my name's sake, because they do not know Him who sent Me.

If I had not come and spoken to them, they would have no sin, but now they have no excuse for their sin.

He who hates me hates My Father also.

If I had not done among them the works which no one else did, they would have no sin; but now they have seen and also hated both me and My Father.

But this happened that the word might be fulfilled which is written in their law, "They hated me without a cause."

Hatred of Christians is evident across the globe, and it does not appear that anything is being done to slow the anti-Christian persecution associated with the global hatred.

U.S. Representative Chris Smith, the New Jersey Republican who chairs the House Foreign Affairs Subcommittee on Global Human Rights, called the widespread persecution of Christians "a genocide." He went on to state, "It is a global phenomenon, but dramatically in the Mideast."[20]

The congressman said that no one is keeping a record of the evidence of the growing persecution that clearly threatens the very extinction of Christianity in the Mideast. No international body, much less the Obama administration, keeps official records of the back-to-back atrocities, the flood of refugees, and the mass emigration laying waste to

Middle Eastern Christendom. Why? We will address that later in this book. For now, consider the breadth of the problem.

Before the seventh- century Islamic conquest, Christians were the Middle East's majority population. As recently as 1910, Christians accounted for 13.6 percent of the region's population.[21] Now their numbers are falling toward zero as the remaining thousands flee the region and untold others are savagely murdered for their faith.

A 2012 Pew Research Center study considered patterns in global migration, which found that the main destination for Christian migrants has been North America and Europe. European countries account for more than four in ten (44 percent) of all Christian migrants, which includes those from the Middle East.[22]

Hundreds of thousands of Middle Eastern Christians have emigrated to the West in recent years to escape faith-based persecution. It is estimated that in the last seven years, at least 110,000 Iraqi refugees have come to the U.S. alone, of which about two-thirds are non-Muslim.[23] Large communities of Iraqi Chaldeans and Assyrians and Egyptian Coptic Christians are relocating to New Jersey, Michigan, California, Florida, and other states. Other Middle Eastern Christians flood communities across Western Europe, and more are waiting to emigrate to safety.

Christian immigration to the West comes in the wake of the devastating downsizing of Christian communities in major Middle Eastern states. In 2003, Syria's Christian minority made up nearly 10 percent of that country's population of twenty-two million, but today, nearly 70 percent are gone, either as refugees to neighboring countries, they emigrated to the West or are dead.[24]

Homs, Syria's third-largest city, provides an example of the Christian exit. In recent years, nearly the entire eighty thousand Christians who lived there were forcibly expelled, as were Christians from all nearby rural areas.[25] Such actions compelled Christian Solidarity International to issue a genocide alert for Syria's Christians and other endangered religious minorities.

In May 2013, Christian Solidarity International also issued a geno-cide alert for Coptic Orthodox Christians in Egypt. That report indi-cates that non-state actors, mostly Salafist extremists, acting with the tacit consent of the government, were creating conditions ripe for geno-cide. Those conditions included attacks on Christian communities and individuals, kidnapping, and driving Christians out of villages. "What we are seeing is a growing trend of 'cleansing society' of Christians," said Dr. Mariz Tadros, a research fellow with the Institute of Develop-ment Studies in the United Kingdom.[26] Many Copts fled the violence with some one hundred thousand Egyptian Copts now relocated to the U.S.[27]

A decade ago, Iraq's Christian population numbered 1.5 million, but today, less than 260,000 remain—and conditions are so bad for the remaining Christians that they may well leave in the near future.[28] For example, the Iraqi city of Mosul was once that country's center of Christian activity, but today, all Christians are largely gone, thanks to ISIS.

Millions of Syrian and Iraqi refugees now live in camps in Turkey, Lebanon, and Jordan, waiting to either emigrate to a better life likely in the West or return to their homes—a dwindling prospect. Large num-bers of those refugees are Christians who have given up hope of ever returning to their former homes.

Turkey claims to shelter nearly two million Syrian refugees; thou-sands of Christians are among them. But Turkey isn't a Christian-wel-coming country; it has seen its indigenous Christian population implode from 13 percent a century ago to as few as 150,000 out of a current population of seventy-two million.[29] Turkey has a long history of anti-Christian persecution, especially among the Armenians, a topic to be addressed later in this book.

For many Christians, emigration or seeking refuge in neighboring countries are the best alternatives compared to remaining to face almost certain death. And it's not just in Syria and Iraq; as Nina Shea explains, Christians across the region are killed for their faith by the thousands each year, and untold other thousands face physical assaults, maiming, rape, imprisonment, torture, kidnappings, banning, or thwarting of their religious practice.[30]

In fact, 2014 was the worst year for Christian persecution—more so than any other year in recent history. And, even though the regional competition is fierce, the Middle East earned first place to lead the world in Christian persecution.

Open Door, a California nonprofit organization, maintains a World Watch List of the top fifty nations that persecute Christians. Not surprisingly, the Middle East leads all other regions, with eleven nations on the list: Iraq (no. 3), Syria (no. 4), Iran (no. 7), Saudi Arabia (no. 12), Yemen (no. 14), Egypt (no. 23), Jordan (no. 30), Oman (no. 39), Turkey (no. 41), UAE (no. 49), and Kuwait (no. 50).[31]

Persecution is a complex reality that makes it difficult to blame specific factors on the pressure Christians face, according to Open Door. However, the organization's researchers found that communities and/or nations characterized by "brokenness" evidence the most persecution.

Middle Eastern countries score very high on the "watch list" of Open Doors USA, the largest network supporting persecuted Christians across the world, because of a combination of factors. Specifically, the Middle East is marked by a lot of tribalism, coupled with four persecution engines (Islamic extremism, religious militancy, tribal antagonism, and ecclesiastical arrogance), and these are driven by complicit autocratic governments and compliant societies.

Middle Eastern societies are especially good drivers for religion-based persecution, because the vast majority is Muslim and peppered with sub drivers such as fanatical movements, radical ethnic group leaders, and the dominance of non-Christian religious leadership at all levels of government and informal society.

Open Door applies these factors to distinguish two main expressions of persecution: "squeeze" and "smash." "Squeeze" is the pressure Christians experience in all areas of life, and "smash" is persecution Christians experience in the form of violence.

"SQUEEZE" THE CHRISTIANS

The Middle East's Muslim majority populations and their Islamic-based governments evidence considerable "squeeze" persecution for Christians.

The "squeeze" on Christians in Egypt is getting worse, according to Dr. Mona Roman, the Coptic Christian Bishop Agathon, in an Arabic satellite television interview. Dr. Roman said that the Egyptian State is often behind the persecution of and discrimination against Christians, such as Muslim abduction of young people, and when Christians provide evidence of the missing person, the state security [lost]...the documents and, according to Roman, "Absolutely nothing [is] done."[32]

The official "squeeze" comes in other ways. "We as Copts are human beings," the bishop said. Muslims can build their mosques, but "as for us, we cannot build anything and that which is already open is being closed.... We, the Copts, are citizens with rights; and we see Muslims get whatever they want, while we are always prevented."

"If anything, the plight of Egypt's Christians has gone 'from bad to worse,'" said the bishop. The cleric explained, "Copts are between a state anvil and aggressor [Islamic radicals] hammers" and they pound away.[33]

Iran's ultraconservative theocracy is among the worst persecutors of Christians. A Google search of media reports between January 2010 and September 2014 found sixty-nine incidents of Iranian government agents arresting citizens for Christian activities.[34] An analysis of other regional governments reveals persecution of Christians as well.

Iran's theocratic government persecutes Christians in a variety of ways—some of the persecution is very subtle through institutions and laws, and other examples of persecution are very overt.

For example, it is illegal for Muslims to convert to Christianity and it is equally illegal for Christians to evangelize. Consider what Iranian officials do to Christians in either instance.

- In February 2010, Reverend Wilson Issavi, sixty-five, was apprehended by Iranian police and then tortured, charged with "converting Muslims," and threatened with execution. He was detained for fifty-eight days.

- On February 28, 2010, Hamid Shafiee and Reyhaneh Aghajary were arrested by Iranian state security in Isfahan and charged with converting from Islam to Christianity. Aghajary was reportedly beaten, and both men have disappeared.

- On September 22, 2010, Pastor Yousef Nadarkhani, thirty-five, was arrested by Iranian government officials, charged, tried, and sentenced to death for apostasy.

- On December 26, 2010, Farshid Fathi, thirty-two, was arrested by Iranian government officials, held in solitary confinement, and subjected to psychological torture, then sentenced to six years of imprisonment for "religious propaganda."

- On March 17, 2011, Masoud Delijani was arrested by Iranian government officials for Christian evangelism. He was imprisoned and eventually convicted of evangelism and holding illegal church meetings.

- On May 5, 2014, Silas Rabbani was arrested by Iranian government agents and then tortured and imprisoned for apostasy—leading Muslims to Christ.

Iran has no tolerance for unauthorized Christian churches and their doctrines, either.

- On July 20, 2011, Leila Mohammadi was arrested by Iranian government officials and kept imprisoned for five months. Eventually, he was convicted of forming a house church and was sentenced to two years in prison.

- In December 2011, Alireza Seyedian was arrested by Iranian government officials who charged, tried, and sentenced him to six years in prison for being baptized.

- On April 7, 2012, the historic Christian graveyard at Ghal'Edokhtar, Kerman, was demolished by Iranian government officials.

- On June 5, 2012, Iranian Revolutionary Guard soldiers shut down an Assembly of God church in Tehran.
- On October 30, 2013, Behzad Taalipas and Mehdi Dadkhah were arrested by Iranian government officials and then flogged with eighty lashes each for drinking alcohol at communion.

"SMASH" THE CHRISTIANS

Christians face widespread and growing violence at the hands of the Muslim majority and especially Islamists, the "smash"-type of persecution.

The trauma suffered by some Middle Eastern Christians is almost too hard to fathom, much less write. A widowed mother of three young children was dumped at the edge of a refugee camp near Mosul, Iraq, in early May 2015 after months of being held by ISIS savages in a room where she was continuously raped by groups of men. The attendants at the monastery where the woman was taken said the state of her body was shocking; the effect of rape was visible.[35]

The Christian woman was totally confused. She couldn't remember who she was anymore, but she did recall her children. After a shower, she went to put on her dirty, ragged clothes rather than the clean ones provided, and she initially fought for the dirty clothes, screaming and pulling her hair. She refused food.

The woman will carry those scars for the rest of her life. That's not atypical of the "smash" persecution more and more Christian women face at the hand of Islamists—sex slaves to be discarded on the human waste pile.

Although a "war" isn't being waged in Egypt, Egyptian Coptic Christians for decades have suffered church burnings and murder at the hands of Muslims. One of the worst days for Coptic Christians was "New Year's Day 2011 when twenty-one Christians were slaughtered and seventy-nine were injured. During a protest in Cairo, twenty-seven were killed and three hundred injured by Egyptian police. An estimated one hundred thousand Copts have recently fled the country."[36]

In the wake of the removal of former Egyptian President Moham-med Morsi, the Muslim Brotherhood leader, more than two hundred churches were attacked, with forty-three completely destroyed by Mus-lim mobs. There were at least seventeen kidnappings of Christians for ransom in August and September of that year alone.[37]

In October 2013, four Coptic Christian children were killed and twenty-four were wounded when gunmen fired on a wedding party in front of the Church of the Virgin Mary near Cairo. A father of one of the eight-year-olds wounded said: "Nobody comes out to tell you hon-estly: 'We have arrested the culprit and they are being subjected to the law.' There is nothing like that."[21] Eyewitnesses of the attack stated that, despite numerous calls for help, ambulances and police only arrived two hours following the shooting.[38]

In March 2010, an Egyptian court acquitted four Muslims for shooting a sixty-one-year-old Coptic Christian thirty-one times before beheading him in a marketplace. The court refused to accept testimony of key witnesses. The victim's attorney said of the verdict, "It sends a clear message that Coptic blood is extremely cheap...this acquittal will make permanent the present culture of impunity enjoyed by Muslim aggressors against Copts."[39]

Killing Christians in Syria and Iraq has become a sport for groups like ISIS. There are numerous reports of atrocities committed against Christians by ISIS and other Islamic groups in that area.

Syria has become a deadly country for Christians. In October 2013, forty-five Christians were killed in the town of Saddad, and the town's fourteen churches were destroyed as well. More than twelve hundred Christians are documented as having been murdered in the Syrian civil war, mostly by Islamic extremists such as an Armenian Christian killed by ISIS for refusing to convert to Islam. A fifteen-year-old Christian girl was kidnapped, repeatedly gang raped, and then killed by a commander in the Jabhat al Nusra, an al-Qaeda affiliate, who married her to make raping the girl permissible under Islamic law, and then he gave her to fifteen different men over the next two weeks.[40]

Iraq is a killing field for Christians as well. On Christmas Day 2013, thirty-seven people were murdered in attacks on Christians. Meanwhile, as Christians were killed, their churches were destroyed, dropping from three hundred to only fifty-seven today.

A Google search of media reports between January 2010 and September 2014 found twenty-three incidents of Iraqi Christians killed in incidents associated with their faith.[41] Other evidence suggests that the following are only a few of many hundreds of similar tragic incidents—but incidents that are not mentioned in the media.

- On September 1, 2014, Salem Matty Georgis, forty-three, a Christian was beaten to death for refusing to convert to Islam.
- On June 21, 2014, a Christian family was attacked by ISIS terrorists, who raped the wife and daughter, and then the husband committed suicide.
- On May 16, 2011, Ashur Issa Yaqub, twenty-nine, a Chaldean Catholic, was abducted, tortured and murdered by ISIS terrorists.

The atrocities committed by ISIS against Christians and other non-Muslims know no boundaries. Some of the most heart-wrenching accounts come from the survivors reported by the United Nation's unit on sex crime. According to Zainab Bangua, ISIS has taken atrocities to a new level.[42]

Bangua visited frontline survivors, focusing on the war on women. He explained that after taking a village, ISIS would execute the men and boys (age fourteen and older) and then separate the women and mothers. Girls were stripped naked, tested for virginity, and examined for breast size and prettiness, according to the report. The youngest and prettiest virgins were sent to Raqqa (ISIS' capital). The report continued:

There is a hierarchy: sheikhs get first choice, then emirs, then fighters. They often take three or four girls each and keep them for a month or so, until they grow tired of a girl, when she goes back to market. At slave auctions, buyers haggle fiercely, driving down prices by disparaging girls as flat-chested or unattractive.

We heard about one girl who was traded twenty-two times, and another, who had escaped, told us that the sheikh who had captured her wrote his name on the back of her hand to show that she was his "property."

CONCLUSION

Christian genocide is occurring in the Middle East, as evidenced by the flood of refugees immigrating out of the region to safer havens and the increasing number of those who are murdered for their faith. The lynch-pin to whether this genocide eliminates all Christians comes down to the influence Islam has on regional governments and their populations. That is why the reader needs to understand the basics of Islamic ideology and its followers before exploring the compelling conditions of historic Christian genocide in the Middle East and why current events point toward not only genocide, but perhaps to the end times.

CHAPTER 2

WHAT DOES ISLAM TEACH ABOUT NON-MUSLIMS AND ESPECIALLY CHRISTIANS?

slam is very different from Christianity and Christendom, according to Bernard Lewis, the West's greatest historian and interpreter of Islam:

> Christianity means a religion, In the strict sense of that word, a system of belief and worship and some clerical or ecclesiastical organization to go with it. If we say Christendom, we mean the entire civilization that grew up under the aegis of that religion, but [it] also contains many elements that are not part of the religion, many elements that are even hostile to that religion.[43]

Islam as a religion embraces "far more than it does in the Christian" world, Lewis explained. Islam is the primary basis of both the Muslim's identity and loyalty. Instead of thinking of a nation subdivided into religions like the mostly Christian United States, orthodox Muslim people think of their religion subdivided into nations. For Muslims, every aspect of their lives—political, economic, and sexual, war making, worship, and even dealings with non-Muslims—is dictated by Islam. No wonder the Western mind has a difficult time understanding the Muslim world and especially how it views and treats non-Muslims.

BASICS TO UNDERSTANDING ISLAMIC TEACHINGS

Islam is defined by a combination of the words of Allah (Arabic for "god") in the Koran and the words of the Prophet Muhammad, the Sunna. The Sunna is based on two texts, the Sira (Muhammad's life story) and the Hadith, a collection of stories about Muhammad.

The trilogy—the Koran, the Sira and the Hadith—comprises all authoritative teachings of Islam. Dr. Bill Warner, of the Center for the Study of Political Islam, explains that Islamic doctrine is based on that trilogy, but only 14 percent is based on the alleged direct revelation from Allah, with the balance (86 percent) taken from the sayings and stories about Muhammad.[44]

The Hadith includes Muhammad's pronouncements that a Muslim should follow. There are as many as six hundred thousand hadiths, but only the most reliable (about seventy-five hundred in ninety-seven books) are said to be recorded in the Sahih al-Bukhari, a collection of hadiths complied by Imam Muhammad al-Bukhari (who died in AD 870). Reportedly, al-Bukhari's collection is recognized by most of the Muslim world to be an authentic collection of reports of the Sunna of the Prophet Muhammad.[45]

The Koran divides humanity into two groups: those who believe Muhammad is the Prophet of Allah and the Kafir (the unbeliever, non-Muslim), profiled in the trilogy as evil and subhuman. Only a small fraction (3 percent) of the trilogy addresses Christian Kafirs, which are the focus of this book. However, where appropriate, other portions of Islamic doctrine are addressed to provide the reader a better appreciation of Islamic teaching.[46]

The Kafir is a very important topic across the trilogy. Two-thirds of the Koran and 81 percent of the Sira address Kafir-related issues. Obviously, this level of attention means the Kafir plays a significant role in the Muslim's life.[47]

ISLAMIC TREATMENT OF CHRISTIANS AND NON-MUSLIMS

Muhammad started his spiritual journey by trying to persuade the local Jewish rabbis in Medina ("the radiant city," the capital of the Al Madinah Region of Saudi Arabia, which contains al-Masjid an-Nabawai ["the Prophet's mosque"]) that he had divine connection to God based on an alleged visit from the angel Gabriel. He expected news of that revelation to compel the rabbis to recognize him as another Jewish prophet. Evidently, Muhammad failed to persuade the Jewish clerics of the linage, which infuriated him and made Jews his instant enemy— and, by association, Christians with whom Muhammad had little contact at the time.[48]

Even though Islam shares significant roots with the Torah (or the Pentateuch, the first five books of the Bible) and Christian Scriptures (Jesus is considered a prophet), the hatred Muhammad had for Jews became a significant part of his many hadiths and the Koran. In spite of that animus, Muhammad recognizes Jews and Christians as special "People of the Book" ('Ahl al-Kitāb—adherents of Abrahamic religions), a clear reference to the Bible. However, Muhammad's "People of the Book" were still Kafirs, unbelievers, for the purpose of Islamic political treatment.

The followers of the Prophet Muhammad take a dim view of all Kafirs—Jews and Christians included—as demonstrated by a long list of approved Muslim views and behaviors for dealing with non-Muslims. The Kafir is to be hated and can be enslaved, raped, beheaded, deceived, plotted against, terrorized, warred against, and humiliated—but must never be a Muslim's friend. Below are what portions of the trilogy state about Kafirs.

They are to be hated: They [Kafirs] who dispute the signs [Koran verses] of Allah without authority having reached them are greatly hated by Allah and the believers. So Allah seals up every arrogant, disdainful heart.[49]

Muslims can enslave the Kafir: When some of the remaining Jews of Medina agreed to obey a verdict from Saed, Mohammed sent for him. He approached the Mosque riding a donkey and Mohammed said, "Stand up for your leader." Mohammed then said, "Saed, give these people your verdict." Saed replied, "Their soldiers should be beheaded and their women and children should become slaves."[50]

A Muslim may rape a Kafir: On the occasion of Khaybar, Mohammed put forth new orders about forcing sex with captive women. If the woman was pregnant she was not to be used for sex until after the birth of the child. Nor were any women to be used for sex who were unclean with regard to Muslim laws about menstruation.[51]

A Muslim may behead a Kafir: When you encounter the Kafirs on the battlefield, cut off their heads until you have thoroughly defeated them and then take the prisoners and tie them up firmly.[52]

A Muslim may deceive a Kafir: Some among them listen to you [Mohammed], but We have cast veils over their [Kafirs'] hearts and a heaviness to their ears so that they cannot understand our signs [the Koran].[53]

A Muslim can plot against a Kafir: They plot and scheme against you [Mohammed], and I plot and scheme against them. Therefore, deal calmly with the Kafirs and leave them alone for a while.[54]

A Muslim may terrorize a Kafir: Then your Lord spoke to His angels and said, "I will be with you. Give strength to the believers. I will send terror into the Kafirs' hearts, cut off their heads and even the tips of their fingers!"[55]

A Muslim can make war on and humiliate a Kafir: Make war on those who have received the Scriptures [Jews and Christians] but do not believe in Allah or in the Last Day. They do not forbid what Allah and His Messenger have forbidden. The Christians and Jews do not follow the religion of truth until they submit and pay the poll tax [jizya], and they are humiliated.[56]

A Muslim must never befriend a Kafir: Believers should not take Kafirs as friends in preference to other believers. Those who do this will have none of Allah's protection and will only have themselves as guards. Allah warns you to fear Him for all will return to Him.[57]

There is even a dehumanizing hadith suggesting that killing a Kafir is not a capital crime:

[Abu] asked Ali, "Do you know of any sources of law that were revealed to Mohammed other than the Koran?" Ali responded, "None except for Allah's law, or the ability of reason given by Allah to a Muslim, or these written precepts I possess." I said, "What are these written rules?" Ali answered, "They concern the blood money paid by a killer to a victim's relatives, the method of ransoming a captive's release from the enemy, and the law that a Muslim must never be killed as punishment for killing a Kafir.[58]

The Koran states that there is hope for the Kafir who submits to Islam—and then the person will go to paradise. However, neither the "path of those who anger you [the Jews] nor the path of those who go astray [the Christians]" will gain paradise. In fact, Muhammad states the same idea another way: "According to Allah, any Jew or Christian that is aware of me, but dies before accepting my prophecy will be sent to Hell."[59]

Muhammad established a very special relationship for Kafirs. Once a Muslim army conquered the Jews at Khaybar (Arabia), the jihadists (those engaged in holy war) seized the Jewish property as the spoils of war. Then the jihadists struck an agreement called a "dhimma" with the conquered Jews in Arabia. That agreement called for the Jews to stay and farm the land, but they must surrender half of their profits to the Muslims. That is apparently the origin of the term "dhimmis," whereby a group of conquered or otherwise subject people come under the protection of Islam in exchange for the fruits of their labor.[60]

The dhimmi practice continues today and translates into a second-class citizenship whereby Muslims dominate and the dhimmi abides by Islamic rules. They pay a heavy poll tax called the jizya; they enjoy limited rights, and the only way out of that status is to convert to Islam or leave.[61]

Muslims like the dhimmi system, which explains why they have imposed it on most of the non-Muslim people conquered over the past fourteen hundred years.

Umar II, aka Umar Ibn Abd al-Aziz, an Umayyad caliph who ruled AD 717 to 720, outlined the expectations of dhimmitude for the newly conquered Christians:

> We shall not build, in our cities or in their neighborhood new monasteries, churches, convents, or monks' cells, nor shall we repair, by day or by night, such of them as fall in ruins or are situated in the quarters of the Muslims.
>
> We shall keep our gates wide open for passersby and travelers. We shall give board and lodging to all Muslims who pass our way for three days.[62]

The Kafirs who lived under dhimmitude were obliged to comply with all Islamic rules. They had to dress differently than Muslims and were to always defer to the Muslims in public. They couldn't display crosses or ring church bells or recite the Gospels aloud, and they were forbidden to build new churches. There were off-limit areas to Kafirs such as Mecca and Medina, and they were never to enter a mosque without permission.

It is noteworthy the U.S. State Department publishes a *Hajj Fact Sheet* for those American Muslims considering participation in the annual pilgrimage to Mecca, a religious duty for all Muslims that must be carried out at least once in their lifetime. The State Department's publication is very clear about non-Muslims: "Non-Muslims are forbidden to travel to the holy cities of Mecca and Medina."[63] However, should a non-Muslim forget about the restrictions, the highway directional signs leading to Islam's holiest cities are very clear: In giant letters above the road are arrows pointing to exits that read "Obligatory for non-Muslims."[64]

Non-Muslims caught inside Mecca or Medina are hauled before a religious judge who can sentence the violator to death if the judge believes the trespasser intended to do something to defame Islam. Whatever the punishment awarded by the judge, it also includes a lifetime ban from ever returning to Saudi Arabia.[65]

INTOLERANCE FOR APOSTATES

Islam strongly condemns apostasy, one who leaves Islam, granting Muslims the duty to kill the guilty. This teaching is very clear in the Koran, the Hadith, and the Sira. The clarity on this issue explains why modern Islamic governments have strong laws on apostasy.

One of the first instances of Islamists striking out against apostasy took place shortly after Muhammad's death. Specifically, there arose wars between Abu Bakr, the caliph, and those who abandoned Islam to revert back to paganism.[66] That episode likely encouraged the emergence of strict apostasy rules, such as the death penalty, which continue in many Islamic countries even today.

Even Kafirs who accept Islam and then revert back are to be killed for apostasy as well. The Hadith states:

A certain Jew accepted Islam, but then reverted to his original faith. Muadh saw the man with Abu Musa and said, "What has this man done?" Abu Musa answered, "He accepted Islam, but then reverted to Judaism." Muadh then said, "It is the verdict of Allah and Mohammed that he be put to death and I'm not going to sit down unless you kill him."[67]

ISLAM'S VIEW OF JESUS CHRIST, WAR, WOMEN, AND SEX

Islam has a lot to say about Jesus Christ, war, women, and sex.

Jesus Christ is not mentioned in the Koran, but the text does mention a man by the name of "Isa" fifty-two times. "Isa" has at least one similarity to Jesus; he was born to the Virgin Mary. Isa became a prophet of Allah who came to earth to predict the coming of Muhammad. He was not crucified and was not resurrected from the dead like Jesus, but he will return to earth to kill the pig, break the cross, destroy churches, end the dhimmi tax, kill nonbelieving Christians, and establish global sharia law. He will also marry, have a family, and oversee forty years of peace before he dies and is buried in Medina.[68]

Muhammad's hadiths outline the Islamic doctrine of Christ, which identifies Him as just another of Allah's prophets and claims the Christian trinity is Allah, Jesus, and Mary.[69] Muhammad said evidence that Christ was a prophet is the fact He spoke from the cradle as a grown man and then went on to heal the blind and the lepers and raise the dead.[70]

Muhammad states that Christ was not crucified or resurrected from the dead, but that Allah took Jesus directly up to heaven. Then Muhammad said:

On the final day, the Day of Resurrection, those who follow Christ but do not believe in his divinity will be blessed. Those who insist that Christ is God, part of the Trinity, and reject true faith will be punished in Hell.[71]

Muhammad believes, as do most Christians, that Jesus Christ will return. But Muhammad has a very different view about Christ's return:

"According to Allah," Mohammed states, "Jesus will soon appear to Muslims as a fair and equitable ruler. He will shatter the cross and slay the swine and cancel the tax levied on Kafirs. Then there will be plenty of money and none will require charity."

Not surprisingly, Muslims also believe the Christian Scriptures are corrupted, because they allegedly conceal Muhammad's superiority to Jesus Christ. Ibn Abbas said:

Muslims, why do you ask the Jews and Christians any questions? The Koran that was revealed to Mohammed contains the latest word from Allah. It has not been altered and you recite it daily. Allah has made clear to you that the Jews and the Christians have distorted the Scriptures that were revealed to them. They have claimed that their alterations are the word of God in order to achieve some material gain.[72]

The trilogy says a lot about war and, not surprisingly, Islamic jihadists have spilt a lot of blood over the past fourteen hundred years. They are estimated to have killed fifty million people, according to Raphael

Moore in *History of Asia Minor*. Of course, the Kafir is the enemy in jihad (holy war), according to Islamic teaching. At least 109 koranic verses call Muslims to war with Kafir. For example, the Koran states:

> And kill them wherever you find them, and turn them out from where they have turned you out.[73] ... You are commanded to fight although you dislike it. You may hate something that is good for you, and love something that is bad for you. Allah knows and you do not.[74] ... But if they turn back, find them and kill them wherever they are.[75] ... Do not be unjust to yourselves regarding them, but fight the Kafirs as they fight you altogether.[76]

Many verses from the Hadith agree with the Koran's endorsement for war. The Hadith states:

> I have been commanded to fight people until they testify that there is no god but Allah and that Mohammed is the Messenger of Allah, and perform the prayer, and pay zakat. If they say it, they have saved their blood and possessions from me, except for the rights of Islam over them. And their final reckoning is with Allah.[77]

The biblical Old Testament is radically different from the Koran regarding calls to war. Koranic verses calling for violence are mostly open-ended, which means they are not bound by time and circumstances and therefore are just as relevant today as they were in the seventh century.

Muhammad was a fighter who laid siege to towns, massacred the men, raped their women, enslaved their children, and claimed their property as spoil. The Sira documents significant jihad under Muhammad's leadership. Specifically, the Prophet reportedly led twenty-seven expeditions and launched another forty-seven jihad campaigns; he inspired his jihadists with booty and threatened them with hell when they hesitated to engage the Kafir.

Participation in jihad is a personal obligation for all Muslims. A jihadist can leave only if he is ill, wounded, or without a weapon—or when the Muslim force faces an enemy at least twice its size.

There is also a communal obligation to participate in jihad even though a Muslim just supports the jihad with money or moral support. "He who provides the equipment for a soldier in jihad has himself performed jihad," said Muhammad.[78] That is likely a comforting statement to the Saudi princes, the Iranian ayatollah, and Persian Gulf monarchs whose deep pockets fund worldwide jihad.

There is no comparison to actually joining the fight against the Kafir, which explains the unprecedented rush today of thousands of volunteer jihadists from ninety countries joining the Islamic State in Syria and Iraq. After all, the Koran states:

> Believers who stay at home in safety, other than those who are disabled, are not equal to those who fight with their wealth and their lives for Allah's cause [jihad]. Allah has ranked those who fight earnestly with their wealth and lives above those who stay at home. Allah has promised good things to all, but those who fight for Him will receive a far greater reward than those who have not.[79]

Islam provides an escape from the sword for the Kafir armies. Specifically, Muslims are to invite Kafir armies to submit to Islam, become dhimmis, and pay the jizya; otherwise, they must face the sword. The Koran states:

> Make war on those who have received the Scriptures [Jews and Christians] but do not believe in Allah or in the Last Day. They do not forbid what Allah and His Messenger have forbidden. The Christians and Jews do not follow the religion of truth until they submit and pay the poll tax [jizya], and they are humiliated.[80]

Once war starts, Islam has rules for the jihadists. They are not permitted to kill women and children unless they are resisting. However, all men—including the elderly and even priests—are fair game. Also, the spoils of war go to the victorious jihadist; the captured children and women become slaves, and the women's previous marriages are immediately annulled. All Kafir property can either be destroyed or taken.

The trilogy of Islamic authority outlines a special place for most women: hell. Muhammad said, "I have seen the fires of Hell and most of its residents are ungrateful women. He was asked, 'Are they Kafirs, or did they show ingratitude to Allah?' He answered, 'They were not grateful to their husbands and not grateful for the kindness shown them.'"[81]

Women are also considered intellectually and religiously inferior to men: "You [women] swear too much, and you show no gratitude to your husbands. I have never come across anyone more lacking in intelligence, or ignorant of their religion than women. A careful and intelligent man could be misled by many of you." That is why, according to Muhammad, the testimony of one man is the equal to the testimony of two women.[82]

The Prophet provides guidance where sex and jihad collide on the lonely battlefield. Muhammad said: "While on jihad without our wives, many of us became sexually frustrated. We asked Mohammed, 'Should we castrate ourselves?' Mohammed forbade that, but did allow us to take a woman as a temporary wife. He recited, 'Oh believers! Do not forswear the good things that Allah has made legal for your enjoyment.'"[83]

Evidently, the ISIS jihadists followed the Prophet's prescription regarding battlefield sex. After all, once the ISIS jihadists conquered villages, the men were killed and the women and children became spoils or slaves.

The Prophet even went so far as to describe the sex act. Muhammad said, "Receiving female slaves as shares of spoils of war, we would practice coitus interruptus with them to avoid unwanted pregnancy. We asked Muhammad his opinion, and he asked us three times, 'Do you really remove yourself?' He then said, 'No soul that is not preordained to exist will be created.'"[84]

The Prophet also approves of sex with captive Kafir women who are married and whose husbands are present. Abu Sa'id Al-Khudri relates that while Muhammad was at the Battle of Hunain, he sent a detachment to Autas and defeated the enemy there. "Although Muhammad's soldiers captured many females, they were reluctant to force sex with them because their husbands were polytheists. Allah, however, then revealed to them that it was permissible as soon as a woman's menstrual cycle ended."[85]

WHEN MUSLIMS IMPOSE SHARIA LAW

In the West, we talk about church and state separation, but the Islamic world is radically different. Historian Bernard Lewis explained: "We think of a nation subdivided into religions. They [Islam] think…of a religion subdivided into nations."[86] Islam defines both their identity and their loyalty—a complete political, cultural, legal, and religious system.

It is critical that non-Muslims understand that the trilogy provides both political theory and legal codes for all aspects of life: banking, family, crime, and foreign policy. Further, the political goal of Islam is to ensure that every constitution is based on sharia—Islamic—law. Further, those sharia-based governments find all Kafir governments offensive to Allah and eventually must be replaced by the sharia.

Westerners ought to be concerned about sharia coming to their shores. Consider how sharia is impacting Europe today.

A growing minority of Muslims are gradually pressing demands for sharia law in their neighborhoods and at the national level. Meanwhile, in many Muslim communities, Islamic imams (title commonly used for an Islamic worship leader) are working the faithful into a frenzy that has evidenced itself in predictable reactions. But Europeans cower in the wake of rising Islamic intimidation.

Sharia principles are enforced through tribunals in some areas in the United Kingdom and, in some cases, in mainstream European courts. Even the European Union is considering cracking down on so-called intolerance or Islamophobia. There are "sharia-controlled zones" in some communities and "sharia patrols" that roam the streets to impose Islamic norms on women and alcohol drinkers.

CONCLUSION

The Islamic mindset is so foreign to the Western mind and culture that it is difficult for even the educated and diplomats to comprehend. There is a built-in assumption in the West that Middle Eastern Muslims are just like us, but nothing could be farther from the truth. Their Koran and their Prophet's hadiths encourage deception and lying in diplomatic relations, as seen by the very different statements made by Islamic negotiators who give one press conference for the Western audience, but then contradict the same major points when giving their remarks to an Islamic audience. Such arrogance and feeling of superiority complement the Koran in their dealings with the West, and it often goes unnoticed.

The P5+1 (five permanent members of the U.N. Security Council plus Germany) nuclear negotiations with Iran is a prime example of the West being taken in by Islamic deception.[87] Amir Hossein Motgahi, an Iranian journalist who defected from his country during the recent nuclear talks, said the U.S. was shilling for Iran at the negotiations. "The U.S. negotiating team [is] mainly there to speak on Iran's behalf with other members of the 5+1 countries and convince them of a deal," Mottaghi told the UK's *Telegraph*. Motaghi previously worked for Iranian President Hassan Rouhani's 2013 election as his public relations manager before joining Iran's state-run Student Correspondents Association.[88]

"My conscience would not allow me to carry out my profession anymore," Motaghi said from political asylum in Switzerland. He explained "there was no 'sense' in becoming a journalist in Iran because he only wrote whatever information was fed to him."[89]

Western people must understand that Islam impacts every aspect of the Muslim's life, and when non-Muslims live in Islamic countries, they are more often than not treated as second-class citizens, or Kafirs. Further, Westerners who engage orthodox Muslims in business, foreign policy, and/or war must appreciate Islamic ideology—especially if Muslim citizens begin to dominate populations and then insist that neighborhoods and/or entire countries allow sharia principles to dictate law and culture.

CHAPTER 3

VIEWS OF MUSLIMS, PRESENT AND FORMER

I t is instructive to consider how Islam impacts Middle Eastern Muslims. Indicators of Islam's influence on current Muslims can be seen in their actions, such as their treatment of non-Muslims displayed daily in news reports as well as in their responses to surveys about their views Meanwhile, Islam's influence is rejected outright by others, especially many former Muslims who deliver powerful testimonies about Islam's tragic impact on their former personal lives as well as entire nations.

Opinion polling is somewhat rare in Middle Eastern countries, in part because of autocratic regimes supported by Islamic clerics who keep a tight rein on outside interference and because opinion polling has the potential to instigate resistance to the status quo. However, a couple of pollsters have navigated the autocratic barriers and enjoy good access; as a result, their findings provide key insights into Muslim views about Islam, certain activities, and Muslim treatment of non-Muslims.

A 2012 survey by the reputable Pew Research Center asked Muslims worldwide about their views on a host of important ideological-related issues. Three-fourths (74 percent) of those surveyed in the Middle East support making sharia the law of the land, and Iraq leads that region by scoring an impressive 91 percent approval of mandating sharia.[90]

The pollsters pursued that line of questioning by asking whether sharia should be applied only to Muslims. Not surprisingly, given the sectarian tensions in Egypt, 74 percent of Egyptian Muslims favor making sharia the law of the land for all people. The poll also found that 88 percent of Egyptian Muslims favor the death penalty for people who leave the Muslim faith, a chilling reminder of just how intolerance is so deep-seated in Egyptian society for apostates much less for non-Muslims.

Another Pew poll conducted in the fall of 2013 found that most (67 percent) people in eleven Middle Eastern countries are concerned about extremism in their faith. It follows that extremist groups like al-Qaeda are reviled by 57 percent of Middle Easterners and the Taliban scores a rejection from 51 percent of local Muslims. However, those figures also demonstrate a sizable plurality of the population at least tolerate if not outright support those groups' extremist views and terrorist actions.[91]

The survey also found considerable support for suicide bombings, which increased from 13 percent in 2012 to 16 percent the following year. Further, substantial minorities in Lebanon (33 percent) and Egypt (25 percent) believe suicide bombings performed in the name of Islam are sometimes justified.[92] If the survey is reliable, that figure translates into a lot of people in Egypt—which has a population of eighty million; 25 percent is twenty million people who believe suicide bombing is sometimes justified. Evidently, such widely held support for extremist groups and suicide bombing explains the terrible treatment given non-Muslim Egyptian (Kafirs—mostly Coptic Christians) and why that country is the center for breeding some of the worst of Islamists, such as the current leader of al-Qaeda, Ayman Mohammed Rabie al-Zawahiri, who was born in and grew up in Cairo, Egypt.

Another survey released in the fall of 2014 by Zogby Research Services polled people in eight Middle East countries (Egypt, Lebanon, Jordon, Iraq, Saudi Arabia, the United Arab Emirates (UAE), Iran, and Turkey). The pollster inquired about the level of concern for Christians and other non-Muslim minorities. It found that in five of the eight Middle Eastern countries, majorities expressed concern over the treatment of Christians and non-Muslim minorities. The greatest concern was expressed by the Lebanese and Egyptians. Lebanon is one of the countries harboring hundreds of thousands of non-Muslim refugees from the Syrian civil war, and Egypt is the home for the oldest and largest Christian minority in the region, a demographic that faces some of the worst anti-Christian discrimination.[93]

Zogby's poll also found that most (two-thirds) of all survey respondents except those in the UAE were concerned about the growth of sectarian divisions. However, the level of concern has radically declined when compared to a similar poll in 2012. That downward trend is especially noteworthy in the UAE and Turkey, as well as in war-affected Lebanon and Iraq. Also, majorities in six of the countries believe the Syrian civil war contributes to increased sectarianism and radicalization.

So, what do these polls say about Middle East Muslims? First, these Muslims are a pretty compliant cohort, given their strong support for sharia law. Second, they are very aware of discrimination against non-Muslims, but evidently that is acceptable—or at least they have no plans to object in the face of imams spouting Islamic law who are supported by autocratic regimes. Finally, there is a significant minority in each country that supports Islamic extremists, to include their use of suicide bombing in the name of Islam.

FORMER MUSLIMS ADDRESS
THE TRUE NATURE OF ISLAM

Resisting the status quo for the average Muslim is dangerous, because Islam has little tolerance for noncompliant believers, much less for apostates. However, some brave Muslims dared to critically look at their faith and the violent situation across the Middle East to become persuaded that they must abandon Islam. Their testimonies are insightful and useful for Westerners who really want to understand the Muslims' motivation, their hatred for non-Muslims, and whether Islam is in fact an existential threat to Christians and other non-Muslims and their nations.

Bosch Fawstin grew up in an American "moderate" Muslim family. Fawstin shared the hard truth about Islam that is demonstrated by many fellow Muslims. He said Islam is about "death and destruction" and it is "here to control…to make life on earth hell." He also volunteered that Jew hatred "is endemic in Islamic culture."[94]

In an interview, Fawstin said his "moderate" Muslim family had fascist views, which explains why they greatly admired Adolf Hitler, the Nazi tyrant who murdered six million Jews in the Holocaust.

It is noteworthy that Egypt's Muslim Brotherhood, a leading radical Islamist group that was started in the 1920s, was in allegiance with the Nazis during the 1930s. At the time, the Brotherhood supported espionage and sabotage against the Western alliance as well as disseminating Hitler's *Mein Kampf* and the fraudulent *The Protocols of the Elders of Zion* to deepen hostility among Arabs for Jews and the West.[95]

Fawstin also said Islam hates women in general and explained that physical abuse of women was commonplace, even in his immediate and extended family. This American Muslim explained that there were even arranged marriages in his community, and girls were taught from an early age to expect physical violence from their husbands.

Another former Muslim's experience isn't all that different from the American Fawstin, even though this man was born and raised in Saudi Arabia. Ali Fadi said, "When I lived in Saudi Arabia, not only did I look at non-Muslims as second class, you would look at non-devout Muslims as second class citizens" as well. He went on to explain that "if Islam has to prosper, be the superior religion, then certain steps must be taken by its followers, including spreading Islam at any cost, including the sword and killing any opposition."[96]

Fadi uses a pseudonym, because leaving Islam for Christianity is an automatic death sentence in Saudi Arabia. Even though he no longer lives under that repressive regime, he wants to protect his family. He explained the Koran teaches that Christ's crucifixion never happened; "that someone else was made to look like Jesus and put in his place," and, of course, Fadi said, the Koran "tells you to hate the Christians and the Jews."

The former Muslim said jihad is a koranic requirement to kill "the infidels, spreading Islam until there is no religion on earth except the religion of Allah." The West is ignorant about the threat because it is "oblivious to what the Koran teaches," said Fadi.[97]

Fadi admits that he grew up wanting to follow in the footsteps of al-Qaeda's leader Osama bin Laden, a childhood hero: "I was willing to go fight and die. And then that opportunity didn't take place." Rather, he decided to attend college in the West, where he met Christians.

"Basically, the more I met people who follow Christ, the more I realized that they are distinct and unique in their character," Fadi testified. "They're kind, they're patient, they're loving, they have moral values, they don't look at others with hatred." In time, Fadi accepted Jesus Christ as his Lord and Savior, a decision that for a Saudi Muslim was a very dangerous one.

"For you to leave Islam, you are leaving your identity, your culture, your community, your family, everything that you grew up to believe to be true," he said. Of course, in Islam, "There is no separation between state and mosque, state and religion."

Fadi warned those Westerners who will listen that they must understand that "Muslims know very well that the best way to conquer is not by the sword anymore." No, he warned that present-day Muslims conquer "by infiltrating the societies, the political systems, and by basically taking their time to grow, to become a majority that at some point, they will have a voice that they can topple things basically to their advantage." They seek to spread sharia law just as is seen in Europe today.

Another former Muslim voice is familiar to YouTube aficionados. Brother Rachid, the son of a Moroccan imam, used a video message to take issue with President Obama's view of the extremist Muslim group Islamic State in Iraq and Syria.[98] On a number of occasions, President

Obama defied every intelligent analysis of Islam and ISIS to assert: "We are not at war with Islam; we are at war with those [ISIS] who have perverted Islam."[99]

Brother Rachid tells Obama in his widely viewed YouTube video: "I can tell you with confidence that ISIL [the "L" is for the Levant rather than the "S" for Syria more commonly seen; "ISIS" is used in this volume] speaks for Islam." Rachid outlined the credentials of ISIS' leader, Abu Bakr al-Baghdadi, who holds a doctorate in Islamic studies. "I doubt you [Mr. Obama] know Islam better than he [Baghdadi] does. He was a preacher and an Islamic leader in one of the local mosques in Baghdad. ISIL's [ISIS] ten thousand members are all Muslims.... They come from different countries and have one common denominator—Islam."

The former Muslim provided Mr. Obama a laundry list of strictly observed indicators that ISIS jihadists embrace koranic teachings. Specifically, ISIS members grow their beards, cut their moustaches, and dress just like the ancient Prophet Muhammad. "They implement Sharia in every piece of land they conquer. They pray five times a day. They have called for a caliphate, which is a central doctrine in Sunni Islam and they are willing to die for their religion," said Brother Rachid.

President Obama said ISIS doesn't speak for Islam because the jihadists behead the conquered. But Rachid dismissed the president's historical ignorance. "In the same way, Islam's Prophet Mohammed beheaded—in one day—between six hundred and nine hundred adult males in a Jewish tribe called Bani Quraiza. In fact, beheading is commanded in the Koran, in Sura 47, 4th verse," Rachid explained.

The same hatred that motivates ISIS was evident in Rachid's homeland. "I grew up in Morocco, supposedly a moderate [Muslim] country. Yet I still learned at a young age to hate the enemies of Allah, especially Jews and Christians." He continued, "We [Muslims] have been brainwashed to hate all of you in our sacred texts, in our prayers, in our Friday sermons, in our education systems. We were ready to join any group that one day would fight you and destroy you and make Islam the religion of the whole world, as the Koran says."

Then Rachid asks Obama two very searing questions: If Islam is not the problem, then why aren't Christians in the Middle East blowing themselves up? Why are Muslims in the West and new converts to Islam joining ISIS?

He said to Obama, "Until you deal with the root [Islam] of the problem, you will be just dealing with the symptoms. ISIS is just one symptom. If it disappears, other ISISs will be born under different names."

Rachid ends his short video message to Obama by prescribing that terrorism must be cut off at the root and suggests a list of targets to begin the culling process:

How many Saudi sheiks are preaching hatred? How many Islamic channels are indoctrinating people and teaching them violence from the Koran and the Hadith? How many Friday sermons are made against the West and freedom and Democracy? How many Islamic schools are producing generations of teachers and students who believe in jihad and martyrdom and fighting the infidels? And finally, how many websites are funded by governments—your allies—that have sheiks that issue fatwas against basic human rights? If you want to fight terrorism, start from there.

MUSLIM SCHOLAR WHO ABANDONED MUHAMMAD FOR JESUS

Perhaps the most compelling and credible former Muslim testimony comes from a man with significant Islamic credentials. Dr. Mark Gabriel, not his given Arabic name but the name he uses to protect his family, was born in Egypt and raised as a devout Muslim. Like some of his childhood peers in Egypt, he memorized the Koran at age twelve and attended al-Azhar schools. He earned a bachelor's, a master's and a doctoral degree at al-Azhar University in Islamic history and culture.

He then served as an imam and lectured for the university.[100] By all accounts, he was a devout Islamic scholar of the highest order.

Gabriel began questioning the validity of Islam while in his early thirties, and before long, after being open with his questions about his faith, he was fired by "the university, kidnapped, imprisoned, tortured, and released."

His search for answers led him to read the Bible, which pointed him to Christ Jesus and eventually to religious asylum in the United States. Here in America, he now employs his expertise in Islam by writing books such as *Islam and Terrorism* and *Jesus and Muhammad.*

Dr. Gabriel provides a great service to Westerners by exposing the truth about Islam. In 2006, a Christian newspaper in Norway ran a critical review of his first book, *Islam and Terrorism.* Gabriel wrote a detailed rebuttal of that review, which was written by Basim Ghoslan from Jordan, a former imam with the Islamic Association of Oslo (*Det islamske forbundet i Oslo*) and at the time the editor of the website islam.no.

The following are a few of Gabriel's responses to Ghoslan's criticisms. The sparring between these Islamic scholars is incredibly helpful for those who may have previously heard similar criticisms but didn't hear reasoned responses such as those Gabriel provides.

Gabriel begins his line-by-line rebuttal with a heartfelt appeal to Europeans facing an onslaught of Islamic propaganda. The same appeal applies to Americans as well, because they must awaken from their gullibility and stupor regarding the very real dangers associated with Islam.

Gabriel warned: "My heart is weeping and crying for the way that many in Europe generally and Norway in particular are still sleeping, not recognizing the danger that is living in the midst of them. This naïveté creates an environment where terrorism can thrive." Gabriel's warning is appropriate, because until recently, Europeans were sleeping, and then incidents of Islamic terror started to awaken the continent. One of the more spectacular Islamic terror attacks occurred January 7, 2015, at the offices of the satirical weekly newspaper *Charlie Hebdo* in Paris, where twelve were killed and eleven others wounded.

Consider a sampling of Ghoslan's criticism and Gabriel's response. Often, critics like Ghoslan begin by attacking the credibility of the former Muslim by questioning his resume. Gabriel said:

> If my picture were shown at Al-Azhar or the mosque, I am not surprised that the people would fail or refuse to recognize me. It has been almost thirteen years since I departed from Al-Azhar, so a few people may have forgotten me or may not recognize me now. But the main reason the people would refuse to identify my picture is because they are ashamed to discuss anything about me. Because I left Islam, I am considered to be a dead person—not just to them in the university or in the mosque, but even for my father and my brothers, who disowned me and have nothing to do with me.

Then Gabriel quoted Jesus Christ from John 10:38 and 14:11: "If you don't believe who I am, at least believe what I do" (paraphrase). Gabriel, in the same way, recited Jesus' words: "If you don't believe who I am, at least listen to what I know" (paraphrase).

Gabriel explained that "it's not the position at the university or the position at the mosque that gives authority to my book. What gives my book authority is the knowledge, experience and courage to speak out." As seen, he speaks with great authority about the Islamic trilogy.

Ghoslan criticizes Gabriel for giving his heart to Jesus Christ after reading Matthew 5:38: "Ye have heard that it hath been said, an eye for an eye, and a tooth for a tooth: But I say unto you, That ye resist not evil: but whosoever shall smite thee on thy right cheek, turn to him the other also." Ghoslan juxtaposes that Scripture with Surah 41:34 to argue that someone who knows the Koran by heart ought to see this verse as beautiful as well. (A Surah or Sura is a chapter of the Koran. There are 114 chapters in the text and each divided in verses [ayat].)[101]

Gabriel confirmed that he knew the Surah verse. However, Gabriel said it isn't the words but the person behind the words that counts. Then he explained that Muhammad, the author of the Surah, was a man of war, not peace: "This man wiped the entire community of Jewish people out of Arabia after they rejected Islam. I saw the history of Islam is nothing but a river of blood as a result of the deeds and the teachings of the founder of this religion."

Then he pointed out the differences between the verses. "Jesus taught, love one another, or, be kind to others, he did not say that this standard applied only to other Christians. The biblical teaching is absolutely general commanding Christians to treat other Christians and unbelievers of any part of the world with the same respect," Gabriel said.

The context of Muhammad's Surah 41:34 addresses how Muslims should treat other Muslims. The Koran states: "The believers are nothing else than brothers (in Islamic religion). So make reconciliation between your brothers, and fear Allah, that you may receive mercy."[102]

Then he points out that when "you come to Muslim treatment of non-Muslims, there is another set of standards. In the same sermon, Muhammad warned those who were not Muslim: 'After today there will no longer be two religions existing in Arabia. I descended by Allah with the sword in my hand, and my wealth will come from the shadow of my sword. And the one who will disagree with me will be humiliated and persecuted.'"[103]

The message, according to Gabriel, is for Muslims to do good to each other, but to "drive all other religions out of Arabia [using the sword]."

Gabriel then explained that Islamic law is based on *al-Ka'saas*, which means "eye for eye and tooth for tooth." He cites Surah 42:40: "The recompense for an injury is an injury equal thereto (in degree): But if a person forgives and makes reconciliation, his reward is due from God: For God loves not those who do wrong."

He cautions that the subsequent verse (Surah 42:41) tells the Muslim to practice *al-ka-saas:* "When an oppressive wrong is done to them, take revenge. And the verse following says, 'And indeed whosoever takes revenge after he has suffered wrong, for such there is no way (of blame) against them.'"

The message is clear, wrote Gabriel. The Koran says forgiveness is best, but an eye for an eye is still good enough. That can't compare with Jesus' teaching that forgiveness is the only option.

Ghoslan walks into Gabriel's verbal buzz saw by asserting that the main message of his book, *Islam and Terrorism*, is that Islam is about holy war and that only terrorists correctly understand Islam.

"The backbone of Islam is jihad…[and] the terrorists see this clearly and act on it," Gabriel explained. He then recounted a series of questions he once posed to a professor at Azhur University. Gabriel said:

Dear Professor, why is our history nothing but a river of blood? Why were the children of Ali, the prophet's cousin, killed by Muslims? Why was the caliph Uthman killed by Muslims? Why was the house of the prophet destroyed in the time of the Umawiyya state through Muawiyya and his son Yazid? Why were Muslims killing and destroying other Muslims, especially when the house of el-Abbas led the Abbasid revolution against the Umawiyya state, and the result was the destruction and the end of that Islamic empire? Dear imam, why do the Muslims historians call the first caliph in the Abbasid state, Abu Abbas the murderer?

We can't change Islamic history, Gabriel opined. Even the Prophet Muhammad set a violent example for the Muslim people. Then Ghoslan said "And the people known by the world as terrorists are the heroes of those who are embracing the full teachings of Islam."

Ghoslan's next jab at Gabriel is steeped in significant theology. The sentences in Gabriel's book that disturbed Ghoslan the most were: "The only way to know for sure that you will get into paradise is to die in jihad. Jihad simply means that Muslims must fight the enemy of Allah until the enemies die or the Muslims die."

Gabriel likely smiled at the opportunity to write about Christian salvation. But he started with a bit of scholarship: "Any Muslim who studied his faith in the Middle East knows that the traditional understanding of martyrdom is that the martyr is guaranteed entrance into paradise.... It is built on the teachings of the Koran and Mohammed as a whole."

Gabriel makes his point using the illustration of a suicide bomber on his way to blow up himself. Ask the bomber, "Why are you going to kill yourself and many innocent people? What are you looking for?" Gabriel suggests the bomber would quote the Koran in response:

O you who believe! Shall I guide you to a trade that will save you from a painful torment? That you believe in Allah and His Messenger (Muhammad), and that you strive hard and fight in the Cause of Allah with your wealth and your lives, that will be better for you, if you but know! (If you do so) He will forgive you your sins, and admit you into Gardens under which rivers flow, and pleasant dwellings in 'adn—(Eden) Paradise; that is indeed the great success. And also (He will give you) another (blessing) which you love,—help from Allah (against your enemies) and a near victory. And give glad tidings (O Muhammad) to the believers. (Surah 61:10–13)

"These verses describe a contract between Allah and Muslims," Gabriel explains. "Why is this contract so important? Because of Islamic teaching about Paradise."

Ghoslan takes aim at Gabriel's assertion that the Koran is about war, and that emphasis continues today. Ghoslan quotes in defense of his view Surah 2:256: "There is no force in the religion."

Gabriel responds with a quote from Surah 8:65:

O Prophet (Muhammad)! Urge the believers to fight. If there are twenty steadfast persons amongst you, they will overcome two hundred, and if there be a hundred steadfast persons they will overcome a thousand of those who disbelieve, because they (the disbelievers) are people who do not understand

Gabriel explained that Muslim scholars refer to this as the principle of *nasikh*.[104] "The idea is that Muhammad's revelations were progressive. A new revelation cancelled out an older revelation," and Muhammad's last "revelations" were very warlike.

"The 'verse of the sword' that Ibn Kathir references is Surah 9:5, which says: 'So when the sacred months have passed away, then slay the idolaters wherever you find them, and take them captives and besiege them and lie in wait for them in every ambush.'

"This is considered by radical Muslims to be the final revelation regarding the treatment of non-believers," said Gabriel.

Ghoslan challenges Gabriel that he has no right to define true Islam. Gabriel says the person who can define true Islam is the person "who memorizes the Koran, the one who studies the commentaries from the different great Muslim scholars, the one who studies Islamic history deeply, the one who has earned the right to make a fatwa (Muslim legal opinion)." Clearly, based on his education and practice, Gabriel is in a position to define "true Islam."

Ghoslan's question about true Islam was prompted by Gabriel's division of all Muslims into three categories. There are secular Muslims who believe only in the good verses of the Koran and reject the jihad verses. The traditional Muslims are those who learn Islam and understand that jihad is part of the faith, but they are afraid to act on it. The Islamists are the third type of Muslims who are violent, the people who practice the real Islam as revealed to the Prophet.

Ghoslan questions Gabriel's assertion that the Koran legitimizes lying. In response, Gabriel describes how Muhammad authorized Muslims to lie and deny their faith in order to protect themselves, which is in an excerpt from his book, *Islam and Terrorism*.

Gabriel paraphrases a hadith that tells about a slave who had become a Muslim and was being tortured by the tribe of Quraysh. The tribe demanded that he forfeit his faith in order for them to stop the torture, so the slave denied his faith. After he was released, he told Muhammad what had happened.

Muhammad asked, "Was anything of that from the heart?" (Meaning, "Was there any change in your faith?")

"The slave answered no."

Muhammad replied, "If they come again, do it again." (Meaning, "If they catch you and torture you again, go ahead and lie to them again.")

In short, Gabriel explained, radical Islamic scholars and terrorist leaders use such stories to develop their philosophy of deceit.

Ghoslan says Gabriel gives a misleading description of Islam's goal to conquer the world. Gabriel responds that he visited the Muslim Brotherhood's website and found under the heading "Who We Are" bylaws that state: "If prayer is the head of the camel, then jihad is the hump of the camel." Gabriel translates: "Prayer is important, but jihad is more important because the hump of the camel rises higher than the head."

"The Muslim Brotherhood website stated that Allah wants Muslims to gain power and use force in order to defend the Muslim homeland from the invader and to establish an Islamic government in the Muslim land. This will allow the Muslims to look forward and start working to establish the worldwide Islamic government," according to Gabriel. He adds that the Muslim Brotherhood's philosophy is based on a deep study of Islam.

Ghoslan suggests that the Koran forbids the use of force in connection with faith. Gabriel soundly refutes that notion with a history lesson:

Dear imam, I wish that what you wrote about Islam were true. I wish you could go back fourteen hundred years and change the facts about Muhammad's life and his successors and to tell me that Islam went out of Arabia and conquered all the nations and the countries, including my own country, Egypt, by peace and not by force. However, if you read the history of Islam, you will see that this is not true. You will see in fact all of Arabia was won for Islam by force. Iran, Iraq, Syria, Egypt and North Africa,

Turkey, most of Eastern Europe, Spain, and Portugal—all these nations went to Islam by force, not by peace.

Did you know that more than two million Egyptian Christians in the first two centuries of Islam in Egypt had their tongues cut off because they refused to speak the language of the Arabic Muslim invaders? Have you heard in these past weeks about the trial of the Turkish writer who was accusing the Uthman calipha in Turkey of killing almost two million Armenians?

I wish Islam were a message of peace from the beginning to our present time.

But, as Gabriel states, "The contents of the Quran are working against peace, but the fact is that it will be almost impossible to touch one letter in the Quran to change it or to reinterpret it."

Gabriel concludes his rebuttal, stating:

My desire is not to cast suspicion on Muslims. I believe that people must separate their feelings about Muslims as human beings from their feelings about the teachings of Islam. I believe Muslims are wonderful, sincere people. They love to serve God and to be obedient to him, but the problem is that they do not have the right direction to do so.

The problem Dr. Gabriel avoids in his response to Ghoslan is whether the Muslims' Allah even exists. Although that is a topic for another book, the fact is that the Muslims' Allah is not the God of the Jews and Christians—especially when one considers the Koran's explicit teachings justifying violence and subjugation of Jews and Christians. Clearly, fourteen hundred years of Muslim violence against the People of the Book should be sufficient evidence to convince even the most jaded skeptic that Islam's god isn't the God of the Bible and in fact doesn't even exist.

CONCLUSION

All Muslims do not think alike and they don't share a common view of their faith. However, majorities of Middle Eastern Muslims share Islam-based views that mitigate against Christians and other non-Muslims from integrating into those societies as equal members. Further, the testimonies of former Muslims indicate that Islam is an all-encompassing and oppressive religion that has zero tolerance for the unbeliever.

It must also be understood that illiteracy rates in the Middle East are higher than in the West. Millions of Muslims only know what they are taught by the imams and therefore are challenged to think for themselves and discern the evil of Islam and the truth of the real and only God. Thus there is a great challenge in not only presenting the truth, but in changing the minds and behavior of Muslims. Nevertheless, there are ways to get the truth into the hands and ears of the Muslims worldwide, and we shall see some ideas later in this volume.

FASCIST ISLAMIC MIDDLE EAST

The contemporary Middle East blames outsiders and especially Christians for its problems as a way of denying Islam's supremacist ideology. This is evident in the distortion of history and the denial of ongoing oppressive actions against religious minorities like Christians.

The first chapter in this section debunks the myths about the Christian Crusades spun by the Islamic world to hide the Middle East's insecurities over falling behind the rest of the world and to clumsily excuse violent jihad.

America's experience with the distortion of the history of the Crusades is relatively fresh. Shortly after al-Qaeda's attack on America on September 11, 2001, President George W. Bush used the term "crusade" to denote the necessity to defeat Islamic extremism. The sycophantic Islam sympathizing media made President Bush pay a price for that choice by characterizing the use of "crusade" as evidence of his insensitivity to Muslims.

Muslim terror leaders quickly jumped on the Bush "insensitivity" band wagon. Al-Qaeda leader Osama bin Laden warned from his cave headquarters in the mountains at Tora Bora that "crusader" Bush would invade Afghanistan "under the banner of the [crusader] cross" as "the leader of the infidels." On the heels of that statement Afghanistan's Taliban leader Mullah Omar crowed that "President Bush has told the truth that this is a crusade against Islam." [105]

Many of Islam's current apologists continue to blame the Crusades for everything gone wrong with the Middle East and Islam. Former Muslim Ibn Warraq attacks that misleading "blame the Crusades" theme in his book *Sir Walter Scott's Crusades and Other Fantasies*. Warraq explains that Islamic apologists distort history when they claim the Crusades were the starting point of Islamic jihad. The fact is the Crusades were launched to save Europe and Western civilization from sharia. [106]

Warraq chronicles Islam's carnage prior to the Crusades. There were countless mass killings and persecutions of Christians and the destruction of tens of thousands of churches before the Crusades. There were burnings of crosses, beheadings of converts to Christianity, and the destruction of Christianity's most holy site, the Church of the Holy Sepulchre in Jerusalem, at the hands of Islamists, as well as the forced taxation of all Christians left alive—to mention just a few of the oppressive abuses suffered at the hand of Islamic conquerors.

The Islamic "crusades" charade continues today. Hiding behind the "crusades" mantra, according to Warraq, "eases the guilty consciences of the Arabs themselves: it is not their fault that they are such abject failures—it is all the fault of the crusaders."

The second chapter in this section applies eight "Universal Conditions for Genocide" to the situation facing Christians and other religious minorities in the Middle East. It begins with evidence that the Middle East is a cauldron in which religion and conflict mix like no other in the world. Further, President Obama's efforts to re-engineer the region to fit his misguided progressive view of the world made the situation much, much worse than had he just left it alone.

The Armenian genocide, which is profiled in the chapter, provides a graphic forewarning of the current Christian holocaust, but once again, the world ignored that crisis until it was too late. The same can be said of the Jewish genocide at the hands of the Nazis and the 1990s genocide in Rwanda.

There are differences with the current Christian genocide and the horror the Ottoman Empire delivered to the Armenians. This time, the holocaust is fueled not directly by the state, but by state surrogates (Saudi Arabia's nexus with ISIS and al-Qaeda), and is encouraged by the pervasive Muslim bias across every Middle East country, which affects every aspect of life. And another difference, like in the case of the Jewish Holocaust, is if the fascists now committing Christian genocide in the Middle East succeed, the genocide won't be contained, but will spread nonstop elsewhere. The only question for the balance of the non-Islam world is this: Will this be allowed to stand?

CHAPTER 4

WHO ARE THE PRIMARY VICTIMS IN THE MIDDLE EAST?

Christians and their universal church get a bad rap from pop culture and some historians, because the Christian Crusades nearly a thousand years ago are incorrectly characterized. Detractors spew myths such as the Crusades were unprovoked attacks by Christians against innocent Muslims and the crusaders were mostly wealthy knights motivated by greed to plunder Muslim lands.

Too often, the medieval Christian Crusades are depicted in such negative and inaccurate ways by the politically correct and historically ignorant. They conjure up negative images of marauding, bloodthirsty, and greedy Christian knights ravaging innocent Muslim homelands, and unfortunately, even those who should know better fall into that trap. Early in 2015, President Obama abused the history of the Crusades to humble his critics by comparing the crusaders to modern-day Islamic extremists who behead children and crucify Christians.

President Obama's address at the National Prayer Breakfast on February 5, 2015, shocked many listeners by demonstrating his shallow understanding of the Crusades. Sadly, Obama used the occasion to lecture Christians that they should not get on a moral high horse in their castigation of Islamic State atrocities by reminding the audience that the

Crusades and American slavery history were also justified in the name of Christ.

The president's choice of the Crusades to encourage humility in denouncing Islamic extremism today makes a clumsy moral-equivalence argument, distorts the facts of history, fuels the insatiable rage of Islamic extremists, and delights the Muslim world, which remains in denial about its savage history.

Obama ended his prayer breakfast speech by acknowledging that "it is sin that leads us to distort reality." Indeed, Mr. Obama's "sin" that morning was the distortion of reality by perpetuating wrong-headed history rooted in Islamic propaganda and therefore largely excusing horrific violence against Christians in the modern Middle East.

Had Mr. Obama consulted historians before misusing a significant historical period to make a terrible values judgment, perhaps he would have exercised better judgment.

Thomas Madden, an associate professor and chair of the department of history at St. Louis University and author of books about the Crusades, wrote:

> The Crusades are quite possibly the most misunderstood event in European history. Now put this down in your notebook, because it will be on the test: The **Crusades were in every way a defensive war**. They were the West's belated response to the Muslim conquest of fully two-thirds of the Christian world. Despite modern laments about medieval colonialism, the [First Crusade's] real purpose was to turn back Muslim conquests and restore formerly Christian lands to Christian control. The entire history of the Crusades is one of Western reaction to Muslim advances. The Crusades were no more offensive than was the American invasion of Normandy.[107] (emphasis added)

Dr. Timothy Furnish, an Islamic history scholar, wrote:

The Crusades, far from being the first time Muslims and Christians fought, were actually merely the first time that Christians, after four centuries of defeats [and lost territory], really fought back.[108]

Dr. James Hitchcock, professor of history and author, wrote:

The Crusades satisfied the requirements of a just war in at least two ways. The Muslims had taken certain Christian territories by force and had thereby denied to Christians, east and west, the opportunity to engage in one of the most important medieval religious exercises, namely, pilgrimages. The concept of the just war not only permits people to defend themselves when directly attacked, it also permits them to go to the aid of others who have been attacked.

It is a major index of the arrogant anti Christian bigotry now prevalent in "enlightened" Western circles that, while the Crusaders are treated as aggressive interlopers against the Muslims of the Near East, little attention is paid to the means by which Islam had come to dominate that region to begin with.[109]

Consider a short history of some important facts about the Middle East and especially the Crusades. The truth should encourage the Christian community and expose those who distort history like Mr. Obama's empty argument that, as he has said many times, Islam is a religion of peace.

MIDDLE EAST HAS A HISTORY OF INTOLERANCE

It is appropriate to emphasize why this text does not examine the detailed back and forth of the violent history between Middle Eastern Muslims and their Christian and Jewish adversaries from the founding of Islam to current times. No doubt atrocities were committed on both sides, and examining the details of the past fourteen hundred years of sectarian conflict may be intriguing for historians, but that exercise serves little useful purpose for those who are trying to sort out the situation in the Middle East today—much less discern whether these are in fact the biblical end times.

The Middle East has a long history of religion-based conflict dating back thousands of years, but the best-known series of wars were the Crusades. Those wars were a response to centuries of Islamic conquests, and the final straw came when Christendom's most holy sites were ripped out of their hands by Islamists.

Before addressing the particulars of the Crusades, the reader needs to put Middle East history into perspective. Consider a review of ancient Middle East history leading up to the time of Christ, which was followed by six centuries in which Christendom spread without significant opposition across the Middle East, North Africa, and Europe. But Christendom's centuries of gains were quickly smashed in the wake of Islam's birth in Arabia about AD 632. Armies of sword-wielding Muslim warriors swooped across much of Christendom, conquering most of the Middle East, North Africa, and the under belly of Europe.

The Christian world failed to mount any meaningful opposition to Islamic aggression for almost four centuries. During those years, Christians lived as second-class citizens under the Muslims' heel until the eleventh century. Christians had finally had enough, and out of desperation to survive, they responded with a somewhat disjointed series of Crusades—armed pilgrimages—that spread across hundreds of years. The results of those campaigns were mixed with mostly short-lived victories for the Christians, but by the thirteenth century, the Muslims once again ruled supreme across the Middle East and Northern Africa.

The residual tensions between modern-day Middle East Christians and their Islamic neighbors are very tender. It is important to put the Crusades into perspective: who fought, why they fought, and the outcomes.

The oldest known civilizations arose in the region of the Tigris and Euphrates Rivers (the Mesopotamia, modern-day Iraq) and Egypt. At the headwaters of the Mesopotamia, eastern Turkey, early people raised animals and planted crops, eventually migrating down the river valleys to form what became known as the Fertile Crescent. Similar development grew up along Egypt's Nile River, forming the first Middle East country, Egypt, about 3100 BC.

Early people known as the Sumerians founded the first civilization in southern Mesopotamia. The area became known as the Cradle of Civilization, which was the home of Abraham, the patriarch of the Jews. The Sumerians also mined ore from which they produced metalwork to trade with their neighbors. Similarly, other early people in what is today's Syria mined silver and Egypt mined gold.

The ancient Middle East experienced constant movement of people seeking new places to live, mostly through the use of force.

CHRISTIANS DOMINATED LARGE SWATHS OF THE MIDDLE EAST PRIOR TO ISLAM'S BIRTH

The West first invaded the region in 334 BC under the leadership of Alexander the Great of Macedonia, who in nine years conquered the entire Persian Empire, which was much of the then modern-day Middle East. At Alexander's death, his successors formed the Seleucid Kingdom in Syria and the Ptolemaic Kingdom in Egypt. These Hellenistic kingdoms introduced Greek culture to the region, which explains why Alexandria, Egypt, was once the center of Greek learning.

Meanwhile, the Seleucids lost a portion of their land to the re-emergent Persian Empire, and the balance fell to Rome in 64 BC. Very soon, Rome annexed Palestine and Egypt as well.

Christianity quickly grew after the resurrection of Jesus Christ during the first century of the Roman era. Churches were established in Jerusalem; Antioch, Syria; Ephesus, Asia Minor; and Alexandria. Christianity became the official religion of Rome's eastern capital, Constantinople (now Istanbul).

It wasn't until the reign of Emperor Theodosius (AD 347–395) that Christianity became the official religion of all the Roman Empire, however. It was under Theodosius that the Holy Land, especially Jerusalem with its shrines and relics, began to attract Christian pilgrims from as far away as Europe.

Therefore, just before the birth of Islam, most of the Middle East, North Africa, and the Mediterranean basin were Christian territories. Orthodox Christianity was the official religion across most of those areas; many Christians lived in Persia (modern-day Iran), and Christian communities were found across Arabia.

EMERGENCE OF ISLAM

The Muslim religion came into being in Arabia early in the seventh century. The Prophet Muhammad claimed to be the last prophet of the biblical God worshipped by Abraham, whom Muhammad called Allah (Arabic for "god" and, more specifically, "the ancient moon god," which explains the crescent moon on many Islamic flags).[110] Almost immediately, Muhammad created a violent and imperialistic movement that consumed most of Christendom's territories by AD 732. Islam is a faith born in war, and it uses the sword as a tool for expansion.

Islam partitions the world into two abodes: the Abode of Islam and the Abode of War. Bat Ye'or, a pseudonym of Gisele Littman, an Egyptian-born British author who writes about Middle East issues, explains the concept of two abodes in *The Dhimmi*:

The jihad is a global conception that divides the peoples of the world into two irreconcilable camps: that of the dar al-Harb, the "Territory of War," which covers those regions controlled by the infidels; and the dar al-Islam, "the Territory of Islam," the Muslim homeland where Islamic law reigns. The jihad is the normal and permanent state of war between the Muslims and the dar al-Harb, a war that can only end with the final domination over unbelievers and the absolute supremacy of Islam throughout the world.[111]

The Muslims' two-abode view of the world explains why non-Muslims must be destroyed, which is precisely what happened for hundreds of years prior to the Crusades. Islamic armies conquered the Christian world—Egypt, Palestine, Syria, North Africa, Spain, most of Asia Minor, southern France, Spain, and the Italian peninsula and surrounding islands were threatened and/or conquered by Muslim jihadists. They even attacked Rome in AD 846. In just over a century, two-thirds of the Roman Christian world succumbed to Islamic jihadists.

Christians attempted to push back with limited success. In the eighth and ninth centuries, Benedictine monks were driven out of monasteries and Papal States overrun. Muslim pirates operated out of bases along Italy's northern coast and France's southern coast.

The conquering Islamic armies forced the people to convert to Islam, except for Christians and Jews, because they were considered "People of the Book." But Christians and Jews lived barely above slave status as second-class citizens in those oppressive Islamic societies.

The centuries under Muslim rule before the advent of the Crusades were mostly peaceful for Christians in part because the Islamic regimes permitted Christian pilgrims from Europe to visit Jerusalem's holy sites. Muslim tolerance waned in the tenth century, when the entrance to the Church of the Holy Sepulchre, the place tradition says is identified as the place both of the crucifixion and the tomb of Jesus of Nazareth, was converted into an Islamic mosque. A few years later, the church's dome was destroyed by fire during anti-Christian riots.[112]

By the early eleventh century, the fanatical Fatimid Caliph al-Hakim, the Muslim ruler of Jerusalem, ordered the destruction of the Church of the Holy Sepulchre. Subsequently, the Byzantine emperor Constantine

IX Monomachus (1042–1055) negotiated the rebuilding of the church shortly before the situation for Christians in the holy lands became very difficult. The tipping point for Christians was the capture of Jerusalem by the Seljuk Turks in 1077, which led to ill treatment of Christians to include denying pilgrims' access to the rebuilt Church of the Holy Sepulchre.

The Seljuk Turks turned violent against Christians in 1065 by waging a campaign against Christian pilgrims in the holy land, which included the massacre by Muslims of twelve thousand Christians only two miles from Jerusalem. Then the Seljuks took their war to the Christian Byzantine Empire, winning a decisive battle in 1071. Allegedly, that battle was "the shock that launched the Crusades," as was the liberation of the holy places, the foremost of which was the Church of the Holy Sepulchre.

CHRISTIAN CRUSADES RESPOND
TO ISLAMIC OPPRESSION

The Crusades were a Christian response to four centuries of Muslim conquests that engulfed two-thirds of the Christian world. Faced with an existential threat to their faith and culture, Christians rose up to defend themselves. That decision was prompted by a desperate plea to Rome from fellow Christians in Constantinople.

The Byzantine defeat at the hands of the Muslim Seljuks persuaded the emperor in Constantinople to appeal to Pope Urban II in Rome for help. The emperor cited the liberation of Jerusalem and other ancient Christian lands as justification for a holy, armed pilgrimage to reclaim the lost Holy Land.

The campaign to reclaim the lost Holy Land was the first significant attempt by Christians to counterattack against Muslims from the inception of Islam four hundred years prior. For those years, Christians experienced deadly and persistent threats from Muslims.

Pope Urban II accepted the Byzantine emperor's appeal by calling for volunteers——knights of Christendom—to mount a crusade. That call reportedly began with a sermon delivered at the Council of Clermont in November 1095, and in that presentation, Urban II set two goals for the Crusaders: the rescue of Eastern Christians and the liberation of Jerusalem and the holy places of Christianity.

Pope Innocent III explained the first goal:

> How does a man love according to divine precept his neighbor as himself when, knowing that his Christian brothers in faith and in name are held by the perfidious Muslims in strict confinement and weighted down by the yoke of heaviest servitude, he does not devote himself to the task of freeing them.... Is it by chance that you do not know that many thousands of Christians are bound in slavery and imprisoned by the Muslims, tortured with innumerable torments?[113]

Professor Madden explains that medieval Crusaders thought of themselves as pilgrims called to perform a righteous act of liberating the Holy Sepulchre. In return for their pilgrimage and related sacrifices, the Crusaders received pilgrimage indulgences from the pope.

Indulgences are a distinctive feature of the penitential system of the medieval Roman Catholic Church, which granted full or partial remission of the punishment of sin. Evidently, indulgences rested on the belief in purgatory, a place in the afterlife where one could continue to cancel the accumulated debt of one's sins. Some of the Crusade-era popes offered "full remission of sins," the first indulgences to Crusaders as an inducement to volunteer.[114]

Popes were not above putting a guilt trip on Christians to volunteer for the Crusades. Pope Innocent III recruited volunteers for the Fifth Crusade in 1215 by writing:

> Consider most dear sons, consider carefully that if any temporal king was thrown out of his domain and perhaps captured, would he not, when he was restored to his pristine liberty and the time

had come for dispensing justice look on his vassals as unfaithful and traitors…unless they had committed not only their property but also their persons to the task of freeing him?… And similarly will not Jesus Christ, the king of kings and lord of lords, whose servant you cannot deny being, who joined your soul to your body, who redeemed you with the Precious Blood…condemn you for the vice of ingratitude and the crime of infidelity if you neglect to help Him?[115]

The pope whipped his would-be holy warriors into a religious frenzy, promising them remission of sins, and sent them to recapture Jerusalem and the land so holy to Christians. Knights, royalty, and peasants "took up the cross" in response to the pontiff's call to action and sewed red crosses to their clothing as evidence of their commission.

The pope and other Crusade preachers used their power of verbal persuasion to muster sufficient volunteers for the armed pilgrimage. They expected the effort would be expensive and potentially cost many lives. But the pope and other Crusade preachers passionately linked the listener's Christian commitment to joining the pilgrimage to recapture the holy sites. At least sixty thousand joined the first Crusade, giving up their reasonably peaceful European lives and worldly possessions to answer the holy call.

Jonathan Riley-Smith, author of *The Crusades, Christianity, and Islam*, wrote that Crusade preachers "had to persuade their listeners to commit themselves to enterprises that would disrupt their lives, possibly impoverish and even kill or maim them, and inconvenience their families, the support of which they would…need if they were to fulfill their promises."[116]

All believers were encouraged to participate, because it was considered a holy mission that included visiting holy sites, performing penance, and praying. But crusading was different than visiting holy sites, because it promised combat and considerable sacrifice, a point not sugar coated by the Crusade preachers.

Most Christian Crusaders left the comforts of family and home ready to face death for God, but a few others saw the call to action as an opportunity to enrich themselves and gain personal glory.

A cross section of European Christians participated in the Crusades, from peasants and laborers to kings and queens. No matter their position in society, joining the Crusades was an expensive affair. Some spent their personal fortunes to win the pope's approval, but as one historian explained, "Few crusaders had sufficient cash both to pay their obligations at home and to support themselves on a crusade."[117]

Taking part in the Crusades involved considerable risk. Imagine leaving the comforts of home—land, vassals, livestock, family, and the nice European weather—to travel months by horseback, foot, and/or ship thousands of miles while facing hunger, dehydration, exhaustion, dysentery, and possible death from disease before attacking the enemy. Certainly the Crusaders considered the cost, and yet many thousands joined the effort to rescue and aid Christians in the East. They comforted themselves by believing it was their calling, the will of God.

Most of the early Crusaders evidently joined for pure reasons, to participate in a holy, armed pilgrimage to recapture Jerusalem and the holy lands for Christians. They expressed sentiments of piety and self-sacrifice as evidenced by the Crusader Odo of Burgundy, who said:

> …the journey to Jerusalem as a penance for my sins…. Since divine mercy inspired me that owing to the enormity of my sins I should go to the Sepulcher of Our Savior, in order that this offering of my devotion might be more acceptable in the sight of God, I decided not unreasonably that I should make the journey with the peace of all men and most greatly of the servants of God.

Indeed, one contemporary chronicler remarked, "The Crusader set himself the task of winning back the earthly Jerusalem in order to enjoy the celestial Jerusalem."[118]

The Crusaders' commitment was more often than not a life-risking decision; the casualty rates during the Crusades were very high: It was 75 percent for the first Crusade, for example.[119]

Once the first Crusade succeeded, most of the remainder of the sixty thousand men who participated returned home. Only a few thousand of the Crusaders remained behind to protect the liberated Crusade states like Jerusalem from the anticipated counterattacks by Muslim armies. In fact, throughout the many Crusades, the Crusaders left behind were always a small minority compared to the overwhelming majority Muslim populations in every country.

Among the elite Crusaders, the Roman pope established a number of military orders in the early twelfth century to oversee operations, most notably the Knights Hospitaller and the Knights Templar. These military-trained knights took vows of chastity and poverty, and their primary goal was to protect and aid pilgrims to the Christian Holy Land. In time, both orders prospered financially, but that was not their initial goal.

There were four characteristics common across the Crusade participants. First, they took a public ecclesiastical vow to join an armed pilgrimage with specified goal of liberating the holy lands, and they displayed a red cross on their clothing as evidence of that vow. Second, the Crusade and its "pilgrims" were endorsed by the pope, who gave the effort his blessing. Third, the Roman Church granted the Crusaders privileges such as protection of family and property during their absence, immunity from arrest during the Crusade, the church's logistics support during the campaign, and exemption from tolls and taxes. Finally, they were granted indulgences after completing their pilgrimage.

Some Crusaders abused their commission for personal gain. Individuals interpreted Urban's words to suit their own ambitions, which tarnished the honorable intentions of the majority. Unfortunately, the "sinful" deeds of the few bad apples were already absolved based on the pope's promise, and such abuses became the fodder of critics through the ages.

CRUSADES BY THE NUMBERS

There were eight Crusades or expeditions to the Holy Land, each with a slightly different objective and fought over a period of approximately two hundred years (1096 to 1272). However, they are understandably thought of as disjointed campaigns, since each was waged over a few years at a time separated by decades.

The First Crusade in 1096 launched four European "armies" that arrived in Constantinople, where Emperor Alexius insisted they swear an oath of loyalty to him. This was his way of ensuring that any territory retaken would come under his control.

Eventually, those European Crusaders and their Byzantine allies retook the Syrian coastal area and most of Palestine, including Jerusalem. Specifically, in June 1099, Jerusalem's governor surrendered to the Crusaders besieging the city. Subsequently, many of the people in Jerusalem were slaughtered as the Crusaders victoriously entered.

The Crusaders established several Latin states or *outremer* (French for "across the sea") in the captured lands: Jerusalem, Edessa, Antioch, and Tripoli. Those Latin states, with their stay-behind Crusader forces, retained control until 1130, when Muslim forces began a new jihad (holy war) to regain control of lost territory.

It is noteworthy that once Muslim forces conquer a land, it is considered to be under Islamic dominion forever. Further, Muslims consider it a mortal affront to the supremacy of Islam if land reverts to infidel ownership.[120] This belief, in part, is driving the Islamic activities witnessed in Europe today.

Once the Crusader county of Edessa fell in 1144, Christian Europe exploded with calls for action and prompted the Second Crusade that began in 1147, which was led by French King Louis VII and German King Conrad III. Unfortunately for those kings and their armies, they lost decisive battles to the Turks at Dorylaeum and Damascus, and most of the Crusaders died. These humiliating defeats ended the Second

Crusade in 1149, and Christian Europe accepted the continued Muslim power as God's punishment for the West's sins.

Meanwhile, there had been numerous Crusader attempts to capture Egypt, but in 1169, Nur al-Din's forces under Shirkuh and his nephew, Saladin, seized Cairo and forced the Crusaders to withdraw. Eventually, Saladin mounted a campaign against the Crusader kingdom of Jerusalem, destroying that Christian army at the battle of Hattin, thus retaking Jerusalem and much of the surrounding territory.

Saladin's victory prompted the Third Crusade (1189–1192), led by Emperor Frederick Barbarossa of the German Empire, King Philip II Augustus of France, and King Richard I Lionheart of England. Unfortunately, Emperor Frederick drowned while crossing a river, prompting his army to head home before reaching the Holy Land. Philip and Richard constantly bickered, which must have influenced Philip to pick up his army and head home after recapturing Acre, a port on modern Israel's Haifa Bay. In September 1191, Richard's army defeated Saladin at the battle of Arsuf and then moved to retake Jerusalem.

Richard reconquered some of the territory lost to Saladin in 1169, but refused to lay siege to Jerusalem after two abortive attempts to secure supply lines from the Mediterranean coast to the inland city. In September 1192, Richard and Saladin made peace and reestablished the former kingdom of Jerusalem—albeit without the city of Jerusalem—although there was a promise of free access to Jerusalem by unarmed pilgrims.

Soon after reinstituting the kingdom of Jerusalem, Pope Innocent III called for a new Crusade in 1198. However, the Fourth Crusade foundered for lack of money and ended as a power struggle between Rome and Constantinople rather than seeking to retake lands lost to Muslims.

The early thirteenth- century, non-Middle East Crusades focused on combating those seen as the enemies of the Christian faith in Europe. Specifically, the Albigensian Crusade (1208–1229) targeted heretical sects of Christianity in France, and the Baltic Crusades (1211–1225) sought to subdue pagans in Transylvania. The Fifth Crusade attacked

Egypt, but lost that fight to defenders led by Saladin's nephew, al-Malik al-Kamil, in 1221.

The Sixth Crusade (1228–1229) was led by Emperor Frederick II, who peacefully regained control of Jerusalem from al-Kamil. But within a decade, Muslims retook the holy city.

The Seventh Crusade (1239–1241) briefly recaptured Jerusalem, but that victory was short-lived as well. In 1244, Khwarazmiam forces enlisted by the sultan of Egypt retook the city.

The Eighth Crusade targeted Egypt and ended in defeat, as did the Fifth Crusade. King Louis IX of France led that Crusade in battle against Egypt at Mansura. Meanwhile, a new Mamluk sultan, Qalawan, defeated the invading Mongols by 1281 and then re-engaged the Crusaders, capturing Tripoli in 1289.

The major Crusades came to an end in 1291 when Qalawan's son and successor, al-Ashraf Khalil, mounted a major assault against the capital of the Crusaders in the region, the coastal port of Acre. The fall of Acre is judged to be the end of two centuries of Crusades in the Holy Land.

POST CRUSADE PERIOD OF MUSLIM SUPREMACY

Muslims reigned supreme after the Crusades, first under the heel of leaders in Egypt, the Mameluke dynasty. In 1258, the Mongols of Genghis Khan conquered Persia and did manage to conquer the Seljuk Turks before the Ottomans rose to prominence by conquering Constantinople in 1453, ending the Byzantine Empire.

The Ottomans quickly established themselves across the region to include the Balkans and Egypt. Eventually, Ottoman control decentralized, which provided an opportunity for Europeans to conduct trade with the East and opened the door to influence and colonial-like control over portions of the Middle East.

France and Great Britain competed for routes across Egypt's Isthmus of Suez, and in 1798, France's Napoleon Bonaparte seized Egypt. But France withdrew under pressure three years later.

Half a century later, France returned to Egypt to construct the Suez Canal (1859–69). However, the French eventually lost operational control of the canal to the British, who established military control over all of Egypt in the 1880s.

But by the end of the nineteenth century, the Ottoman Empire was faltering, and the Christian European nations had become world powers. It is at this point in time that the Crusades were dredged up from the depths of history to be used by both Christians and Muslims for purposes that had little, if anything, to do with what had actually happened.

CONCLUSIONS

There are a number of conclusions to take from the history of the Crusades. First, there is no justification for Muslims to cite the Crusades as the reason for hatred of the West. After all, the Muslims were the aggressor that prompted the Crusades and won most of the battles, denying Christians the permanent liberation of the Christian Holy Land. Perhaps that is why the Crusades were mostly forgotten in the Islamic world until Arab revisionist history books created myths about unprovoked Western attacks and greedy Europeans plundering of Muslim lands.

No wonder generations of Arab school children have been taught that the Crusades were a clear case of good versus evil. According to some Arab history texts, rapacious and zealous Crusaders swept into a peaceful and sophisticated Muslim world, leaving carnage and destruction in their wake. This false history was exploited by the likes of al-Qaeda leader Osama bin Laden and radical Islamists like Mehmet Ali Agca, the man who attempted to assassinate Pope John Paul II and who stated, "I have decided to kill Pope John Paul II, supreme commander of the Crusades."

Most disappointing, however, was the statement President Obama made at the 2015 National Prayer Breakfast. President Obama said:

> You see ISIS is a brutal vicious death cult that, in the name of religion, carries out unspeakable acts of barbarism, terrorizing religious minorities like the Yazidis, subjecting women to rape as a weapon of war, and claiming the mantel of religious authority for such actions.
>
> And lest we get on our high horse and think this is unique to some other place, remember that during the Crusades and the Inquisition people committed terrible deeds in the name of Christ.[121]

Obama added, "There is a tendency in us, a sinful tendency that can pervert and distort our faith." Given the facts about the Crusades, Obama is guilty of his admonition not to pervert and distort the truth.

Second, the Crusades were armed pilgrimages undertaken by mostly pious warriors fighting to remove the oppressive yoke of Muslims and restore Christian holy sites for future pilgrims. Unfortunately, some promoted the myth that Christian Europeans joined the Crusades for booty, plunder, and the establishment of colonies. The evidence demonstrates that few of the Crusaders enriched themselves as a result of the pilgrimage; rather, far more lost their fortunes in order to participate. The Crusades were not a land-grab either, as evidenced by the small garrisons left behind and the requirement to keep returning forces to the holy lands to reclaim land taken by Muslim invaders.

Finally, the Crusaders were no more brutal than necessary. Steve Weidenkopf, a lecturer of church history at the Notre Dame Graduate School of Christendom College, explained that the rules of eleventh-century warfare were harsh. "Standard practice at the time dictated that a city that refused to surrender at the sight of a siege army would suffer any and all consequences of a successful siege; this is why many cities agreed to terms before commencement of the siege," he wrote.[122] Crusaders allowed Muslims who surrendered to keep their faith, property, and livelihood.

The truth about the Crusades debunks the secular and Muslim mythology that Islam was victimized by power-mad popes and Christian fanatics seeking booty. Unfortunately, those distortions continue today, and the very same oppression and rank discrimination experienced by Christians at the hands of Islamic fascists and societies continues today across the Muslim world—but especially in the modern Middle East.

CHAPTER 5

AGE-OLD CHRISTIAN-ISLAM TENSIONS

Makings of Christian Genocide

W hy are Christians suffering to the point of extinction in the Middle East? Is the crisis really that dire?

There are a number of competing views that may explain the Middle East crisis. One of the more popular views is especially controversial. Harvard professor Samuel Huntington asserts that Islam has "bloody borders" and predicts that the dynamics of civilizational conflict in the post-Cold War era will intensify the phenomenon. His notion of a "clash of civilizations" holds to three points: Civilizations are defined by religion; conflicts involving Islamic civilization will be common and violent; and Islamic civilization will be the greatest threat to Western civilization.[123]

Huntington's theory is widely embraced, and as a result has influenced Western government policies. Advocates of that theory argue that the clash between Islam and Christianity explains the Middle East conflicts that target minority Christian populations.

Another view that might explain the tragedy of anti-Christianism in the Middle East is the nexus of Islam and conflict.

A bevy of empirical research suggests that Middle Eastern conflicts should be particularly frequent and intense because of religious factors. Those factors tend to exacerbate ethnic conflict and feed discrimination against minority faith groups like Christians. Political behavior is particularly influenced by religious differences between groups. This is especially true given the region's high level of autocracy combined with the particular importance of religion.

An analysis of the Minorities at Risk (MAR) dataset provides further insight into the nature of the Middle East's ethno-religious conflicts. MAR dataset research, which considered 267 politically active ethnic minorities throughout the world, discovered that religious factors surface considerably more often in the Middle East than in other world regions. That analysis led researchers to conclude that religion is more important in Middle Eastern conflicts than elsewhere, which means that while Islam, the region's dominant religion, may provide a partial explanation for the conflict, it cannot provide a full explanation.[124]

Perhaps the other ingredient that can explain Middle East conflicts and the associated violence against non-Muslims is the fact that the region is the most autocratic and least democratic in the world. That linkage, the Islamic faith and autocratic governments, may explain the propensity for conflict because of cultural and historical momentum than anything else.

Proponents of this research conclude that somehow delinking Islam from autocratic governments will lead to a far less oppressive and discriminatory environment. U.S. President Barack Obama appears to be such a proponent, which might explain his attempt to re-engineer the Middle East discriminatory culture beginning with his June 2009 speech at Cairo University.

President Obama began his Cairo speech with "a greeting of peace from Muslim communities in my country: *assalaamu alaykum*" (greeting for Muslims meaning "peace be on you"). But that greeting was an indirect slap in the face to America's mostly (70.6 percent) self-identifying Christians who are left out of the president's vision for the Middle East.[125]

Then Obama used his speech to indirectly attack Huntington's theory about the Islamic threat for the West. "I know there are many—Muslim and non-Muslim—who question whether we can forge this new beginning.… Some suggest that it isn't worth the effort—that we are fated to disagree, and civilizations are doomed to clash."

Unfortunately and naïvely, Obama in his speech ignored the Middle East's ruinous history and sent a message of appeasement to Islamist objectives: The U.S. will respect and accept conservative forms of Islam.

President Obama's appeasement message at Cairo and his hands-off policy over the subsequent years encouraged Islamic extremists who seized the historic opportunity to grab power. Soon the entire region exploded with unrest, and the so-called Arab Spring fueled revolutions that toppled autocratic governments, led to civil war, and put every regional government on edge.

Long before Obama's Cairo speech and the emergence of the so-called Arab Spring uprisings began to metastasize the cesspool of Islamic fascism across the Middle East, every regional country was already unwelcoming to non-Muslims. But the Arab Spring put Islamic extremism on steroids, which has become the casus belli for what is becoming a modern Christian holocaust in the faith's very cradle.

RISE OF THE MIDDLE EAST'S CHRISTIAN GENOCIDE/HOLOCAUST

The Middle East has a violent history as outlined in the previous chapter, but the savagery of wars never reached the point of genocide, that is, until the twentieth century. Specifically, the Armenian genocide—the systematic destruction of all or a significant part of a racial, ethnic, religious, or national group—occurred when two million Christian Armenians living in Turkey were eliminated from their historic homeland through forced deportations and massacres mostly between 1915 and 1918. The Turkish authorities demolished entire Christian Armenian cities and any remnants of Armenian cultural heritage, including price-less masterpieces of ancient architecture.[126]

The Turkish authorities were fearful that the Christian Armenian population was planning to align with Russia, the Ottomans' enemy. As a result the Turks made the decision to annihilate the entire Armenian population, which started by rounding up Armenian leaders, educators, writers, clergy, and dignitaries. They were jailed, tortured, and hung or shot. Then Armenian men were arrested and executed by death squads. The women, children, and elderly were subjected to death marches into the Syrian Desert, where they were thrown off cliffs, burned alive, or drowned in rivers. Finally, children were coerced into denouncing their Christian faith and embracing Islam, and the young boys were forced to endure circumcision as required by Islamic custom.

A gripping account of one such early incident is related by David Kupelian, the *WorldNetDaily* editor who is an Armenian and great grandson of Steelianos Leondiades, an Armenian pastor. Kupelian's maternal grandmother, Anna Paulson, daughter of Steelianos, described the scene based on the account of the lone survivor.

Protestant minister Leondiades traveled to the Turkish city of Adana to attend a pastors' conference in 1909. Anna Paulson, the pastor's daughter, said: "Some of the Turkish officers came to the conference room and told all these ministers—there were seventy of them, ministers and laymen and a few wives: 'If you embrace the Islamic religion you will all be saved. If you don't, you will be killed.'"[127]

Pastor Leondiades, who spoke for the group, asked the Turkish officers for a few minutes to make a decision. At the end of the brief respite—a time used for prayer and Bible reading—none of those Christian men and women would renounce their Christian faith and convert to Islam.

"And then," Anna Paulson said, based on the lone survivor's testimony, "they were all killed. They were not even buried. They were all thrown down the ravine."

The world knew at the time (late 1890s through the end of World

War I) that the Turks were guilty of genocide, but did little more than protest. Even the *New York Times* ran one hundred articles in 1915 alone documenting the forced death marches of Armenian victims. Today, archives are stacked high with countless photos, films, and personal accounts of beheadings, shootings, and burning under the brutal Ottoman caliphate.[128] Yet, even with overwhelming evidence, today the Turkish government refuses to acknowledge culpability for the Armenian genocide.

Henry Morgenthau, the U.S. ambassador to Turkey at the time, documented the planned genocide of Armenians by Turkish soldiers and the incitement of Turkish Muslims to kill their Christian neighbors. At the height of the Armenian genocide, Morgenthau wrote to Washington about their forced exile: "When the Turkish authorities gave the orders to these deportations, they were merely giving the death warrant to a whole race."[129]

The Western powers expressed outrage at the time to the Turkish government and warned of consequences. But those warnings had no effect, which encouraged other rogues. In fact, years later, a young German politician, Adolf Hitler, used the feckless Western reaction to the Armenian tragedy as justification for genocide when he decided to do the same to the Polish people: "Thus for the time being I have sent to the east only my 'Death's Head Units' with the orders to kill without pity or mercy all men, women, and children of Polish race or language. Only in such a way will we win the vital space that we need. Who still talks nowadays about the Armenians?"[130]

The world community eventually formulated a consensus on genocide, albeit too late for the Armenian genocide by the Ottoman Empire and the Jewish Holocaust by Nazi Germany during World War II. In 1951, the United Nations adopted the recommendations of the Convention on the Prevention and Punishment of the Crime of Genocide (CPPCG).[131]

The CPPCG, which was ratified by 146 states, including most of the Middle East countries, defines genocide as the intent to destroy in whole or in part a national, ethnical, racial, or religious group by killing the members; causing serious bodily or mental harm; inflicting on the group conditions of life calculated to bring about its physical destruction; imposing measures intended to prevent births; and forcibly transferring children to another group.

Tragically, many of the universal conditions for genocide codified by the CPPCG are evident in the Middle East today.

Dr. John Eibner, the chief executive officer of Christian Solidarity International, a human rights nongovernmental organization, said: "Conditions for genocide against non-Muslim communities exist in varying degrees throughout" the Middle East.[132] The crisis of survival for non-Muslim communities is especially acute in Iraq, Syria, Egypt, Iran, and the Palestinian territories.

Neil Hicks with Human Rights First agrees with Eibner. "The future of Christians in the Middle East is very bleak," he says. "What has happened in Iraq and Syria is de facto ethnic cleansing of Christians."[133]

Former U.S. Representative Frank Wolf says ISIS' butchery of Christians in the Middle East meets the U.N.'s definition for genocide. "It is genocide. It meets the test of genocide," Wolf explained. Meanwhile, President Obama is mute on the issue and refuses to use the "g" word to describe the eradication of Christianity from its birthplace.[134]

The ongoing cleansing of Middle Eastern Christians takes place amidst many of the same conditions seen a century ago in Turkey during the Armenian genocide as well as the Jewish Holocaust.

Consider eight genocide-related conditions on full display in Middle Eastern countries today. These were adopted from Christian Solidarity International's list of "Universal Conditions for Genocide."[135]

First, there is an absence of integrating institutions in most of the Middle East countries. The region's Islamic governments and their societies have a long history of little tolerance for non-Muslim religious groups and no apparent institutional willingness to integrate those groups.

Egypt illustrates the absence of non-Muslim-friendly integrating institutions better than other countries, because Egypt has a significant Christian minority. Even though Coptic Christians are 10 percent of Egypt's population, most Egyptian institutions are biased against them, and that includes government-controlled Islamic institutions that have special influence inside Egypt's government.

Egyptian Islamic institutions have special influence because they are wholly controlled by the federal government. Cairo maintains control over all Muslim religious institutions, appoints and pays all Sunni Muslim imams, licenses all mosques, monitors sermons, and even officially sanctions the interpretation of Islam. Allegedly, such control is intended to prevent religious extremism and terrorism—but it can also be used by Muslim bureaucrats to discriminate against non-Muslims.[136]

Muslim clergy also have power in Egypt's government because of Article 2, holdover language from the 1971 constitution, which states: "The principles of Islamic Sharia are the principal source of legislation." Further, Article 4 appears to grant Islam's Al-Azhar University scholars a special consultative role in reviewing religiously significant legislation, which, under sharia, means virtually every aspect of life. Al-Azhar University in Cairo is Egypt's oldest degree-granting university and renowned as "Sunni Islam's most prestigious university."[137]

Evidently, the tight Islam-state relationship gives the state-paid imam and his Muslim surrogates great influence over the affairs of government to include something as simple as whether to approve a Christian's request to either build or repair a church.

Christians who want to build a new church must obtain a presidential decree, or if they want to repair an existing structure, they must obtain the approval of the Muslim-dominated regional government. Both permissions are difficult, if not impossible, to obtain.[138] It appears that the Ministry of Interior, which oversees regulations governing building permits, strongly discourages even the request to construct a new church by imposing nearly impossible barriers such as requiring a new church project to be located at least one hundred meters away from the nearest mosque. In addition, the neighboring community must approve the construction project, a nearly impossible proposition in an overwhelmingly Muslim country where anti-Christian views run strong.

In Egypt, there is also a major institution that fans the flames of hostility rather than integration of Christians. Specifically, "Al-Azhar, the world's preeminent Sunni Islamic institution, has contributed its share to widespread hostility for Christians by publishing a pamphlet declaring the Bible a corrupted document and Christianity a pagan religion."[139] No wonder Christian missionaries are forbidden and, if found, are immediately deported by Egypt's authorities.

Even Egypt's law enforcement and army seem to be biased against Christians. An incident in July 2013 reported by Amnesty International indicated that Egyptian security forces "stood by and failed to intervene during a brutal attack on Coptic Christians in Luxor… [They] left six besieged men—four of whom were killed and one hospitalized—to the mercy of an angry crowd."[140]

The Egyptian military is a hypocritical institution when it comes to Coptic Christians. Specifically in the wake of the June 2013 ouster of Muslim Brotherhood leader and former President Mohammed Morsi, Islamic mobs destroyed dozens of churches. At the time, the military promised to rebuild those churches, but according to the *Global Post*, "The army's work to rebuild the churches has been slow. Even the help they do provide is partial" and some churches never received any help.[141]

The Anba Moussa Church was completely destroyed in the 2013 riots, for example. "Nothing has been moved since the day a mob burned and looted the church and priest's apartment. They took everything, down to the doorframes and the toilet seats, after driving a car through the front doors. Only an ever-thickening layer of dust attests to the passage of time," reports the *Global Post*. Where is the Army and President Abdel Fattah el-Sisi, who promised to patch up religious-based differences?

Egypt typifies the lack of meaningful institutions to help integrate non-Muslim minorities across the region. Not only does Egypt lack such institutions as well as the will to correct the problem, but like many other Middle Eastern countries, it actively discourages Christian practices such as public Christian worship, which in some states is illegal. A number of governments like Saudi Arabia requires all citizens to be Muslims and Riyadh, the Saudi capital, even has laws that label conversion to another religion like Christianity an apostasy, a crime punishable by death. The Saudis also prohibit non-Muslims from entering the cities of Mecca and Medina, Islam's holiest cities—a topic addressed later in this volume.

Some Middle East countries that at least allow Christians to publicly exist have laws that prohibit their churches from displaying crosses or erecting bell towers. Others prohibit Bibles, crucifixes, statutes, carvings, and other Christian symbols. A number of regional governments even prohibit non-Muslim clergy from entering their country for any reason.

Second, there is a perception that minority religious groups are politically subversive. Most Middle Eastern governments oppress Christian communities on political, security, and economic levels with the objective of reducing their influence and their physical presence.

Iran illustrates the issue as well as others. Since his June 2013 election, Iranian President Hassan Rouhani failed to deliver on his campaign promise to strengthen civil liberties for religious minorities. Specifically, the numbers of Christians now in prison in Iran for their faith increased over the past year, as did the incidents of physical attacks, harassment, detention, and arrests.

Since 2010, according to a U.S. State Department report, Iranian authorities arbitrarily arrested and detained about four hundred Christians throughout the country. As of February 2014, at least forty Christians were either in prison, detained, or awaiting trial because of their religious beliefs and activities. One of the most publicized cases is that of an Iranian-born American pastor.

In January 2013, Saeed Abedini, the American pastor, was sentenced in a trial without due process to eight years in prison for "threatening the national security of Iran" for his activity in the Christian house church movement. There is no evidence that Abedini sought to undermine the Iranian government.[142]

Unfortunately, the case of Pastor Abedini is not that uncommon in present-day Iran. A 2014 United Nations report found that the Islamic Republic's Bible believers are more persecuted than ever. Iran continues to imprison Christians for their faith, and evangelical Christians are charged with "threats to national security." The report indicates that at least forty-nine Christians were among 307 religious minorities being held in Iranian jails as of January 2014.[143]

Davood Irani, an Iranian Christian convert who hosted a home church, described the circumstances surrounding being charged with crimes against national security due to his Christian faith.[144] His case illustrates how Islamic states like Iran treat Christians as politically subversive.

Mr. Irani was born in Sari, Iran, in 1976 and fled that country after discovering that both he and his wife had been sentenced to two years of imprisonment on charges of acting against national security and other unspecified political charges, based solely on the practice of his Christian faith.

Mr. Irani provided his story to the Iran Human Rights Documentation Center on March 2, 2014.

"I became a Christian on August 28, 2005," Irani said. "Although I was born into a non-religious Iranian family like everyone else I was forcefully deemed a Muslim from birth." After becoming a Christian, he moved to Tehran to be near other Christians, where he eventually served as a home church director whose membership never exceeded ten people.

About noon on December 7, 2009, there was a knock at his door, Irani explained. He thought his landlord was knocking, but after opening the door, he was met by five agents from the Iranian Ministry of Intelligence (MOI). Two of the agents were armed.

The MOI agents presented no warrant, but quickly entered Irani's apartment and meticulously searched his dwelling, confiscating every Christian-related item: pictures, books, a cross, and much more. They even took his personal computer, which was never returned.

Irani and his wife were soon whisked away in government sedans to the Number 100 Detention Center, known in Shiraz as *Pelak-e Sad*. Before entering the detention facility, they were blindfolded and then taken inside, where they were placed in wooden cabins designed for interrogations and then handcuffed to a table.

One of the arresting agents announced to an evidently more senior official who entered the cabin that they had "arrested the suspect." Irani and his wife were next questioned separately.

The agents told Irani that he was charged with apostasy, spreading propaganda against the Islamic Republic, and for his membership in groups opposed to the Islamic Republic. Later, according to Irani, he was also charged with insulting Islam.

The day after his arrest, the MOI agents took the couple to the Islamic Revolutionary Court's procurator's branch, where they were arraigned. The procurator spoke to them about their Christian beliefs, and the procurator specifically said they were Christian Protestants. Then the procurator charged that being a Protestant meant that they were "protesting," which is an offense. "He said that [because of being a Protestant] I was supposed to do something against the norm," Irani said. The official expected them to confess, according to Irani, but neither he nor his wife capitulated.

Irani said he was afterward interrogated daily for perhaps a month, both in the morning and in the afternoon. Interrogators would tag team Irani. One would ask questions and the other would discuss religious matters, trying to convince Irani about the error of his beliefs. At one point, the official accused Irani of being associated with Elam, a Christian organization in the United Kingdom and U.S. dedicated to spreading Christianity in Iran.[145]

During the course of the daily examinations, Irani said the MOI agents had no problem, saying that his crime was apostasy—but he was never charged with apostasy. "They would focus on the political aspects of the case," Irani explained. At one point, the agents said that if Irani continued to evangelize, "a car would strike me." Then the agents explained that if he spoke about his faith, "maybe something would happen to me. 'Anyway, you have a wife. You may go on a trip,'" the agents would say.

Irani was soon transferred to Abelabad prison, a "frightening and unfortunately an unhygienic prison." Even though he was in Abdelabad for only ten days, he became sick but was denied medical attention. His wife only spent half of that time in the facility. Both were soon released on bail after pledging to stop their Christian activities—a promise they did not keep.

Although the MOI agents told him he was barred from leaving the country, in June 2011, Irani and his wife flew from Imam Khomeini Airport to the Republic of Georgia.

Irani's story ends well because he escaped certain imprisonment. But thousands of other Iranis, Christian men and women, live in Middle East countries afraid that at any moment the local MOI will knock on their door and change their lives forever.

Irani's case and hundreds of other stories about heavy-handed Islamic regimes clamping down on Christians illustrate the paranoid government view that these people are political subversives who seek to topple their governments. Perhaps that would be an outcome of spreading the gospel of Jesus Christ, but not their primary focus.

Third, there is a prevalence of religiously discriminatory ideology. Both Middle East governments and their mostly Islamic societies embrace an Islamic ideology that inherently discriminates against Christians and other religious minorities.

The fact that most Middle Eastern governments codify Islam as the state religion and or prohibit non-Islamic public worship creates a poisonous environment for Christians. This public discrimination is witnessed in the schools, by many public figures (especially government-supported clerics), and government-owned and privately owned regional media.

A study by Pew Research Center's Forum on Religion in Public Life found that the Middle East has the highest instances of government restrictions on religion and social hostility toward religious communities than any other region in the world. The three worst Middle East countries are Saudia Arabia, Iran, and Egypt.

Consider evidence of religious-based discrimination in their public schools.

Egypt's government publishes school textbooks filled with intolerant content that incites violence against non-Muslims. The same is true in other Middle East countries like Iran.

A study by Freedom House examined the textbooks used in Iranian schools to teach the country's children and not surprisingly found the texts weave suspicion and contempt about non-Muslims. Further, the textbooks present a particular interpretation of Shi'a Islam that fits the regime's political and ideological interests.[146]

Textbooks obviously help shape and socialize the next generation, which the ayatollah and his clerical regime fully appreciate. That's why they use the educational environment to imprint religious lessons that would educate a generation familiar with the Islamic republic's discourse and dominant views. Additionally, it is noteworthy that the ministry of education created separate textbooks for boys and girls.

As expected, Iran's educational system is mandated to include "religious education" and "purification" training that are consistent with Shi'a culture and traditions. A grade 7 social science text states, "The people in the Islamic community must take on the responsibility of putting into practice Islam's social laws—under the coherent organization of the Islamic government. They must carry out these laws with certainty and power and, in this way, provide for the security of the Islamic community."

Iranian textbooks address non-Muslim minorities and explain the approved attitude toward non-Muslim religions. "We must believe in and respect all of the divine prophets," states a grade 6 religious studies textbook. "We believe that they have come from god...based on Islamic laws, we have the duty to treat the followers of Moses and Jesus—who are known as Jews and Christians—well and respect their rights."

Note what a grade 6 Iranian history textbook states about Jesus Christ:

> With his pleasant words and good disposition, Jesus invited people to worship the one and only God and to avoid cruelty. He supported the deprived and victims of cruelty. God had given him the power to heal the sick. Jesus' teachings angered the Romans, who worshipped multiple gods and had become used to treating their people and slaves in a cruel and oppressive manner. In spite of all this, Jesus continued to travel to various cities and villages and to invite the people to practice monotheism and do good deeds.

Not all Iranian textbooks are so neutral or complimentary of the Christian faith. Specifically, a grade 8 Islamic culture and religious studies textbook reads:

> The source of differences in, and the existence of, various religions were propagators of various new religions who, upon the arrival of the new prophet, opposed him and did not accept him as the prophet. For example, when Jesus appeared among the Jews and asked people to practice the true teachings of Moses, most of the Jewish authorities and elders did not accept his mission as a prophet and rose in opposition to him. If these learned Jews had not opposed the mission of Jesus as a prophet and had followed him, this dichotomy and difference would not have come about. At the time of his appearance, the honorable Prophet of Islam, too, introduced himself as following in the path of all the prophets and complementing their work and asked Jews and Christians to put their faith in him. However, this time as well, in spite of the fact that the coming of the Prophet of Islam had been promised in the Torah and the Bible,

the Christian and Jewish authorities and elders denied his mission as a prophet and rose in opposition to him. If at that time, the Jewish and Christian authorities and elders had accepted the mission of Mohammad as prophet, this difference would not have come about.

Even the eleventh-century Crusades earned special mention in an Iranian grade 7 history textbook:

The Pope too issued a decree saying that since Jesus had lived there, Jerusalem had to be taken back from Muslims. Thus, the invasion of the Islamic World started. Christian soldiers... started towards Jerusalem. On their path, they murdered people and pillaged and plundered their property and, after occupying Jerusalem, too, they killed a large number of Muslims.... Some time later, under the leadership of Salahuddin Ayubi, Muslims took Jerusalem back. Finally, the Crusades ended with the defeat of the Europeans.... By observing the advanced civilization and the cultural progress of Muslims, they became aware of their own backwardness and strove to use the scientific and intellectual achievements of Muslims.

Saudi school texts are just as anti-Christian as those in Iran. A 2011 study by the Center for Religious Freedom at the Hudson Institute, *Ten Years On: Saudi Arabia's Textbooks Still Promote Religious Violence,* found that Saudi school texts continue to encourage violence and extremism as an integral part of national textbooks, particularly those on religion.

Five million Saudi students are fed a steady diet of Islamist extremism, and as the controlling authority of the two holiest shrines in Islam, Saudi Arabia disseminates its hateful religious propaganda to millions of Muslims attending the annual Hajj, the pilgrimage to Mecca Muslims must make at least once in their lives.

Saudi Arabia's oil wealth helps the kingdom spread its textbooks and other propaganda free of charge across the world. The Saudi Education Ministry ships the material to many Muslim schools, mosques, and libraries worldwide. This fact cannot be underemphasized. Lawrence Wright wrote in his book, *The Looming Tower*, that while the Saudi people are only 1 percent of the world's population, they fund "90 percent of the expenses of the entire faith, overriding other traditions of Islam." That is why the material they produce is significant.[147]

The Hudson Center for Religious Freedom identified a number of intolerant and violent textbook passages that were discovered in previous studies as well. Specifically, there are Saudi schoolbooks that glorify jihad and martyrdom, and another blames Jews for virtually all sedition. For example, militant jihad is exalted in a 2010–11 public school textbook as a "profitable trade" that "saves from painful punishment."

The study also identified passages regarding polytheists and infidels. A twelfth-grade monotheism textbook advocates killing and robbing polytheists which, according to the texts, include Shiites and some Christians because of their belief in the Trinity. Although other 2010–11 schoolbooks no longer sanction outright killing and robbing, they do state that "infidels" should be fought under certain conditions.

The books use a highly offensive lexicon for non-Muslims and inflate the facts. Christians are sometimes referred to as "Crusaders" (al-Qaeda's terminology), infidels, polytheists, and apostates. Various texts also misrepresent the actual percentages of Muslim minorities in the West, perhaps to suggest that those Muslims face dire circumstances as minorities in "infidel" lands.

Some texts suggest that "Islamic jihad" has not gone far enough in ridding Muslim countries of colonial control. They also address the issue of Muslims converting to Christianity, suggesting that Christian and American schools located in the Middle East are really evidence of a new "crusades." The study also notes that the "crusader"-related concern is why groups like al-Qaeda and Nigeria's Boko Haram ("Western education is forbidden") reject Western education.

Some Saudi schoolbooks prime the student for future jihad. A twelfth-grade book asserts that Muslim minorities in non-Muslim occupied "Islamic lands" like the Balkan states, Romania, and Kashmir in India are encouraged to adopt a belligerent worldview, according to the Hudson Center, that seems designed to prepare the students for future hostilities based on religious identity. Some twelfth-grade texts even explicitly promote militant jihad for "spreading Islam" by "fighting unbelievers."

The Center for Religious Freedom points out that the Saudi education system's method of rote learning is ideally suited for Islamic indoctrination, which is evidently what happens. That rote learning starts in first grade and becomes more virulent as the student progresses. Radical Wahhabi religion courses are favored over traditional math and science courses that leave Saudi youth prepared for terrorism rather than the modern workplace.

Middle East Islamic leaders are frequently tethered to their governments and are seldom restrained in their anti-Christian comments that tend to incite violence. Saudi Imam Issa Assiri of the Sa'eed bin Jubair Mosque in Jedda, Saudi Arabia, applied his understanding of Islamic ideology to incite violence against non Muslims. The imam said Jews and Christians only understand the sword, a reference to the January 2015 al-Qaeda-sponsored attack on the Paris magazine that depicted a satirical cartoon of the Prophet Muhammad. He used that view to espouse the obligation of Muslims to kill Christians and other non-Muslim people.

An analysis of Saudi Friday sermons demonstrates a source of the prevalence of religiously discriminatory ideology permeating the Middle East. Three things should be understood about the Saudi clerics' allegiance and influence. First, many of these imams are funded by the Saudi government; and second, all Muslim men are expected to attend Friday worship at their mosque. Finally, all Islamic clerics, whether Saudi or American, are incredibly powerful people, and their words have consequences—especially in countries where Islam is backed by autocratic governments.

The Middle East Research Institute compiled Saudi sermons into categories that impact views about non-Muslims and the West. Some sermons identified Christians and Jews as infidels and enemies of Allah. A sermon delivered by Sheikh Abd al-Muhsin al-Qadhi at the al-Salaam mosque in al-Unayzah referred to Christianity as a "false faith." Then the imam said, "We will review their history, full of hate, abomination, and wars against Islam and the Muslims."[148]

Another Saudi imam was highly critical of the pope's visit to the region at the time. The imam accused the pope of being a descendant of the Spanish inquisitors "who tortured the Muslims most abominably… they are the descendants of those who led the crusades to the Islamic east, in which thousands of Muslims were killed and their wives taken captive in uncountable numbers. They are the perpetrators of the massacres in Bosnia-Herzegovina…in Kosovo, in Indonesia, and in Chechnya." Another imam at a Mecca mosque claimed the pope's visit was proof that "Christian missionaries are invading the Islamic world."

A number of imams rejected calls for religious harmony. At Al-Rahmah Mosque in Mecca, Sheikh Marzouq Salem Al-Ghamdi said:

If the infidels live among the Muslims, in accordance with the conditions set out by the Prophet—there is nothing wrong with it provided they pay *jizya* to the Islamic treasury. Other conditions are…that they do not renovate a church or a monastery, do not rebuild ones that were destroyed, that they feed for three days any Muslim who passes by their homes…that they rise when a Muslim wishes to sit, that they do not imitate Muslims in dress and speech, nor ride horses, nor own swords, nor arm themselves with any kind of weapon; that they do not sell wine, do not show the cross, do not ring church bells, do not raise their voices during prayer, that they shave their hair in front so as to make them easily identifiable, do not incite anyone against the Muslims, and do not strike a Muslim.… If they violate these conditions, they have no protection.

Imam al-Rahmah's statement is evidence that the so-called clash of civilizations between East and West remains alive. After all, many of the clerics in Saudi mosques rely on a steady diet of Western and non-Muslim statements and behaviors to illustrate the struggle.

Some imams take a very practical approach to address the clash of civilizations by calling on fellow Muslims to vaccinate their children against Western influences. They call on Muslims to educate their children to jihad and to hate Christians. Sheikh Muhammad Saleh Al-Munajjid said in a sermon:

> Muslims must...educate their children to Jihad. This is the greatest benefit of the situation: educating the children to Jihad and to hatred of the Jews, the Christians, and the infidels; educating the children to Jihad and to revival of the embers of Jihad in their souls. This is what is needed now.

WOMEN IN ISLAMIC SOCIETIES

Women's rights are often the subject of Saudi imams' sermons that the clerics cite as evidence of the West's decadence and contrariness to the truth. Evidently, some Saudi imams believe that the status of women in society is a matter of life and death, and they see the West's preoccupation with the status of women in Islamic countries as an attempt to undermine Islamic society.

In a sermon at the Al-Huweish Mosque in Al-Taif, Sheikh Muhammad Al-Nimr explained:

> The enemies of Islam...know that the woman is a double-edged sword, and that she can be transformed into the most dangerous weapon of destruction [of Islamic nations]. Thus, the woman has suffered from most of the conspiracies to shatter the Islamic

nation—because the woman has a group of traits allowing her to either build or destroy the nation.

Permitting women to leave the home, so that they rub up against men in the marketplaces and talk with people other than their chaperones—with some even exposing parts of their bodies prohibited from exposure—are forbidden acts, a disgrace, and lead to destruction. The first crime perpetrated by the Israelites was letting their women loose when they were adorned, so that they would stir up *Fitna* [inner strife]. For this, Allah punished them with the plague.

SUPPORTIVE MEDIA

Much of the Middle East's media is influenced if not outright controlled by their governments as evident in reporting and commentary.

One of the best known accounts of religious-based historical revisionism is perpetrated by the Iranian regime, which consistently denies the Jewish Holocaust. Tehran uses its Holocaust denial propaganda to claim that Israel's existence is illegitimate. Specifically, on January 28, 2015, the day after the International Holocaust Remembrance Day, the *Fars News Agency*, which is affiliated with Iran's Islamic Revolutionary Guard Corps (IRGC), headed by Iranian Supreme Leader Ali Khamenei, published an article titled, "The Holocaust an Example of the West's Rewriting of History Based on Superpower Interests." That article states that the "Holocaust lie" was being exposed worldwide, and Holocaust reports are based on falsified and unsubstantiated documents that fail to prove any mass extermination of Jews or any decision by the Nazis to carry out such an atrocity. Further, the article said Hitler's anti-Semitism was used as an opportunity to concoct the myth of the Holocaust in order to promote the establishment of a state for the Jews.

Arab commentary can best be judged by examining the bias demonstrated regarding a familiar incident. On January 7, 2015, as mentioned previously and to illustrate the bias, three gunmen killed twelve French citizens and critically wounded five others in an attack at the headquarters of the French satirical magazine *Charlie Hebdo*. The magazine is widely known for lampooning Islam and the Prophet Muhammad. Previously, the magazine's Paris office was completely destroyed by a Molotov cocktail attack in November 2011 in response to an edition that also contained caricatures of the Prophet.

A week after the *Hebdo* attack al-Qaeda in the Arabian Peninsula's media organ, al-Malahem, released a video featuring Nasser bin Ali al-Ansi claiming credit for the attack on the French magazine headquarters. Al-Ansi claimed that al-Qaeda core leader Ayman al-Zawahiri ordered the attack and that it was coordinated by Anwar Al-Awlaki. Al-Ansi said, "We clarify to the Ummah [community of Islamic peoples] that the one who chose the target, laid the plan and financed the op is the leadership of this organization."

There was no shortage of Arab comment regarding the Paris incident, and most of it was not sympathetic to the French, thus revealing their bias.

Arab states and their leaders were quick to condemn the attack, but then tried to portray that such attacks are evidence of a global phenomenon that hurts Arab countries. The exception was the Syrian foreign ministry, which blamed France itself and stated, "Syria had warned time and again of the dangers of supporting terror…and that this terror would come back to bite those who supported it."[149]

The Arab press covered the Paris incident by publishing hundreds of articles that for the most part condemned the attacks but universally claimed they did not represent the world's Muslims or their religion. Some of the reports stressed that the Muslims did not have to apologize for the assaults, because France had brought the attacks upon itself mostly due to its wrongheaded foreign policy, which "supports terror" or racism against domestic Muslim communities. Yet others claimed that the French deliberately provoked Muslims by "insulting the Prophet," making France responsible for the incidents.

Some liberal Arab writers called on the Muslim public to condemn the attack. They emphasized that even insulting Islam's Prophet and faith were not justification for the killings.

Most of the Arab media's attention focused on the *Charlie Hebdo* shooting and very little even mentioned the attack on the kosher supermarket. That incident that took three lives earned press comments but ignored the clear anti-Semitic character.

It is noteworthy that the government-owned press was far more critical. Almed Mansour, a presenter on the Qatari-owned Al-Jazeera channel, lambasted fellow Arab journalists for their response to the Paris incident.

> The Muslims' self-degradation and their submission to the crusader west following the attack on the French newspaper *Charlie Hebdo*, in supplication for [the West's] forgiveness and absolution, are a source of sorrow and anguish. This, especially since the West has waged consecutive Crusades against the Muslim world ever since [former U.S. president] George W. Bush announced the anti-Iraq crusade in 2003. It is the West that is perpetrating acts of killing and terror. The French are the terrorists who kill Muslims day and night. French history is suffused with the killing of Algerians during the 130 years of [French colonial] occupation. [For example,] in one massacre [carried out] in a single day in 1945 they killed forty-five thousand Algerians who came out to demonstrate against them. Furthermore, they used Algeria and its people as a nuclear testing ground. In the same way, the Zionists are waging incessant terror against the people of occupied Palestine, and the Americans and their allies are committing acts of killing and terror in Iraq, Egypt, Libya, Syria and in many places worldwide.

The Saudi government daily *Makkah* also attacked Western countries, accusing them of cultivating terror organizations to advance their interest:

The terror whose crimes the West is now condemning is originally of Western manufacture. [The West] cultivated it during the 1980s, when it played a major role on its behalf in the East-West struggle in Afghanistan. But now that this terror has grown stronger, bared its teeth and eroded the status of these [Western] countries, they consider it a vile thing that must be uprooted.

The Egyptian government's daily *al-Ahram* editorialized, accusing the West of supporting and legitimatizing terror organizations for years while ignoring Egypt's call to combat terror:

The West must now understand that it has made some shameful mistakes for which it is paying dearly today. This, because it opened its arms to several extremist movements and insisted on embracing them, viewing them as oppositions to regimes in the region that could be recruited to serve its interests whenever it wished…. Following the attack on the French newspaper *Charlie Hebdo* in Paris… [The West] should have admitted its mistaken policy towards these terror movements that flourished and grew under its wing for decades while it provided them with a cover of legitimacy and support.

Middle East governments and their Islamic societies proliferate religiously discriminatory ideology through most public outlets such as those just profiled: schools, clerics, and the media. Clearly that ideology is designed to propagandize their populations and implant false teachings with the sole purpose of government control over the thoughts and actions of the people as has been common with autocratic governments down through history. In short, Islam by itself would not stand; it must be propped up through constant deception and unrelenting control.

Fourth, religious discrimination is institutionalized in law and social custom. Non-Muslims in the Middle East are at a distinct disadvantage in all aspects of existence. Christians in particular face systematic discrimination in most Middle Eastern countries due to religion-based repressive laws and policies that restrict freedom of thought and conscience. Such laws and policies result from combining autocratic governments that declare official religions with Islamic jurisprudence, which is at the heart of Middle Eastern legal systems.

That is the profile of most of the Middle East, but on paper, those states claim to be like the rest of the world's states, which tend to encode religious freedom in their constitutions. In fact, most (65 percent) Middle Eastern regimes have religious freedom clauses in their constitutions, but that freedom is subject to a variety of limitations due to country customs, morality, and extraconstitutional law. Specifically, those constitutional limitations more often than not provide the legal pretext to their respective autocratic regimes to violate religious freedom. For example, state courts use those constitutionally based religious freedom qualifications to bypass or disregard their constitutions' encoded religious freedom commitment.

Those qualifications were inserted into the constitutions so the autocratic regimes could appear on the world stage as being supportive of religious freedom. Further, more often than not, the regimes tend to use the national security trump card to disregard constitutional religious freedom clauses. The Islamic Republic of Iran illustrates the point.

Iran discriminates against Christians in many of its laws. A 2003 study by the Switzerland-based International Federation of Human Rights documents the basis of that discrimination in Iran's constitution and penal and civil laws.[150]

Iran's religion-based discrimination is based on two guiding principles. First, one must understand that divine law—Shi'a Islam—is the unique source of legitimacy and political power in Iran. The second principle is that as Iranians wait for the reappearance of Shi'a Islam's Twelfth Imam, the Imam's earthly representative and interpreter of divine law is the spiritual leader or the grand ayatollah. This concept is known as the *velāyat-e faqīh* ("spiritual leadership") and serves as the cornerstone of every aspect of the Islamic Republic of Iran's governance.

Therefore, Islam is the religion of the state, which is conceived as an institution and instrument of the divine will. Further, in this system better known as a clerical oligarchy, divine truth and clerical authority are inseparable.

This clerical oligarchy under Article 110 of Iran's constitution grants all powers to the spiritual leader, grand ayatollah. He exercises absolute control over virtually every aspect of life: the judiciary, the army, the police, the radio, the television, and all the political leaders and government institutions.

It is noteworthy that Article 12 of Iran's constitution grants special status to three religious minorities:

> Zoroastrian, Jewish, and Christian Iranians. These are the only recognized religious minorities, who, within the limits of the law, are free to perform their religious rites and ceremonies, and to act according to their own cannon in matters of personal affairs and religious education.

It is wonderful that Iran recognizes Christians as a religious minority and that the constitution guarantees them general rights. However, the overwhelming evidence is that Christians face severe discrimination in Iran when compared to Muslims.

Even though Iran's constitution grants Christians freedom to perform their religion "within the limits of the law," Iranian authorities have the discretion to impose important limits to the Christian's right to exercise his faith and to subject him to considerable state scrutiny and interference.

Iran is particularly vigilant to curb proselytizing by evangelical Christians. In fact, conversion from Islam to Christianity is considered apostasy and may be punishable by death. Additionally, Christians complain they are discriminated against in their employment and mobility and generally say they are treated as second-class citizens.

That second-class status is evident in their inability to participate in

Iran's government. Only Muslims are allowed to take part in the elected government of the Islamic Republic and to conduct public affairs at a high level. Further, non-Muslims are not eligible to become members of parliament, with the exception of four seats specifically designated for Zoroastrians, Jews, and Christians.

Article 14 of the Iranian constitution reads, "The government of the Islamic Republic of Iran and all Muslims are duty-bound to treat non-Muslims in conformity with ethical norms and the principles of Islamic justice and equity, and to respect their human rights." However, in practice this article only applies if the Christian refrains "from engaging in conspiracy or activity against Islam and the Islamic Republic of Iran," which is totally left to the discretion of local clerical authorities to define.

Iran's penal code also demonstrates the Christian's second-class status because for many criminal offenses, the punishment is significantly harsher for the Christian. For example, a Muslim man who commits adultery with a Muslim woman is punished by one hundred lashes, but a Christian man who commits adultery with a Muslim woman is subject to the death penalty. A similar disparity is evidenced regarding homosexuality.

The federal penal code states that homosexuality "without consummation" between two Muslim men is punishable by one hundred lashes, but if the "active party" is Christian and the other Muslim, the Christian is subject to the death penalty.

Similar disparities are evident in civil law. The civil code discriminates against Christians each time a Muslim is involved in an inheritance case. Specifically, the law states that a Christian is not allowed to inherit property from a Muslim, and if one of the beneficiaries of a Christian happens to be a Muslim, that person—no matter how distant his relationship with the deceased—will collect the entire inheritance.

Iranian marriage law discriminates against Christians. An Iranian Muslim woman is not permitted to marry a Christian man, but a Muslim man may marry a Christian woman. Evidently, the latter is allowed because in that culture the man is deemed to be the dominant partner.

Egyptian civil law governing marriage and divorce is biased against Christians as well. Muslim men can marry Christian women, but Muslim women can't marry Christian men. A similar bias is evident when a Christian mother who seeks a divorce from an abusive Muslim husband. Christian women seldom get custody of their children in divorce cases, even though the law states they are entitled to custody. That's the reality, thanks to Muslim-favoring family courts.[151]

Discrimination is also widely evident in the job market and government service. Very few Coptic Christians ever reach senior government positions with the military or security services, and no Christian has ever served as a governor in a country with twenty-seven governorates.

Egypt's legal system, like that in Iran, discriminates against non-Muslims, especially when it comes to faith-related issues. Article 98(f) of the Egyptian penal code prohibits citizens from "ridiculing or insulting heavenly religions or inciting sectarian strife." Authorities use this blasphemy law to detain, prosecute, and imprison members of religious groups whose practices deviate from mainstream Islamic beliefs or whose activities are alleged to jeopardize "communal harmony" or insult Judaism, Christianity, or Islam.

It should not surprise anyone that Egyptian Christians are more often than not sentenced for blasphemy in that country's Islamic court system. Some 40 percent of the blasphemy defendants are Christians, a high percentage when compared to Egypt's approximately 10 percent Christian population.

Egyptian courts are serious about enforcing the country's blasphemy laws. Consider the 2011 criminal "contempt of religion" or blasphemy case against Ayman Yousef Mansour, a seventeen-year-old Coptic Christian. Mansour was sentenced to three years in prison for insulting Islam and the Prophet Muhammad on a Facebook page. Another widely reported case was appealed in September 2012, and the Egyptian court upheld the conviction and a three-year prison sentence for Coptic teacher Bishoy Kameel, who posted cartoons defaming the Prophet on Facebook.[152]

There was a similar blasphemy case in Kuwait in June 2012. A Kuwaiti court sentenced a blogger, Hamad al-Naqi to ten years in prison for Twitter messages insulting Islam, the Prophet, and his wife, as well as Saudi and Bahraini leaders. Al-Naqi claims someone hacked his Twitter account and he professed his innocence.[153]

It is fortunate for al-Naqi that he wasn't tried after the Kuwaiti parliament increased the criminal penalty for blasphemy to a death sentence in 2013.

Saudi Arabia has laws like Iran, Egypt, and Kuwait that criminalize apostasy and blasphemy, but it also has laws against criticism of the regime. Consider the case of an Islamist Muslim, Hadi al-Mutif, who remains on Saudi's death row for a sentence of apostasy dating back to 1994 that was based on an offhand, allegedly blasphemous remark he made as a teenager. Trial lawyers argue that the judge in the case was biased against Isma'ili Muslims, a branch of Shia Islam, and the teenager's trial was neither fair nor transparent.

Evidently, al-Mustif has suffered during his long incarceration to the point that he attempted suicide on numerous occasions. Reportedly, he suffers from both physical and psychological health problems, yet remains in prison more than twenty years later.

A Saudi blogger was accused of insulting Islam in a post, and for that he was sentenced to one thousand lashes, delivered "very harshly," fifty at a time, plus ten years in prison. Raif Badawi, a thirty-one-year-old Saudi blogger and father of three who is ill and frail, will most certainly perish as a result of the punishment. Badawi expressed forbidden thoughts by questioning the nature of his society and going public with them. Specifically, he wrote: "Muslims in Saudi Arabia not only disrespect the beliefs of others, but also charge them with infidelity—to the extent that they consider anyone who is not Muslim an infidel. They also, within their own narrow definitions, consider non-Hanbali [the Saudi school of Islam] Muslims as apostates. How can we be such people and build...normal relations with six billion humans, four and a half billion of whom do not believe in Islam?"[154]

Even though Middle Eastern countries present the façade of religious freedom, most demonstrate rank discrimination in their laws and enforcement of those laws against Christians.

Fifth, state and non-state actors spew hateful propaganda that portrays members of minority religious communities as subject peoples, aliens within society, or subhuman creatures. This is a particularly serious problem for Christians living in the Middle East today where the region's largest Christian population, the Coptic Church, is especially threatened.

The U.S. State Department's religious freedom report found a dangerous level of violent sectarian attacks targeting Egypt's Copts. This occurred both before and after former President Mohamed Morsi's tenure in office, and all was carried out without consequence or accountability. For example, shortly after Morsi's ouster on July 3, 2013, violence against Christians skyrocketed. On August 14, the day the Egyptian security forces dispersed pro-Morsi protesters, violent religious extremists and thugs launched a coordinated series of attacks on Christians and their property throughout the country. At least seven Copts were killed and more than two hundred churches and other Christian religious structures, homes, and businesses were attacked.

The violence problem against Coptic Christians isn't just laid at the feet of Morsi's Islamist followers; the government and its surrogates share some responsibility. Specifically, state-controlled media and government-appointed imams use their platforms to ridicule Christianity as "perverted" and "false." Even the Egyptian army has published an article labeling Christians as "infidels," and reportedly police participate in attacks against Copts and too often fail to arrest those who attack innocent Coptic Christians.

Christians are treated as subhuman in some Middle East countries as well. Muslims have no fear of exploiting "infidel" women and children in the Middle East—for example, the ISIS terrorists allegedly hosted a "female slave market in Deir ez-Zur," a Syria region that was 20 percent Christian in the summer of 2014.

A media report regarding the ISIS slave market fits some uncomfortably widely held Islamic views about the treatment of non-Muslims and treatment of "the spoils of war" endorsed by the Koran. Abu Ishaq al-Huwaini, a popular Salafi preacher in Egypt, said in 2011 that after jihadi conquests, the properties and persons of "infidel" (read "Christian and other non-Muslim") inhabitants are to be seized as *ghanima*, or "spoils of war," and can be taken to "the slave market, where slave-girls and concubines are sold." Huwaini referred to these sex slaves with the dehumanizing name *ma malakat aymanukum*—"what [not whom] your right hands possess." Further, in Koran 4:3, Allah commands Muslim men to "marry such women as seem good to you, two and three and four…or what your right hands possess."

Another source of evidence regarding Middle East actors spewing hateful propaganda about non-Muslims and especially Christians, which are often lumped in with the entire West, are Islamic clerics. They tend to be more often than not the default leaders in most Islamic countries.

Many Islamists portray the West as the enemy of Islam and openly declare that the U.S. and its allies have declared war on Islam, which makes waging jihad the personal duty for every Muslim and makes all Westerners deserving of annihilation. Of course, it doesn't seem to matter to these radicals that most American and other Western leaders declare Islamic extremists—not all of Islam—the enemy.

Even though most Muslims consider Christians "People of the Book," many Islamic clerics and their more radical associates accuse Christians to be no better than idolaters because, according to his Koran commentary, *Fi Zilal al-Qur'an*, Sayyid Qutb states "that the Jews and Christians claim that Allah has offspring, which makes them not only infidels but polytheists." That's why, according to the Middle East Media Research Institute (MEMRI), Friday sermons often refer to Christians and Jews as enemies of Allah.[155]

Jews earn special hateful criticism from some so-called Islamic scholars. They are described as "apes and pigs," meant to be a dehumanizing slur based on three koranic verses that "state that some Jews were turned into apes and pigs by Allah as punishment for violating the Sabbath."[156] Christians should take no comfort in their exclusion from this demeaning description, because more often than not, Christians are lumped in with Jews by Islamists.

The imam of the al-Haram Mosque in the Islamic holy city Mecca, Sheikh Abd ab-Rahman al-Sudayis, said:

Read history and you will understand that the Jews of yesterday are the evil forefathers of the even more evil Jews of today: infidels, falsifiers of words, calf worshippers, prophet murderers, deniers of prophecies…the scum of the human race, accursed by Allah, who turned them into apes and pigs…. These are the Jews—an ongoing continuum of deceit, obstinacy, licentiousness, evil, and corruption.

Many Islamists perceive that the West is engaged in a crusade against Islam and as a result must be fought. That was a favorite declaration of al-Qaeda leader Osama bin Laden, who declared jihad against all Jews and crusaders. On February 23, 1998, the London Arabic-language daily *al-Quds al-Arabia* published bin Laden's declaration of jihad, which said that killing Americans is a commandment for every individual Muslim. Evidently, America's intelligence community didn't take the threat seriously or we would have been better prepared when al-Qaeda struck on September 11, 2001.

Bin laden wrote:

Killing the Americans and their allies—both civilians and military personnel—is a commandment for every individual Muslim who can do this, in any country in which he can do this, in order to free the Al-Aqsa Mosque and the Al-Haram Mosque from their grasp, and so that their armies will leave all the lands of Islam defeated and no longer a threat to any Muslim. This is in compliance with the words of Allah: "Fight the polytheists all together, as they fight you all together [*Koran* 9:36]" and "Fight them until civil strife ceases altogether" [*Koran* 8:39].

Al-Qaeda founder bin Laden is joined by others calling for the annihilation of the West. Some Islamists prophesy that America and the Jews will meet their end as did Pharaoh and the people of Noah and the two ancient tribes "Aad and Thamoud," which "according to the Koran rejected the message of Allah and were consequently annihilated."

One such Islamist, Seif al-Din al-Ansari, wrote an article, "The Infidels Will Be Obliterated," stating:

Allah made annihilating the infidels one of his steadfast decrees. According to the [divine] natural law of alternating fortunes, Allah said: "[Allah will] obliterate the infidels' [*Qur'an* 3:141]. It inevitably follows that this wisdom [of the decree] has become the way according to which life is lived—particularly the aspect of struggle in life.

Clearly some Islamists see the efficiency of using nuclear weapons to fulfill their call to annihilate the Jews, Christians, Israel and all the West. One such believer is Sheikh Nasser ibn Hamed, a Saudi cleric with al-Qaeda links, wrote, "A Treatise on the Ruling Regarding the Use of Weapons of Mass Destruction against the Infidels." Perhaps the treatise was testing the water among fellow Islamists and clerics to clarify Islamic law's view on the permissibility of using nuclear weapons.

Sheikh Hamed evidently concluded that Islam would permit the use of weapons of mass destruction to annihilate the infidels. The sheikh stated that "it was permissible to use weapons of mass destruction against ten million Americans specifically, and against infidels in general, and the support for their use could be found in Islamic religious sources."

There is no shortage of hateful speech from either state or non-state Middle East actors who portray Christians and their associates like the

Jews as subject peoples, aliens within those societies, and as subhuman—apes and pigs.

Sixth, mobs or individuals use violence against members of vulnerable religious communities. The incidence of anti-Christian violence is pervasive across the region; much of the recent carnage is addressed earlier in the book. Such use of violence seems to permeate autocratic Islamic environments.

Egyptian Christians are clearly targets of Islamist violence. Dr. Mariz Tadros labels the mobilization of Egyptian Islamist groups "untriggered violence" used to drive Christians out of their villages. "What we are seeing is a growing trend of 'cleansing society' of Christians," Tadros said, a term that was unknown before the Arab Spring revolution.

A *Frontpage* report elaborates on a despicable tactic used against Egyptian Christian girls. An investigation exposed a Muslim ring operating out of the Fatah Mosque in Alexandria that uncovered a systematic "religious call" plan, where Muslim high school boys were urged to approach Coptic girls, nine to fifteen years old, and manipulate them through sexual exploitation and blackmail. Clearly their plan was to sexually compromise Christian girls by defiling them and humiliating them before their parents, thereby forcing them to flee from their homes and convert to Islam.

Joseph Hakim, a Lebanese native and president of the International Christian Union, states that the jihadi forces within the Syrian opposition and Hezbollah, the Iranian military proxy in Lebanon, have used the conflict in Syria to ethnically cleanse the Christians. Hakim states the indigenous Christian minority in Syria is being "forced out of their native cities, towns, and villages" and they are being slaughtered, their churches are being firebombed, priests are being beheaded, and bishops are being kidnapped. "I feel that I am being accurate in calling what is happening genocide," Hakim said.

The incidents of ISIS' violence against Christians through crucifixion, burning, burying alive, beheading, or simple execution with a bullet are well-documented and likely to continue. In fact, such barbaric behavior is likely to continue and may expand if immediate action isn't taken to arrest such groups and governments and their societies that seed such hate-filled violence against the most vulnerable.

Seventh, state and non-state actors engage in habitual discrimination by oppressive practices, including violence, against vulnerable groups in society. Christians are frequently targeted by many Middle East actors just because of their faith, especially in the worst of Middle Eastern cases like Syria.

The civil war in Syria has ushered in a stark Islamization that resulted in the increase of attacks on Syrian Christians now subject to religious cleansing, targeted killings, massacres, attacks on churches and abductions. The United Nations independent commission of inquiry on Syria warned: "Entire [minority] communities are at risk of being forced out of the country or of being killed inside the country." More than three hundred thousand Syrian Christians have fled that country and those Christian refugees in Turkey report that they are unwelcomed at Turkish government refugee camps because Islamic rebel groups like Jubhat al-Nusra, the Syrian al-Qaeda affiliate, impresses young men from those camps into fighting against the Syrian regime.

The State Department alleges that Iran continues to engage in systematic, ongoing, and egregious violations of religious freedom, including prolonged detention, torture, and executions based primarily or entirely upon the religion of the accused. This record of behavior justified the U.S. government's decision to designate Iran for the fourteenth year in a row as a "country of particular concern" under the International Religious Freedom Act. That designation grants the government the right to impose trade and funding sanctions for the offending nation. However, in Iran's situation, it remains under a host of economic sanctions due to its nuclear weapons program.

Unfortunately, religious freedom conditions in Iran worsened in the wake of the disputed 2009 presidential elections. "Killings, arrests, and physical abuse of detainees have increased, including for religious minorities and Muslims who dissent or express views perceived as threatening the legitimacy of the government," states the 2013 report by the U.S. Commission on International Religious Freedom (USCIRF). In fact, hundreds of Iranians remain detained from 2009, according to the USCIRF.

The commission's report indicates that during 2013, the Iranian government brought national security cases against members of religious minority communities and individuals for alleged crimes such as "confronting the regime" and apostasy. Similar behaviors were evident in the run-up to the June 2013 presidential elections as security forces increased crackdowns on scapegoat religious minorities.[157]

Iranian authorities continue to use oppressive practices against Christian groups. They raid church services; harass and threaten church members; and arrest, convict, and imprison Christian laymen and leaders. Evangelical Christians are subjected to special attention, harassment, and sometimes imprisonment, according to the USCIRF. Perhaps that is because former Iranian President Mahmoud Ahmadinejad expressed a widely held official view that called for an end to all Christianity in Iran, which explains why the Tehran government requires evangelical groups to submit membership lists.[158]

Even though the Iraqi constitution guarantees religious freedom, that country continues to have one of the worst records of violence against Christians, the reason most have fled the country. Those few Christians who remain in Iraq face official discrimination, marginalization, and neglect to a large part because Islam is the state religion and the fundamental source of all legislation that states no law may contradict "the established principles of Islam," which are not defined.

The Middle East also has hundreds of non-state terrorist or otherwise anti-Christian entities as well. The worst of these may well be ISIS, the self-declared Islamic caliphate. Recently, ISIS' web site posted a statement about its agenda:

We will conquer your Rome. We will break your crosses and
enslave your women by the permission of Allah, the exalted.
This is his promise to us: he is glorified and he does not fail in
his promise. If we do not reach that time, then our children and
grandchildren will reach it and they will sell your sons as slaves
at the slave markets.

ISIS has been faithful to its promise to be desperately violent. Mark
Arabo, a prominent Chaldean-American businessman, soberly said,
"There is a park in Mosul where they [ISIS] actually beheaded children
and put their heads on a stick and have them in the park."[159]

"The world hasn't seen this kind of atrocity in generations," Arabo
told *CNN*. Although genocides are tragically part of human history, the
genocide now perpetrated by ISIS against Christians and other minorities is especially extreme.

There is developing evidence that ISIS seeks a chemical weapons
capability that may make its killing capability more destructive. On
February 3, 2015, the *Daily Beast* reported that one of ISIS' chemical weapons experts and longtime jihadist was killed by a U.S. airstrike
near Mosul, Iraq. Abu Malik, a Saddam Hussein-era weapons of mass
destruction specialist, was assembling a stockpile of specialized gear,
according to the U.S. Central Command. U.S. officials referred to the
prospect of former Saddam regime chemical specialists joining ISIS as a
"nightmare" scenario.

Last year, ISIS terrorists occupied the Muthanna facility, which still
contains a stockpile of remnants from Saddam's old chemical warfare
programs. Then again, it is widely reported that the Syrian regime has
used chemical weapons on adversaries—and it is quite possible that
remnants of those weapons are now in the hands of ISIS.

Remember that Saddam Hussein used chemicals against non-Muslim minorities, and more recently, Syria allegedly did the same in several cities. The proliferation of weapons of mass destruction will only
increase the death toll among minorities.

Finally, the country or region is notable for the widespread militarization of society and/or the widespread influence of non-state terrorist groups or militias. Most of the Middle East countries are militarized in part because of their autocratic regimes, but also because their countries are crawling with non-state terrorist groups and militias.

The Middle East is the focal point of the world's largest arms buildup, and much of those weapons came from America. That buildup started decades ago, but one only needs to look at the sale of arms in the last ten years to understand the stark militarization of the region.

The Middle East continues to be the most highly militarized region in the world, a conclusion reported by the Bonn International Center for Conversion (BICC). Four of the top ten countries on the BICC's list are in the Middle East: Israel, Syria, Jordan, and Kuwait. But all the other regional countries follow close behind them. "This high level of militarization, together with general rearmament projects involving arms imports from all over the world, is contributing to a further destabilization of the area and can lead to the use of violent means to resolve internal as well as external conflicts, as in Syria," said Jan Grebe, researcher at BICC, in commenting about the results of the GMI.[160]

"The scale of rearmament in the Middle East is unparalleled," she said. Some of these states spend over 7 percent of their gross domestic product on military expenditures, significantly higher than the average 2.5 percent elsewhere in the world.

Over the past decade, the U.S. sold Saudi Arabia and five other Persian Gulf states over $20 billion in military weapons. More recently, President Obama followed suit in 2010 with a $60 billion arms deal with Saudi Arabia; by 2012 regional military expenditures amounted to $128 billion, or a 60 percent increase over a decade earlier. Such militarization bolsters Sunni petro-states' concerns about a possible attack from a nuclear-armed Iran, the Saudi's arch enemy. Further, the ongoing supply of weapons to Gulf monarchies gives the U.S. leverage in the Middle East.

The fear is that these militarized countries will have a tendency to share their newly acquired technology among like-minded neighbors or use those arms against one another or against internal enemies such as non-Muslim minorities. Not surprisingly, Iran already shares deadly military technology with rogues. On February 2, 2015, IRGC's Aerospace Force commander, Brigadier General Amir Ali Hajizadeh, told the BBC that Iran is providing Syria, Iraq, the Palestinian Territories, and terror proxy Hezbollah with missile technology as well as the means to build radar systems and drones.

Iran's willingness to share sophisticated military technology could very well escalate regional tensions into a global security threat. Specifically, Iran "faces no insurmountable technical barriers to producing a nuclear weapon, making Iran's political will the central issue," according to Marine Lieutenant General Vincent Stewart, director of the Defense Intelligence Agency, in testimony to the House Armed Services Committee on February 4, 2015. The real possibility that Iran may soon become a nuclear weapons power and may share that technology with other rogue state and non-state actors escalates exponentially the militarization of the Middle East. Further, an Iranian nuclear weapon will unquestionably spark an arms race with rival Saudi Arabia, which likely already has a back-room deal with ally Pakistan to buy a fleet of shiny new nuclear arms.

Evidence of a Saudi Arabian-Pakistani back-room deal for the transfer of nuclear arms surfaced in May 2015. Saudi Arabia's Deputy Minister for Religious Affairs Abdul Aziz Al-Ammar visited Pakistan in May 2015 to clarify Pakistan's view of the Yemen conflict, which pits Saudi Arabia's proxy forces against Iran's proxies. During a speech to a Pakistani audience packed with clerics and government leaders, Al-Ammar called Pakistan "our friend-country" and then said something very revealing: "Pakistan's atom [bomb] is not of Pakistan alone but is of the world of Islam." Al-Ammar's evident effort to recruit Pakistan to side with Saudi Arabia's fight against rival Iran in Yemen and then in practically the same breath claim Pakistan's nuclear arsenal really belongs to "the world of Islam" is indeed very curious. In fact, that message was likely meant to signal Tehran that, as many have long suspected, Saudi Arabia and Pakistan have a secret deal to transfer nuclear weapons to Riyadh if Iran threatens the kingdom. Clearly, Iran's active support of the Houthi rebels in Yemen is more evidence that the Saudis feel threatened by Iranian aggressiveness on the Arabian Peninsula.[161]

The Middle East also has many competing terrorist groups and networks. The U.S. State Department has designated sixty groups, of which twenty-four are in the Middle East as foreign terrorist organizations. Most of the sixty organizations are Islamist extremist groups, nationalist/separatist groups, or Marxist militant groups. The Middle East's Islamist terror groups without exception embrace a radically anti-Christian ideology that explains their involvement in committing atrocities against Christians.

Hundreds of militia groups across the Middle East also embrace a radically anti-Christian ideology. Some of those groups are aligned with local governments, such as the Shi'ite militias in Iraq that fight alongside the Iraqi security forces but answer to their real leaders in Tehran, Iran, while others like the Shi'ite al-Houthi rebels in Yemen, who fight against that government, compete domestically for power with the terrorist group al-Qaeda in the Arabian Peninsula.

The chaos unleashed by the wars in Afghanistan, Iraq, and the 2011 Arab Spring led to the rise of many powerful militias—including Islamic extremist groups—across the Middle East. Too often, local governments are hard-pressed to control the spread of these militia groups and their influence as proxy security forces. In fact, like the Kurdish Peshmerga—regional militia—in northern Iraq, the government in Baghdad is pleased to support that militia group because it has assumed responsibility for fighting ISIS, a shared enemy.

These militias are potentially very dangerous even for their government allies because they are self-governed and selectively unaccountable. Further, they tend to embrace extremist Islamic views that too often lead them to discriminate against Christians.

CONCLUSIONS

The aforementioned collection of eight conditions evident across the Middle East demonstrates that the region is a tinderbox ripe for Christian genocide. This volatile situation must not be left to percolate; otherwise, the problem will worsen, and not only will Christians be annihilated, but the cancer could very well spread to other regions like the United States.

Dr. Richard Landes, director and cofounder of the Center for Millennial Studies at Boston University, said of the dire situation in the Middle East that "in the old days [Yishuv days], when the Muslims rioted and massacred Jews, they'd say, 'first the Saturday people, then the Sunday people.' Now that the Jews have a state and can defend themselves, they've moved on to the Sunday people, and the only place Christians are safe is where the Saturday people have sovereignty."[162]

Landes added:

The really sick part of this picture is that the Christians in the West not only won't come to the defense of the Sunday people in the Muslim world, but rather, seem fixated on not letting the Saturday people defend either themselves or the Sunday people who live among them. With their Western enemies behaving so self-destructively, it's a good time to be a jihadi.

GLOBAL COMMUNITY'S FINGERPRINTS ON GENOCIDE

There is plenty of blame to go around for the catastrophic mess in the Middle East. The last section demonstrated how the volatile combination of Islam and autocratic governments contributes to the nightmarish situation now confronting regional Christians. This section demonstrates that outsiders, especially the great powers, contribute to the region's dysfunction and thus by association, genocide.

Chapter 6 profiles the causes of regional instability that reflect some of the conditions for genocide explored in the last section, but considers regional conditions from an instability causing perspective. Then the major non-American powers' agendas are explored, as well as how—not surprisingly—those agendas serve the great powers' domestic agendas, which tend to contribute to Middle East instability.

Chapter 7 examines in detail President Obama's Middle East policies to demonstrate that with no exceptions he contributed not just to Christian genocide in the region, but also to the region's growing instability. This outcome is to a large degree due to Obama's fixation on getting a nuclear deal with Iran (his foreign policy legacy) at the expense of regional stability.

Unfortunately, the Iran deal is likely to fail for reasons that become evident most every news cycle.

As an incentive to earn Tehran's nuclear deal cooperation, Obama avoided taking a lead role in virtually every brewing crisis in the region that involved an Iranian interest: Lebanon (tensions with Israel), Iraq (return only in a support role with Iran leading), Syria (failed "red line" on chemical weapons use for Iran's ally), and now Yemen (al-Houthi, an Iranian proxy, creates a Shia foothold on the Arabian peninsula). Such American cooperation with Iran helped the Persians become the dominant power in the Middle East, which makes Shia Islam the dominant religion by force if not by numbers.

Of course, team Obama will argue their Middle East strategy in all these crises is to get regional allies to take the lead, but perhaps the unintended consequence for America's global allies is that they can no longer rely on U.S. leadership, the region falls deeper into chaos, and the Christian genocide continues unabated.

CHAPTER 6

CHAOTIC REGION
DEFIES SOLUTIONS

Christians will be free of the threat of genocide only with a radical transformation of the Middle East—and then only if the necessary reforms are generated from within the Islamic system. Many people thought the 2011 Arab Spring was that transformational movement, but the series of rebellions collapsed, and now autocratic governments returned to those countries with a vengeance: Civil wars still rage in Syria and Yemen; and Islamic extremists like ISIS and al-Qaeda use the chaotic period to carve out new and more dangerous roles. Internal Islamic reforms appear to be impossible at this time, if ever.

The post-Arab Spring Middle East is arguably worse than before the revolutions for other reasons than a return of autocratic governments. Today, the region continues to be seized by more violence as well as by a host of intractable problems that no nation or people seem able to solve—and all evidence points to more of the same for the foreseeable future. This inevitably means the eight conditions that contribute to Christian genocide outlined in the previous section of this book are likely to get worse for Christians, and those same conditions could accompany the transnational Islamic violence now spewing from the Middle East to the rest of the world.

There is no shortage of recommendations to address the region's intractable problems, but few ever succeed, such as the Arab Spring uprisings. In fact, America's failures to address Mideast problems have accelerated under President Obama's leadership, which will be explored in the next chapter.

Middle East experts make a living analyzing the region's many problems and then recommend solutions, but even they tend to be pessimistic about the region's future. Some are so bold as to suggest cause-and-effect relationships between the region's terrible social symptoms and the escalating instability. But outsiders, especially the big powers (U.S., Europe, Russia, and China), do little to address the social problems wracking the region. An outline of big power agendas is considered later in this chapter.

The very reputable Washington-based Center for Strategic and International Studies (CSIS) compiled a book of Mideast social data that the authors admit is of questionable reliability. Nevertheless, it is the best available, and the authors suggest that the information may help us understand some of the region's causes of instability.[163] Certainly the statistics provide key insights about the region's challenges, helping us to put recent events such as the Arab Spring into perspective and suggesting whether there is any hope to resolve these challenges in order to secure long-term stability.

A complimentary CSIS publication to the social data book provides a useful context when considering the list of troubling Middle Eastern symptoms. Jon Alterman, CSIS' senior vice president and contributor to a new book, *Religious Radicalism after the Arab Uprisings*, wrestles with theories that might explain the persistence of religiously inspired Mideast violence as well as the region's significant social challenges.[164]

Alterman admits that religious and sectarian conflicts have deepened and accelerated in recent years, as evidenced by the so-called Arab Spring uprisings. He admits that one possible theory regarding the persistent violence is that "Islam [the faith of the vast majority of Middle Eastern people] is a religion that brooks no compromise and is bent on domina tion; it has bloody borders because it is a religion of conquest."[165] Then Alterman suggests an alternative view, a more politically correct theory to explain the discord in the Arab world: "The region's modern politic" is to blame for persistent violence. That's a reference to the autocratic nature of most of the region's governments, which allegedly fuel the causes of instability.

Not surprisingly, like many other scholars and policy experts who wrestle with the region's problems, Alterman avoids labeling Islam as being responsible for the region's instability, much less blames the religion for contributing to the dire symptoms. He states, "It is hard to accept the idea that Islam is uniquely receptive to violence given the justifications religion has given for violence throughout the world. And yet, other regions [in the world] have emerged from colonialism without the high levels of endemic violence of the Arab world."[166]

That sounds as if Alterman believes the "Islam is to blame theory" is potentially the culprit peering from behind the region's many problems. In fact, Islam may be at the root of the region's instability, but most of the Mideast's autocratic leaders won't admit the obvious, because Islam is an important partner in keeping the people under heel. And of course, Western officials run at the very thought of blaming Islam for the region's problems out of fear of being labeled an Islamaphobe or worse. That is why Western governments look at the Arab world's malaise and call for the only solution they understand: a knee-jerk call for Western-style democratization. But recent Western efforts and encouragement of locals to democratize Mideastern states have produced some bad outcomes in places like Iraq, Egypt, and Iran (after massive pro-democracy protests that followed that country's June 2009 presidential election).

Why should Islam be considered a contributor to the region's intractable problems that encourage instability and by association promote Christian genocide?

It is essential to understand that the majority of Middle Eastern Muslims believes Islam plays a large and positive role in politics, according to a 2012 Pew Research Center survey. The Middle Eastern respondents to Pew's poll believe the Koran should hold sway over all law, and strong majorities of Muslims like the Jordanians want their government to strictly follow the Koran (72 percent) while other populations, like the Islamic-majority Turkey, want their government to follow the values and the principles of Islam (17 percent strictly follow and 44 percent follow values and principles).

Islam's importance to Middle Eastern populations has an indisputable influence on the region's culture, and as a direct result, it significantly influences social symptoms identified by the CSIS data that contribute to regional instability. In short, the root of dysfunction, at least in part, is inherent in Islam.

Before considering CSIS' data, the reader should accept a brief diversion to better understand Islam's prescription for every aspect of its followers' lives. There is no part of life outside Islam's influence for the Muslim. In fact, the Sunna, which accounts for 86 percent of Islamic teachings, attributes all knowledge to Allah and Muhammad and the Prophet's seventh-century hadiths (stories) that cover everything imaginable. Hadiths are used by Islamic clerics to influence every aspect of modern Islamic life, from politics to economics and even the subordinate roles for women. Take health issues, for example. There are hadiths that state if someone has a fever (above-normal body temperature), the increased heat comes from the "fires of Hell." According to another hadith, only Allah can predict a child's sex before birth; so much for modern ultrasounds.

These teachings and the underlying ideology make orthodox Muslim populations and their clerics great partners for the region's mostly autocratic regimes. Further, the marriage between Islamic orthodoxy and autocratic governments is the rational mind's worst enemy and a mystery to most Western-minded people.

This Islam-fascist marriage forbids critical thought because criticism of the status quo and the Prophet's teachings cannot coexist with authoritarian thinking. Question Muslim authority or the local autocratic government's decisions, and quickly, the liberal-minded, freedom-seeking citizen is threatened or worse. Also, truth has no meaning in an authoritarian Islamic culture; truth is what the imam espouses and what the government enforces.

A Saudi official confirmed that modern truth will not interfere with seventh-century Islamic truth. "Bandar Al-Khaybari, a preacher with the Saudi Ministry of Islamic Affairs in Al-Madina, claimed that the Earth is fixed and does not revolve around itself, during a series of lectures held in the Sharjah emirate, between January 28 and 31 [2015]. The lectures were posted on the Internet."[167]

Therefore, the inherent dysfunction in Islam is its foundation in deception and a resultant radicalization of the population.

Now consider the data collected by CSIS and then examine how those dire social symptoms contribute to the region's ongoing instability and what this might portend for the future. Further, unless these symptoms are mitigated, there is little chance to reverse Christian genocide.

Anthony Cordesman, a respected international security analyst, is the lead author for the CSIS data study entitled, "The Underlying Causes of the Crises and Upheavals in the Middle East and North Africa: An Analytic Survey." Cordesman admits that the chaotic situation in the Mideast can't just be blamed on political dynamics; rather, there is a "current pattern of politics, religion, and ideology…shaped by major tribal, ethnic, sectarian, and regional differences within a given nation."[168] Those dynamics are influenced by the quality of governance, internal security systems, justice systems, and progress in social change, according to Cordesman.

The CSIS study indicates that there is no reliable way to assess "the deep underlying structural impact of factors like demographics and economics on unrest." However, the study states that, in spite of serious reservations about the current data, "no one can realistically address the current upheavals…without considering such factors."[169]

Soberly and before launching into the data, Cordesman states, "The entire set of indicators warn that the 'Arab Spring' is likely to involve a decade of more political, economic, and social unrest. The causes of unrest are deep, complex, and involve structural problems in governance, demographics, and economics. None can be solved in a few months or years."

The CSIS study also states that the region's upheavals can be blamed on much more than politics, religion, and terrorism. There are underlying causes to the upheavals that vary by individual nation, such as demographics, economics, internal security and justice systems, governance, and social change. Five of those "causes" and the potential consequences are outlined below.

First, the region has governments that are rigid and/or repressive regimes that lack peaceful civil and political alternatives to autocratic rule. This is disturbing to the young people who filled the streets of Arab capitals in 2011 calling for the ouster of the autocrats and in with real freedom and democracy.

The Arab Spring promised to be transformational, but quickly the authoritarians re-emerged using the same old tools—religious authorities to rally support, suppression to silence dissent, and use of state largesse to build alliances. Meanwhile, the young liberals faded and the Islamic extremists carved out a new niche. Today, the Islamic extremists occupy ungoverned spaces in the Levant and elsewhere, poised to continue to advance their radical agenda. As a result, the few young liberals have no place to go except the West.

Another unintended consequence of the Arab Spring uprisings was a fissure among the Islamist community. So-called jihadi-Salafists, religious and social reformers who seek to return to seventh-century Muslim practices, rebelled against al-Qaeda's authority and pushed extremist leaders to declare the caliphate, forcing jihadists to pick sides. These medieval aspirants embrace a goal of waging jihad to reestablish an Islamic political structure and society—a far cry from liberal calls for freedom of faith and voice for people of all faiths.

This outcome is defeating to those who sought transformation Western style. Rather, they face the continuation of conflict and deep resentment for autocratic governments. They will live under the oppressive thumb of Islam in the foreseeable future.

Second, the Middle East as a region lags behind much of the world in per capita gross domestic product (GDP). While American GDP per capita was $47,111 in 2010, the average per capita GDP across the Mideast and North Africa was just $6,488. That figure is revealing when one considers the impact on jobs and standard of living. A similar disparity exists within the Mideast, with Kuwait leading with a GDP per capita ratio of $46,970 in 2012 compared to Jordan's ratio at $4,788.[170]

Much of that wealth is tethered to the flow of oil and its price, which exposes regional economies to the volatile global oil market. Further, the region has very limited industry and agriculture to compete with the rest of the world. Take away oil and, frankly, there is little to attract outside investment—and besides, there is little incentive for outsiders to invest in the region because of the Islamic and autocratic regimes.

Third, the region's one-product economy is problematic in part because it produces too few jobs for a mushrooming population. The CSIS data evidences the region has experienced a massive population growth since 1950, a trend that is expected to continue at least through 2030, possibly 2050. The region has an average fertility rate of 3.1 children per woman compared with 1.9 in the U.S.[171] Further, the rapid population growth has been mostly in urban areas, creating special problems such as the growing lack of water, education, health care, energy and high cost of food. Food costs are skyrocketing; more than 40 percent of the average Jordanian's consumption expenditures are for food alone.

The current employment picture is discouraging for the youth bulge. Regional governments plow in available funds to create jobs, mostly state sector and inefficient state industry jobs, but that is unlikely to be sufficient to meet the growing demand. Regrettably, many of those jobs are little more than make-work positions marked by underemployment, and wages tend to be insufficient to meet the financial needs of those who want to marry and raise a family.

The 2011 Arab Development report identified many problems that hurt the region's employment. Specifically, massive government subsidies and a focus on the services sector has led to little industrialization and low-value-added services have become the main employment. Further, the region has an overreliance on foreign labor which denies locals work.

The Arab region already has a 9.3 percent unemployment rate (down from 12 percent in the 1990s) compared to 6.6 percent for other developing regions, and youth unemployment across the region is 24 percent, double the world average. Unfortunately, the future doesn't look promising, because the youth population is outpacing employment growth and the education system fails to produce graduates with the skills to find meaningful, productive jobs.

The 2011 Arab Development report identified a significant regional challenge: Arab unemployment. "Arab unemployment is fundamentally a demand-side problem…the growth return of education is low since misguided policies do not enable the country to translate the accumulated knowledge into ideas, innovations, and new productive activities," the report states.

The combination of a youth bulge and too few meaningful jobs discourages many otherwise productive people who then begin to look elsewhere. The lucky few will leave the region to pursue their dreams in places like Europe and America. Some youth will become dissatisfied with the lack of a meaningful jobs, evidence in part to the obvious failed governance. That lack of jobs potentially contributes to increased dissatisfaction, which could lead to a turn to religious extremism.

Fourth, the region's autocratic governments lean on their security forces and justice system to keep the population under heel. The data clearly shows that most of the governments are notorious for weak and corrupt justice and law enforcement systems that alienate many citizens. Oppressive police tactics anger the people and contribute to deep-seeded mistrust in their leaders. Also, the court systems, according to the data, lack fairness and transparency. Civil criminal justice is perceived as somewhat arbitrary and too often leads to excessive punishments; detention facilities are often very inadequate.

We saw in an earlier chapter how Egypt's justice system was in league with Islamic leaders. Clearly, the abuse of the rule of law discourages Egypt's Coptic Christians, who get harsher treatment just because of their faith. But so do other citizens who push against the government's goads. The perception of abuse of authority and fear of government justice alienates many; for some, it's enough to drive them into the arms of extremists and for yet others, its drives them out of the country.

Survey data demonstrates that a wide swath of Middle Eastern people perceive their civil institutions to be corrupt as well. Specifically, a 2013 Transparency International Global Corruption Barometer found high perceptions of corruption in Egypt for political parties (72 percent), parliament (71 percent), and the legal system/judiciary (65 percent). Egyptian police are perceived to be corrupt (78 percent) and the country's military less corrupt (45 percent).

Fifth, the region has significant ethnic, sectarian, and tribal differences that create a clash within a civilization. The age-old internal Islam fight between the Sunnis and Shias is very serious, as evidenced over the last decade in Iraq, a country divided by sectarian tensions and constantly on the edge of sectarian civil war. Then, of course, there are Islamic extremists of many colors, but the most prominent in 2014 and 2015 is the ISIS, which kills and or subjects every ethnic, tribal, and/or religious group that lacks the same extremist baggage.

The increase of Islamic extremism is a concern for many Middle Eastern people, and yet a sizable minority admits they support Islamic extremists. A Pew Research Center survey found concern for extremism as high as 81 percent in Lebanon, and yet in Egypt, al-Qaeda enjoyed favorable views by one in five citizens (19 percent) in 2012. The balance of the region fits in between these extremes, which means there is an unsettling level of sympathy for extremists.

The failure of Egypt's Muslim Brotherhood to hold onto power after its 2012 election illustrates the clash within a civilization. Although the

Brotherhood had long aspired for power, once it got that power, it was quickly lost because of what is known as the *ikhwanat al-dawla,* the "Brotherhoodization" of Egypt. The group couldn't resist the desire to force its strict interpretation of sharia law on the country and even on non-Muslim people. This indicates that Islam's influence is pervasive in the region's most populated country, but evidently enough oppose the Brotherhood's radical agenda.

The Middle East is a broken region in many respects. The CSIS' "causes" for instability addressed above wouldn't be so tough to resolve if not for the marriage of Islam and autocratic regimes that create a culture of intolerance. But that marriage is here to stay, and more often than not serves the interests of the big outside powers.

Former deputy director of the Central Intelligence Agency, John McLaughlin, wrote a paper, "The Great Powers in the New Middle East," demonstrating that outside (non-Mideast) interest and investment for the most part won't touch the five "causes" of instability outlined above, much less target the region's Islamic-autocratic regime marriage, the true culprit. These great powers use their money and influence to meet their national needs while fueling some of the causes of regional instability.[172]

Outside power Russia has three goals for the Middle East, according to McLaughlin. Russia wants to consolidate its sphere of influence in the "near abroad," tighten domestic political and economic control, and restore its influence in the region—especially in the realm of fighting terrorism.

Fighting terrorism in the region serves Moscow's domestic concerns and to some degree helps regional authorities in their quest to reduce Islamic extremists. Russian President Vladimir Putin has been an opponent of Islamic extremism since the two Chechen wars in 1994 and 1999 in which jihadi fighters from the Middle East flooded into Russia through the Pankisi Gorge in Georgia.

On other fronts, Moscow creates more tension between the Iranians and its Sunni neighbors by helping Tehran develop its nuclear program. Even though Moscow says it opposes Iran acquiring a nuclear weapon, it still helped the regime develop a nuclear network that has the potential to develop a weapon—a reality not lost on the Saudis and Israelis.

Russia also helps the Syrian regime sustain its civil war. Moscow maintains an active port facility in Syria (Tartus Port) through which arms flow to President Bashar al-Assad's military that to date has killed perhaps two hundred thousand of its citizens and created the situation that led to the rise of the ISIS now morphing across the region.

Outside power China has a simple Middle East policy formula that has nothing to do with the causes of regional instability: energy security = economic development = political stability, according to McLaughlin. After all, Beijing sees the Middle East as little more than a filling station for China's escalating, energy-hungry economy. Until recently, Beijing could care less about the region's internal problems.

The U.S. decision to shift naval resources to the Asia-Pacific as a check on Chinese aggression created some angst for Beijing's reliance on American power to secure Middle East energy trade routes. Further, China now realizes U.S. energy dependence is shifting away from the Middle East because of American domestic extraction of shale gas and oil. That means the U.S. is slowly leaving the region's security to others, like the Chinese; in fact, China has responded by rapidly growing its navy to protect the sea lanes between the Persian Gulf and home ports.

China is also concerned about Middle East terrorism. Although it has made limited investment in the region's fight, that could change—especially if the restive population of Xinjiang Province in Western China starts to see Islamic extremists start to flow in from the Middle East. Keep in mind that Chinese Uyghurs are ethnic cousins of Turkey's Uyghurs, which creates an opening to expand the Islamist caliphate into mainland China as well.

Finally, past efforts to address causes of instability in the Middle East by Europeans and the U.S. have been both self-serving and philosophical. For many decades, Western firms set up offices in Gulf States to exploit the oil wealth and provided those regimes with significant ongoing incentives to keep pumping oil. Meanwhile, the West—perhaps out of a sense of collective guilt—called for political and economic development.

The Europeans hoped against history that they could partner with Middle Eastern nations much as they have with Eastern Europeans. Unfortunately, the Middle Eastern autocratic regimes haven't shown the same enthusiasm for cooperation and democratization, as evidenced by the former Soviet satellites like Estonia, Poland, and Ukraine. Rather, the Middle East's dictators are primarily interested in economic and military assistance that maintains the status quo, and the West can stuff the democracy and calls for human rights.

The Western powers also returned to the region out of necessity to stop the Islamic extremists from breaking out of regional wars to infect the West. That happened after the September 11, 2001, attacks on America and brought the great powers together to cooperate, albeit temporarily, among themselves and with the regional regimes that reluctantly agreed out of guilt into cooperating, even though they helped fuel much of the extremism.

Regional malaise and government dysfunction will continue, and no amount of outside effort and influence can fix the intractable causes of Middle East instability. Only an internally and widely supported effort that removes or at least moderates the destructive influence of Islam and autocratic regimes can begin to mitigate the instability and the conditions that contribute to Christian genocide. The chance of this happening anytime soon is nil to none.

CHAPTER 7

PRESIDENT OBAMA'S POLICIES

Their Contribution to the Madness

President Obama's Middle East policy is a total failure; worse, his actions directly contribute to broader instability and the killing of many innocents. His failures condemn the region to many years of future chaos. Expect Obama, the consummate foreign policy bystander, to do little more through the balance of his administration than to manage the policy quagmire he helped create.

Obama came to the job with a thin resume devoid of foreign policy experience, and his performance is rounded out by his own naïvete and inexperience. He was elected on the basis of celebrity and sloganeering: "Hope and Change." He is likely to end his two terms with little positive to boast about: He ended the Iraq war until it resumed; his necessary war (Afghanistan) continues and may expand; our best ally, Israel, is now treated as an enemy; Guantanamo, which he promised to close, remains operational although he continues to release dangerous murderers like the Taliban five sent to Qatar in exchange for an American soldier taken captive; and he got al-Qaeda mastermind leader Osama bin Laden thanks to SEAL Team Six, but more serious threats like the Islamic State and its franchises now threaten everyone across the globe.

Oh, and he was awarded the Nobel Peace Prize based on promises to be transformative; he ought to return the award for malpractice.

Rather than apply himself to learning the job, he spent most of his presidency enjoying the trappings of celebrity, vacationing, and more than 230 golf outings.[173] Wiser men would have invested in the job and learned, but not Obama; he checked out of the presidency and lost interest, thus shirking his constitutional responsibilities. That left American foreign policy on the skids and the country in grave danger.

This tragic outcome is both by design and default. Obama began his presidency with zero foreign policy experience, but described himself as a smart man and "student of history." Whose history he studied isn't clear, however. He wasn't smart enough to appreciate the complexity of his new job, and he recruited similarly ill-equipped talent that helped cement failure. He brought into the administration rank amateurs, third stringers who are mostly sycophant campaign workers, political hacks, and non-credentialed academics with no meaningful real-world experience. That combination ensured that the administration's foreign policy would be deeply flawed and dangerous.

Obama's selection of third stringers for his international staff isn't hyperbole. This author knows professionals who have been in National Security Council (NSC) meetings with Obama officials. These acquaintances explained that the NSC staff is inexperienced, and yet they use their bully positions to dictate actions to seasoned intelligence and security professionals. One acquaintance who visited the White House to participate in multiple meetings on sensitive Middle East issues reported how uninformed and out of touch with reality some NSC appointees were about vital issues.

This acquaintance said that once, Obama came to one of the NSC meetings, and the sycophant staffers fell all over themselves in deference to Obama. They told Obama what he obviously wanted to hear, according to my acquaintance, rather than what the president needed to understand about the security situation, which led to more mistakes.

Juxtapose Obama's sycophant staff with the president's pro-Muslim background; then one begins to understand why his Mideast policy is so dysfunctional and dangerous.

Evangelist Franklin Graham says Obama is biased to Muslim groups because of the president's personal history. This bias, says Graham, will lead to persecution of Christians in America if left unchecked. But it clearly impacts the president's Mideast policies, which are blindly biased to Muslims, and his naïvely progressive view of the world.[174]

Graham said:

> We're going to see persecution in this country because our president is very sympathetic to Islam and the reason I say that…is because his father was a Muslim, gave him a Muslim name, Barack Hussein Obama. His mother married another Muslim man, they moved to Indonesia, he went to Indonesian schools. So, growing up, his frame of reference and his influence as a young man was Islam. It wasn't Christianity, it was Islam.[175]

Graham said that Obama opened the doors of the White House to Muslim groups who are shaping foreign policy, including how the administration views Israel and events across the Middle East. "There are Muslims that have access to him in the White House," the evangelist said. "Our foreign policy has a lot of influence now, from Muslims. We see the Prime Minister of Israel being snubbed by the President and by the White House and by the Democrats and it's because of the influence of Islam. They hate Israel and they hate Christians, and so the storm is coming I believe."

Obama brought to the White House a promise to transform international relations, which at the beginning of the administration generated considerable enthusiasm. In fact, that support prompted the Nobel Foundation to award him the Nobel Peace Prize in anticipation of work to be done. Even Harvard University's Joseph Nye gushed over Obama's international prospects: "It is difficult to think of any single act that would do more to restore America's soft power than the election of Obama to the presidency."[176]

Obama's foreign policy failures are extensive and incredibly dangerous for the U.S. and, on balance, much of the world community, which for decades depended on America's steady hand in global matters, now view us with great suspicion and Obama's failures have emboldened our enemies as well.

Consider seven Obama Mideast foreign policy disasters and then their consequences for the nation, and the Christians who are caught in an Islam-fueled genocide in part thanks to Obama's rank failures.

LIBYAN POLICY SET THE PACE FOR OBAMA FAILURES

The Obama administration's 2011 war in Libya is a total failure. It was a war of choice for Obama—like Iraq was for President Bush—with no vital U.S. national interests at stake and without a clear military plan. Sound familiar? Now that Libya is a failed state, the chaos spawned a new haven for another Islamic State franchise and another platform for exporting terrorism to Europe and beyond.

Prior to the 2011 war, the U.S. had then dictator Colonel Muammar Gadhafi in his place. He may have been a psychotic monster, but he was cooperating with U.S. interests in a troubled neighborhood. Just prior to launching Operation Odyssey Dawn, the U.S. was about to open a new embassy; Gadhafi was cooperating by helping round up his weapons of mass destruction stockpiles (chemical munitions); Westerners were returning to invest; oil and gas were flowing; and Gadhafi had a stranglehold on the Islamists—plus he provided the U.S. intelligence community considerable information to track terrorist cells throughout the region. All that good was thrown away by Obama for nothing of value in return.

In February 2011, the Libyan government faced an uprising, to which President Obama issued an ultimatum to Gadhafi: End the threat to civilians in "days, not weeks" or suffer the consequences. Evidently, the dictator didn't react fast enough to Obama's "red line" and Obama's foreign affairs trio—Hillary Clinton at State, Samantha Power (an NSC staffer with a Pulitzer Prize for a book on genocide), and Susan Rice (UN ambassador)—persuaded Obama to order the bombings that turned Libya into a terrorist paradise.

Obama secured a U.N. Security Council resolution to establish a no-fly zone in Libyan airspace, to authorize robust enforcement measures for the arms embargo, and "to take all necessary measures…to protect civilians and civilian populated areas under threat of attack."

Obama's war began March 19, 2011, with cruise missile strikes to eliminate Gadhafi's air defense network, which was followed by months of bombing strikes by mostly French and British warplanes supporting a ragtag militia ground element backed by allied special forces. Early on, Obama officially passed the military mission to the North Atlantic Treaty Organization (NATO) so he could declare that the U.S. "led from behind," whatever that meant. In fact, the U.S. did most of the heavy lifting and certainly paid for most of the operation's costs to include supplying the munitions dropped throughout the "war."

After Gadhafi's regime fell, Libya disintegrated into a patchwork of independent Islamist groups fighting among themselves and with the government for control. The weak central government that emerged couldn't hold the fragile country together, much less restore central authority or the rule of law. Evidence of the instability played out on September 11, 2012, when Islamists attacked the U.S. diplomatic mission in Benghazi, killing Ambassador Chris Stevens and three other Americans.

The Obama administration ignored the rising threat that led to the four deaths. After the attack, Obama blamed the deaths on nonexistent protesters reacting to an obscure film that allegedly insulted the

Muslims' Prophet when, in reality, the facts point to an act of terrorism aimed at U.S. officials. That investigation continues and in time may implicate former Secretary of State Hillary Clinton for malfeasance.

Obama's invasion of Libya was a foreign policy mistake from the beginning that created another failed state and a haven for Islamist radicals to include an ISIS franchise that chops off Christian heads.[177] It has now further destabilized the region.

TEAM OBAMA'S MISSTEPS IN SYRIA

Early in the Obama administration, then Senator John Kerry, chairman of the Senate Foreign Relations Committee, visited Damascus, Syria, to meet with President Bashar al-Assad. Kerry said in a press conference during the visit: "President Barack Obama's administration considers Syria a key player in Washington's efforts to revive the stalled Middle East peace process. Syria is an essential player in bringing peace and stability to the region."[178]

While bombs were dropping over Tripoli, Libya, Obama's Secretary of State Hillary Clinton praised Syrian President Assad as a "reformer." Clinton promised the U.S. would not intervene on behalf of Syrian civilians revolting against Assad as it had done in the case of Libya. Then Secretary of Defense Robert Gates got the same talking points from the NSC. He told CBS' *Face the Nation* that the U.S. would not enter the conflict in Syria as it had in Libya.

CBS newsman Bob Schieffer noted that President Assad's father, Hafez Assad, had "killed twenty-five thousand people at a lick" in the town of Hama in 1982. Then he said the new regime was firing on civilians again. "Why is that different from Libya?" Schieffer asked Clinton.

"There's a different leader in Syria now," Clinton said. "Many of the members of Congress of both parties who have gone to Syria in recent months have said they believe he's a reformer."[179]

Obviously, Kerry and Clinton aren't very good at judging Assad's character. He became a butcher worse than his father. Both Kerry and Clinton eventually reversed their glowing endorsement of Assad as Syrian bodies piled up and the flow of refugees out of Syria turned from a trickle to a flood. Now that civil war is in its fourth year with no end in sight.

By late summer 2011, Obama declared that Assad must relinquish power, but the administration did nothing to advance that goal. Rather, the administration sought to hide behind the U.N.'s skirts and cried foul when Russia and China predictably exercised their Security Council veto to block effective action against Syria.

Obama's NSC stuffed any serious effort to stop Assad. They offered Syria's fledgling opposition only humanitarian aid even though they begged for weapons. Obama's "jayvee" NSC team overruled the advice of then CIA Director David Petraeus, then Secretary of Defense Leon Panetta, and Chairman of the Joint Chiefs of Staff General Martin Dempsey to provide arms aid. Meanwhile, Russia and Iran loaded down Assad's regime with arms, and Tehran's Revolutionary Guards Quds Force arrived to advise thousands of Lebanese Hezbollah volunteer fighters to join the war defending Damascus.

Foolishly, Obama made matters more difficult for himself, and he shot his already marginalized credibility by announcing a "red line" against Assad using chemical weapons. Predictably, Assad's blatant use of chemical weapons against his people was indisputable, and Obama then threatened to launch a military reprisal against the Assad regime. But Obama backed down from that threat and hid behind a request to Congress for authorization to take military action. It's nice when you can pass the buck to Congress, which rightly saw no national interest to justify bombing Syria.

Russian President Vladimir Putin rescued Obama from further embarrassment by proposing to dispatch international inspectors to disarm Syria's chemical weapons arsenal. This served Russia's purpose of bolstering its influence in the region while making Obama look feckless, again. Of course, Assad never gave up all the weapons, and small chemical attacks will continue as long as that civil war festers.

The nexus of Obama's war against ISIS and the Syrian civil war has some interesting consequences as well. One, Turkey, a NATO ally, is cooperating with Obama to train Syrian rebels to fight ISIS, but Ankara insists that Obama do more to remove Assad, something Obama refuses. Meanwhile, from the perspective of Syrian refugees and those citizens trapped in the war's cross-fire, a growing portion of the innocents understandably believe the U.S. is siding with Assad. After all, they see the U.S. striking Assad's enemies such as ISIS and other Islamic extremist groups but never targeting regime forces.

Obama's policy regarding Syria is a failure in that it has encouraged Assad by doing nothing and allowed Assad's supporters like Russia and Iran to fuel the war to fit their geopolitical interests. Expect the civil war to continue, and Christians will either die or leave—ISIS provides no real alternative.

REDUX BUSH: OBAMA SQUANDERS AMERICAN BLOOD, TREASURE

Iraq was functioning albeit with the help of U.S. troops when Mr. Obama became president in January 2009. That country was quiet, daily violence was low, and then team Obama declared that it could not get an agreement from Baghdad to leave forces behind. The truth is the administration didn't try hard enough. After all, Obama made clear in his 2008 campaign that Iraq was the wrong war, which he promised to end. Certainly Obama knows our enemies in Baghdad can read!

In December 2011, the president ordered the withdrawal of all American forces. Obama used the occasion to declare at Fort Bragg with 82nd Airborne Soldiers at his back that Iraq was "secure" and "stable." Vice President Joe Biden, who voted for the war as a senator, boasted that withdrawing forces might become the Obama administration's "greatest achievement."[180]

The president's decision to completely withdraw American forces from Iraq violated another of his promises made in 2008. Then candidate for president, Obama wrote an op-ed for the *New York Times* entitled "My Plan for Iraq." Obama promised in that editorial to retain a residual military force in Iraq and warned that "we must be as careful getting out of Iraq as we were careless getting in."[181]

Literally weeks after the dust from American forces' departure settled, along Iraq's southern border with Kuwait, the fabric of the Iraqi government that was formed at considerable cost to America in blood and treasure quickly frayed. The Baghdad government, under the care of Iranophile Prime Minister Nouri al-Maliki, turned back on his sectarian stripes and tossed most of the Sunnis out of government, then cut them off from funding as well as turned the Iraqi security forces back into a patronage organization, with senior ranks sold to the highest bidder. Meanwhile, al-Qaeda in Iraq awoke newly empowered to take on the sectarian Baghdad regime and its ally in Syria, already enmeshed in a protracted civil war.

Until the spring of 2014, Obama foolishly downplayed the threat posed by the re-emergent Islamists in Iraq and Syria, and he all but ignored panicked warnings from Kurds and the Iraqi government that the crisis was out of hand. Send help!

Once Obama was forced by public opinion, the intelligence community, and his fellow Democrats who expressed alarm at the terrorists' gains and the obvious genocide, the president carved out time from golf and social events to admit that he had no strategy to defeat what he previously called a "jayvee" group [ISIS] that posed little threat to the U.S.—or at least no more of a threat than street criminals pose for a big city mayor. Anyway, Obama decided to launch airstrikes against the ISIS and promised he would build a coalition "to destroy and defeat" the Islamist threat that consumed much of eastern Syria and northern Iraq.

Obama's commitment to "destroy and defeat" ISIS lacked believability. By comparison, before President George W. Bush launched operations into Iraq in 2003, which Obama opposed as a senator, Bush secured multiple U.N. resolutions and congressional approval, and formed a broad "coalition of the willing." Obama took America back into Iraq with none of that, which is a sign of weakness and evidence of yet another failed foreign policy.

Likely what Obama wants in Iraq today is to avoid the legacy of a complete renewal of the former American effort that he abandoned in 2011. Of course, he also wants to avoid an ISIS triumph that could destroy the Iraqi regime and permanently establish the so-called caliphate and further embolden Tehran.

So Obama is seeking a minimalist solution using an air campaign and a few trainers of Iraqi and Kurdish forces. But that strategy has important skeptics like his military adviser, General Martin Dempsey, who publicly distanced himself from Obama, indicating that a greater U.S. ground presence may be required. This too is unlikely to end well.

OBAMA TRUSTS PATHOLOGICAL LYING IRAN ON NUKES

Obama's record with Iran is perhaps his most dangerous and misguided policy failure yet. Certainly the most important issue regarding Iran is that nation's nuclear weapons program, which threatens to engulf the region in an arms race and, based on the hatred spewing from the theocracy's top leaders, is an existential threat to our best regional ally Israel.

Iran is also a terrorist-sponsoring state—it formed terrorist proxy Hezbollah in 1982—and one of two states today propping up the Syrian regime, which to date has butchered at least two hundred thousand of its own citizens. Then again, Iran has by its opposition to the Islamic State's actions in Iraq become America's erstwhile ally. After all, both the U.S. and Iran supply arms, trainers, and air power to Iraq in the common cause of defeating ISIS fighters, which makes Tehran the enemy of my enemy or, as the adage goes, our friend. The major difference is that Iran's Revolutionary Guard Corps' Quds Forces are embedded with Iraqi Shia militia like the Badr Brigade and Iraqi security forces, which together fight ISIS trying to recapture large swaths of land lost to the terror group in 2014. Meanwhile, U.S. forces kept their powder dry inside Iraqi bases training new Iraqi recruits.

Iran's very active role and success aren't lost on Baghdad, much less on the rest of the region. While Iran builds up credibility, the U.S. is seen, thanks to Obama's policies, as cowering inside bases out of harm's way.

Defeating ISIS is important, but Iran's nuclear weapons program is the more pressing geopolitical issue and likely to become Obama's major foreign policy failure. Once all the smoke settles from Obama's legacy nuclear deal with Iran, we either are left with a nuclear Iran or so much ambiguity that no one knows whether the mullahs in Tehran have atomic weapons or not. In either case, the situation is very serious and enough to spark a Middle East arms race.

The prospects of either outcome brought Israeli Prime Minister Benjamin Netanyahu to Washington to speak to a joint session of Congress on March 3, 2015, where he made a strong case to avoid a bad deal. Obama was unhappy with the prime minister's visit and made his displeasure known by sending his representatives to the press to announce that the administration considered the Israeli's speech unhelpful. Of course, it appears that any outcome with Iran that is acceptable to Obama will provide no real guarantee that Israel will accept, because a nuclear weapons-armed Iran—real or presumed—poses an existential threat to Israel.

Obama's options to deny Iran a nuclear weapon were admittedly limited. A military strike would produce many unsavory repercussions, including plunging financial markets, skyrocketing oil prices, and a significant spike in regional tensions. The president virtually eliminated any such strike on his watch by his words, and the mullahs know that gave them great leverage at the nuclear negotiations they delayed numerous times. Meanwhile, they insisted on relief from congressional sanctions for their further cooperation.

As if Obama's strategic messages that the U.S. would not strike Iran over its nuclear program weren't enough, our strategic partner in the talks, Russia, decided to strengthen Tehran's hands just as the negotiations were winding up. Specifically, Moscow announced its intent to sell and deliver in 2015 the S-300 sophisticated air defense system to Iran, which significantly ratchets up the regime's defenses against any air strike either from the U.S. and/or Israel.

Isn't it a twist of fate that Obama strongly opposed the war President Bush launched against Iraq in 2003—which at the time was justified on flimsy evidence about Saddam Hussein's weapons of mass destruction—but now Obama emboldens Iran to cross significant nuclear thresholds while ignoring significant undisputed intelligence about that nation's atomic weapons progress? Of course, such hypocrisy is lost on an inattentive American public, but not on the Persian negotiators who laughed at our negotiating and strategic messaging incompetence.

At this writing, it appears that Iran has all the ingredients for a nuclear weapon—enriched uranium, triggering mechanisms, and ballistic missiles equipped with special weapons capsules, as well as telemetry based on past satellite launches. Further, in spite of so-called severe sanctions, Tehran manages to import sensitive Western microelectronics and power supplies for military and nuclear energy systems.

The evidence of such illegal acquisitions is well established. For example, on April 16, 2015, the U.S. District Court in Texas indicted five individuals and four companies on twenty-four counts related to illegally exporting sensitive military microelectronics and power supplies to Iran. The illicit procurement network is estimated to have "obtained at least approximately twenty-eight million parts valued at approximately $24 million from companies worldwide and shipped these commodities to Iran." The technologies, according to the indictment, went to the Atomic Energy Organization of Iran and the Iranian Centrifuge Technology Company.[182]

Evidently, Iran successfully bypasses sanctions to outfit its nuclear programs. Imagine what Tehran can do once the "severe" sanctions are removed thanks to President Obama's agreement.

There is also the matter of Tehran's close relationship with nuclear-power partner Pyongyang and the presence in Iran of hundreds of North Korean weapons specialists, which makes a Persian nuclear-weapons capability a foregone conclusion. It is just a matter of the mullahs giving the military the go-ahead.

The Obama administration's agreement with Iran leaves the regime with no more than a one-year breakout option that does not resolve forever the threat. Further, the questionable effectiveness of inspections by the UN's International Atomic Energy Agency (IAEA) and Iran's record of cheating make any assurances Tehran provides fallible at best. Just think about how ineffective the IAEA was at keeping North Korea from its quest for nuclear status.

The IAEA has repeatedly failed to completely monitor Iran's nuclear program. In such a vast country—more than twice the size of Texas—in which clandestine activities are the cornerstone of politics, IAEA inspectors cannot ensure that Iran is not moving forward to obtaining a nuclear bomb. Former secretary of state under President Nixon, Henry Kissinger, pointed out: "Nobody can really fully trust the inspection system or at least some may not. This is something I would hope gets carefully examined before a final solution is achieved."[183]

That situation leaves the region and world a more dangerous place, having merged nuclear weapons power with ideological Islamists, religious motives, and regional hegemonic ambitions. The next president faces a far more difficult problem thanks to Obama.

OBAMA ALIENATES ISRAEL, FAVORS TERRORIST PALESTINIAN

President Obama has an icy relationship with Israeli Prime Minister Benjamin Netanyahu. Leaked administration slurs about the Israeli calling him a "coward" and "chickensh-t"[184] are consistent with Obama's own 2011 open-microphone smear of Netanyahu during the G-20 summit in Cannes in which the president said, "You're fed up with him [speaking with then French President Nicolas Sarkozy], but I have to deal with him even more often than you."[185]

The tension stretches across Obama's tenure in the White House. In the wake of the January 7, 2015, Islamic attack on a kosher market in Paris, Obama said it was a "random attack," not an attack on Jews. That was a slap at Jews and the nation of Israel.[186]

The Obama-Netanyahu troubled relationship could be part personality conflict, but Obama's distaste for the Israeli is likely more based on some fundamental disagreement about his views of the Israeli-Palestinian stalled peace process.

Two outstanding issues divide the parties: Palestinian terrorist attacks and Israeli settlements. Palestinians don't want to stop the terrorist attacks or haven't made a serious enough effort to convince the Israelis. Also, the Israelis tend to support some eventual trade of the West Bank, but only in exchange for the vast majority of the Jewish settlements in the West Bank.[187]

Unfortunately, the Obama administration tried to restart the collapsed peace process without consulting the Israelis by making a settlement freeze the centerpiece of its strategy. The Israelis accepted a limited halt that did not impact housing construction in East Jerusalem. But Obama pushed for the freeze in Jerusalem as well, which no Israeli government would accept without significant verifiable Palestinian security guarantees—and those are unlikely to be forthcoming.

Obama's insistence on a construction discontinuation in East Jerusalem hardened the Palestinian position on the issue, a position Palestinian Authority President Mahmoud Abbas embraced as a condition for resuming talks. Thus the talks became stalemated, thanks to Obama's one-sided policy. Then, like piling on, Abbas pushed the United Nations to endorse unilateral Palestinian statehood as the only path to peace which further alienated the Israelis.

Obama showed just how biased he is for the Palestinians during the 2014 Israel-Hamas war in Gaza. At the time, Obama contributed to an op-ed in the left-wing Israeli newspaper *Haaretz*, "Israel Conference on Peace." Obama called for the two-state solution and declared that "peace is the only true path to security for Israel and the Palestinians."[188]

Obama used the article to praise Abbas as a peace partner, but failed to offer similar praise for Netanyahu. While praising Abbas, he ignored the renewed violence from Hamas against Israel and the role that the Fatah-Hamas unity pact had played in undermining peace talks earlier that year. Obama's own State Department considers Hamas a terrorist organization, which evidently has no bearing on the president's calls for negotiations.

OBAMA TOSSED A GOOD ALLY
UNDER THE BUS FOR ISLAMISTS

Mr. Obama boasted at his 2015 State of the Union speech that we live in a "safer, more prosperous world." On the heels of that empty proclamation, yet another Obama foreign policy failure emerged: Yemen. A few months prior to Obama's speech, he called attention to the situation in Yemen to declare it the model for other countries.

In February 2015, Shiite al-Houthi rebels, Iranian allies, seized control of the capital. Quickly, the American and other Western country embassies emptied, and the nation descended into failed state status.

Yemen had long hovered near failed-state status for years. Remember, Yemen has a long history of radicalism: In 2000, the USS Cole was attacked in the Yemeni port of Aden; in 2009, an American airliner came close to being blown up by the Yemen-trained "underwear bomber" Umar Farouk Abdulmutallab; and radical cleric Anwar al-Awlaki instructed Fort Hood jihadist Major Nidal Hasan, who murdered thirteen soldiers in 2009. Besides, Yemen exported many jihadists to battlefields, and many were taken off battlefields and shipped to the Guantanamo Bay detention facility.

In 2011, Secretary of State Hillary Clinton visited Sanaa, Yemen, to announce the U.S. policy there was to develop a "unified, stable, democratic and prosperous Yemen where civil society has room to operate but al-Qaeda does not."[189] Clinton announced that American aid would double and called for a "rebalancing" of priorities.

Throughout the subsequent years, team Obama insisted that our Yemen policy was a great success. In June 2014, Obama praised Yemeni President Abdu Rabbu Mansour Hadi as a "committed partner" to the U.S. and boasted that "we have been able to develop their capacities without putting large numbers of U.S. troops on the ground at the same time as we're got enough counterterrorism capabilities."[190]

Obama really put himself out on a limb by bragging about Yemen being the "model" for trouble spots like Syria and Iraq. The president said Yemen is a model because of the "wide-ranging national dialogue that took a long time, but helped give people a sense that there is a legitimate political outlet for grievances."[191]

On January 19, 2015, Yemen's al-Houthi rebels stormed the presidential palace in Sanaa and surrounded the prime minister's residence January 20. The Shiite al-Houthis claimed they were not interested in directly ruling Yemen, but wanted to influence Yemen's federal system. They are, however, interested in controlling the area within the boundaries of the old kingdom of Yemen or the Yemen Arab republic.

In late March, Saudi Arabia with Gulf emirates started an air, sea, and ground campaign against al-Houthi rebels, which by early May 2015 had killed twelve hundred, and three hundred thousand had fled their homes to escape the fighting. Although talks will take place in 2015, a long-term solution to the Shia-Sunni stand-off in Yemen, much like those in Syria-Iraq, are not anywhere in sight.[192]

What's clear is that Obama's model crumbled, and now the upstart Shiite group is calling the shots in Yemen, which expands Tehran's regional sphere of influence. Today, for the first time, there are direct flights from Tehran to Sanaa.[193]

OBAMA EMBRACES BROTHERHOOD
OVER SECULARISTS

Obama spoke at Cairo University in June 2009 promising a new start for the Middle East. He turned his eyes back to Egypt less than two years later in the wake of the chaotic Arab Spring, using that opportunity to dump a tired old ally, President Hosni Mubarak. At the time, Obama praised the "passion and dignity" of Egypt's protesters, which included many Muslim Brotherhood supporters, as an "inspiration" to people around the world. He said, "I have an unyielding belief that you [Egyptians] will determine your own destiny."[194]

Obama's favorable view of the Brotherhood is due partly to Hillary Clinton's trusted aide, Huma Mahmood Abedin. Abedin, Hillary's deputy chief of staff, longtime aide, and the daughter of parents involved in the Muslim Brotherhood leadership, steadily moved the secretary and Obama by association toward the Muslim Brotherhood. Specifically, Abedin convinced Clinton that to "control" the outcome of the Arab Spring, the U.S. needed to back moderate Islamist parties like the Muslim Brotherhood.[195]

Clinton evidently persuaded Obama to follow that course of action as things exploded in Cairo. That likely explains the president's praise for antigovernment protesters even though it alienated regional partners like the Saudis, according to an Arab official quoted in the *Wall Street Journal*.[196] Arab leaders are rightly concerned that Obama's push to oust Egyptian President Hosni Mubarak reflected incredible naïveté about the strength of Egypt's Islamists' opposition. In 2009, Obama demonstrated similar gullibility by inviting the Brotherhood to attend his speech at Cairo University.

The Brotherhood's election prospects at the time were especially bright because the democratic opposition was fractured and the Brotherhood already commanded a third of the vote. Besides, Shakyh Qaradawi, the most prestigious Brotherhood cleric, claimed that in a

Muslim country, secular reformers will never beat those who say "Islam is the solution" (the Brotherhood's slogan) and because, according to a recent Pew poll, 95 percent of Egyptians favor an Islamic-leaning government.[197]

Brotherhood apologists argued that the group, which was closely allied with the Nazis in World War II and embraced a theology based on Wahhabism, extremist Islam, did not aim to create an Islamic theocracy in Egypt like the one in Iran. Rather, its spokesmen claim it is a nonviolent charitable and educational organization with Islamic roots.

Mohammed Habib, a former deputy leader of the Brotherhood, told *Radio Liberty* at the time that he rejected the suggestion that the organization aimed to create an Iranian-like Islamic theocracy. "We want a democratic government based on genuine political plurality," he said.[198]

But Habib's claim of "political plurality" did not agree with the Brotherhood's strategic plan used in seventy countries. That plan calls for Islamic dominance through subtle integration, becoming part of the national social and political life and the application of sharia law.

The Brotherhood's supreme guide, Muhammad Badi, is not a pluralist, but he does advocate violence. Both Badi and then al-Qaeda leader Osama bin Laden were devoted followers of Sayyid Qutb, a fundamentalist scholar who advocated Islamic holy war and the chief developer of doctrines that legitimize violent Muslim resistance.

In 2010, Badi demonstrated his radicalism in a series of sermons. He said that "waging jihad is mandatory" for all Muslims, especially against Israel and the United States. He called for "all forms of resistance for the sake of liberating every occupied piece of land in Palestine, Iraq, Afghanistan, and all [other] parts of our Muslim world." He also said the United States can be defeated through violence since it is "experiencing the beginning of its end and is heading toward its demise."[199]

Both Badi and his predecessor outlined their political plans for Egypt at the time. Badi said the Koran should "become our constitution," and in 2007 then supreme guide Muhammad Mahdi'Akef drafted the Brotherhood's political platform.[200]

That platform read that Islam will be the state religion and Islamic sharia "is the main source for legislation." The Supreme Council of Clerics—similar to Iran's all-powerful Guardian Council—will exercise veto power over the legislature.[201] Non-Muslims and women are barred from the presidency, and the 1979 Camp David Peace Accords with Israel will be put to referendum, which means certain defeat in the Muslim majority country. And tourists visiting Egypt must "be in line with Islamic principles, values, and laws," which will put a serious damper on Western tourism.[202]

Team Obama knew Mohamed Morsi's Muslim Brotherhood was a radical group that would never democratize Egypt. But for reasons as yet revealed, Obama's staff put out the word that the Brotherhood was "largely secular," in spite of their long record of radical Islamic statements and advertising their long-term objectives.

Plainly, the Obama administration was surprised once Morsi's radical Islamism quickly alienated the majority of the Egyptian people after the election. Obama expected the practical responsibilities of governing to moderate the Brotherhood's views, but once in power, Morsi let loose his Islamic minions, who persecuted Egypt's Coptic Christian minority, cracked down on pro-democracy groups, and imposed severe restrictions on freedom of press and religion. Eventually, his excesses forced the country's army to conduct a coup on July 3, 2013.

Morsi, who sent aides to Washington to consult with the Obama administration, evidently felt no need to temper their Islamist ambitions, because the Obama administration refused to use its annual $1.5 billion aid to leverage a different approach. No wonder many Egyptians resent Obama for courting the Brotherhood and failing to mitigate some of Morsi's radicalism before the coup.

Once again, Obama ended up on the wrong side of history embracing radical Islamists.

OBAMA HAS NO FRIENDS
STANDING AND PLENTY OF DEAD

What are the consequences of Obama's failed Middle East policies? His failed Mideast policies have made America irrelevant by his avoiding tough decisions and standing back to let events drift. Certainly he made tough speeches, but seldom did Mr. Obama follow through with his words with meaningful action. He is a paper tiger and our enemies know it. We have become a useless ally and an ineffectual opponent.

For years, Mr. Obama never missed an opportunity to blame former President Bush for Mideast mistakes, but those same mistakes only got worse under Obama. Obama also alienated our only regional friend, Israel, setting that relationship back a decade or more. He pushed other former friends like Egypt into the arms of the Russians and would-be friends in Iraq, Yemen, and Libya into chaos.

Mr. Obama's worst failure will be on Iran. He will likely be perceived as the president who allowed Iran to acquire nuclear weapons capability, replete with delivery systems, and further upset the balance of power in the region, triggering an arms race that will ultimately affect America's homeland.

Mr. Obama also has lots of Christian blood on his hands. Obama's Mideast policy failures exacerbated Christian sufferings by growing regional instability. Specifically, his policies in places like Libya, Syria, Iraq, and Egypt contributed to the demise of Christian-friendly governments that were replaced by radical Islamic regimes far more prone than before to persecute Christians.

FUTURE IMPLICATIONS AND END-TIMES PROPHECY

This section answers two compelling questions: What are the implications for the Middle East and the rest of the world if the Middle East becomes void of Christians? Is the Christian genocide in the Middle East another clue that the world is quickly entering the end times?

Chapter 8 addresses the implications for the Middle East if the region is cleansed of all Christians. Certainly, firsthand reports from the region suggest that Christian hope is threadbare.

Charmaine Hedding with the Shai Fund, a nonprofit humanitarian assistance and development organization, reported in April 2015 about the growing hopelessness among Christians in Erbil, Iraq. Ms. Hedding said, "The lay people have had enough and if given the chance, would leave." But she fears that "the Christians will be abandoned," which means they will be left in a Muslim area that could turn on them at any moment.

Should Christians across the region like those in Erbil actually flee for safety or worse, then the entire Middle East will suffer irreparable harm. Specifically, the Christian contributions to the region over the last two millennia are momentous. The void Christians leave will be filled not with charity and love, but with fundamentalist, Islamic fear.

Chapter 9 considers the global implications of a Christian genocide. Here the Nazi genocide of European Jews is used to illustrate the possible implications for Middle East Christians at the hands of Islamists and their collaborators. Further, we explore the widespread religious-based hatred in the Middle East that encourages genocide, as does the plague of apathy in the West that prevents any serious effort to help the suffering. Finally, there is a massive effort by some Muslims and so-called progressives to criminalize Christian-based behavior that directly impacts Middle East believers, but is also a growing cancer in the West as well.

Chapter 10 addresses whether the current events in the Middle East are clues leading to the end times. We review end-times prophecies across the Bible to suggest how to interpret the crises that are popping up more frequently and that pose great danger for Christians today.

Finally, Chapter 11 provides an explanation of Islamic eschatology to help the reader understand both the motivation of Islamist fighters who seek to usher in the end times and how end-times biblical and Islamic prophecies are very different.

CHAPTER 8

WHAT WILL HAPPEN IN THE MIDDLE EAST IF CHRISTIANS ARE GONE?

I f Christians were to vanish from the Middle East, the key to understanding the implications lies in the recognition of the Christians' impact on the political life of the region. Under the current circum stances, Christians will never play a significant political role in the region; rather, they will continue to be at best a marginalized minority. In fact, that status appears to be diminishing as Islamic extremism grows, and therefore the current grave situation makes a Christian genocide all the more likely in the coming years.

Dr. Fiona McCallum, with the School of International Relations, University of St. Andrews, Scotland, wrote a very insightful paper entitled "Christian Political Participation in the Arab World," which helps put the Christian community's participation in Arab countries into proper perspective.[203] She wrote that Christian participation in the political life of an Arab nation takes place in three main areas. First, they can participate in the electoral process, receiving votes and gaining seats in parliaments. Second, they can serve in ministerial cabinets or as advisers to government executives. Finally, the average Christian citizen can participate in the political process by casting a vote for various strata of elections.

This level of political participation sounds fair until you realize that Muslim-majority states treat token Christian participation unequally. Christian political participation is shaped by strategies dictated by the ruling authoritarian regimes that institutionalize religion-based quotas and award minorities political clout based on their loyalty. Underlying these strategies is the fact that religious identity continues to be the crucial factor in determining the Christian's level of political participation, and even the ruling elite won't buck the Muslim majority to favor Christians.

It should also be understood that Middle Eastern Christians are not a monolithic group, which means they are not all treated alike across the region's countries. They are scattered into relatively small enclaves across the region, belonging to different denominations with multiple identities, tribes, and ethnicities—some with greater political influence than others. Greek Orthodox, Greek Catholic, and Protestant churches are best at being politically active by working closely with their Arab neighbors. They have perhaps the most political clout. There are Armenian Christians who survived the early twentieth-century Ottoman genocide and resettled in various Arab lands. They have less clout than the aforementioned groups, and the Assyrians never quite succeeded in establishing a separate ethnicity in their homeland of Iraq, which means they are rather politically impotent. Other church groups such as Aramaic, Syriac, and Coptic have tried to establish separate identities with mixed results. The Egyptian Coptic Christians are somewhat successful due in part to their significant population (maybe eight million and rapidly declining due to anti-Christian compelled immigration), but not without considerable internal resistance from Islamists within the region's largest Arab population.

The Christian community's participation in Middle East politics must be understood within the context of regime authoritarianism as well. Christians have tended to stay close to the ruling elite, who govern with an iron fist and reward political patronage rather than rely on the majority Muslim population—which isn't especially sympathetic to non-Muslim minorities. That explains why Christians have in the past aligned themselves politically with tough men like the former Egyptian President Hosni Mubarak of Egypt, the Syrian Assad family, the Hashemite Kingdom of Jordan, and even the former Iraqi dictator Saddam Hussein. Christians had to choose their poison to survive in the hostile Islamic cultures, and sometimes they had to bed down with some very unsavory characters in order to have any leverage and protection from hostile Islamists.

Christians are also pragmatists about where they live. They understand that in the Middle East, religion in general retains social significance and therefore it continues to influence political affairs and the accompanying rights and privileges. After all, Islam is the official religion in Arab countries, and sharia law is the source of most legislation. There fore, the political role of Christians depends on not just the political elite with which they are aligned, but also on the prevailing majority interpretation of the Koran and the various hadiths of the Prophet Muhammad as they relate to non-Muslims. As expected, most of the Prophet's teachings aren't especially generous to non-Muslims, as we saw earlier in the book.

Islam does recognize the right of *ahl al-kitab* (People of the Book) to worship and, as long as they accept their second-class *dhimmi* ("covenanted people") status in society, they can survive and some flourish. Further, Christians are generally granted the opportunity to participate in the political process and society in general. However, the Muslim makes certain that many important public positions such as the head of state and commander of the army are off-limits to non-Muslims.

Christians are limited in their individual political participation based on national formulas as well. It is possible for a Christian to stand for office and be elected based on competence and political views rather than religious identity, but this is rare. The idea is that the Christian must portray himself as a "secularist" in such situations. But even in such a secular system, Christian identity is never totally ignored. That's why most Arab governments have a quota system for minority groups based on their percentage of the overall population. For example, in Jordan, Christians are allocated nine parliamentary seats (out of 150) and in Iraq, Christians have been assigned five out of the eight seats for all non-Muslim minorities. The Iraqi parliament has 328 seats.[204]

Political participation is not solely confined to token representation within parliament either. In Jordan, cabinets usually have a couple of Christian ministers, and in Iraq, one Christian was appointed to the thirty-two-strong cabinet in 2005. There have been exceptions, such as Michel Aflaq, a Greek Orthodox school teacher who helped found the Arab Ba'th Socialist Party. Aflaq demonstrated that Christians at one time enjoyed the opportunity to participate in the Arab nationalist movement, but he was the rare exception.[205]

Christians led two Palestinian nationalist movements and others played roles in the Kurdish national movement. Until 2003, Iraq had a Christian, Tariq Aziz, who served as Saddam Hussein's deputy prime minister although he represented himself mostly as a secularist.

Even though some governments have Christian ministers, and a few senior military officers are Christian, a Christian will never be head of an Arab state. In fact, most of the Arab constitutions declare that the religion of the head of state must be Islam, and in some countries the level of Christian participation in national institutions is limited by tradition, not law.

It is also well established that religious identity remains a crucial component in determining how regimes deal with Christians. That glass ceiling will always limit the Christian's political power and could change at the whim of the political elite.

We saw just how fragile support is for Christians with the election of the Muslim Brotherhood in Egypt. Before Brotherhood leader President Mohammed Morsi was ousted in 2013, Christians experienced significant discrimination and now they are back to just being second-class citizens, and the normal level of persecution continues.

Unfortunately, the shift of power in the Middle East, thanks to Islamic extremism, accelerated by the Arab Spring, puts the politically marginalized Christian at greater risk. However, even though Christians are marginalized in their political power, they are still citizens with a rich history of contributing to the betterment of their individual countries.

Now consider the Christian community's collective contribution to the Middle East and what the region risks should Christians be forced out of the holy lands.

CALLS FOR CHRISTIANS TO LEAVE OR CONVERT

Not surprisingly, some Middle East Muslims call on Christians to convert to Islam to avoid extermination at the hands of Islamic State terrorists while others believe the only solution to Christian genocide is emigration from the Middle East. But becoming Muslim to avoid death or abandoning the Christian's ancient homeland isn't in the best interest of the region's Muslim population, because Christians have enriched the Middle East and will in the future given the opportunity. Muslims should do whatever possible to keep Christians contributing to the future of the region for their own welfare.

Fortunately, Christians through the past two thousand years have clung to their faith and countries in spite of being routinely targeted for extermination. Christians survived for hundreds of years in spite of Muslim oppression leading up to the eleventh-century Crusades. They survived the Mongol invasions of the thirteenth century, and Armenian Christians survived the twentieth-century massacres at the hands of the Ottomans. Christians will hopefully endure the current reign of terror at the hands of Islamic extremists, who are tacitly supported by the region's oppressively discriminatory Islamic governments.

If Christians are killed or abandon the Middle East to escape genocide, they will leave a social vacuum that will be quickly filled by a return to the Dark Ages, thanks to the growing intolerance of extremist Islam now sweeping across the region. In the past, Christians played an invaluable role on many fronts, influencing regional governments by promoting a democratic and pluralistic society and contributing much to the region's successes.

Middle Eastern Christians have fostered a subculture that produced outstanding citizens focused on creating a moral ecology that promotes human rights and family unity, a vibrant economy, diverse education for all people, hospitals, orphanages, and professional classes that man the region's middle class. They generally have been outstanding patriots. Those virtues and contributions could quickly fade if Christians leave the region, and the Middle East will be worse for their departure.

Jordan's King Abdullah agrees with that view. The king said, "The protection of the rights of Christians is a duty rather than a favor. Christians have always played a key role in building our societies and defending our nations."[206]

CHRISTIAN CULTURE PRODUCES VITAL RESULTS

Christian contributions can be traced to the Bible's influence on their way of life, which forms their unique culture. Their lifestyle reflects the teaching of Jesus Christ, who gives a hungry world meaning and purpose to life and influences the behaviors that make Christians outstanding, reliable, and productive citizens.

Consider Christian teaching that molds their culture and makes them valued citizens even in the Middle East and in spite of Muslim hostility.

Christians believe in the centrality of forgiveness in Jesus Christ's teachings, which makes them helpful at reducing sectarian discrimination in pluralistic societies. They believe Jesus Christ is the Savior of all mankind, but they are also respecters of others' rights to freedom of belief and expression. They may disagree with others' theology, but that won't stop the Christian from caring for the non-Christians and treating them with love and compassion—all in the name of Jesus Christ.

Unlike other religious figures, Jesus Christ came not as a warrior but as a loving Savior to heal and forgive our sins (behaviors that displease and separate us from God). Christ's thirty-three-year earthly ministry was lived as a peacemaker, a servant, a healer, a teacher, and an outstanding citizen who respected the governing authorities and religious leaders to the point of His death on the cross. Christians are to emulate Christ's example to their present world, and that's an example that contributes to a healthy Middle East.

Christ's teachings are captured in the New Testament, which touches on virtually every aspect of the Christian's life and influences their daily behaviors. One of the least understood of Christ's teachings is His command for the Christian to avoid being worldly. Rather, Christians are commanded to impact the world for the gospel (good news) of Jesus Christ by being Christ-like to the world—giving, peaceful, caring. Although they are in the world, they are called to be different for Christ's sake.

The apostle Paul instructed in Romans 12:2 that the Christian is not to conform to the world; he should not reflect the world's sin and waywardness, but be "transformed by the renewing of [his] mind" that he may "prove what the will of God is, that which is good and acceptable and perfect."

Paul's instruction is for the Christian to constantly seek to please his living Savior and be mindful through constant prayer and devotion to God's Word to be other focused. Christians are to think about others and their needs before themselves and be charitable and caring. Those are virtues evidenced by orthodox Christians, which makes them especially good citizens and neighbors.

The New Testament teaches the Christian to cling to righteousness (2 Corinthians 6:14) and to minister to the needs of orphans and widows (James 1:27) as well as to take care of their families, working diligently for the cause of Christ.

The Bible teaches about the role of the husband, which encompasses provision and protection for his wife and children: "Anyone who does not provide for their relatives, and especially for their own household, has denied the faith and is worse than an unbeliever" (1 Timothy 5:8, NIV). "Husbands, love your wives and do not be harsh with them" (Colossians 3:19, NIV).

Christian teaching about marriage and family life are welcomed in modern nations because the family is considered the primary building block of society.

The Christ-forgiven and forever-saved Christian is called to be a witness for Jesus to the world. He said in Matthew 5:13–16 (NIV):

You are the salt of the earth. But if the salt loses its saltiness, how can it be made salty again? It is no longer good for anything, except to be thrown out and trampled underfoot.

You are the light of the world. A town built on a hill cannot be hidden.

Neither do people light a lamp and put it under a bowl. Instead they put it on its stand, and it gives light to everyone in the house.

In the same way, let your light shine before others, that they may see your good deeds and glorify your Father in heaven.

Christians are salt and light making disciples by sharing the gospel in a winsome and peaceful manner through loving and caring for the unbeliever. That's the type of person societies should seek. Yes, Christians are commissioned to "go therefore and make disciples of all the nations, baptizing them in the name of the Father and the Son and the Holy Spirit, teaching them to observe all that I commanded you; and lo, I am with you always, even to the end of the age" (Matthew 28:19–20, NASB).

These ambassadors for Christ (2 Corinthians 5:20) are to conduct themselves with wisdom toward outsiders—unbelievers like Muslims—making the most of the opportunity. They do so not with a sword but with a caring and giving heart.

What kind of culture grows out of such teaching? Christian culture embraces Christ's redemption and restoration, which is renewal of the whole of life. The Christian hopes for the ultimate release of humanity and the earth from the bondage of sin, which is the church's task of salvaging a sin-wrecked creation.

Bishop Awa Royel, Bishop of California for the Holy Apostolic Catholic Assyrian Church of the East, explained the Christian church in the Middle East is important for humanity. Christianity provides hope for mankind because God stepped into history in order to show His solidarity with man. Christianity is a salutary faith in that it offers salvation to all humanity, Muslims as well.[207]

Christians are taught to live out Christ's teachings in tangible ways. If they do so, they create a beautiful culture that is attractive to non-Christians.

One of the foremost Christian authors of the past century was C. S. Lewis, who wrote a marvelous book, *Mere Christianity*, in which he created a word image of the perfect Christian culture.[208] It's a very attractive picture for every region of the world and shows the appealing Christian potential for the Middle East.

> All the same, the New Testament, without going into details, gives us a pretty clear hint of what a fully Christian society would be like. Perhaps it gives us more than we can take. [First] It tells us that there are to be no passengers or parasites: If man does not work, he ought not to eat. Everyone is to work with his own hands, and what is more, every one's work is to produce something good: There will be no manufacture of silly luxuries and then of sillier advertisements to persuade us to buy them. [Second] And there is to be no "swank" or "side," no putting on airs. To that extent, a Christian society would be what we now call "leftist." On the other hand, it is always insisting on obedience—obedience (and outward marks of respect) from all of us to properly appointed magistrates, from children to parents, and

(I am afraid this is going to be very unpopular) from wives to husbands. Thirdly, it is to be a cheerful society: full of singing and rejoicing, and regarding worry or anxiety as wrong. Courtesy is one of the Christian virtues; and the New Testament hates what it calls "busybodies."

If there were such a society in existence, visitors should come away with a curious impression. They should feel that its economic life was very socialistic and, in that sense, "advanced," but that its family life and its code of manners were rather old-fashioned—perhaps even ceremonious and aristocratic. Everyone would like some bits of it, but it's likely that very few would like the whole thing. That is just what could be expected if Christianity is the total plan for the human machine. Everyone has departed from that total plan in different ways, and each person wants to make out that his own modification of the original plan is the plan itself. This is found again and again about anything that is really Christian: Everyone is attracted by bits of it and wants to pick out those bits and leave the rest. That is why we do not get much farther; and that is why people who are fighting for quite opposite things can say they are fighting for Christianity.

The Christian culture Lewis describes—a benevolent monarchy—will exist only during the Millennial Kingdom when Christ rules and is physically present on earth. Until then it will not be a reality anywhere much less in the Middle East, but it does provide a perspective regarding what such a miracle would look like, a glimpse of heaven on earth. However, some of the values, beliefs, and practices evidenced by Christians in Lewis' Christian culture are very desirable for all humanity, even the Middle East today, and in fact they have in the past been evidenced in that region.

Middle East Christians deliver some of those outcomes in tangible ways to their neighborhoods and nations. Christians have historically introduced a disproportionate number of critical services, such as establishing universities, schools, hospitals, centers for healing, and much more compared to other faith-based groups in their society.

Pope Benedict XVI outlined the very significant contributions made by the Catholic Church in the Middle East. The pontiff said:

> For many years, the Catholic Church in the Middle East has carried out her mission through a network of educational, social and charitable institutions. She has taken to heart the words of Jesus: "Whatever you did for one of the least of these brothers and sisters of mine, you did for me" (Matthew 25:40, NIV). The proclamation of the gospel has been accompanied by works of charity, since it is of the very nature of Christian charity to respond to the immediate needs of all, whatever their religion and regardless of factions or ideologies, for the sole purpose of making present on Earth God's love for humanity.[209]

Geoffrey Blainey, a historian of Christianity, likened the Catholic Church to a positive welfare state: "It conducted hospitals for the old and orphanages for the young; hospices for the sick of all ages; places for the lepers; and hostels or inns where pilgrims could buy a cheap bed and meal."[210] Of course, Christian charity is not just to help those in need, but also to allow the grace of God to work through the Christian to conform that person to the image of Christ and bear witness to the world of that grace.

Following Christ as indicated in Mark 8:34–35 means, "Then he called the crowd to him along with his disciples and said: 'Whoever wants to be my disciple must deny themselves and take up their cross and follow me. For whoever wants to save their life will lose it, but whoever loses their life for me and for the gospel will save it'" (NIV). Christians are called to do good works for the glory of Christ.

That perspective explains why hundreds of Christian institutions across the Middle East serve the frail, the elderly, the handicapped; hospitals and social and education programs exist for the good of all. They serve local people without regard for their faith with openness and compassion.

Middle East Christians have a reputation for doing very well in business as well. They are over-represented in the region's middle class as merchants and skilled craftsmen. But discrimination and threats have driven many away from Middle East communities where they previously owned businesses that are now closed and the jobs are gone.

Christians continue to make significant contributions to education in the Middle East. Traditionally, Arab schools teach rote learning, which reinforces dogmatic Islam. But Christian education tends to be well-rounded, addressing the arts, sciences, mathematics, and literature.

The Catholic Church has been a particular leader in education across the Middle East. The Catholic Church established universities, as well as primary and secondary schools where there were parishes and missions. The numbers of Catholic education institutions across the world is staggering: 125,016 primary and secondary schools and 1,046 universities—— many hundreds are still serving in the Middle East.[211]

The high quality of Christian education in the Middle East has unwittingly contributed to the diaspora of the Christians. "The Christian schools that helped to educate Christians in the Gaza Strip and in the West Bank indirectly, without intending to do it, have encouraged the diaspora of the Christians…and they did that through giving quality education to Christians," said Alex Awad of the Bethlehem Bible College. Christian education "was a blessing to these individuals, but it hurt the community as a whole," he said.[212] In other words, it is easier for educated Christians to emigrate because of better job opportunities abroad.

Christians who remain in the region tend to remain active in their societies. The Lutheran-based Diyar Consortium in Bethlehem indicates that nearly half of Palestinian civil institutions are Christian and they are one of the largest employers after the Palestinian Authority, providing jobs for both Christians and Muslims.[213]

The Bible also teaches Christian citizenship, loyalty that every state should want in its people. Several biblical principles provide insights regarding the scope of a Christian's responsibilities regarding his or her state.

Jesus confronted the Pharisees using a Roman coin:

Tell us, then, what is your opinion: Is it lawful to pay the census tax to Caesar or not?'

Knowing their malice, Jesus said: "Why are you testing me, you hypocrites?

Show me the coin that pays the census tax." Then they handed him the Roman coin.

He said to them, "Whose image is this and whose inscription?"

They replied, "Caesar's." At that he said to them, "Then repay to Caesar what belongs to Caesar and to God what belongs to God."

When they heard this they were amazed, and leaving him they went away. (Mathew 22:18–22, New American Bible, Revised Edition [NABRE])

The common interpretation of this Scripture is that Jesus instructs that the church and government have jurisdiction over different spheres. Christ asks whose image is on the coin. Of course, the correct answer is "Caesar." The implication is that the listener ought to then ask: "Who has the image of God on them?" The answer to the implied question is that human beings have the image of God on them. The principle is that the government and the church share a common obligation to advance the good of those made in God's image.

That means Christians are respecters of all human beings and look out to advance the good of all men with respect for race, color, creed, faith, and national origin. Christians should be blind to these differences, which makes them less inclined to discrimination.

The Bible teaches the Christian to be just in his dealings, a virtue of good citizenship. The Christian is taught to love his neighbor (Luke 10:27), and the parable of the Good Samaritan encourages the Christian to help the stranger in trouble (Luke 10:29–37).

Fighting injustice is a principle throughout the Old Testament as well, and the Ten Commandants (Exodus 20:2–17) outline justice precepts about worshipping God, honoring parents, being faithful to spouses, not coveting, being truthful, and respecting human life. These principles translate into broader applications such as religious liberty, right to life, private property rights, traditional marriage, parenting, and integrity in public life.

Justice instruction in the Bible produces a Christian community's "moral ecology," a concept advanced by Robert P. George.[214] Just like well-crafted advertisements attract customers to buy products, the same concept applies when instilling theological truths in a population. Jesus' teaching using parables creates a "moral ecology" that promotes justice in the Christian culture, according to George.

The Christian Scripture makes it clear that Christians are expected to obey the law because governments are established by authority from God. The apostle Paul writes in Romans:

> Obey the rulers who have authority over you. Only God can give authority to anyone, and he puts these rulers in their places of power.
>
> People who oppose the authorities are opposing what God has done, and they will be punished.
>
> Rulers are a threat to evil people, not to good people. There is no need to be afraid of the authorities. Just do right, and they will praise you for it.
>
> After all, they are God's servants, and it is their duty to help you. If you do something wrong, you ought to be afraid, because these rulers have the right to punish you. They are God's servants who punish criminals to show how angry God is.
>
> But you should obey the rulers because you know it is the right thing to do, and not just because of God's anger.
>
> "You must also pay your taxes. The authorities are God's servants, and it is their duty to take care of these matters.

Pay all that you owe, whether it is taxes and fees or respect and honor." (Romans 13:1–7, CEV)

Christian culture makes the believer willing to mediate differences, and Christians act as a liberalizing force in the Middle East, where intolerance and fundamentalism is on the rise. Christians in that region have trended to become an increasingly neutral group politically, mostly out of necessity.

Christians are also instructed to be respectful of non-Christians.

The Christian is to "live such good lives among the pagans that, though they accuse you of doing wrong, they may see your good deeds and glorify God on the day he visits us" (1 Peter 2:12, NIV).

Peter expands on the honorable treatment to unbelievers to government: "Submit yourselves for the Lord's sake to every human authority: whether to the emperor, as the supreme authority, or to governors, who are sent by him to punish those who do wrong and to commend those who do right (1 Peter 2:13–14, NIV).

Peter concludes his instruction on government with: "Show proper respect to everyone, love the family of believers, fear God, honor the emperor" (1 Peter 2:17, NIV).

Christians are known for promoting human rights. The Bible and Christian theology influenced both philosophers and political activists. Jesus' teaching calls on the Christian to demonstrate compassion for the stranger, a trait any society should laud and seek in its citizens. Christianity also promotes the status of women and condemns infanticide, divorce, incest, abortion, and marital infidelity. These are all positions most Muslims support.

The tiny Christian presence in the Middle East has made an oversized and positive contribution in every aspect of the region's history. Those contributions will vanish if Christians emigrate and the region implodes with Islamic extremism.

There is an argument that, given the circumstances, Christians should abandon the Middle East and let it implode. Would their absence really be noticed and would in fact the region truly be worse without them? Further, as we saw earlier in this chapter, many Christians compromise their faith in order to survive and that hurts their witness as well as diminishes their impact for Christ.

What we don't know with any certainty is how many Christians in the region are truly living Christ-centered lives. That's key if a Christian culture is ever to have an impact on the region's radicalized Islamic culture. Absence Christian obedience to the Word of God and being led in their daily lives by the Holy Spirit, their usefulness as the light and salt of Matthew 5 is marginal or nil.

That's a tough decision for any Christian to make, because remaining—even for orthodox Christians focused on being Christ-like in a dangerous region—may mean certain death or at best a miserable physical life. Leave or stay? That's the question. But whatever the answer, the outcome could have a serious and long-lasting impact on the region and the rest of the world.

CHAPTER 9

GLOBAL IMPLICATIONS OF MIDDLE EAST CHRISTIAN GENOCIDE

We examined the universal conditions for genocide earlier in the book, but now we will compare the current situation in the Middle East with the best known modern genocide, the Jewish Holocaust. The Nazi genocide of European Jews in the 1930s and 1940s illustrates similarities with the ongoing Islamist cleansing of Christians in the Middle East, and that comparison suggests possible implications for the future world.

JEWISH HOLOCAST

German Nazism emerged as a fascist, totalitarian threat to the world and especially to the Jews prior to and during the Second World War. The Nazi regime under the leadership of tyrant Adolf Hitler perpetrated the murder of six million Jews, the mass murder best known as the "Holocaust," which is a Greek word meaning "sacrifice by fire." Why did it happen? Jews were considered "inferior" to the "racially superior" German race, and Hitler targeted them for death because they were "unworthy of life."[215]

Hitler was appointed the German chancellor following his Nazi Party's electoral success in 1933. Quickly, the Reichstag, Germany's parliament, passed the Enabling Act, legislation that transformed the old Weimar Republic into the Third Reich, which put Hitler in total command. Then, using his new dictatorial powers, Hitler, known as the Führer, a German title meaning "leader or guide," set a course to eliminate all Jews from Germany and establish a new order of Europe *(Neuordnung Europas).* Hitler proclaimed: "This year 1941 will be, I am convinced, the historical year of a great European new order."[216]

Hitler's new order included the creation of a pan-German racial state to ensure the supremacy of an Ayran-Nordic master race, massive territorial expansion, as well as the annihilation of the Jews.

At the time, most of Europe's nine million Jews lived in countries under Nazi Germany's control. By the end of the Second World War, the Germans and their allies murdered nearly two-thirds of all European Jews as part of their so-called "Final Solution," the Nazis' decision to exterminate all European Jews.

There are at least five parallels evident between the Nazi genocide of European Jews and today's Christian genocide in the Middle East. Those five parallels don't necessarily mean more genocide is forthcoming elsewhere in the world, much less the Middle East. However, if some of the same ingredients long associated with the Nazi atrocities against the Jews and now being replicated by Islamist terrorists against Christians aren't stopped, then more Christian persecution if not genocide ought to be expected elsewhere.

TOTALITARIAMISM INCREASES RELIGIOUS-BASED GENOCIDE

Totalitarianism, the political system in which the state holds total authority over the society and seeks to control all aspects of public and private life, often brings out the worst in mankind. The world saw that manifestcd in the rise of the German Führer to power. Adolf Hitler was guided by racist and authoritarian principles whereby he eliminated individual freedoms.

Shortly after the Reichstag's Fire Decree on February 28, 1933, there was a total suspension of basic civil rights, and the Third Reich became a police state, a totalitarian regime. All opponents to the new dictatorship became subject to intimidation, persecution, and discriminatory legislation.[217] Jews were quickly and specifically targeted for the incremental removal from every aspect of society before being murdered or shipped to work and death camps.

Heinrich Himmler was the *Reichsfuehrer* (Reich leader) of the Nazi SS (*Schutzstaffel*; protection squadrons), the second most powerful man in Germany at the time and responsible for conceiving and overseeing the "Final Solution." On October 4, 1943, in Poznan at an SS gathering, Himmler justified the Holocaust with the following words:

> In front of you here, I want to refer explicitly to a very serious matter.... I mean here...the annihilation of the Jewish people.... Most of you will know what it means when one hundred corpses lie side by side, or five hundred or one thousand.... This page of glory in our history has never been written and will never be written....We had the moral right, we were obligated to our people to kill this people which wanted to kill us.[218]

The same totalitarian impulse that drove Nazism in the 1930s today drives radical Islamism in the Middle East and perhaps elsewhere. From the Islamic State's campaign to conquer Iraq and Syria to the extremist mullahs in Iran and al-Qaeda to the Taliban and the Persian's proxy al-Houthi militants of Yemen, these totalitarians are gaining power and threaten all liberty, especially for non-Muslims.

The Nazi and Islamist examples demonstrate an unmistakable pattern of totalitarian impulses that result in terrible atrocities. What we must watch for elsewhere in the world is the spread of similar impulses where fanatical leaders gain absolute and permanent authority and seek to transform humanity in every aspect of their existence without any accountability to any law or institution.

The source of these evil impulses is difficult to identify. Some popular culture documentaries (*The Morning of the Magicians*) and books (*The Occult Roots of Nazism*) suggest the Nazis were fascinated with the occult, and Himmler, for example, had "visions of himself as the reincarnation of a medieval German emperor."[219] The occult allegation appears to have originated with a 1938 German expedition into Tibet to find a hidden population of Aryan supermen in the Himalayas, the roots of the Aryan race.[220] The research staff at the U.S. Holocaust Museum in Washington dismisses the occult allegation as "inaccurate."[221] However, the evil impulses behind Nazi atrocities are still unexplained.

Even though the source of Nazi evil may not be fully understood, it clearly existed and continues to exist today. Specifically, the implication of such an evil impulse for the world should totalitarian Islamists like the Nazis before them manage to succeed in cleansing the Middle East of Christians, then other evil totalitarians present or future will be encouraged to abuse and murder their unwanted citizens as well. Unfortunately, we already see evidence of significant anti-Christian discrimination by totalitarians today and in some places where persecution is approaching genocide. Specifically, the 2015 World Watch List by Open Doors, a sixty-year-old ministry that empowers Christians in oppressive countries, ranks fifty countries where persecution of Christians is the most severe, and not coincidentally, most of those nations have majority Muslim populations and evidence some degree of totalitarianism.[222]

Open Doors reported that "authoritarian governments seek to control all religious thought and expression as part of a comprehensive plan to control all aspects of political and civic life." That is why "these governments regard some religious groups [such as Christians] as enemies of the state because they hold religious beliefs that may challenge loyalty to the rulers." That's horrible news for Christians, who account for almost one-third of the world's population and reside in every totalitarian leaning country across the world. For example, in North Korea, Christians are part of the "hostile" class,[223] and more than one hundred thousand are now in labor camps for their faith.[224]

FAITH-BASED GENOCIDE
INVITES COLLABORATORS

The Nazi inspired Holocaust was a systematic, bureaucratic, state-sponsored effort to eliminate all Jews. To do that the regime recruited many collaborators to help commit some of the worst atrocities against the Jewish people. For example, many of the German occupied nations, the so-called European Axis Partners, cooperated with the Nazis in the "Final Solution" by promulgating anti-Jewish legislation that led to deporting their Jewish citizens and/or shipping them off to killing centers or labor camps.[225] The "Final Solution" was the Nazis' plan to annihilate the Jews of Europe.

One occupied country that cooperated in Hitler's Final Solution was France. The government of Vichy France enacted the *Statut des Juifs* (Jewish laws), which restricted Jews' rights and even established internment camps, arrested Jews, and aided in their deportation to killing centers in Poland.

Other Axis partner states had fascist organizations like the Hlinka Guard in Slovakia, the Iron Guard in Romania, and the Ustasa in Croatia that murdered thousands of Jews while local authorities approvingly watched from the sideline or helped facilitate the deportation of Jewish residents.[226]

There are similarities with the treatment of Jews under Nazi control and non-Muslims today in Middle Eastern countries. Some Islamic extremist groups like ISIS murder Christians like fascist organizations did Jews, but it is the hands-off behavior of Middle Eastern governments that demonstrates the similarities with the Nazis. Not only are Christians treated as second-class citizens by those governments (in most cases by law), but many are targeted by their governments for their faith through either neglect or outright persecution as indicated earlier in countries like Iran.

The implication for the rest of the world is that Islamists will find other collaborators across the world to carry on Christian persecution, either through direct recruitment or by inspiring lone-wolf adherents via the Internet. After all, some Islamist groups espouse a "Final Solution" for all non-Muslims, such as the Iranian regime, which calls for the elimination of the state of Israel. Some of the region's Sunni Islamic leaders even call for the elimination of all Christian places of worship and open expression of Christian worship.

Unfortunately, there is evidence that such persecution is growing globally. In 2014, "more Christians worldwide live[d] in fear for their lives than at any time in the modern era," according to Open Doors USA. In fact, Christian persecution reached historic levels in 2014, with approximately one hundred million Christians facing possible serious consequences for merely practicing their faith, according to Open Doors. If current trends persist, the year 2015 could be even worse.[227]

Soberly, David Curry, president of Open Doors, said: "In regions where Christians are being persecuted as central targets, the trends and issues we track are expanding."[228]

HATE FUELS GENOCIDE

The Holocaust is history's most extreme example of anti-Semitism, prejudice against and hatred of Jews. The word "anti-Semitism" was coined in 1879 by German journalist Wilhelm Marr. He said the term not only meant hatred of Jews, but also hatred of various liberal, cosmopolitan, and international political trends often associated with Jews, such as equal civil rights, constitutional democracy, free trade, socialism, finance capitalism, and pacifism.[229]

Modern anti-Semitism gave birth to a political dimension that became associated with nationalism, whose adherents often used to denounce Jews as disloyal citizens. In fact, the nineteenth-century, xenophobic "Voelkisch Movement" ("People's Movement") established the notion of the Jew as "non-German," which influenced the theories of racism embraced by the Nazi Party and gained popularity by promoting anti-Jewish propaganda. Hitler's book *Mein Kampf* ("My Struggle") called for the removal of all Jews, and is even used today by white supremacist groups to engender hatred for non-whites.

Christians in the Middle East suffer similar prejudice and hatred evidenced by the Nazi regime for Jews. An October 2014 Pew Research survey provides evidence of that hatred, which states that Middle Eastern people "name religious and ethnic hatred most frequently as the greatest threat to the world." [230] In fact, one in three (34 percent) of all those surveyed across the region believe religious and ethnic hatred is the top world threat, and this Pew survey took place before ISIS conquered large portions of Iraq and Syria in 2014. No doubt evidence of hatred and prejudice against non-Muslims is the highest ever in war ravaged areas of the Middle East.

One such area is Lebanon, which has the largest percentage of Christians in the Middle East. Lebanese respondents to the Pew survey recorded the highest level of concern, with 58 percent identifying religious and ethnic hatred as the top threat. Specifically, religious hatred is the top concern among Lebanese Christians (56 percent), Shia Muslims (62 percent) and Sunni Muslims (58 percent). Significant levels of concern about hatred were also evident in the Palestinian territories, Tunisia, Egypt, and Israel as well. [231]

The implication is that hatred for Christians, the world's largest religious group with 2.3 billion believers, is contributing to genocide in the Middle East and that hatred could grow like a cancer elsewhere, sparking further persecution or worse. That's a finding of the 2014 Pew survey, which reports that "publics across the globe see the threat of religious and ethnic violence as a growing threat to the world's future."[232] Hatred and racism are ugly and are evidently spreading like a cancer, propelled in part by the likes of Islamic extremism.

The incidence of anti-Christian hatred is accelerating in the form of deadly violence, especially in Africa at the hands of Islamists. For years, the Boko Haram, a Nigerian Islamist group that has aligned with ISIS since early 2015, uses kidnapping, murder, and destruction of Christian facilities to terrorize the Nigerian people and their neighbors. In February 2015, twenty-one Egyptian Coptic Christians were ceremonially beheaded somewhere along Libya's Mediterranean coastline by extremists also affiliated with ISIS. In March 2015, al Shabaab, a Somalia-based terrorist organization, an al-Qaeda franchise, stormed Garissa University in eastern Kenya, separated the Christians from the Muslims, and then executed as many as 147 young Christians. An al Shabaab spokesman told the BBC at the time that it attacked the college because "it's on Muslim land colonized by non-Muslims."[233]

Hate fueled by religious bigotry is very much alive today, and Christians are more than ever before falling victim to such treachery.

APATHY ABOUT FAITH-BASED GENOCIDE

European Jews died because of American apathy in World War II. How many Middle East Christians must die today because of a similar apathy?

Rescuing European Jews facing genocide in World War II was not a priority for the U.S. government. During the 1930s, as it became clear that the Nazis were carrying out the genocide of Jews, the U.S. State Department made it very difficult for them to obtain entry visas. Clearly, the State Department's view was that America's economic woes, a national depression, intensified grassroots anti-Semitism, and xenophobia were of higher concern; therefore, Jewish immigrants were unwelcomed. In fact, just before entering the Second War, the U.S. further tightened immigration rules by delaying visa approvals on the grounds of national security, which seriously impacted Jews desperately seeking to flee Nazi death squads.[234]

Making matters worse, early in the American involvement in the Second World War, the U.S. State Department received a secret report on the Nazi policy to annihilate the Jews. Plainly, the department sat on that report for months, ostensibly to confirm its authenticity. Meanwhile, a copy of the same report came via British channels to the American Jewish leader Stephen Wise, the president of the World Jewish Congress. Wise pressed the U.S. government to release the report, and finally, on December 17, 1942, the U.S., Great Britain, and other Allied governments announced the Nazi intention to murder all Jews albeit many months after the initial report.[235] How many Jewish lives were lost to Nazi gas chambers and firing squads because of the delay in announcing the shocking truth about the Holocaust?

Those with inside knowledge about American policies regarding the Jewish genocide at the time must have thought there was a conspiracy to downplay the Holocaust, and their suspicions were well founded. In 1938, then U.S. President Franklin Roosevelt called for an international conference to address the Jewish refugee crisis. Roosevelt brought together representatives from thirty-two nations at a conference in Evian-les-Bains, France, in July of that year. But he set low expectations up front by reassuring the conferees that "no country will be expected… to receive a greater number of immigrants than is permitted by existing legislation." Only the Dominican Republic agreed to accept as many as one hundred thousand refugees.[236] Once again, the world turned its back on the tragic situation facing millions of European Jews.

The U.S. media was especially slow about reporting Jewish genocide early in Hitler's reign of terror. The *New York Times*, America's so-called newspaper of record, for much of the 1930s deemphasized the mass murder of Jews in its coverage, even though the Nazi violence started as early as 1933. Finally, the major Western media awakened to the tragic situation for the European Jews on November 9, 1938 when a massive wave of violence known as *Kristallnacht* ("Night of Crystal") erupted.

At the time, there were Germany-wide, state-sponsored waves of violence that resulted in the death of ninety-one Jews, the destruction of hundreds of synagogues and many Jewish businesses, and the arrest of thirty thousand Jewish men who were quickly shipped to prisons and concentration camps. Two months later, the world press, now awakened to the tragedy, reported that Hitler warned the German Reichstag that a new world war would mean the annihilation of the Jews.[237]

Even after the American media began reporting the Jewish genocide, there continued to be widespread apathy across the country. Americans, like many people in parts of the world not impacted by the war, fell victim to pro-Nazi and anti-Semitic propaganda that retarded their understanding and eventual response to the Holocaust. For example, the ever-bureaucratic American government debated what to do as the Jewish population was being exterminated before their eyes. "At the heart of the argument was the question of responsibility," states a blogger writing about American apathy leading up to World War II, "because it is on that conception that acceptance or denial to act hinged."[238]

The blogger applauds America's pivotal albeit late role in the Second War and the liberation of the Jewish people from the Nazis. However, he argues that "the mere numbers, methods, and length of time of the oppression and extermination of the Jews were enough justification to warrant the moral urgency." Yet many Americans and others, at least early in the crisis, were reluctant or unwilling to sacrifice American lives and treasure to rescue the Jews facing genocide. The ethical dilemma they faced was "to kill or let die," which, as the blogger quotes Freda Kirchwey from *While the Jews Die,* America was indicted for being "accessories to the crime."[239]

Today we see a similar lack of urgency—an apathy—regarding Christian genocide in the Middle East, and modern America is rightly charged with being an accessory to the crime. Specifically, the Obama administration allows many hundreds of thousands of Middle Eastern Christians to languish on dangerous battlefields or in refugee camps inside Syria, Iraq, Jordan, and Turkey, where they are subject to constant

Islamist violence and have little hope of ever returning to their homes—much less emigrating to the West or elsewhere. Where is America's leadership helping Christians with no hope of returning home to find a safe place? Not only is the West failing to provide an escape for Christians, but it is doing a poor job of protecting them in the region's cauldron of war, as evidenced by the carnage and lack of support.

Matthew VanDyke, founder of Sons of Liberty International, a group that trains Christians to defend themselves against Islamists in Iraq, told this author that a 330-man Christian unit guarding the few remaining Christians in Northern Iraq has too few weapons with which to fight. Mr. VanDyke and his small band of former U.S. Soldiers and Marines trained the Nineveh Plains Christian unit guarding the frontline against ISIS terrorists. However, that unit only has one hundred AK-47 Russian-made rifles and two pick-up trucks as of April 1, 2015. The U.S. government, which ships tons of weapons to Baghdad, fails to demand that the Shia-dominated Iraqi government share some of those weapons with non-Muslim groups like the Christians north of Mosul who face the most danger.[240]

Further, Western journalists are so jaded regarding Middle Eastern Christians that they run from reporting on the dire situation in Iraq, Mr. VanDyke said. Western media, with the exception of *Fox News* and the *TheBlaze*, refuses to deal with Christian genocide, and most Western media reporters in the region, according to VanDyke, label anyone helping the Christians as "crusaders." "They keep all Christians at arms' length while demonstrating more concern about alienating Sunnis," Vandyke explained.

That attitude may explain why Western media was slow about reporting the dire situation for non-Muslims in the Middle East. But the problem isn't just the lack of good reporting. Rather, there are few Westerners affected by the ongoing genocide. A general apathy about the situation has crept into Western populations; few Americans and even fewer American Christians are bothered with the plight of Christians in faraway Syria and Iraq.

Unfortunately, American apathy about the plight of Iraqi Christians has affected U.S. government decisions. Specifically, the Iraq war initiated by President George W. Bush had the unintended consequence of setting up the conditions for the destruction of that country's ancient and large Christian population. The Bush administration was told about the impact of its decisions for Christians. One of the worst decisions was made by Bush appointee Paul Lewis Bremer III, an American diplomat who led the occupational authority in Iraq following the 2003 invasion.

Bremer decided in 2003 to disband the Iraqi army, which released hundreds of thousands of security personnel to join the follow-on sectarian blood bath that rocked the country for years. That blood bath wasn't contained until Mr. Bush's 2008 surge in the Anbar Province finally stabilized the violence, although only temporarily. Meanwhile, most Christians fled Baghdad for what they perceived would be safer grounds around Mosul in northern Iraq.

The second U.S. government decision that contributed to the current genocide was made by President Obama. Mr. Obama satisfied his 2008 campaign promise to withdraw all U.S. forces from Iraq, but that decision, which took effect in December 2011, gave opportunity to Islamic extremists to re-emerge and eventually morph into what became the Islamic State now terrorizing much of the region and rapidly spreading to Africa and Central Asia. As reported earlier, ISIS terrorists killed or exiled virtually all Christians from Mosul in 2014.

Those U.S. government contributions to the genocide of Christians in Iraq haven't outraged the American public, however. Rather, the American Christian public still seems indifferent to the massive suffering of fellow believers. That apathy is reflected in the lack of public awareness campaigns and in the absence of activism such as that seen during the Vietnam War. Likely, that apathy is explained in part because few Americans have any flesh in the fight and they know that Mr. Obama has no intention of starting another war in Iraq. However, as of this writing, the U.S. has nearly three thousand military personnel in Iraq who are in danger and could face hostile action.

Just as the world ignored the atrocities against the Jews until most of the murders were history, the same appears to be the case today in the Middle East. Christian genocide may be complete by 2017 and the world yawns indifferently.

Lebanese member of Parliament, Samy Gemayel, said on March 1, 2015, that if the U.S. and the international community do not intervene, Christians may be completely driven out of the Middle Eastern Arab countries within two years. Gemayel is a senior member of the Phalange Party and a Lebanese Christian whose father Amin was the country's president.[241]

Gemayel warned that Christians are victims of two extremist forces fighting each other. "Today all the moderates in the region are taken between two big extremist powers," he said. "On one side you have ISIS and on the other side you have the Islamic state of Iran."

Gemayel continued:

So you have two Islamic states with two very extremist ideologies fighting against each other. And the moderates are stuck in a sandwich between these two powers

Unfortunately the Christians are paying the price all over the region and that's why we have been calling for the international community to do something about the Christians all over the region. That means support. And they are left alone.

Gemayel warned that "maybe in two years you will not have Christians in the region anymore except in Lebanon because we are strong and we are still defending ourselves."

The implication for the rest of the world is that governments and their societies tend to downplay or ignore such threats, even as all the evidence of genocide mounts. There is apathy even within the Western church about the plight of fellow Christians.

Former Congressman Frank Wolf, a man who has traveled the world and seen some of the worst persecution, was in Iraq in early 2015. He visited Christian refugees in Erbil who approached him to ask why the Christian church in the West doesn't care about their plight. He had no good response.

A growing number of Christians in the region are desperate and would leave given the chance. Even Christian refugees of the war in Syria now in Jordan, Lebanon, and Turkey refuse to join refugee camps because of the danger from Islamists in those same camps, and yet Christians in the West and their governments are doing little to help.

Christians trying to hold on in their country face terrible conditions as well. Mr. VanDyke said the Iraqi Christians in the Nineveh Plain find themselves trapped between unsympathetic Sunni Arabs, ISIS terrorists, and the Kurdish Peshmerga. They have no friends in the region. Even the Kurds treat the Christians poorly. VanDyke cited the example of the one thousand-home Christian village of Tel Isqof that was looted by Kurdish Peshmerga fighters in 2014.

Apathy and political correctness are a poisonous combination that does not threaten just Christians facing genocide in the Middle East: That same mindset is dangerously seeping into the West as it relates to Muslims. For example, Europe's complacency regarding the threat posed by nonintegrating Islamic people is just beginning to harvest severe consequences.

Those consequences accumulated for many years, such as the train bombing in Spain and the subway bombing in London. One of the most recent consequences for Europe took place in early 2015. On January 7, 2015, in the wake of Islamists' murder of twelve people at the offices of *Charlie Hebdo* in Paris, President Obama used the occasion to criticize Europeans for failing to do enough to integrate Muslims. *Charlie Hebdo* is a French satirical weekly magazine that previously depicted the Prophet Muhammad in a cartoon. "Our biggest advantage is that our Muslim populations, they feel themselves to be Americans," Obama said at a White House press conference. "There are parts of Europe in which that's not the case. And that's probably the greatest danger that Europe faces.... It's important for Europe not to simply respond with a hammer and law enforcement and military approaches to these problems."[242]

In the wake of many terror attacks, Europe struggles to push off its apathy to better integrate Muslim immigrants by seeking stricter immigration controls, as well as more community policing. This movement to clamp down on immigration is an acknowledgement of what German Chancellor Angela Merkel admitted was that German multiculturalism had "utterly failed."[243]

In spite of Obama's claim that Muslims in America have integrated, there is growing evidence the problems of nonintegration are coming to America as well. For example, National Intelligence Director James Clapper said more than 180 American jihadists are fighting in Iraq and Syria for ISIS.[244] There is also plenty of evidence that many so-called lone-wolf, Islamic jihadists are in America and they intend to do in this country what others are doing in Europe. With enough time, they will try to impose sharia law. Given the European example, America will witness ever-growing Islamist attacks bent on the destruction of our form of government and the Christian church.

One of the latest such "lone-wolf Islamic jihadist" attacks took place May 3, 2015, on organizers of a best depiction of the Prophet Muhammad event in Garland, Texas. Stratfor indicates that event demonstrates the likely type of Islamist attacks in the short term. Stratfor Global Intelligence is an Austin, Texas, geopolitical intelligence firm that provides strategic analysis and forecasting around the world.

The two Muslim gunmen were fatally shot in front of the event after wounding a security guard. One of the shooters, Muslim convert Elton Simpson, according to FBI records, attempted to travel to Somalia to join al Shadaab, an al-Qaeda-affiliated group. Just prior to the Garland attack, Simpson posted a message on Twitter that he pledged allegiance to the Islamic State.[245]

Not surprisingly, two days after the shooting in Garland, ISIS claimed responsibility for the attack. The claim came in an audio message from ISIS' Al Bayan radio station, based in the Syria city of Raqqa. The ISIS announcer described the shooters as "two soldiers of the caliphate" and promised: "We tell America that what is coming is more bitter and harder and you will see from the soldiers of the Caliphate what harms you."[246]

Apathy is dangerous, especially when it comes to Islamists. Much of the West sits on the sideline too focused on its own comforts to help Middle East Christians facing genocide. That same apathy will come home to roost for Westerners who fail to recognize the Islamic threat growing in their communities as well.

CRIMINALIZING PUBLIC BELIEF

The Nazis used propaganda and intimidation to win over the German public to support their radical anti-Jewish agenda. A sophisticated propaganda effort led by Joseph Goebbels sought to manipulate and deceive the German people to support the Nazis' program. Goebbels used a message of national unity and a utopian future that facilitated the persecution of Jews who were excluded from the Nazi vision of the "national community."[247] We see similar anti-Christian propaganda doing the same today.

Goebbels, Hitler's master propagandist, portrayed Germany as a victim "held in bondage by the chains of the post-World War I Versailles Treaty and denied the right of national self-determination." The Führer's propaganda goal was to justify military action as righteous and necessary for self-defense. In fact, prior to Germany's attack on Poland in September 1939, the Nazis launched a media campaign to create a faux threat as a pretext to justify the coming invasion as an appropriate defensive action given Poland's alleged "atrocities."[248]

Just prior to Hitler's planned invasion of Poland, the Nazi regime staged a border incident to make it appear that Poland initiated hostilities. Evidently, twenty-two men dressed in Polish uniforms "attacked" a German radio station at Gliwice. Hitler used that fabricated pretext to announce his decision to send troops into Poland the next day in response to the alleged Polish "incursions." Meanwhile, the Third

Reich's press office avoided the use of the word "war"; rather, it directed that media reports were to indicate that German troops were sent to beat back Polish attacks. This spin made Germany appear to be the victim and thus justified Hitler's incursion into Poland.

Just as Hitler's propagandists portrayed Germany as a victim in order to create a pretext to carry out their plan, today's Middle Eastern Islamists and some Arab regimes portray themselves as victims of Christian "crusaders" and Zionists. They spin tales that arouse Muslim populations to fanatical behavior that is then tapped by totalitarians to justify harsh treatment of Christians and other non-Muslims.

That treatment in Iraq, according to Reverend Franklin Graham, is genocide. "I'm just frightened that the Christian community in Iraq is going to be completely wiped out," he said. Graham said the problem is broader than Iraq; it is evident elsewhere in the Middle East. He explained that the Islamic Republic of Iran has placed tough restrictions on the Farsi-speaking Christian churches to the point where they too "will soon be gone" and just "die off."[249]

Former Congressman Frank Wolf saw the same situation in Iraq. He illustrated the heart-wrenching anti-Christian choices people in Iraq face today. When Wolf was in Iraq in early 2015, he spent a week in Kurdistan, near Irbil, talking with Christians. One Christian man told Mr. Wolf about his wife who had breast cancer and went to a Mosul hospital for treatment.[250]

Islamic State terrorists controlled the Mosul hospital beginning mid 2014 and when the woman with breast cancer presented herself for scheduled chemo treatment, she was told to either convert to Islam or leave without treatment. She refused to convert, as did her husband. The woman later died for lack of treatment. This story is very common among Christians in the region, and especially in the war-torn areas like Iraq and Syria.

The implication for the rest of the world given the examples of Nazi and Islamic manipulation of public opinion is that criminalizing belief makes it easier for other oppressors to control those with deeply held religious views. There are signs of this happening in Great Britain and even in America, and it will get worse if we remain on the same track.

British Christians can't take their faith into the workplace without jeopardizing their employment. In England, that government criminalizes Christian speech and practice.

George Hargreaves, a British politician and head of the Christian Party, received a complaint regarding his billboard advertisement. "Yesterday I got a letter from the advertising standards authority over complaints saying that my billboard that says Britain is a Christian country is offensive to atheists and other religions and it incites hatred against them. What nonsense," he said. But such an official complaint is just indicative of the movement to criminalize Christianity in England, Hargreaves said.[251]

Andrea Minichiello-Williams, the director for Christian Concern for Our Nation, warns that if British Christians don't step up now, the nation is on a path to eventually criminalize the practice of Christianity in public.

"There's been a massive move by the secularist lobby to privatize religion," Minichiello-Williams said. "You can have faith so long as it doesn't affect you in the workplace. So long as you don't bring it into the workplace. 'Just make it private. It can't be public. It can't affect what you do in the public square.'"

So-called homosexual rights are a hot button issue that is often associated with the criminalization of public Christianity in Britain. British citizen Christian Kwabena Peat was forced to attend homosexual sensitivity training at her work, a session taught by an open lesbian. "One of things that she said was, she asked the question, 'What makes you think that to be heterosexual is natural?' At which point, I walked out," Peat told the Christian Broadcasting Network.

Peat then wrote a letter to the trainer explaining her Bible-based position on homosexuality and exclaiming that God loved her and so did Peat. Then Peat was suspended for her letter.

"They said that by me telling them about the word of God, it constituted harassment and intimidation," Peat said. She was later reinstated, but such cases abound in Great Britain as Christians are told not to speak about God in the workplace or they could be punished for offending homosexuals or Muslims.

Lawyer Paul Diamond defends Christians facing discrimination charges in England. "In the United Kingdom the homosexual agenda is militant," Diamond said. "The power shift began in about 2000, and they've been arresting Christians, jailing Christians for hate crimes, shutting off grants, constant litigation with the government, constant aggression."

"Your Christian values are wicked and evil, and that's what they want everybody to believe," Diamond explained.

Islam enjoys similar protection against Christian beliefs in Great Britain as well. A British Broadcasting Corporation broadcast, *Bone Kickers*, showed a violent Christian beheading a Muslim, a twisted view given the avalanche of beheadings at the hands of Islamic extremists in the Middle East in 2014 and 2015. Undeniably, Britain's politically correct government television network put a practicing Muslim in charge of all religious programming, which sanctioned the distortion.

Criminalization of Christian belief is coming to America, warns both Minichiello-Williams and Diamond. This is going to happen "if you liberalize the laws as President Obama has done," Minichiello-Williams said.

"We know what's going to happen to your 40 percent church attendance," Diamond added. "It's not going to be 40 percent. It's going to be 20 percent, when the federal and state government start saying that if you criticize homosexuality, the hate crimes laws will apply to you Christians."

Reverend Franklin Graham believes President Obama's "progressive" views are forcing "a new morality" on America, a "morality that does not include God" and which is "an anti-Christ movement."

Yes, Obama's "new morality" is criminalizing Christianity in America. Even though the majority of Americans are Christians, their beliefs and associated behaviors are not treated with respect and the consequences can be severe.

Consider some recent examples of the "anti-Christ movement" persecuting American believers that aren't all that different from what we saw early in the Nazi and Islamic campaigns against Jews and Christians:

A Christian food for the hungry ministry in Lake City, Florida, operated for thirty-one years until state officials threatened to cut-off U.S. Department of Agriculture food supplies. The government officials insisted the ministry must remove portraits of Christ, the Ten Commandments, a banner that read "Jesus is Lord," and stop giving out Bibles.[252]

In 2011, two men were arrested and charged with misdemeanor offenses for reading the Bible outside the Department of Motor Vehicles in Hemet, California. A court later found the men "not guilty of any offenses," but not based on their rights to free religious expression. Rather, the court determined that the law the prosecutors tried to invoke was likely unconstitutional, as it gave law enforcement too much power over public gatherings. It is reasonable to ask: Would two Muslims reading the Koran outside a public building also be arrested under similar circumstances? Likely not, and that should outrage all Americans.

Obama's "new morality" also creates a too-common scenario whereby Christians acting on their deeply held religious views refuse to endorse homosexual "marriage." A Christian baker in Colorado faces jail time for refusing to make a cake for a homosexual wedding. The owners of the Masterpiece Cakeshop declined to make a cake for a homosexual wedding, stating it conflicted with their Christian beliefs, which evidently could land them in jail, according to attorney Nicolle Martin.

Government restrictions on Christian services are one step closer to criminalization. The U.S. National Park Service adopted a policy requiring churches wishing to hold baptisms in public waters needed to apply for a special permit at least forty-eight hours in advance. The Park Service stated the permits were necessary to "maintain park natural/cultural resources and quality visitor experiences, specific terms and conditions have been established."

Rep. Jason Smith, a Missouri Republican, wrote the Park Service, threatening to bring the matter before the full Congress. Quickly the Park Service reversed its policy, stating to the congressman in a letter, "As of today, the park's policy has been clarified to state that no permit will be required for baptisms within the Riverways."

Criminalizing Christian belief is already a serious problem across much of the Middle East, which contributes to the conditions for genocide. There is growing evidence that the same trend is just beginning here in America. What we don't know at this point is whether Christianity will eventually be criminalized in the West and, as a result, bring about conditions promoting genocide as we now see in the Middle East. That may not be such a far-fetched outcome given the domestic situation. It is past time for the Christian church to take action to reverse the trend now before reaching the point of no return.

CONCLUSION

There is a growing sense among many across the world that increasing violence, in the Middle East in particular, points to a build-up to global war. Ethnic and religious hatreds, apathy, and the criminalization of faith are spreading. Bible prophecy offers a look into such things to come and suggests at the very least they are stage-setting for what lies just ahead—a time that Jesus said would be the worst that would ever be upon earth.

Has this generation entered what is known as the *end times*–or—*the end of days,* as it is sometimes termed? Does the bloodlust that saturates theological ideologies driving the perpetrators of genocide signal satanic rage that will not end until Armageddon brings consummation of man's ability to wage war? A look at end-times implications is in order.

CHAPTER 10

ISRAEL & ISLAM

Are These the Prophetic End Times?

The previous chapters in this section address the implications of a Christian genocide for the Middle East and the broader implications of that outcome for the rest of the world. This chapter and the next wrestle with two complex, although related questions: What clues do we find in biblical prophecy to suggest these might be the end times? What does Islamic eschatology say about the end times?

There are many very good books about Bible prophecy and end-times prophecy. This is not one, although a more detailed account of biblical prophecy as it related to end times is available at the appendix, Biblical Prophecy 101. The intent here is to provide an overview of the immediate crisis growing in the Middle East as it relates to biblical prophecy, whereas Christian genocide across the region is a significant indicator or clue of a much broader issue—the end-times scenario with the nation Israel in the bull's eye. Further, we will briefly consider the apostle Paul's characterization of end-times man and demonstrate why Islamists fit that description.

ISRAEL AT THE CENTER OF END TIMES

For the Muslim world, Christians are an extension of the Jewish people and the modern nation Israel. Therefore, destroying all aspects of Christendom across the Middle East for many Islamic extremists and especially ISIS terrorists is by association doing the same to Israel, their ultimate target. It is with this view in mind we briefly explore end-times biblical prophecy.

There is no doubt whatsoever in the thinking of those who view Bible prophecy from the premillennial position (the view that Christ will return to earth before the thousand-year kingdom of God begins) that Israel is the number-one clue of just how near is the time of Christ's return. Since the Lord will return to earth in His Second Advent at the very end of the seven-year period known as the Tribulation, based upon issues and events of these troubled days, that hellish era looks to be near, indeed.

Issues and events involving Israel are literally lighting up the spiritual radars of those who observe the times from the biblically prophetic perspective. Not a day passes that doesn't bring reports of matters involving the Jewish state that can be considered to have end-times relevance.

Before looking at some of these, it's important to consider one of the prophecies most directly relating to this topic. Even the secular neophyte to Bible prophecy, if he or she is an observer of world news on a regular basis, should find the foretelling interesting.

The Old Testament prophet Zechariah prophesied:

The burden of the word of the LORD for Israel, saith the LORD, which stretcheth forth the heavens, and layeth the foundation of the earth, and formeth the spirit of man within him.

Behold, I will make Jerusalem a cup of trembling unto all the people round about, when they shall be in the siege both against Judah and against Jerusalem.

And in that day will I make Jerusalem a burdensome stone

for all people: all that burden themselves with it shall be cut in pieces, though all the people of the earth be gathered together against it. (Zechariah 12:1–3)

Every Islamic neighbor state of modern Israel has at the head of those governments those who protest that Israel is an illegitimate "occupier" of the land upon which the Jewish state sits. From the time even before Egypt's Gamul Abdul Nasser (1918–1970), Arab Islamist leaders have threatened to wipe Israel off the map. As a matter of fact, most of those nations do not even show Israel on their maps, so strongly do they see it as a hated enemy.

The Middle East is ablaze with militant actions and reactions by Israel's avowed enemies. Strangely, Israel, which sits in the middle of all the turmoil, is not as of this writing involved in the fighting.

Iran, the nation that sits in the area of ancient Persia, seems the instigator of much of the warring activity by Islamists that are of the Sunni and of the Shia varieties. The Iranian leadership lusts after the huge petroleum fields of Saudi Arabia and is hegemonic for the entire region.

All the while, the growing threat from ISIS troubles both Iran and Saudi. Islamist states like Jordan—which, along with Saudi and Egypt and others—fight in coalition against the terrorist groups like Yemen's al-Houthi and ISIS affiliates that threaten them. It is a wildly weird amalgamation of antagonists among family, in effect. The hostilities certainly bear out the angel's prediction to Hagar, Sarai's handmaiden, who bore Ishmael, Abram's son, when Sarai and Abram decided, wrongly, to produce a child in order to fulfill God's promise that Abram would have an heir:

And he will be a wild man; his hand will be against every man, and every man's hand against him; and he shall dwell in the presence of all his brethren. (Genesis 16:12)

Abram's name was changed to Abraham, and Sarai's name was changed to Sarah. As promised by God, they produced a son, Isaac. The birth took place when they were well beyond childbearing years. Isaac became the progenitor of the nation Israel. Jacob, Isaac's son, fathered twelve sons. Jacob's name was changed by God to Israel.

Animosity and hatreds have been at the center of these peoples in the Middle East ever since Abram and Sarai decided to take things into their own hands regarding producing an heir. It is playing out again today in that region, and it is scheduled to get infinitely worse before Jesus Christ returns to establish His millennial throne, which the Bible calls the "throne of David," referring to the most famous king of Israel.

Despite the fact that Israel temporarily might not be in the direct line of fire from its distant relatives who surround it, the Jewish state is always in Satan's sights, thus Israel is never out of the center of controversy. No matter which way the cameras and microphones of global media might temporarily turn to cover issues and events, it's certain that they will soon be focused again on Israel, and more specifically on Jerusalem.

Israel—the Jewish race—is the people through whom the Savior of the world, Jesus Christ, was brought into the world to rescue all human beings. The creation called mankind individually and collectively is perishing because of sin into which man is born. Sin is rebellion against the God of heaven, and fallen man must be redeemed through God's chosen way—the sacrificial offering of His Son on the cross two thousand years ago. The Scripture most Christians learn as very young children is:

> For God so loved the world, that he gave his only begotten son, that whosoever believeth in him should not perish, but have everlasting life. (John 3:16)

Christians believe this is why Satan—Lucifer, the fallen one—so hates Israel. This hatred is reflected daily in headlines while the world continues to set the stage for Zechariah 12:1–3, as mentioned earlier.

Sadly, Israel's plight is to increasingly become hated by all nations of earth until the one called Antichrist attempts to do what Hitler desired to do—annihilate the Jewish people. The "beast's" persecution will be much worse than that of Hitler and the Nazis, according to the words of Christ. Speaking specifically about Israel's dire situation during the last seven years of human history, Jesus said the following.

> For then shall be great tribulation, such as was not since the beginning of the world to this time, no, nor ever shall be. (Matthew 24:21)

One day, when that time of ultimate holocaust is finished and Christ rules from the throne of David in Jerusalem, Israel will be the apex nation of the Millennial Kingdom. From this present hour until that time, however, the Jewish state—and all of mankind, because of rebellion and treatment of God's chosen people—is in for a time of geometrically progressing troubles.

WORLD OUTCRY FOR PEACE

Wars and rumors of wars were among the first end times troubles Jesus prophesied in the Olivet Discourse (Mark 13, Matthew 24, and Luke 21). The forewarning implied that these would be unprecedented in terms of the deadly effects they would have on mankind. Remember, Jesus went on to say that it would be the most troubled time in history. He said further:

> And except those days should be shortened, there should no flesh be saved: but for the elect's sake those days shall be shortened. (Matthew 24:22)

Many believe that the two great world wars of the twentieth century were among the wars Christ was foretelling in this most profound teaching. They were indeed horrific in terms of those killed and wounded, and accounting the tremendous damage done. However, it's not certain that the Lord was including those as being among the wars and rumors of wars He mentioned—chiefly because of the numbers of human beings that Bible prophecy states will be killed due to violence during the Tribulation.

When tallying the number of those who will die during that future time, the number reached will total perhaps as much as three-fourths of the world's population. Much of that death will, as seen in the prophecy involving the kings of the east, involve military slaughter. That force will, itself, account for one-third of the deaths. This, of course, means that many billions will die.

Prior to the very end of World War II, mankind didn't have the capability to inflict this level of death. The splitting of the atom changed all that. It's been said that an all-out nuclear war could end human life on the planet. Whether that is true, only God knows. And, of course, He has assured through His prophetic word that that will not happen.

It certainly appears, however, that nuclear war will be a part of inflicting this kind of devastation upon human life—and, the possibility of such warfare is a visceral part of the thinking of many today. As the possibility of such war has turned into the likelihood that such weapons will be unleashed at some point soon, there is a growing outcry for peace throughout the world.

The Bible has something to say about this outcry for peace as it relates to end times:

> For when they shall say, Peace and safety; then sudden destruction cometh upon them, as travail upon a woman with child; and they shall not escape. (1 Thessalonians 5:3)

This prophecy by the apostle Paul refers to a time just before Christ's return, when the "day of the Lord" is about to begin. There will be a great outcry for peace, just like that heard today in daily news reports.

Diplomats have for decades been shuttling from around the world to Jerusalem and other cities in the Middle East in quest of a pathway to making peace between Israel and that nation's enemies. The concerned diplomats instinctively understand that this is the one place on earth where nuclear conflict is most likely to ignite.

Israel is allegedly the only nation of the immediate region with nuclear weaponry—which has, in "human terms," kept it from being totally destroyed. But closely on Israel's heels as nuclear armed states are Iran and Saudi Arabia. Iran has all the ingredients for a nuclear arsenal: uranium, weapons technology and a phalanx of long-range missiles with which to deliver atomic warheads. Building a nuclear weapon is only one decision away for the radical mullahs in Tehran. Meanwhile, Saudi Arabia has an arsenal of Chinese-built nuclear capable missiles and there is widespread credible evidence to believe the Saudis have an arrangement with nuclear-armed friend Pakistan to deliver nuclear warheads for a price.

The phrase "in human terms" (above) applies because Israel is God-guaranteed to never be destroyed. Again, like in Zechariah 12:1–3, God says in Jeremiah that Israel will be His chosen nation forever.

> This is what the Lord says, "He who appoints the sun to shine by day, Who decrees the moon and stars to shine by night, Who stirs up the sea so that its waves roar—the Lord Almighty is His Name;
>
> Only if these ordinances vanish from My sight," declares the Lord, "will the descendants of Israel ever cease to be a nation before Me." (Jeremiah 31:35–36)

Although outnumbered by armies much greater in force, Israel defeated those nations in 1948 at its birth. It defeated even greater numbers of enemies when attacked in 1956, when opposed in 1967, and when again attacked in 1973.

Now, Iran seemingly has a clear path to developing its own nuclear weapon. The diplomats, rather than striving to make certain that hate-filled regime doesn't get such a weapon, instead put ever-increasing pressure on the tiny Jewish state to agree to a peace that would have it give up the tiny sliver of land that it has won and defended against all odds. There cannot be peace, the diplomats foolishly believe, until there is a "two-state solution," a so-called Palestinian state next to Israel. This means that tiny Israel, which is the size of New Jersey, must give up to enemies—those who are blood-vowed to erase it from existence—land that was deeded to that people by God Himself.

END-TIMES NUMBER-ONE CLUE

Bible prophecy foretells that there is a man who will step onto the stage of history who will guarantee a peace pact between Israel and its enemies. Apparently, the whole world will be involved, and will think that long-elusive peace is here at last.

It's important to look at what the great prophet Daniel had to say about this—until this point in history—unachievable making of "peace."

> And after threescore and two weeks shall Messiah be cut off, but not for himself: and the people of the prince that shall come shall destroy the city and the sanctuary; and the end thereof shall be with a flood, and unto the end of the war desolations are determined.
>
> And he shall confirm the covenant with many for one week: and in the midst of the week he shall cause the sacrifice and the oblation to cease, and for the overspreading of abominations he shall make it desolate, even until the consummation, and that determined shall be poured upon the desolate. (Daniel 9:26–27)

This "prince that shall come" is none other than Antichrist, the "first beast" of Revelation 13. He will be able to do what no one else has been able to do. establish peace in the Middle East. It will, apparently, also be considered to be world peace, at last achieved.

But, a thorough reading of that prophecy portends the worst of all possible results. Daniel foretells that the "peace" that this "prince" will "confirm" will bring about death, destruction, and all but total decimation to planet earth and its inhabitants. Daniel says it will be peace "that will destroy many" (Daniel 8: 25). Isaiah the prophet said the following to the Israel of that future day about this coming "peace they will make under the confirming hand of Antichrist":

> Because ye have said, We have made a covenant with death, and with hell are we at agreement; when the overflowing scourge shall pass through, it shall not come unto us: for we have made lies our refuge, and under falsehood have we hid ourselves....
>
> And your covenant with death shall be annulled, and your agreement with hell shall not stand; when the overflowing scourge shall pass through, then ye shall be trodden down by it. (Isaiah 28:15, 18)

This is what brings about the prophecy as given by Jeremiah the prophet:

> Alas! for that day is great, so that none is like it: it is even the time of Jacob's trouble; but he shall be saved out of it. (Jeremiah 30:7)

Israel (a remnant of the people) will be saved by the returning Messiah, Jesus Christ, at the very end of the Tribulation. But, before that rescue, that nation's persecution will be great once its leaders agree to the covenant of false peace the world foists upon it.

Is there such a process at present that could produce this covenant of false peace that will be destructive to Israel and the entire world? Why, yes, as a matter of fact, there is. Ever heard of the "Roadmap for Peace"?

It's very likely that the number-one clue that we are in the end times is the incessant attempt to force peace on Israel. This "peace" apparently will require a "two-state" solution that will further divide God's land, which He promises Israel. This is something for which the world of anti-God rebels will pay a most profound price. Joel the prophet says the following:

> I will also gather all nations, and will bring them down into the valley of Jehoshaphat, and will plead with them there for my people and for my heritage Israel, whom they have scattered among the nations, and parted my land. (Joel 3:2)

That punishment will be *Armageddon.*

PERILOUS TIMES

The apostle Paul wrote that in the last days, perilous times will come. In the original Greek language, this phrase could be translated as "raging insanity," certainly an appropriate title for what we see today in the Middle East.

Paul then identified a number of characteristics of end-times man—certain anti-God traits that will mark that final generation at the end of the age. Here's a look at some of the traits that seem to fit within the evil activity being inflicted upon Christians and others by Islamist murderers.

Paul said in 2 Timothy 3:1, "This know also, that in the last days perilous times shall come. For men shall be…"

"…lovers of their own selves"

The great appeal to many jihadists—probably to all of the young men who are attracted to fight with ISIS, Hamas, Hezzbolah, al-Qaeda, al Shaabad et al—are the seventy-two dark-eyed virgin women promised to them if they die martyrs in the cause of spreading Islam.[253]

Some psychological studies conclude that suicide can be a form of self-love, in a perverted, irrational sort of way.[254] Remember the nineteen young jihadists, convinced by Osama bin Laden to fly the passenger jets into the World Trade Center towers and into the Pentagon on September 11, 2001? There have been accounts of how they prepared in especially sexual ways immediately preceding the suicide missions.[255]

This seems a self-gratification that defies all rationale. Yet, to those who hold to the fundamentals of the Koran, blowing up one's self to advance the cause of Allah is a noble act, deserving of as much pleasure in the afterlife as fantasy can conjure.

This characteristic—"lovers of self"—permeates the male-dominated Muslim culture. Women are at best treated as property, subject to indignities by most men within such societies who think only of their wants and needs.

"...covetous, boasters, proud"

There is no more obvious manifestation of the term "covetous"—in thinking on nations wanting what belongs to other nations—than the desire of Israel's Islamist-controlled neighbors to take for themselves the tiny piece of real estate upon which the Jewish state sits. They have launched several major attacks in modern times, as mentioned before, to try to accomplish that goal.

Those enemies have never stopped raging against Israel, proudly and boastfully vowing even today to push every Jew into the Mediterranean Sea:

> It is the mission of the Islamic Republic of Iran to erase Israel from the map of the region. (2002)[256]

> Israel is a hideous entity in the Middle East which will undoubtedly be annihilated. (2010)[257]

The great powers have dominated the destiny of the Islamic countries for years and…installed the Zionist cancerous tumor in the heart of the Islamic world…. Many of the problems facing the Muslim world are due to the existence of the Zionist regime. (2012)[258]

The world community of nations, represented by membership in the United Nations, for the most part proclaims Israel to be an illegal occupier of land belonging to Palestinians without a homeland. In actuality, those very enemies are themselves occupying vast portions of land that God granted Abram, Isaac, and Jacob's progeny. The Almighty will one day see to it that His *chosen people* fully inherit what is rightfully theirs.

"…unholy, without natural affection"

Throughout history, the pagan cultures most rebellious to the God of heaven have committed the most heinous atrocities to their fellow man. Since its founding, Islam has contributed among the most brutal of such anti-God people, butchering women, children, and even infants in order to satisfy their bloodlust as well as to instill abject fear in the minds of its enemies.

Today, daily reports chronicle news of Christians and others being beheaded, the heads of women and infants placed on stakes throughout the villages they invade. These beastly hordes are "without natural affection."

"…trucebreakers, false accusers, fierce"

It is well known that the Koran excuses lying to Allah's enemies if it puts forward the cause of subjugating anyone who is not a Muslim.[259] History—even recent history—is replete with cases of broken treaties by Islamist leaders. Yasser Arafat, who, as a terrorist before becoming aggrandized by the world press as the chairman of the Palestinian Authority, fit the "perilous times" characteristic of being "fierce." This butcher, even of his own people, comes to mind as one infamous for lying and cheating whenever and wherever he could do so. The hapless Palestinian masses he ruled with an iron, terroristic fist were the victims of his nefarious dealings with Israel and the international community.

Like Arafat, today's Islamist leaders falsely accuse Israel of brutalizing the Palestinian people, when Israel does more to help those poor people than even the U.N. and others who falsely accuse the Jewish state. Arab citizens of Israel enjoy a standard of living higher than that of Arabs living in practically any Islamist nation on earth.

"...having a form of godliness, but denying the power thereof"

Muslims bow to the east toward Mecca and perform rituals to demonstrate to the world how they honor their god, Allah. They have been given wide latitude in America to demonstrate their form of "godly" behavior, while Christian rights are noticeably in decline within this nation, which was founded on Judeo-Christian principles.

Christians, rather than being granted the same privileges, in most Islamist countries are murdered and cut to pieces in many cases, as seen lately, while the likes of ISIS slaughter thousands upon thousands of defenseless people during their genocidal rampages.

All are expected to agree with the politically correct view that Islam is not at fault for these aberrant adherents to that "peaceful" religion. There is, however, less than scant observable evidence that the so-called vast majority of Muslim believers protests the beastly deeds of those murdering and slaughtering innocents by the thousands. It is still etched in the memory of many Americans that on Tuesday, September 11, 2001, the streets of many Islamist-ruled nations were filled with celebratory gunfire and the traditional giving and receiving of candies after the Trade Towers fell in New York City.

Such form of religiosity that celebrates bloodshed, rather than embraces love of fellow man, is assuredly a major signal that this generation is witnessing end-times behavior.

IS THE END NEAR?

Is this the generation that has entered the end of days? If the likes of ISIS and other apocalypse-driven Islamist militants have their way, it very much appears that all that is happening in the Middle East has end-times implications.

One observer of these matters who does so from the biblical prophecy standpoint states the following:

> One of the most intriguing and disturbing developments of our times is that we now have two nation states—the Islamic Republic of Iran and the Islamic State—driven by adherents to apocalyptic, genocidal forms of End Times theology. The Iranian leaders hold to a Shia brand. ISIS leaders hold to a Sunni brand. But both are driven by a belief that their messiah is coming and judgment with him. The Iranians believe they must lay the groundwork for the messiah (Mahdi) to come and build his caliphate or kingdom. ISIS isn't waiting. They have launched a jihadist rampage to build the caliphate now, so that the Mahdi will come soon.[260]

The following excerpt from a thorough examination of what is considered the most dangerous of Islam's jihadist agents of terrorism and genocide urges an understanding of just what the world faces, regarding Islam's eschatology:

> The reality is that the Islamic State is Islamic. Very Islamic. Yes, it has attracted psychopaths and adventure seekers, drawn largely from the disaffected populations of the Middle East and

Europe. But the religion preached by its most ardent followers derives from coherent and even learned interpretations of Islam.

Virtually every major decision and law promulgated by the Islamic State adheres to what it calls, in its press and pronouncements, and on its billboards, license plates, stationery, and coins, "the Prophetic methodology," which means following the prophecy and example of Muhammad, in punctilious detail. Muslims can reject the Islamic State; nearly all do. But pretending that it isn't actually a religious, millenarian group, with theology that must be understood to be combated, has already led the United States to underestimate it and back foolish schemes to counter it.

That the Islamic State holds the imminent fulfillment of prophecy as a matter of dogma at least tells us the mettle of our opponent. It is ready to cheer its own near-obliteration, and to remain confident, even when surrounded, that it will receive divine succor if it stays true to the Prophetic model....

Ideological tools may convince some potential converts that the group's message is false, and military tools can limit its horrors. But for an organization as impervious to persuasion as the Islamic State, few measures short of these will matter, and the war may be a long one, even if it doesn't last until the end of time.[261]

The scriptural clues indicating that we are in the prophesied end times are numerous. The prophetic mega-clue is Israel's miraculous rebirth as a nation, people, and language in 1948 and its continual survival despite numerous attempts at annihilation. Israel's troubles continue to mount as prophesied: the formation of Islamic State with affiliates boldly proclaiming its intent to destroy Israel and the West, world pressure on Israel to embrace a bad "two state" solution with the Palestinians, and a general call for peace yet labeling Israel as the "burdensome stone" blocking peace. An honest evaluation of these issues by a Western mind shows the absence of logic; there is no reason for such hatred. It appears to be nothing less than raging insanity.

But the Christian armed with a modicum of prophetic insight knows there is an unseen spiritual force creating these perilous times and driving the world toward the abyss, the end times: Satan. Satan created and uses Islam to accomplish his goals, and he will not cease until Jesus condemns him to eternity in hell.

Are these the end times? They certainly have all the trappings backed by Scripture.

CHAPTER 11

ISLAMIC ESCHATOLOGY

Muslim View of the End Times

slamic eschatology—end times—motivates Muslim extremist groups like ISIS and therefore it warrants the reader's consideration, especially as it relates to Christian genocide in the Middle East and the religion's broader global agenda.

It is important to understand that the most fundamentalist Muslim believers are driven by an apocalyptic theology. They want more than anything else to ultimately bring about a final military conflict so their version of the messiah (what the Shia call their Mahdi, "guided one") can come and establish worldwide sharia rule on behalf of Allah. In other words, they seek war and terrorism that will bring worldwide chaos as the perfect condition to bring forth their messiah.

In some sense, the Christian, premillennial view of end-times things and fundamentalist Islam's view of eschatology seem alike. They are not.

Islam proposes that it is both fact and preferable that death and destruction fill the whole earth, and that Armageddon erupts so everyone will be made to bow the knee to Allah or be killed. The Bible presents the fact that the Tribulation (the seven years of great, worldwide trouble leading up to Christ's return) is something that is, sadly, self-engendered by man—the tragic result of mankind's sinfulness and rebellion against a God who loves all people and wants them to repent and receive redemption through Christ's sacrifice on the cross. God gives people volition (free will) to choose to accept Christ—or not.

The god of Islam, fundamentalists like ISIS believe, directs them to hate their enemies, non-Muslim. Yet the true God of heaven directs that the greatest of all commandments is to love one's neighbor.

The Koran doesn't give much in the way of prophecy. It does, however, predict that on the last day when history ends, the dead will be raised and judged according to their deeds in life.

The second-holiest Islamic material and the source of Islamic jurisprudence is the "Hadith," which includes the Sunnah, the way or path the Prophet Muhammad lived his life. Islamic scholars compile hadiths into different collections of "hadith" texts, such as books for Sunnis by Sahih al Bukaria and Sahih Muslim. Earlier, it was explained that there are as many as six hundred thousand hadiths, but only a few (seventy-five hundred) are captured in ninety-seven books. Although none of the hadiths or the collections of hadiths are claimed to be revelations directly from Allah, they are the source of most of Islam's eschatology.[262]

The prophetic utterances within the Hadith are so scattered throughout that it is difficult to pin down details. That is, it is hard to put together any sort of easily discernible timeline of end-times events. Scholars of Islam don't for the most part try to put together any such chronology. Like scholars who look at Bible prophecy, there is often disagreement on the timing of prophesied events.

As alluded to earlier, some of Islam's prophecy seems similar to that outlined in the Bible. Many, including this author, believe that Muhammad plagiarized the Koran and the hadiths from the Bible. Remember that Muhammad didn't get his "revelation" until centuries after the prophecies of the Christian Bible were written. In addition, he was illiterate and thus could not do research or record his thoughts. A great number of biblical scholars have no doubt whatsoever that the Prophet got inspiration for his religious concoction from otherworldly sources, but not of the heavenly sort.

HADITH END-TIMES OVERVIEW

Despite the unstructured nature of Muhammad's "prophecies" collected in the Hadith, here's an overview of things to come, according to Islam's most revered prophet.

Teaching within Islam offers a number of signs that will indicate the end of the world. Many are quite similar to those given by the Bible, and some of the signals occur simultaneously. Again, they can be common to Christianity's teachings, but many are totally unique to Islam.

Teachings about end-of-days world conditions and events seen as common to both Islam and Christianity include apostasy, false prophets, increasing immorality, wars, political corruption and turmoil, and natural disasters.

One interesting end-of-days focus comes from the Islamic State's infatuation with Dabiq, a small town in northern Syria six miles from the Turkish border. Specifically, ISIS terrorists often recite a hadith that provides great insight into the group's eschatology:

> The Last Hour would not come until the Romans land at al-a'Maq or in Dabiq. An army consisting of the best (soldiers) of the people of the earth at that time will come from Medina (to counteract them).[263]

The hadith's importance to ISIS is traced to the group's founder, Abu Musab al-Zarqawi, who said in September 2004: "The spark has been lit here in Iraq, and its heat will continue to intensify…until it burns the crusader armies in Dabiq." Many ISIS propaganda videos end with the image of a fighter carrying the group's large black banner accompanied by an audio clip of al-Zaraqawi mentioning Dabiq.[264]

Dabiq is a small town of a couple thousand residents, but it played a strategic role in history and, for a growing number of Muslims, will be very significant in the future. Specifically, Dabiq is the site of the decisive battle of Marj Dabiq between the Ottoman Empire and the Mamluk Sultanate in 1516. Islamic eschatology, at least according to ISIS, indicates that Dabiq sets up the "final confrontation" in which Muslim forces defeat invading Roman (Christians—Europeans and Americans). That Muslim victory will mark the beginning of the end of the world, the apocalypse.

ISIS isn't subtle about the importance given to Dabiq. The group calls its magazine *Dabiq*, its TV station is called Dabiq, and all its propaganda refers to the town. Remember the beheading of Peter Kassig? The masked executioner said over Kassig's body, "Here we are, burying the first American crusader in Dabiq, eagerly waiting for the remainder of your armies to arrive."[265]

Islam has its own version of an antichrist. He is not mentioned in the Koran, although he is central to Islam's end-times eschatology as given in the Hadith. The Dajjal will, it is said, be a one-eyed Jew with "infidel" written across his forehead. He will be born in Iran to parents who have the child after thirty years of apparent inability to have children.

The Dajjal, whose name is defined as "deceiver" or "liar," will declare himself to be divine, and will demand that he be worshipped. He will take to himself absolute authority as he rules without mercy.

He will have an army, along with a following of seventy thousand Jews and seventy thousand Tartars. He will conquer all the world except for Mecca and Medina, and will reign for a period of forty days.

Members of the Sunni strand within Islam hold that Jesus (Isa), at the Second Coming, will return to the Mount of Olives. Jesus will then move swiftly to Damascus and will attack the Dajjal. After pursuing him into southern Israel, Isa (Jesus) will kill the Antichrist. This dispatching of the Antichrist will take place "at the gate of Ludd" (modern-day Lod, near Tel Aviv) Every single Jew will also be wiped out in this battle. Shi'ite Muslims differ in that they believe that the Dajjal will be killed by the Mahdi, the Twelfth Imam, who is their savior and has the power to work miracles. Like the Antichrist, the Mahdi will establish Jerusalem as his capital, from which he will rule the earth.

It is interesting that the Koran teaches that Jesus was never crucified, buried, or resurrected. He, it says, was taken into heaven before He could be killed by enemies. But, He will have to come back so, among other reasons, He can die like every other man.

Once Jesus kills the Dajjal, it is taught, the Gog-Magog attack from the north will take place. These two great armies will come against Jesus and His friends in Jerusalem. (See the Prophecy 101 appendix for details on the Gog-Magog attack.)

This Jesus, a Muslim in the Islam version, according to the Hadith, will cry out to Allah. Allah will send a deadly swarm of insects to deal a death blow to the invaders. Jesus, it is claimed, will then declare Islam as the one, true religion.

After this event, the Mahdi— the Islamist version of the Messiah—will force every person to convert to Islam. Jesus will reign over an Islamist theocracy for forty years. He will marry and have children. During His rule, the Muslim version of the millennial like earth will produce peace on earth, perfect weather, massively bountiful crops, and tranquility among animal life. All weapons of war will be made into productive tools for conducting life in utopian fashion.

Jesus will die and be buried beside Muhammad at Medina, where He will await resurrection along with everyone else who has died. According to this eschatology, when Jesus dies, all believers will die, too. Only unbelievers will be left, and will be forced to convert to Islam or die.

Following Jesus' death, a series of events take place moving toward the very end of days. A "good beast," produced out of the earth, wearing Solomon's ring and carrying the rod of Moses, comes forth to confront all unbelievers with a message to accept Islam. All who refuse to convert and believe in Allah will have "Infidel" scrawled across their foreheads.

Next, great suffering ensues when smoke envelopes earth and a massive earthquake occurs. Huge landslides, one in Asia, one in the West, and one in the East take place. The sun rises in the West. Great fires break out south of Eden (Yemen). This drives everyone to Syria, where all are gathered for the day of resurrection.

Next, there are three trumpet blasts. The first produces terror in the hearts of all people. A second trumpet—the "trumpet of the swoon"—kills everything on earth and in heaven. Allah is the only being left alive. He then will declare his sovereignty once the earth is void of life. He will at that time create new heavens and a new earth.

With the third trumpet's blowing—heard only by Allah—the resurrection of the dead begins. There is but a single resurrection in Islam. Heaven's inhabitants are first to resurrect. At the same time, the bodies within the earth reconstitute and rejuvenate. When those bodies are prepared, Allah blows the third trumpet and the spirits of the dead—just and unjust—rejoin with their bodies. They come out of their graves naked at that time.

While Muhammad is the first to resurrect and come forth, Abraham is the first to be clothed by Allah and will sit facing Allah. Muhammad is next clothed, and sits at the right hand of Allah.

There is an interval of time between the resurrection and the final judgment called the Day of Final Reckoning. This interval will be marked by great suffering for all people except for the prophets and certain devout Muslims, hand-picked by Allah.

Following the Day of Reckoning, Allah descends from heaven and the judgment begins. Allah weighs the good against the bad in what Islam calls "the Scale." When the judgment is completed, everyone, led by Muhammad, has to cross a bridge over the abyss to hell. The unjust fall into hell and the others are delivered across.

These have great thirst from their ordeal and drink from the Pool of the Prophet to quench their intense thirst. There is at that time a period of intercession at the pool, where Muhammad begins to make intercession for Muslim believers before Allah so that they may be allowed entrance to paradise. The angels, prophets, martyrs, and faithful, at the same time, intercede for the condemned who have an "atom of faith" in their hearts. Allah allows all of the faithful to enter paradise, and he also rescues a large number of people from hell.

In Islam, heaven is the eternal abode only for Allah and Muhammad. There are seven heavens below that. The levels beneath the abode of Allah and Muhammad contain Old Testament personalities. The first layer holds Adam; in the second are found Jesus and John the Baptist. The third layer is where Joseph is; Enoch is in the fourth; Aaron is in the fifth; and Moses and Abraham reside in the sixth and seventh layers. All others who are considered just after judgment reside in "the Garden," which is a perfect environment that caters to all the desires of the faithful. Ordinary Muslim men receive forty virgins each, and jihadi martyrs receive seventy-two each.

Hell has seven levels among its compartments. Specific levels are reserved for Christians, Jews, idolaters, hypocrites, etc. It is a place of torment where inhabitants are tortured by demons.[266]

While the biblical and Islamic accounts of the end times have some vague similarities, they are essentially polar opposites. The Bible is based on the love of God, who desires that all come to Him, but people are free to choose. The Koran and Islamic teachings are based on hatred and subjugation of unbelievers. The true God is the God of love while Allah is a hateful warrior. Perhaps most disturbing today is that Islam is duty- bound to bring about the chaos that they believe is what their god needs in order to conquer the world. Ultimately, the Bible is clear that they will bring about their own destruction and the end of Islam. In the meantime, expect increasing Islamic inspired wars and terrorism aimed at Israel, America, and Christians worldwide.

WHAT MUST BE DONE TO STOP IT?

Every effort to stop Christian genocide in the Middle East has failed. Western governments seem impotent to force Middle Eastern countries to take the actions necessary to stop the Islamists from killing Christians. Those same Middle Eastern governments refuse to treat their Christian citizens as equal partners, and are complicit in the ongoing genocide of their Christian citizens. Christians in growing numbers seek to escape the region, but Christian majority countries like the U.S. exhibit mostly disinterest and dicker around with limited military action to stop the Islamist onslaught. Meanwhile, Islamists continue murdering the few remaining Christians in the Middle East.

Frugal Western and American humanitarian aid has limited impact to alleviate the continuing catastrophe. Pleas for weapons so that Christian enclaves can try protecting themselves go unanswered while those in the West wring their hands and debate, creating a lot of hot air. Western governments are hopelessly incompetent as daily more Christians die due to the escalating persecution across the Middle East.

Western Christians aren't any better than their incompetent governments. While the dwindling Christian communities across the Middle East hunker down trying to survive, their Western brethren go about their lives totally apathetic about the plight of fellow Christians in distant lands. Of course, if the current trend continues and genocide soon voids the Middle East of most Christians as expected, the implications outlined earlier in this book could begin to threaten Christians across the rest of the world and especially in the West. Then those same apathetic Christians will regret having been so complacent, but by that point, they will have little leverage or hope.

So what should be done?

Ideally, if the U.S. had a president who wanted to defeat Christian genocide in the Middle East, he would lead the effort. An American president who cared would immediately host an emergency cabinet meeting and direct the formulation of a strategy to stop the genocide. Next, a concerned commander in chief would speak to the nation from the Oval Office to press his case for defeating Christian genocide, warning that the implications of failure in the Middle East may well impact America and the rest of the free world.

The president's strategy should be very simple and focused. He would explain the dire situation facing Middle Eastern Christians and warn that the time is short. The president would outline a very simple goal and strategy. His goal would be a Middle East where Christians enjoy truly equal treatment like their Muslim neighbors, and where Islamist extremists no longer threaten Christians or anyone else.

Then the president would outline a three-part strategy to reverse the Christian genocide in the Middle East. First, he would declare that any group or country that participates in violence against Christians because of their faith is an enemy of the United States. That means the U.S. would use every element of national power—diplomatic, informational, economic, military—to defeat those enemies to include military action as appropriate.[267]

Second, the president would declare that any country that supports those enemies to include trades with such an enemy of the U.S. would also be considered an enemy as well, subject to the same treatment.

Third, the U.S. would welcome all Christians seeking to emigrate from those anti-Christian enemy countries either to other safe havens in that region or to America.

Fourth, the president would announce that the U.S. would take the lead to establish—with the full cooperation of foreign partners in the region or elsewhere—refugee centers for Christians where they would be protected from Islamists and provided humanitarian assistance and then help to relocate those Christians.

Finally, the president would direct the Secretary of State to develop a foreign policy that makes religious freedom a top priority.

The president would end his Oval Office speech by announcing that he directed his national security team to work with all departments to develop an interagency campaign plan to implement his strategy. He would then promise to closely consult with the Congress on his campaign plan to win their support, and would do so within two weeks.

Unfortunately, Mr. Obama will never do the above. His past actions demonstrate that he is unwilling to help distressed Christians—and, in fact, he is very pro-Muslim.

Americans must then wait for a future president who appreciates the seriousness of the threat for Christians in the Middle East and the related implications for America. However,

by the time the U.S. gets a new president who potentially
could be sympathetic to the dire situation facing Middle East
Christians, it may already be too late for those people as well as
for the inevitable fallout for the rest of the world.

Therefore, the Christian world needs to come together to
develop a strategy and its own campaign plan to stop Christian
genocide in the Middle East. Christians from across the globe
need to help develop a simple strategy and what ought to be
called the "Never Submit Campaign Plan to Save Middle Eastern
Christians."

The campaign title "Never Submit," introduced earlier,
comes from a response to the meaning of Islam and the choices
ISIS gives innocent Christians. Islam means "submission," and
ISIS terrorists give Christians three choices: leave, convert to
Islam, or "face the sword."[268]

The "Never Submit" campaign plan is outlined in detail
across the following four chapters. The recommendations in
these chapters are not prioritized, and should be understood as
requiring immediate, simultaneous implementation.

CHAPTER 12

CHRISTIAN LEADERS WHO STOOD IN THE GAP

A Call for New Voices to Stand Against Christian Genocide

There are too few Christian voices today opposing the genocide of fellow believers in the Middle East. It is instructive to look at similar crises in history and understand how Christian leaders at those times came to the forefront to stand in the gap.

Three such Christian leaders stood in the gap when their peers were cowed by the opposition: an Englishman, a German, and an American. Where are such Christian leaders today who are willing to stand in the gap as fellow believers suffer genocide in the Middle East and as global Christian persecution worsens?

CHRISTIAN ENGLISHMAN STOOD IN THE GAP

Early in this book, William Wilberforce (1759–1833) was introduced as the Christian British parliamentarian who led the charge to end slavery. At that time in the late 1700s, slavery was considered vital to the British Commonwealth's economy, and as a result, very few people thought anything could be done about it. Wilberforce was one of the few who thought otherwise. He invested his life to eliminate slavery, a goal that only started after his evangelical conversion experience in 1786 followed by his public vow to dedicate his life to moral reform.

Wilberforce's spiritual rebirth helped him realize that God gave him position and skills for the moral work before him. He said: "My walk is a public one. My business is in the world, and I must mix in the assemblies of men or quit the post which Providence [God] seems to have assigned me."[269]

Soon Wilberforce became absorbed with the issue of eliminating slavery. "So enormous, so dreadful, so irremediable did the trade's wickedness appear that my own mind was completely made up for abolition," Wilberforce wrote. "Let the consequences be what they would: I from this time determined that I would never rest until I had effected its abolition."[270]

Wilberforce's determination to eliminate the "trade's wickedness" was evident to his peers who called him and his evangelical friends "the Saints," but that effort took him eighteen years before the initial success in parliament and, like many before him, it came at a price.[271]

He began in 1789 making a three-and-a-half-hour speech before the British Parliament to introduce legislation to end the slave trade. At the time he was vilified, and subsequently, one friend feared that Wilberforce would be "carbonated [broiled] by Indian planters, barbecued by African merchants, and eaten by Guinea captains" for his antislavery campaign that threatened the privileged merchants' livelihood.[272]

Public opposition to his efforts was complemented by the steady drag of illness on his physical stamina. Two years prior to his long speech to parliament, he had a near-death illness that left him in constant pain, for which he took opium and continued to do so for twenty years. For the balance of his life, Wilberforce suffered many bouts of debilitating sickness and often had to remove himself for long periods in order to recuperate.

Wilberforce stood in the gap, overcoming great political and physical barriers to defeat the scourge of slavery.

GERMAN PRIEST STOOD IN THE GAP

Dietrich Bonhoeffer stood in the gap against the genocide of Jews at the hands of the Nazis. For his opposition he was ultimately arrested and executed, but he remains a symbol of opposition to Adolf Hitler, and Bonhoeffer's views on Christianity remain influential today.

In 1931, Bonhoeffer was ordained a priest in the German Evangelical Church in Berlin during a troubling time for Germany, a country wracked by the Great Depression, and shortly before the election of the controversial Nazi Party.

Bonhoeffer opposed Adolf Hitler's racist philosophy and often publicly criticized the Nazi Party as an idolatrous cult of the Führer. Shortly after Hitler became chancellor in 1933, Bonhoeffer's German Evangelical Church welcomed Hitler's government. In spite of Bonhoeffer's membership, he wrote an essay assailing Nazi persecution.

Bonhoeffer's opposition to Nazi interference in church affairs led to the formation of a breakaway church—the Confessing Church, which he helped found with Martin Niemoller. The Confessing Church stood against the morally corrupted, Nazi-supported German Christian movement, which compromised with the Nazis to retain its clerical authority.[273]

Hitler's ironclad totalitarian rule quickly clamped down on all Christian leaders, especially those clergy opposing Nazi rule. Soon Christian seminaries were shuttered, and many members within the Confessing Church became reluctant to oppose Hitler. But a few clergy like Bonhoeffer, a professed pacifist who had tried to oppose Hitler through religious action and moral persuasion, changed their strategy, coming to believe that force was appropriate to remove Hitler.

Bonhoeffer worried that he might be required to take an oath to Hitler or be arrested for his public opposition to the Nazis, so he left Germany to accept a lecturing position at Union Seminary in New York in 1939. But soon he was overcome with guilt for abandoning his fellow Christians. He wrote fellow theologian Reinhold Niebuhr the following:

I have made a mistake in coming to America. I must live through this difficult period in our national history with the Christian people of Germany. I will have no right to participate in the reconstruction of Christian life in Germany after the war if I do not share the trials of this time with my people.[274]

After returning to Germany and in spite of Gestapo tracking, Bonhoeffer became a double agent with the German military intelligence, the Abwehr, traveling to churches supposedly to collect information for the expansion of Nazism. Instead, he helped rescue Jews and worked for the expansion of the anti-Nazi resistance.[275]

An encounter with Visser't Hooft, the general secretary of the World Council of Churches, exposed Bonhoeffer's conviction. "What do you pray for in these days?" asked Hooft of Bonhoeffer. "If you want to know the truth, I pray for the defeat of my nation," said Bonhoeffer.[276]

Bonhoeffer's cover in the Abwehr afforded him valuable information to share with the German resistance movement and to help German Jews escape to Switzerland. Those activities were eventually discovered, which led to Bonhoeffer's arrest in April 1943.

For the next year and a half, Bonhoeffer was imprisoned at Tegel military prison. He used that time to continue his writings that are read today, such as *Ethics*, still sold by Amazon.[277]

During his incarceration, Bonhoeffer ministered to his fellow inmates. Payne Best, a British army prisoner at Tegel, wrote: "Bonhoeffer was different, just quite calm and normal, seemingly perfectly at his ease…his soul really shone in the dark desperation of our prison. He was one of the very few men I have ever met to whom God was real and ever close to him."[278]

Bonhoeffer was given a cursory court martial and then transferred to the extermination camp at Flossenbürg, where he was executed on April 9, 1945, alongside six other resisters.

Bonhoeffer was a Christian leader who stood in the gap. He could have remained safely in America, but he chose to return home to make a difference in the name of Christ.

AMERICAN BAPTIST PASTOR
STOOD IN THE GAP

Martin Luther King Jr. (1929–1968) was a Baptist minister and nonviolent civil rights activist who stood in the gap against the injustice of segregation in America. He was the driving force behind the 1963 March on Washington, the Civil Rights Act of 1964, and the Voting Rights Act of 1965. The U.S. celebrates King's life with an annual federal holiday on his birthday.

In 1963, King wrote one of the most compelling letters ever written while in a Birmingham, Alabama, jail cell where he was detained as a participant in nonviolent demonstrations against segregation. The letter was written to eight white religious leaders in the south who had labeled King's activities in Birmingham "unwise and untimely."[279]

King accepted the white religious leaders' criticism as sincere from "men of genuine good will," but he used the occasion to outline how the religious leaders had abandoned their calling to oppose injustice. That letter eerily applies today to the American church and her leaders who ignore injustice against fellow believers facing genocide in the Middle East.

Consider King's critique of the 1963 Birmingham injustice and the seven parallels to the ongoing genocide and rank mistreatment of Christians in the Middle East today.

RESPOND TO INJUSTICE

King went to Birmingham at the invitation of locals to "engage in a non-violent direct-action program...because injustice is here." He compared his journey to that of the apostle Paul, who carried the gospel of Jesus Christ to the Greco-Roman world. King wrote: "I too am compelled to carry the gospel of freedom beyond my particular hometown." After all, "I cannot sit idly by in Atlanta [his home town] and not be concerned about what happens in Birmingham [146 miles away]."

"Injustice anywhere is a threat to justice everywhere," King wrote. "We are caught in an inescapable network of mutuality, tied in a single garment of destiny. Whatever affects one directly affects all indirectly."

Birmingham, according to King, was "the most thoroughly segregated city in the United States" at the time. The city had an "ugly record of police brutality" and "unjust treatment of Negroes in the courts is a notorious reality."

Birmingham's blacks were clearly treated as second-class citizens. King spoke of the "unsolved bombings of Negro homes and churches" and the humiliating racial signs in local stores. All efforts to negotiate with Birmingham's civil and economic leaders proved to be fruitless in spite of repeated promises otherwise.

King said the South was "bogged down in the tragic attempt to live in monologue rather than dialogue." Those in power didn't want to dialogue, because the "privileged groups seldom give up their privileges voluntarily," King explained. He continued: "We know through painful experience that freedom is never voluntarily given by the oppressor; it must be demanded by the oppressed."

The parallels to the Middle East are stunning. The current Middle East is like the Birmingham of 1963 but on steroids. The Arab region is the most thoroughly bigoted place on earth, with a record of brutality, unjust treatment, and genocide regarding Christians.

Christians in the Middle East today, like African-Americans in 1963, are second-class citizens treated like Kafirs (unbelievers), as the Koran teaches, and the region's governments support their Muslim majority, which makes them complicit in the persecution of non-Muslims. King would remind us "injustice anywhere [Birmingham or the Middle East] is a threat to justice everywhere."

Today we need Christian leaders to demand equal treatment for all Christians and other non-Muslims in the Middle East, leaders who will stand in the gap to stop those mostly totalitarian regimes from ignoring the cries of the oppressed.

UNTIMELY AND JUST WAIT

King addressed the issue of "untimely." He admits that he had "never yet engaged in a direct-action movement that was 'well timed' according to the timetable of those who have not suffered unduly from the disease of segregation." Then he rejected the word too often used about his movement: "wait." He said "wait" always meant "never."

"We have waited for more than three hundred and forty years for our God-given and constitutional rights," King said. Then he outlined "stinging darts of segregation" and said you want us to "wait." He profiled those "stinging darts" below:

But when you have seen vicious mobs lynch your mothers and fathers at will and drown your sisters and brothers at whim; when you have seen hate-filled policemen curse, kick, brutalize, and even kill your black brothers and sisters with impunity; when you see the vast majority of your twenty million Negro brothers smothering in an airtight cage of poverty in the midst of an affluent society; when you suddenly find your tongue twisted and your speech stammering as you seek to explain to your six-year-old daughter why she cannot go to the public amusement park that has just been advertised on television, and see tears welling up in her little eyes when she is told that Funtown is closed to colored children, and see the depressing clouds of inferiority begin to form in her little mental sky, and see her begin to distort her little personality by unconsciously developing a bitterness toward white people; when you have to concoct an answer for a five-year-old son asking in agonizing pathos, "Daddy, why do white people treat colored people so mean?"; when you take a cross-country drive and find it necessary to sleep night after night in the uncomfortable corners of your automobile because no motel will accept you; when you are humiliated day in and day out by nagging signs reading "white" and "colored"; when your first name becomes "nigger" and your middle name becomes "boy" (however old you are) and your last name becomes "John," and when your wife and mother are never given the respected title "Mrs."; when you are harried by day and haunted by night by the fact that you are a Negro, living constantly at tiptoe stance, never knowing what to expect next, and plagued with inner fears and outer resentments; when you are forever fighting a degenerating sense of "nobodyness"—then you will understand why we find it difficult to wait.[280]

Today in the Middle East, Christians are being killed by murderous Islamic extremist groups and others are forced into exile. Even those Christians who remain behind face many of the "stinging darts" King describes above.

The Middle Eastern governments and the majority of their Muslim people would tell Christians and other non-Muslims to "wait," and any attempt to change things now would be "untimely." Nonsense. We need stand-in-the-gap leaders to demand an end to the persecution of Christians in the Middle East.

UNJUST LAWS

King said, "The cup of endurance runs over and men are no longer willing to be plunged into an abyss of injustice." He explained there are two types of laws: "There are just laws, and there are unjust laws." As St. Augustine wrote, King said, "An unjust law is no law at all." That's especially true of laws used to deny people their freedom.

"All segregation statutes are unjust because segregation distorts the soul and damages the personality," King wrote. He quoted St. Thomas Aquinas, who said unjust law is a human law that is not rooted in eternal and natural law, the very epitome of segregation statutes.

King illustrated unjust and just laws. He explained that he was arrested in Birmingham for parading without a permit, which on its face appears to be just. But when "the ordinance is used to preserve segregation and to deny citizens the First Amendment privilege of peaceful assembly and peaceful protest, then it becomes unjust."

"We can never forget that everything Hitler did in Germany was 'legal,'" wrote King. Then he said it was "illegal" to aid Jews in Hitler's Germany. King then said, "If I had lived in Germany during that time [the Nazi era], I would have aided and comforted my Jewish brothers even though it was illegal."

Middle Eastern governments are mostly governed by Islamic-influenced laws that are tragically unjust to non-Muslims. As a result, Christians are discriminated against because of their faith, not because they are bad citizens. If Dr. King were alive today, he would stand in the gap demanding that Middle Eastern governments amend their laws to make them just for Christians and other non-Muslims.

PROTECT THE ROBBED AND PUNISH THE ROBBER

King expressed grave disappointment with the "white moderate." The white moderate was "more devoted to order than to justice" and was a "greater stumbling block in the stride toward freedom" than the Ku Klux Klan. He accused the moderates of setting a timetable "for another man's freedom; who lives by the myth of time and who constantly advises the Negro to wait until a 'more convenient season.'"

King wrote that the white moderate's "shallow understanding from people of good will is more frustrating than absolute misunderstanding from people of ill will." Then he rhetorically asked, "Isn't this like condemning the robbed man because his possession of money precipitated the evil act of robbery?" He answered the question by stating that "society must protect the robbed and punish the robber."

King's white moderate in the modern context is the Western government or international organization like the United Nations that is deathly afraid of offending Muslim nations (King's "robber"). They tell the Christians (King's "robbed") who are tragically suffering in the Middle East to wait until a "more convenient season" to gain their freedom and, for that matter, to save their lives.

The world needs men and women like Dr. King ready to punish the oppressive Middle Eastern governments and not ask the savaged Christians to wait for their freedom, much less allow genocide to continue until the region is void of all Christ followers.

A RELIGIOUS HURRY

King received a letter from a white brother that read, "All Christians know that the colored people will receive equal rights eventually, but is it possible that you are in too great of a religious hurry? It has taken Christianity almost two thousand years to accomplish what it has. The teachings of Christ take time to come to Earth."

Dr. King labels that statement "a tragic misconception of time." He went on to label the "religious hurry" statement as "strangely irrational" as if "in the very flow of time that will inevitably cure all ills." Dr. King concludes, "We will have to repent in this generation not merely for the vitriolic words and actions of the bad people but for the appalling silence of the good people."

King said that human progress "never rolls in on wheels of inevitability," but "comes through the tireless efforts and persistent work of men willing to be coworkers with God, and without this hard work, time itself becomes an ally of the forces of social stagnation."

Christians in the Middle East are in a "religious hurry" because their survival is at stake and they know that without help, progress is not inevitable. In fact, unless good men stand in the gap taking on the hard work of freeing the Middle East Christian, there will never be freedom.

BE AN EXTREMIST

Dr. King dismissed being labeled an extremist for his nonviolent direct action. He explained that he tried to channel normal and healthy discontent "through the creative outlet of nonviolent direct action."

Many past leaders were extremists, King argued. "Was not Jesus an extremist in love?—'Love your enemies, bless them that curse you, pray for them that despitefully use you.'" The apostle Paul was an extremist: "I bear in my body the marks of the Lord Jesus." Martin Luther said, "Here I stand; I can do no other so help me God."

"I had hope that the white moderate would see this," King said, then answered, "Maybe I expected too much."

He continued:

I guess I should have realized that few members of a race that has oppressed another race can understand or appreciate the deep groans and passionate yearnings of those that have been oppressed, and still fewer have the vision to see that injustice must be rooted out by strong, persistent, and determined action.

The Middle East needs Christian extremists like Dr. King to stand in the gap as did Jesus, Paul, and Martin Luther.

DISAPPOINTED IN CHRISTIAN LEADERS

Dr. King admits to disappointment "with the white church and its leadership." He acknowledges some that stood against segregation, but "despite these notable exceptions, I must honestly reiterate that I have been disappointed with the church."

King admits that he fully expected the "support of the white church. I felt that the white ministers, priests, and rabbis of the South would be some of our strongest allies." But he was disappointed because he heard "numerous religious leaders call upon their worshipers to comply with a desegregation decision because it is the law, but I have longed to hear white ministers say, follow this decree because integration is morally right and the Negro is your brother." Sadly, Dr. King admitted, "I have watched white churches stand on the sidelines and merely mouth pious irrelevancies and sanctimonious trivialities."

He opined that "there was a time when the church was very powerful. ....in those days the church was not merely a thermometer that recorded the ideas and principles of popular opinion; it was the thermostat that transformed the mores of society." He explained that they were powerful because "they were too God-intoxicated to be 'astronomically intimidated.' They brought an end to such ancient evils as infanticide and gladiatorial contest. Things are different now."

"The contemporary church is so often a weak, ineffectual voice with an uncertain sound. It is so often the arch supporter of the status quo." He continued, "If the church today does not recapture the sacrificial spirit of the early church, it will lose its authentic ring, forfeit the loyalty of millions, and be dismissed as an irrelevant social club with no meaning for the twentieth century."

Dr. King concludes his letter expressing great disappointment with Christian leaders and the contemporary church. It would appear that if Dr. King were here today, he would express similar sentiments about the failure of the church and her erstwhile leaders to stand in the gap.

CONCLUSION

Where are the Kings, Bonhoeffers, and Wilberforces of today—Christian leaders standing in the gap defending Christians facing genocide at the hands of Middle Eastern terrorists and righteously resisting the treatment of Christians and others treated as second-class citizens by Islamic governments?

CHAPTER 13

HOW CAN THE GLOBAL CHRISTIAN COMMUNITY HELP?

The global Christian community should begin by acknowledging the truth: The Islamic world is at war with Christianity. Of course, saying Christians are at war with Islam is not politically correct in most Western cultures, but, as the Reverend Franklin Graham said: We are at war with Islam, "no question about it." Further, it doesn't matter that leaders like President Obama refuse to call our long conflict a war with Islam. The circumstances we find today may not be to our choosing, but they are indeed a war—and the casualties are mounting.

A Christian leader who wants to remain anonymous because of his work with the indigenous church in the Middle East said our Islamist enemy is very dangerous. He explained that many orthodox Muslims in the Middle East "are spending thirty hours a day trying to figure out how to kill us. Meanwhile, we in the West are distracted by ball games and Hollywood but our enemy isn't playing games. We need to be very aware what our enemy is up to."[281]

The most important dimension of the war with Islam is the spiritual. The key to fighting a successful spiritual war is finding the biblical balance, which begins with dealing with our own sin through prayer and then obediently preparing ourselves to be used by God to confront the evil (Ephesians 6:10–18).

Ephesians 6 directs Christians to prepare for warfare by putting on the full armor of God and knowing that our enemy is controlled by spiritual forces: Satan.

> Finally, be strong in the Lord and in his mighty power.
>
> Put on the full armor of God so that you can take your stand against the devil's schemes.
>
> For our struggle is not against flesh and blood, but against the rulers, against the authorities, against the powers of this dark world and against the spiritual forces of evil in the heavenly realms. (Ephesians 6:10–12, NASB)

Christians should take spiritual war seriously by employing all God-given means to defeat the enemy. Those means include at least the six following actions common to martial parlance: understanding the commander's intent, knowing the enemy, providing the necessary logistics, providing security, employing information operations, and protecting noncombatants.

COMMANDER'S INTENT

Our preparation for the battle begins with prayer—understanding the commander's (God's) intent. How should Christians pray and what should they pray for regarding Christian genocide in the Middle East?

They should pray earnestly and in detail, beginning by staying personally right with God about their own sin. Then Christians should heed the exhortation in Hebrews 13:3 (NIV) to "continue to remember those in prison as if you were together with them in prison, and those who are mistreated as if you yourselves were suffering."

Todd Nettleton, director of media and public relations for the Voice of the Martyrs, has met with Christians facing persecution in the Middle East, and he said their primary request is for fellow believers to keep praying. They say, "Pray that we will be faithful to Christ in spite of the persecution." Nettleton also calls on Christians to encourage and strengthen those facing persecution. Fellow believers need to know that they are not alone. He mentioned speaking with a Christian who had been a hostage who told him she knew Christians were praying for her. Somehow, God through his Holy Spirit let her know that believers were lifting her up in prayer—she was not alone, she said. God honors prayer, Nettleton said.

Nettleton met with an Iraqi pastor who asked believers to pray that God will call on Christians to remain in Iraq in spite of the persecution. Many Iraqi Christians are rightly concerned about their safety and future. But, as the Iraqi pastor said, Christians are needed to stay in Iraq to preserve the all-important pluralism—the salt and light of the Christian.

David Curry, the chief executive officer of Open Doors USA, said we should pray for the safety of believers in the Middle East. He also exhorts Christians to pray for Muslims who are suffering because of ISIS and other terrorist groups. Curry calls on Christians to pray for those persecutors—the ISIS-like extremists—that they might "have a Saul to Paul conversion [Acts 9:1–19]."

Not surprisingly, Curry indicated that many Middle Eastern Christians have lost hope that they will ever move back to their homes abandoned as a result of ISIS attacks and other persecution. He encourages Christians to pray that our brothers and sisters know that they aren't forgotten. We can do that through our gifts and communications through social media networks and our missionary representatives helping in the region.

Tom Farr, the former director of religious freedom at the U.S. State Department under both Presidents Clinton and Bush, said we should pray—and especially as congregations—for fellow believers facing faith-based persecution in the Middle East. He also exhorts Christians to pray "for our government to do what it is capable of doing to help the Christians."

Another Christian leader who works with indigenous churches in the Middle East said, "God will not waste persecution in martyrdom. He will make use of this crisis." He encouraged Christians to "pray that there will come a day when Jesus Christ is honored throughout the Middle East…pray for the endurance of believers and especially for the Muslim background believers who face special threats."

Todd Nettleton with the Voice of the Martyrs challenges believers to "beat the drums" for fellow Christians suffering persecution. He outlines three things Christians should do to "beat the drums." First, they should pray specifically for Christians suffering. Second, Nettleton explains Christians should educate themselves so as to target their prayers. There are groups like Voice of the Martyrs, says Nettleton, that publish material and host websites providing details about fellow believers facing persecution—names, places and circumstances—to help believers target their prayers. Finally, Nettleton encourages Christians to respond to whatever God puts on their hearts to do.

KNOW YOUR ENEMY

The Chinese military philosopher Sun Tzu wrote: "If you know the enemy and know yourself you need not fear the results of a hundred battles."[282] That means to defeat our enemy we require an understanding of ourselves first and then we must understand our enemy's plans, capabilities, thoughts and desires.

We understand ourselves—strengths and weaknesses—through prayer and seeking God's guidance in His Word and then obeying His direction.

We know our enemy—Islamists—in part by exploring as we did earlier in this book Islam's teachings (plans and desires). Those "know-the-enemy" teachings are applied in various ways by Middle Eastern governments, local imams, as well as Islamist groups that collectively persecute Christians.

The missing part of "know the enemy" is understanding the orthodox Muslim thinking process, which results in a peculiar worldview reinforced by Islamic culture and teaching to produce a certain percentage of Islamic extremists, Islamists. That view is totally alien to the West, but understanding it is critical if Christians are to ever defeat orthodox Islam's tragic influence on Muslims and help the Muslim to come to Christ.

The case of Dzhokhar Tsarnaev, a Muslim man convicted on multiple charges in the 2013 Boston marathon bombing that killed three people and injured more than 260, illustrates the orthodox Muslim belief system by association. (Tsarnaev's older brother, Tamertan, died after being shot and run over by his younger brother in the wake of the Boston bombing.) The boys' mother, Zubeidat Tsarnaev, responded to her youngest son's March 2015 "guilty on all charges" verdict by labeling Americans "terrorists" and proclaiming her son's innocence in spite of overwhelming evidence to the contrary.

In an interview, Zubeidat Tsarnaev, who is a Muslim living in Dagestan (southern Russia), insists on her Chechen sons' innocence. "My sons are innocent, as innocent as all those who are being killed by your [U.S.] country," Zubeidat Tsarnaev wrote in text messages to Vocativ via WhatsApp following the verdict. "Today they are killing Muslims, and tomorrow will come your turn and he who doubts this is deeply mistaken!!!!!"[283]

"How can a mother feel whose son is in the claws of a predator preparing to tear him to pieces like meat???" she wrote. "They will pay for my sons and the sons of Islam, permanently!!! The tears of their mothers will be fuel for them in hell, and also their blood, I am doubtless and eternally glad that I know this from the words of the creator, not just anyone's words!!!!!!"

Mrs. Tsarnaev is a grieving mother who desperately wants to believe the innocence of her sons. But she expressed no remorse for her sons' vicious crimes; rather, she evidenced an orthodox Muslim condemnation of others—an alien response to Western minds, but too typical of someone coming from an Islamic culture.

Todd Nettleton cautions Christians not to hate Muslims for their belief system, but blame Islam. "Expose Islam's teaching and then teach them [Muslims] the truth about Jesus Christ," Nettleton said. It is in that vein the following is provided to help the reader appreciate Islam's impact on Muslims, people who need to hear the truth that salvation is theirs through Jesus Christ.

Nicolai Sennels, a Danish psychologist, who did groundbreaking research regarding the psychological differences between Muslims and non-Muslims, helps the Westerner understand the impact Islamic culture has for the Muslim's way of thinking. Specifically, he found the major differences in worldviews between the Muslim and non-Muslim Westerners are in the realm of anger, aggression, irresponsibility, and insecurity.[284]

Sennels' research is based on "immigrant criminal behavior" and the comparison between non-Muslims and Muslims in therapy. He found that the Danish Muslim population accounted for about 70 percent of crime in Denmark, though that population comprises a low percentage of Denmark's overall population.

Nancy Korbin, author of *The Banality of Suicide Terrorism: The Naked Truth about the Psychology of Islamic Suicide Bombing*, reviewed Sennels' work on criminal Muslims in Denmark. Korbin conducted her own interviews of Muslim prison detainees in Minneapolis and came to similar conclusions as Sennels. She wrote:

> Like Sennels, I came away with a similar sense that Western law enforcement and the general public did not understand why there was so much crime in the Muslim population. And why there has been this problem of jail house converts to Islam who then becomes radicalized through contact with other criminal Muslims during incarceration.

Islam is the perfect religion to give justification for those who feel under attack and to maintain the eternal "victim's fantasy." Islam incites, encourages and permits hatred of the Jew and jihad. It's perfect for a fragile personality that has the need to hate and the need to have an enemy.

Sennels adeptly outlines the key problems of why Muslims are not able to integrate into Western culture. She continued:

We are dealing with nothing more than paranoia. Sennels stresses that the West must set boundaries because otherwise they will kill you. This kind of rage is malignant borderline behavior as in serial killing. We must come to understand such politically incorrect observations as Sennels does in order to connect the dots concerning criminal Muslims even though it is brutal.

Sennels' book, *Criminal Muslims: A Psychologist's Experiences from the Copenhagen Municipality* (Free Press Society, 2009), outlines his experiences with Muslims based on hundreds of therapy sessions. He found that "Muslim culture has a very different view of anger and in many ways opposite to what we experience here in the West." For the Westerner, expressions of public anger and the use of threats are discouraged and often lead to feelings of shame and loss of social status. The opposite is true for Muslim culture, however.

Aggressive behavior and especially threats are expected in the Muslim culture as "a way of handling conflicts and social discrepancies," wrote Sennels. A Muslim is expected in his culture to respond in a threatening manner to insults or social irritation otherwise he/she is seen as weak, undependable.

By comparison, the Westerner considers aggressive behavior a weakness, as not having control of oneself. The Islamic expression of "holy anger" is just the opposite, according to Sennels. For example, the "Muslims' aggressive reaction to a picture showing their prophet as aggressive, completely confirms the truth of the statement made by Kurt Wester-gaard in his satiric drawing." Westergaard is a Danish cartoonist who created the controversial cartoon of the Islamic Prophet Muhammad wearing a bomb in his turban. This depiction met with strong reactions from Muslims worldwide, and as a result, Westergaard received numer-ous death threats and was a target of assassination attempts.

The teaching point is that Westerners tend to handle disagreements through dialogue while the Muslim views that approach as a sign of weakness and a lack of courage. The Muslim will see that response as a weakness and an invitation for exploitation.

KNOW YOUR ENEMY: LOCUS OF CONTROL

Muslim and Western cultures tend to be radically different in terms of locus of control, a psychological term describing whether people experi-ence their life influenced mainly by internal or external factors. Western-ers tend to be mainly influenced by inner forces—points of view, ways of handling emotions, ways of thinking and relating to others, motivation, and ways of communicating.

Muslim culture is very different. "They have strict external rules, tra-ditions and laws for human behavior. They have a god that decides their life's course," according to Sennels. Their religion is very directive, and Muslim clerics dictate virtually every aspect of life: politics, child rearing and how to deal with outsiders.

Therefore, the Muslim's locus of control helps understand the indi-vidual's freedom and responsibility. The Muslim is taught that outer rules and traditions are more important than individual freedom, which leads them to ask about life's consequences: "Who did this to me?" and "Who has to do something for me?"

Thus Islam-influenced societies tend to have people with fewer feel-ings of guilt and a tendency to demand others adapt to the Muslim's wishes and desires. This explains Muslim demands that Western societies accept Islamization and why too often the Muslim displays a victim mentality.

The teaching point is that Westerners must understand that orthodox Muslims tend to blame others for their problems, like Zubeidat Tsarnaeva blamed "Americans" for her sons' crimes. In fact, Dr. Sennels told this author that we must "remind them [Muslims] and the world about Muslim self-responsibility."[285]

KNOW YOUR ENEMY:
SELF REFLECTION & RESPONSIBILITY

Sennels explains that many Westerners feel it is "our standards" that determine real consequences for people. As a result, Westerners tend to avoid setting strict boundaries, because they want to avoid making people feel as if they are being punished. However, that shows a lack of understanding when dealing with people from Muslim cultures.

Sennels quotes a Danish philosopher, Soren Kierkegaard, to make the point: "If one truly wants to help a person, we should first of all start by finding where he is. This is the secret to the art of helping. Anyone who cannot do this is arrogant."

The Westerner needs to understand that people who grew up in a Muslim culture with an outer locus of control will tend to exercise little self-reflection and self-responsibility. That fact should influence how one deals with such people.

Sennels came to the following conclusion based on his extensive experience in giving therapy to Muslims and how to deal with Muslims from outer-locus-of-control societies now living in the West.

We should not permit the destruction of our cities by lawless parallel societies, with groups of roaming criminal Muslims overloading of our welfare system and the growing justified fear that non-Muslims have of violence. The consequences should be so strict that it would be preferable for any antisocial Muslims to go back to a Muslim country, where they can understand and be understood by their own culture.

This factor goes back to how especially boys are raised differently in Western and Muslim cultures. In the West, parents tend to give children a short leash—strict expectations—and as they get older, the leash is lengthened. By the time they are adults, they are expected to have learned enough to handle whatever life throws at them.

Muslim cultures are very different. Children enjoy great freedom early in their lives, and as they age, cultural and religious restrictions are piled on. Parents and the local imam make choices (about wife/husband, education, and job) for the Muslim young adult.

Young adult Muslims from Islamic societies tend to need structured environments and standards. Otherwise, they will not self-police their behavior and expect others to tell them what to do rather than making mature decisions for them. But don't expect Muslims to engage in self-reflection, Dr. Sennels told this author. "Questioning Islam is punished by death for Muslims."

KNOW YOUR ENEMY: MUSLIM IDENTITY

The Muslim identity is more important than any other. Sennels found that his Muslim clients who were second- and third-generation immigrants did not feel Danish, and in fact, "many of them were even more religious and hateful towards non-Muslims than their first generation immigrant parents." That's a common finding across other European countries.

A French survey showed that only 14 percent of that country's nearly five million Muslims see themselves as "more French than Muslim." A similar study in Germany found that only 12 percent of Muslims saw themselves as more German than Muslim. And a Danish survey similarly found that only 14 percent of Muslims identified themselves as "democratic and Danish."

Sennels also suggests Muslims will not entertain the integration of non-Muslims as equals, which means that Muslims tend to live together in Muslim-only neighborhoods, create their own Islamic parallel societies, and continue to have less respect towards non-Muslims.

The Muslim culture is resilient and intolerant of outside influences, and it grows more so with succeeding generations. Add to the mixture the Muslim tendencies toward isolation, crime, and aggression and one can readily see that the mixture is unstable and explosive: the perfect mindset for a real, growing, and present danger to Europe and America.

KNOW YOUR ENEMY: HONOR

The West is well aware of mass rage from Muslims at the publication of caricatures of their Prophet. The conclusion is that Muslims are easily offended.

Sennels explains that Muslim culture tells its men "that criticism must be taken completely personally and met with childish reactions." That's a result of a culture that makes Muslim men "stiff and develop fragile, glass-like, narcissistic personalities."

Sennels' observation may be correct, but some leading Muslims reject that part of the Islamic culture. Abdurrahman Wahid, former president of Indonesia, a Muslim-majority nation, rejected those who use violence to "defend" Islam:

Nothing could possibly threaten God who is Omnipotent and existing as absolute and eternal Truth.... Those who claim to defend God, Islam, or the Prophet are thus either deluding themselves or manipulating religion for their own mundane and political purposes. We witnessed this in the carefully manufactured outrage that swept the Muslim world several years ago, claiming hundreds of lives in response to cartoons published in Denmark. Those who presume to fully grasp God's will, and dare to impose by force their own limited understanding of this upon others, are essentially equating themselves with God and are unwittingly engaged in blasphemy.[286]

The teaching point Dr. Sennels told this author about "honor" is not to be afraid to tell the truth even though it might hurt Muslim sensibilities.

Knowing your enemy, as Sun Tzu said, means you need not fear a hundred battles—or for that matter, a hundred Muslims. Understanding the Islamist—the orthodox, extremist Muslim—requires a study of Islamic teachings that he takes literally, but it also calls for a comprehension of the Muslim's worldview as well.

PROVIDING THE NECESSARY LOGISTICS

General Dwight D. Eisenhower wrote, "You will not find it difficult to prove that battles, campaigns, and even wars have been won or lost primarily because of logistics."[287] Winning the war with Islam to save Christians in the Middle East from genocide requires a lot of logistical support.

The number of displaced people in the Middle East is staggering. One report indicates there are over eight hundred thousand displaced in Kurdistan alone.

"According to the United Nations, if it operates at 100 percent efficiency, it can only take care of 40 percent of these desperate people."[288] Of course, the United Nations is not accounting for outside nongovernmental organization assistance and individual nations, like the United States, which provide humanitarian assistance via the United States Agency for International Development.

Refugees International, an organization that monitors the global refugee problem, paints a sobering, country-by-country picture of the refugee crisis in the Middle East. The worst refugee crisis is in Syria, which has 6.5 million internally displaced persons (IDP) and another 9 million who are vulnerable and in need of humanitarian assistance. Already, more than 2.4 million Syrians fled that country's civil war for neighboring countries.[289]

Iraq has a similar IDP crisis. That country has roughly two million IDPs, and most of the Christians in that group are in the Kurdistan region of northern Iraq. Many live outside of organized refugee camps where social services are underdeveloped and ill-equipped to handle the ever increasing heavy load.[290]

Jordan is home to more than six hundred thousand Syrian refugees living in two camps designed for only a quarter of that population. Other Syrian refugees live in Jordan's urban areas away from the camps, yet they totally rely on aid for their very basic daily needs. Further, Jordan's Palestinians, which account for half the country's total population, are still considered refugees from Israel. Hundreds of thousands of those Palestinians continue to live in refugee camps even after more than sixty years after the 1948 Israel-Arab war, which drove them into exile.

Lebanon is host to refugees from Iraq, Syria, and Israel. More than four hundred thousand Palestinians remain in Lebanon in a dozen camps, some which have existed there since the 1948 war as well. Meanwhile, more than half a million Syrian refugees flooded into Lebanon in the wake of the civil war. Many of those refugees live with Lebanese host families, taking the load off refugee camps and other refugees from Iraq, which are straining Lebanon's ability to sustain the growing demands.

Other regional populations are vulnerable as well. Yemen's fragile situation has forced many people to flee violence and now gather in makeshift shelters and depend on international aid.

Throughout the region, the number of Christians displaced among the masses of total refugees is difficult to estimate. However, we know with some accuracy that Christians account for about 5 percent of the region's overall population, which means there are somewhere between 7.5 and 15 million Christians and most live (or lived) in Egypt, Syria, and Lebanon.[291]

The growing refugee population across the Middle East is stretching even the best efforts to keep up with the demand. For example, a 2015 United Nations report states that "several overlapping crises and humanitarian emergencies, the Middle East is likely to witness further internal and external displacement, with vast numbers of existing refugees and internally displaced people requiring direct humanitarian support." The report indicates that to maintain basic services and essential needs for millions, considerable resources will be needed for the foreseeable future. In fact, the U.N. report indicates its financial requirements for the region increased from $506 million in 2011 to $1.7 billion in 2015.[292]

What is the global Christian community doing to help relieve the suffering?

Reverend Franklin Graham said Samaritans' Purse is helping by providing shelter and food, and by working with Christian congregations. It isn't enough, however. He admits that Christian ministries are limited in what they can do "due to the danger of being there." Then he explained, "The only safe places for Christians in Syria are areas controlled by the Syrian government." That's because the refugee camps are crawling with Islamists who target Christians.

Graham warned that Christian refugees are truly desperate. They "lost their homes, have little money and they need basic necessities. They do not want to leave but the situation is too dangerous." Meanwhile, Christians elsewhere indicate they are desperate to leave.

David Curry with Open Doors said the body of Christ must take a very human approach to the crisis. He illustrated the resistance to go to the region using the biblical account of Jonah, whom God called to preach to Nineveh (northern Iraq), but Jonah ignored God's calling and ended up in a whale's stomach.[293] Curry said Christians "need to go to them [refugees] with the loving message of Jesus—both other Christians and Muslims.

Todd Nettleton with Voice of the Martyrs said once immediate needs are met, Christians need to think long term. He explained that in the Middle East, the average length of time refugees are displaced is twelve years. In fact, Nettleton said, some of the current refugees, such as Christian Iraqis who left Baghdad years ago for Mosul, have been displaced many times. They were forced out of Mosul in 2014 and now live in more temporary housing in Irbil.

These people need permanent homes, and that requires more help than nongovernmental organizations can provide, which means that governments and international organizations like the U.N. must step in with permanent solutions. These people must move from weathered tent homes without clean water and sewage systems to more permanent housing with services. They need jobs to provide them income rather than waiting in line for the next meal. Their children need education, they need good medical care, and most of all, they need hope of a better life.

Providing the logistics associated with this war is daunting. The hurt is growing among all people in the Middle East, but especially among minority religious groups like Christians, who are persecuted at every turn because of their faith.

PROVIDING SECURITY

The wars being fought in the Middle East today are a combination of sectarian civil wars and insurgencies. It is instructive for Christians who want to help fellow believers in the Middle East to understand what the U.S. military doctrine says about operations related to an insurgency.

Then Lieutenant General David Petraeus oversaw the writing of America's counterinsurgency doctrine while serving as the commander for the Army's Combined Arms Center at Fort Leavenworth, Kansas. Subsequently, he took command of the multinational coalition in Iraq, leading the surge in 2008 that successfully suppressed the insurgents and regained stability for that country.[294]

Petraeus' manual states: "You cannot fight former Saddamists and

Islamic extremists the same way you would have fought the Vietcong, Moros, or Tupamaros; the application of principles and fundamentals to deal with each varies considerably." The general concludes that "a successful counterinsurgency campaign requires a flexible, adaptive force led by agile, well-informed, culturally astute leaders."

Those culturally astute leaders understand that the people are the center of gravity of the operation, which explains why it is critical to provide for the population's physical security. "During any period of instability, people's primary interest is physical security for themselves and their families," states the field manual. "When HN [host nation] forces fail [as in Iraq and Syria] to provide security or threaten the security of civilians, the population is likely to seek security guarantees from insurgents, militias, or other armed groups."

Christians caught in the ground war in the Middle East find themselves facing a physical security crisis. Christians in particular indicate that there are no safe places and their governments are consistently failing them. Thus, as Petraeus' manual states, the population seeks alternatives. Two such alternatives are emerging among Christians in the region, and the global Christian community must decide whether it is going to help with one or both of these initiatives.

There are no safe places for Christians in the region, and that has been true for a long time. For example, in 2003, the American invasion of Iraq replaced tolerance for Christians under Saddam Hussein with sectarian violence that drove most Christians away. Similarly, the 2011 Arab Spring forced Christians to take sides between secular and Islamic forces in places like Syria. Even though Syrian Christians accepted the limited safe havens provided by President Bashar al-Assad, others in the country were either expelled by Islamists or murdered.

Those expelled became refugees cast into the region's most troubled areas. That situation is getting worse as the number of refugees grows, and many of the current refugee camps and so-called safe areas are in jeopardy because ISIS and its Islamist affiliates aim to create "Christian-free" zones in those very same places.

This security situation for Christian refugees creates two possible alternatives for the global Christian community to consider.

First, the global Christian community should consider whether to help create security enclaves for endangered minorities like Christians. The U.S. did something similar when it created no-fly zones over northern Iraq in the 1990s to prevent Iraq's dictator, Saddam Hussein, from coming north to attack the Kurds. A similar idea was floated by the current Turkish government in 2014, but the Obama administration rejected such an approach to protect refugee camps along the Syria-Turkey border.

Not surprisingly, Christian aid leaders are mixed about the proposal to create security enclaves for Christian refugees. Reverend Graham said, "That would be nice if we could do that," but he admitted that would take soldiers, a view Voice of the Martyr's Nettleton echoed. Farr, the former State Department official, believes it could be a temporary measure, but he suggested another security alternative: We should "provide enough training to Kurds and Christians to defend themselves and even if it means more [U.S.] boots on the ground."

The idea of training and arming a Christian force to defend the indigenous church is becoming a reality, but it is not uniformly supported. Open Doors' David Curry said, "We are to be a spiritual movement…a military Christian force is not the answer."

Matthew VanDyke, mentioned previously, is the founder of Sons of Liberty International, a group focused on training Christian militias to defend themselves against the likes of ISIS. In early 2015, VanDyke and five former U.S. military volunteers ran a three-week basic training camp for 330 Christians living in the Nineveh plain. Even though the Christian force only had a third of the individual weapons required, they are stepping up to the challenge of defending their homeland. Of course, as VanDyke said, in the Nineveh Plain, Christians prefer to have their own province and not to share with the Kurds, whom VanDyke says they can't trust.

Trust is a big issue for the Christian community in the Nineveh

Plain, and the Kurds broke that trust in 2014. Specifically, according to VanDyke, soon after ISIS abandoned Tell Isqof, a Christian village in the Nineveh Plain, the Peshmerga (the Kurdish militia) moved in and looted the thousand-home Christian community. He said after that incident, the Christians dislike the Peshmerga as much as they dislike ISIS.

"Their future does not look good," VanDyke cautions. The Christians find themselves located between hostile Sunni Arabs on one side and the "can't-trust" Kurds on the other. Christians are understandably pessimistic about being a super minority in such a troubled area, which might explain why they are seeking to arm themselves.

A *Wall Street Journal* reporter filed a story on the new Iraqi Christian militia in the Nineveh Plain in early 2015. That reporter wrote that the Christian militia members complained that they were abandoned by Iraqi government forces in 2014, and as a result, they created a force to keep their homes safe from ISIS. Further, as one young militia leader said, "I want to defend our own lands, with our own force."[295]

More than two thousand Christians signed up to defend their Christian community—one Christian town, al Qosh, and three small villages remain free. These men hold out hope that the U.S. will give them equipment to fight ISIS. They believe that support is guaranteed by the 2015 U.S. National Defense Authorization Act, which includes $1.6 billion to train and equip fighters including those in the Nineveh Plain.

A senior aide with the U.S. House of Representatives' Armed Services Committee confirmed the underlying authority in the Defense Authorization Act does allow for assistance to "local security forces with a national security mission." He went on to say, "So potentially that could include some Christian groups."[296]

Unfortunately, the Christian militia—much less other non-Shia fighters in northern Iraq—will never see any of the 2015 U.S. security assistance aid. In fact, proposed legislation for fiscal year 2016 to require the Pentagon to set aside a quarter of the security assistance to Iraq for Kurdish and Sunni fighters drew a harsh protest from the Shia majority government in Baghdad and a threat from Cleric Moqtada al-Sadr, the leader of the Mahdi Army militia that fought Americans beginning in 2003.

"If the time comes and the proposed bill is passed, we will have no choice but to unfreeze the military wing that deals with the American entity so that it may start targeting American interests in Iraq and outside of Iraq when possible," Sadr said.[297] Sadr's response to the American desire to help non-Shia fighters opposing ISIS is more evidence that Iraq is further fracturing along sectarian lines and may never become whole again.

An American, a former U.S. soldier, said U.S. officials in Erbil know about his group's efforts to help the Christian militia, but the U.S. doesn't want to get involved. "The Americans want to stay away from this because their view is, if you train the Christians, you're starting some crazy religious war," the former soldier said. "Well, ISIS beat you to it."[298]

The Nineveh Plains Christian force has counterparts in Syria and Lebanon as well. The leader of Lebanon's Syriac Union Party, Ibrahim Murad, urged British officials to provide arms to "Christian opposition fighters" in Syria. He appealed to British Member of Parliament Brooks Newmark in an April 2015 meeting in Beirut. Murad said he briefed the British parliamentarian on the "suffering of Syriac and Christian communities" in Iraq and Syria as a result of ISIS' brutality.[299]

Fox News reported about residents in a small Lebanese Christian village on Syria's border taking up arms to defend themselves from Muslim extremists. "We all know that if they come, they will slit our throats for no reason," said one villager.[300]

Lebanese Christians are rearming because their very survival is at stake. So, they are setting up self-defense forces in anticipation of Syria's civil war spilling into their country. Meanwhile, the sale of weapons on the black market has climbed sharply, according to *Fox News*.

Umm Milad, a young Iraqi refugee now in Lebanon, said her family fled after ISIS fighters painted the letter "N" for "Nasrani"—an archaic term used to refer to Christians—on their home in Mosul. Milad said, "We are scared. We don't want to go back. We want to go anywhere else. Canada or America." That fear makes some refugees desperate to arm themselves until they can leave the region.

So what is the global Christian community to do in order to improve the security of Middle Eastern Christians? It is doubtful that, without local government and international endorsement, any nongovernment group can establish a Christian enclave. However, Christians can lobby their governments to press for the creation of a safe haven for Christians.

On the second point, many Christians across the world own personal firearms with which they hunt and protect themselves and their families. America's founders were mostly Christian believers, and all were armed to protect their interests and used those weapons when the British tried to rob the colonies of their freedom. What's the difference in the Middle East today for Christians who are forced out of their homes at gunpoint and no legitimate government rushes to defend them? Christians ought to be able to defend themselves, and that might mean they form militias.

Christians should encourage their governments to work with regional governments to arm, train, and integrate Christian militia as security forces much like America's National Guard but focused only in Christian areas.

EMPLOYING INFORMATION OPERATIONS

In 2006, then Secretary of Defense Donald Rumsfeld said:

In this environment, the old adage that "A lie can be halfway around the world before the truth has its boots on" becomes doubly true with today's technologies...the longer it takes to put a strategic communication framework in place, the more we can be certain that the vacuum will be filled by the enemy and by news informers that most assuredly will not paint an accurate picture of what is actually taking place.[301]

We see Rumsfeld's observation in spades almost every day delivered by the extremist Islamic State in terms of its sophisticated recruitment of vulnerable Western youth via the Internet and very well-produced shocking videos of yet another atrocity meant to seed fear.

The ongoing war with Islamists devastating the Christian population in the Middle East involves diverse enemy audiences like ISIS, supportive Islamic governments, captive Muslim societies, a sympathetic Muslim diaspora, and the underlying Islamic ideology.

The West successfully fought an ideological war with the Soviet Union. Winning the Cold War took the employment of the various instruments of national power (diplomatic, information, military, and economic). The same would be necessary to win an ideological war with Islam's audiences. However, at this point, the West and especially the pro-Muslim Obama administration is not about to wage such a war, but the global Christian community is already engaged and moving rapidly in that direction.

The global Christian community must do what it can to fight Islamic ideology, and that includes some form of information operations. Information operations are analogous to a political campaign—presenting a coherent message that convinces an audience(s) to be sympathetic to one candidate and to oppose another.

It is instructive to consider how the military views information operations. The U.S. military's Joint Publication 3-13, *Information Operations*, defines the term as "the application, integration, and synchronization of information related capabilities to influence, disrupt, corrupt, or usurp the decision making of target audiences to create a desired effect to support achievement of an objective."[302]

How can the global Christian community use information operations to help Christians in the Middle East? There are four ways that will help, which parallel the military's definition.

First, there is a massive hunger for truth and receptivity for the gospel of Jesus Christ in the Middle East. Part of a Christian information operations campaign ought to be the use of social media to reach out to Muslims in the name of Christ to share the gospel.

Tom Doyle, author and Middle East expert, cited the case of a young Saudi woman who came to Christ through the Internet, which illustrates the power of social media. The young Saudi woman never met another Christian face to face, explained Doyle. One day, her brother who worked for the Saudi secret police noticed something different about his sister. "Why are you so happy?" he asked. And he asked suspiciously, "Are you a Christian?" She acknowledged Christ as her Savior. "You have two hours and then we will kill you," her brother told the girl. She went to her room and wrote a poem, which in part says: "May the Lord guide you Muslims that you might love others. We follow Jesus the messiah."[303]

The girl's brother murdered her as promised, and then he lit her body on fire after removing her tongue for speaking the truth.

Doyle said that when Muslims in the Middle East come to faith in Jesus Christ, they must ask themselves two tough questions: "Am I willing to be persecuted for my faith?" and "Am I willing to die for Jesus?" In spite of such dire consequences for accepting Jesus, according to Doyle, more Muslims than ever before are coming to Christ.

Too often, the problem isn't the Muslim's receptivity to the gospel, but the Christian's fear of sharing Christ, even via social media. Doyle reminds us that the Bible calls on Christians three hundred times not to fear. We are called to eschew fear and hate and to love our enemies.

Second, expose the lies of Islam. The media in the Arab world is strictly controlled by autocratic, Islam-influenced regimes. Christians should counter the constant stream of lies and distortions with an information operation to influence Muslim people to turn on their governments and their hate-spewing imams.

Doubting Christians should turn to a great source of Islamic media analysis. The Middle East Research Institute chronicles the hate-spewing,

Islamic-favoring media and the almost daily diatribes of hatred coming from mosques across the region. Visit http://www.memri.org/ to view videos and their translations as well as to see the latest articles distorting truth.

Third, use information operations to create a global backlash against Islamic extremism and stop their use of social media to recruit vulnerable youth. This will require Christians to aggressively seek vulnerable Muslims in their communities to win them to Christ before they are radicalized by the likes of ISIS.

Finally, encourage governments to use their electronic surveillance and cyber-attacking tools to find, monitor, and then shut down Islamic extremist activities.

Defeating the Islamic ideology is very difficult and could take a long time, as demonstrated by the West's decades-long Cold War. The global Christian community must play a critical role, even if the politically correct governments abdicate their responsibility.

PROTECTING NONCOMBATANTS

Christians are literally dying to get out of the Middle East. There are a variety of ways to help Christians escape persecution—but don't count on the Obama administration.

Christian leaders working with Middle East refugees provide sobering accounts of the sad situation facing Christians seeking to escape persecution. Those Christians at greatest risk are the Muslim background believers (MBB), because there is no safe place for them in the region. One Christian leader told this author about a Saudi woman who came to Christ and later escaped to Lebanon, at which point her family put a bounty on her "infidel" head. As she approached the U.S. Embassy in Beirut, according to a knowledgeable source in Lebanon, "She saw the bounty hunters and never went for her interview. She assumed that someone in the embassy tipped off the hunters."

Another Saudi who converted to Christianity also came to the U.S. Embassy in Beirut. According to a knowledgeable source in Lebanon, "She was told [by a U.S. Embassy official] that if they gave her entrance to the U.S., since she is an MBB, it would appear that the U.S. was giving preferential treatment to Christians." That statement seems odd but not surprising, because the Obama administration gives preference to Muslims to emigrate from the Middle East.

Last fall, WorldNetDaily reported Syrians would be the next big wave of Muslim refugees coming to the U.S., an estimated seventy-five thousand Syrian refugees over the next five years. Evidently, the U.S. accepts Middle East refugees only cleared by the U.N. High Commissioner on Refugees (UNHCR).

The State Department announced that it will accept nine thousand UNHCR-cleared refugees from Syria in 2015, but none will be Christian. The U.S. will only take those Syrians who are "persecuted by their government." Clearly, Christians are being killed by ISIS and other Muslim rebels, not by the Syrian government. So Christians must go to the back of the line and besides, the United Nations decides who the U.S. even considers for immigration, an organization well known for its socialist, anti-Christian, anti-Jewish, and anti-American actions.

"There is no doubt the majority of Syrians to be admitted to the U.S. will be Muslims because it would be unlikely there would be a 'security risk' with the Christians," according to Ann Corcoran with Refugee Resettlement Watch.[304]

Christians caught in the Islamist crossfire aren't as endangered as Muslims threatened by the Syrian government. So they must be sacrificed, because the Obama administration considers Muslims threatened by Assad better immigration candidates. This view is reminiscent of the tricks President Franklin Roosevelt's State Department played with the Jews seeking to flee Nazi Germany.

Roosevelt's State Department made it virtually impossible at the time for German Jews to provide the extensive documentation required to obtain a visa. Below is the actual list of documents a Jew was required to provide when seeking a visa to enter the U.S.[305]

- Five copies of the visa application
- Two copies of the applicant's birth certificate
- Quota number (establishing the applicant's place on the waiting list)

In addition, a Jew was required to have two sponsors:

- Close relatives of the prospective immigrant were preferred
- The sponsors were required to be US citizens or to have permanent resident status, and they were required to have completed and notarized six copies of an Affidavit of Support and Sponsorship

Supporting documents required included.

- Certified copy of most recent federal tax return
- Affidavit from a bank regarding applicant's accounts
- Affidavit from any other responsible person regarding other assets (affidavit from sponsor's employer or statement of commercial rating)
- Certificate of Good Conduct from German Police authorities, including two copies of each:
  - Police dossier
  - Prison record
  - Military record

Other government records required about the individual included:

- Affidavits of Good Conduct (after September 1940) from several responsible disinterested persons

- Physical examination at U.S. consulate
- Proof of permission to leave Germany (imposed September 30, 1939)
- Proof that prospective immigrant had booked passage to the Western hemisphere (imposed September 1939)

According to religion-based Middle East and North Africa immigration statistics, the U.S. doesn't favor Christian immigration in spite of significant persecution. In fact, nearly twice as many Muslims as Christians were granted visas to emigrate to the U.S. over the past twenty years.

The most lopsided part of the disparity in Christian versus Muslim immigration from the Middle East and North Africa is in terms of the percentages. The overall percentage of Muslims legally emigrating from that region increased from 35 percent to 47 percent of the total, whereas for the same region and period, Christian immigration remained flat, 2 percent to 3 percent of the overall Christian immigration. Meanwhile, immigration from the Middle East and North Africa over the same period doubled. Further, even though Christians are by far the most persecuted religious group in the overwhelmingly Muslim region (Middle East and North Africa), far fewer Christians (between 254,000 and 381,000) were permitted to legally immigrate than Muslims (527,000) over the twenty-year period.[306]

Based on State Department policy, it would appear that the disparity in religion-based immigration will continue to favor Muslims for the foreseeable future. So how can the global Christian community help Middle Eastern Christians emigrate? There is a legal way and a not-so-legal way.

The legal immigration route is the most preferred, but moves at a pace set by state bureaucracies. We saw how the U.S. made immigrating virtually impossible for Jews, and plainly, the Obama administration is putting in place similar restrictions for Middle East Christians today.

Christians need to lobby their respective governments to streamline the visa-granting process and increase the number of Christians their governments will permit. Further, Christians must be prepared to help the immigrating Christians with the means to sustain them once they arrive to include money and jobs. This will require sacrifice for the body of Christ.

The alternative to legal immigration is an illegal approach, but as Dr. King said, "There are just laws, and there are unjust laws." Immigration laws that favor Muslim over Christian immigrants are unjust laws. But Christians who choose to violate those laws must be prepared to be held to account for their infraction.

Christians can establish an underground railroad much like Christians did in the American South before the Civil War to help fugitive slaves escape to the North. The South lost one hundred thousand slaves between 1810 and 1850 thanks to the so-called Underground Railroad.[307]

The Underground Railroad, named after the emerging steam railroads at the time, was a secret network of people who provided hiding places, food, and often transportation to fugitives trying to escape slavery. As the fugitives traveled, they were provided directions for the safest route to the North.

Those who helped the slaves escape were "conductors," and the stops along their escape route were called "stations" and "depots." Conductors helped the escaping slaves get from one station to the next, often traveling with the escapee, and then handed the fugitive to the next conductor. "Engineers" were the leaders who provided the slaves food, shelter, and money, as well as hid the slaves from those trying to catch them.

Christians could establish a similar "underground railway" today to help fellow believers escape the persecution in the Middle East. The exact mechanisms for such a railway could vary—air, land, and sea—and selecting the most desperate will be a challenge, but likely the MBB will be near the top. Further, the "stations" and "conductors" would likely be different for those leaving Syria than those trying to escape Iran.

Once the immigrating Christian arrives, no matter how (air, land, sea), he must decide whether to seek permanent status by filing for political asylum or, if the person arrived through illegal means, he must decide whether to remain an illegal immigrant and blend into the society. Clearly in the U.S. today, that is not such a chore, but not something glorifying to our Lord.

CONCLUSION

A review of the Muslim mindset provides a helpful understanding of the Christians' enemy, Islamists. That understanding is instructive on how to deal with the threat of Islamic thought and behavior in the Middle East, Europe, and at home. However, it is also crystal clear that President Obama has set the policy for dealing with Christian refuges and aiding the Christians who stay behind in a direction that will mean an increased danger to America and the Middle East Christians. All Christians must be called to take action to defeat this wrongheaded policy and turn the ship of state in the direction of what God will bless.

CHAPTER 14

POLITICALLY ACTIVE CHRISTIANS AND MIDDLE EAST GENOCIDE

Christians should participate in the "Never Submit" campaign to help save fellow believers in the Middle East and possibly bring America back from the brink of moral self-destruction. Such a campaign requires Christian Americans to engage their government and political campaigns for the glory of God.

A "Never Submit"-like campaign to influence government and the political process is a bold plan, given that most Christians today are either too afraid to buck the secular culture, too distracted by their over-busy lives, and/or don't believe Christians should play in politics. This misguided and sad state of affairs was predicted by a French lawyer nearly two centuries ago.

In the 1830s, Alexis de Tocqueville, a French low-level judge, made a remarkable, eight-year journey through America to observe democracy in action. That journey was chronicled in de Tocqueville's book entitled *Democracy in America*, which turned out to be "perhaps the greatest commentary ever written about any culture by any person at any time."[308]

De Tocqueville probed into every aspect of American culture with particular emphasis on the role of the American citizen. "No novelty struck me more vividly...than the equality of conditions," de Tocqueville wrote, a reference to how Americans were treated equally, a strange concept for a European accustomed to the rigid hierarchical aristocratic society in Europe.[309]

Part of America's uniqueness was her deep respect for law, according to de Tocqueville. He observed that Americans held the power to change the laws they disliked while participating in law enforcement, a strange dichotomy from the Frenchman's perspective.

He was especially concerned that in America's democracy, the majority is always considered right. De Tocqueville believed the majority could learn to abuse that power, thus creating the "tyranny of the majority," a phrase adopted from the title for chapter 8 in *Democracy in America*. For example, de Tocqueville observed that the American white majority discouraged free blacks from voting, evidence of the intolerance of the majority for minority rights. Further, to be fair to the text, de Tocqueville also expressed the view, "I do not think that the white race and the black race will come to live on an equal footing anywhere."[310]

The Frenchman warns that the equality-focused Americans might eventually abandon their interest and involvement in self-government. That diminished involvement by citizens would create an expansive government that would produce "a network of petty, complicated rules," said de Tocqueville. He feared that American equality would morph into a new form of slavery—citizen slaves answering to government.[311]

One symptom of the citizens' dwindling interest in government that de Tocqueville describes is that society's best men avoid elected office. He observed that too often those serving in public office were the most corrupt and least educated—such as then President Andrew Jackson, whom de Tocqueville described as a "man of violent character and middling capacities."

It is worth noting that de Tocqueville referenced the significant role Christianity played in public life at the time. Although he acknowledged by the time of his visit in the 1830s that "America has already become much weaker" in terms of its original "Puritan rigor," he called attention to a late-nineteenth-century law passed by the Massachusetts legislature that forced citizens to observe Sunday as a day for worship and reflection. The law's preamble states: "Sunday observance is in the public interest…it leads men to reflect upon the duties of life and the errors to which humanity is so prone." The law explicitly closed all shops, prohibited most travel on Sunday, and imposed a monetary fine for those who regularly missed church services.[312]

The Frenchman also noted that American politics and Christianity were inseparable at the time. De Tocqueville wrote that the English Americans "brought to the New World a Christianity that I cannot portray better than by calling it democratic and republican: this will singularly favor the establishment of the republic and of democracy in public affairs. From the onset, politics and religion found themselves in order, and they have not ceased to be so since."[313]

De Tocqueville concludes *Democracy in America* with a sobering prediction: "It depends on themselves [Americans] whether equality is to lead to servitude or freedom, knowledge or barbarism, prosperity or wretchedness."[314]

CHRISTIANS CALLED TO POLITICAL ACTION

Juxtapose de Tocqueville's prediction about the possible outcomes for America's democracy experiment with biblical injunctions for Christians to participate in the political process. Unfortunately, de Tocqueville's prediction is coming true, which leaves America with servitude, barbarism, and wretchedness—a result in part attributable to the parting of "politics and religion" in public affairs.

More than a century later, Dr. Martin Luther King Jr. warned American Christians not to abandon their biblical responsibility to engage in public affairs (government). The Baptist pastor called Christians to stand for justice in civil society, something evidently lost since de Tocqueville's time. King warned: "The church must be reminded that it is not the master or the servant of the state, but rather the conscience of the state. It must be the guide and the critic of the state, and never its tool."[315]

Christians participate in America's political process in order, as Dr. King said, to be "the conscience of the state." When they are rightly informed and motivated, they change the character of the political debate and often the course of government. Further, Richard Doster, the editor of *byFaith*, a publication of the Presbyterian Church in America, wrote an essay on the issue in which he said: "They [Christians] bring the moral standards of God's kingdom into the civic realm and thereby become agents of his common grace—of his provision for those who believe as well as those who don't."[316]

"When God commands us to love our neighbors, He means to love them holistically," Doster elaborated. That means Christians care about their neighbors' spiritual and physical welfare as well as about government policies that protect all families, the unborn, and even fellow Christians caught in genocide far away.

Biblically-based Christians as opposed to cultural Christians (or "Christmas and Easter Christians") should exhibit a vision that "holds the world [and especially their government] accountable," according to Prison Fellowship Ministries founder Charles Colson. Further, they understand that changing society starts with changing the hearts of people first.[317]

Richard John Neuhaus, a Roman Catholic priest and prolific writer, describes the importance of "dual citizenship," the simultaneous citizenship in heaven and earth. Heavenly citizenship occurs once we are born again by faith in Jesus Christ (Matthew 4:17) and become "new creatures" (2 Corinthians 5:17) indwelt by God's Holy Spirit (1 Corinthians 3:16). Then the born-again Christians' focus turns to eternal things, and we consider ourselves ambassadors of Christ to the world (Ephesians 2:18–19).

Our earthly citizenship is associated with the place of our physical birth or our adopted homeland, and is evidenced by voting, obeying the law, being a good neighbor, and paying taxes, among a long list of other civic obligations. The coincidence of "dual citizenship"—heavenly and earthly—acts to compel the Christian citizen to give a moral account of his country by passing on the country's virtues "to citizens of the next generation" and, as theologian Carl Henry said, Christian citizens "work through civil authority for the advancement of justice and human good."

Doster identifies three important outcomes when "dual citizens" participate in politics.

First, Christians participating in politics keep their government accountable. God places Christians in positions where they are given the opportunity to counsel and/or confront secular leaders on issues of moral consequence. Daniel advised King Nebuchadnezzar (Daniel 4), Joseph advised Pharaoh (Genesis 41), Mordecai counseled King Aha-suerus (Esther 10), John the Baptist confronted King Herod (Luke 3), and Paul spoke to Governor Felix "about righteousness and self control and the coming judgment" (Acts 24). Untold numbers of Christians through the ages were divinely appointed to advise unsuspecting secular leaders; but to be useful, those believers had to take advantage of their appointments in spite of the obstacles placed in their paths.

Second, Christians bring transcendent (the most valuable and enduring) Christian values to our godless culture. Modern American culture is rapidly transforming into what German philosopher Fried-rich Nietzsche called the god-is-dead phenomenon. That phenomenon is evidenced by everyday Americans who do and say some of the most bizarre and immoral things, and yet they are not held accountable even by Christians who should know better and yet say nothing.

Chuck Colson clarified Nietzsche's concept: It isn't that God is dead, but that He is irrelevant. Colson said God was declared dead, "because we live, play, procreate, govern, and die as though he doesn't exist." After all, to make Him seem irrelevant, modern America removed God from classrooms and offices, tore down crosses, removed the Ten Command-dants from the public square, and so much more to the disgrace of this country, and yet so few Christians spoke up in protest.

When biblical Christians participate in the political process, they act as the proverbial salt and light of Matthew 5, introducing Christian values into the marketplace of ideas. Those values are derived from the teachings of Jesus such as love of God, fidelity in marriage, forgiveness of sins, and others that are communicated to the god-is-dead culture to temper the pervasive evil.

James Boice, the first president of Southern Baptist Theological Seminary, wrote, "Religious people are…the only citizens who actually advance the nation in the direction of justice and true righteousness." Colson said Christianity provides the transcendent moral influence on culture as well as a transcendent ordering of society.

Third, Christians provide a restraining influence on government. The church, not government, promulgates a moral vision for the country. Doster illustrates the point by citing the teaching of Southern Presbyterian Pastor Robert L. Dabney, who taught that Christians "should bring their Christian conscience, 'enlightened by God's word,' into the civic realm. Christians need to be involved, Dabney believed, not to force their morals onto society as a whole, but to advocate for justice, show respect for life, and support the powerless."

These outcomes are reason enough for the Christian to participate in the politics of government. However, the Bible also assumes that Christians will participate in government because it instructs them on how to get involved in the world for Christ.

Their involvement is critical, because "Christianity is the soul of Western civilization. And when the soul is gone, the body putrefies," wrote Christopher Dawson, a twentieth-century British culture and Christendom author. That's why Christians must be responsible "dual citizens" by getting involved in government to address moral and justice issues to secular leaders in order to influence their policies on morally charged issues such as slavery, abortion, and, for that matter, America's foreign policy impacting Christian genocide.

Doster concludes his essay with an exhortation that Christians must "plunge into social and political problems, not with the hope of ushering in Christ's kingdom, but to provide a glimpse of something better, to exhibit our hope for what's to come." But American Christians face a barrier to taking the plunge into today's god-is-irrelevant culture.

There is a danger that American Christians might be robbed of their obligation to "plunge into social and political problems," especially if President Obama and his progressive allies get their way. Catholic Cardinal Raymond Burke issued a warning about the so-called progressive threat to the Christian's religious obligation to engage government.

> [President Obama] wants to restrict the exercise of the freedom of religion to freedom of worship; that is, he holds that one is free to act according to his conscience within the confines of his place of worship but that, once the person leaves the place of worship, the government can constrain him to act against his rightly-formed conscience, even in the most serious of moral questions.[318]

Retired U.S. Army Lieutenant General William G. "Jerry" Boykin, former deputy undersecretary of defense for intelligence under President Bush and the current executive vice president at the Washington-based Family Research Council, agrees with Cardinal Burke. "The church today is accepting something our founders never intended. It is accepting the freedom of worship rather than freedom of religion. That's what Hitler did to the church in Germany," Boykin said.[319]

Hitler persuaded the German church to keep its moral views inside the sanctuary and out of the public square. That's why, as mentioned earlier, Dietrich Bonheoffer broke from the German Christian (Deutsche Christen) movement to form the Pfarrernotbund (the forerunner to the Confessing Church). General Boykin warns that if the church in America accepts freedom of worship over freedom of religion, as did the German Christian church, "it will have no moral authority and won't be able to influence anything in the public discourse."

Therefore, American Christians must quickly grasp the initiative before their voices are silenced by progressives like Obama who could use law or cultural manipulation. That's why the body of Christ in America needs to launch a "Never Submit"-like campaign that provides, as Doster wrote, "a glimpse of something better" for the culture by calling fellow Christians across America to lobby their government and engage political campaigns to address Christian genocide in the Middle East and by association redirect America to Christ.

What follows is an agenda of activities for the "Never Submit" campaign on behalf of fellow believers facing genocide. The campaign agenda focuses on the two federal government departments best equipped to play decisive roles in the fight to stop Christian genocide in the Middle East: the State and Defense departments.

CALL TO ACTION AT THE STATE DEPARTMENT

The State Department oversees foreign policy for the president, who is constitutionally responsible for setting the course of the nation's foreign affairs. Therefore, the president working through the State Department has many tools with which to fight Christian genocide in the Middle East.

First, the State Department staffs U.S. embassies across the world with appointees and Foreign Service officers who represent the president in all interactions with foreign governments. It should be the policy of the U.S. government to address religious freedom in every meeting with those foreign parties.

Todd Nettleton with Voice of the Martyrs said, "The biggest thing State can do is make [religious freedom] part of the agenda all the time." It is important that the U.S. be seen talking about religious freedom so other nations understand it is a priority.

General Boykin expects the State Department to do more than talk. He wants the American government to pressure Middle East governments to pass laws that protect Christians from persecution, and he would use diplomatic and economic pressure, withholding foreign military sales[320] as well as all other forms of U.S. aid to compel those governments. At the end of the day, Boykin said, "They will be Muslim and hate Christians...[after all] we really can [only] expect to modify their behavior, not change their theology."

Second, the U.S. is a party to the 1948 Convention on the Prevention and Punishment of the Crime of Genocide. Christians should push the government to declare the violence against Middle East Christians as genocide.[321]

It took the U.S. forty years to finally ratify the genocide convention. The Genocide Convention Implementation Act of 1987 binds the U.S. to the provisions of the 1948 convention. Specifically, if a party to the convention [like the U.S.] determines that genocide is occurring such as what is now happening with Christians in the Middle East, then that party is obligated to undertake appropriate actions to prevent it and to punish the guilty parties.

Unfortunately, the convention has done little to prevent or stop genocide in the past, such as the slaughter in Rwanda that claimed eight hundred thousand lives. In fact, the U.S. more than once avoided labeling the Rwanda slaughter as genocide, which by treaty would have triggered the obligation to respond under Article 1 of the convention.[322]

One such effort to avoid labeling Rwanda as genocide occurred in 1994 with State Department spokeswoman Christine Shelly. She floundered when asked whether Rwanda was experiencing genocide. Shelly said "acts of genocide" were occurring in Rwanda, but she wondered out loud how many "acts of genocide" constituted genocide.[323]

Finally, in 1998, President Clinton went to Rwanda "... to pay the respects of my nation to all who suffered and all who perished in the Rwandan genocide." Clinton used his remarks to call upon world governments to accept blame for failing to act against what was clearly genocide. "The international community, together with nations in Africa, must bear its share of responsibility for this tragedy, as well," Clinton said. He continued, "We did not act quickly enough after the killing began. We should not have allowed the refugee camps to become safe havens for the killers. We did not immediately call these crimes by their rightful name: genocide."[324]

President Obama is repeating President Clinton's failure to take immediate, decisive action when the killing began. Sadly, in spite of the mass killing of Christians in Iraq and Syria, President Obama has yet to declare the Middle East situation genocide, perhaps to avoid triggering our treaty obligations. Even President Obama's draft legislation requesting authority to use military force against ISIS employed deliberately vague language, perhaps to avoid treaty obligations. That language acknowledges ISIS has committed "despicable acts of violence," but then falls short of declaring a genocide, stating "whereas ISIL [ISIS] has threatened genocide and committed vicious acts of violence against religious and ethnic minority groups, including Iraqi Christian, Yezidi, and Turkmen populations."[325]

Clearly, the Obama administration is waiting until Christian bodies are piled high before declaring the situation a genocide as it was in Rwanda. Time is wasting, which is why American Christians must immediately insist that the president make a simple declaration that many Middle Eastern Christians face genocide and then take appropriate action.

Third, in 1998, Congress passed and then President Bill Clinton signed the International Religious Freedom Act (IRFA), which strengthened U.S. religious freedom advocacy on "behalf of individuals persecuted in foreign countries on account of religion." The act established an ambassador-at-large for international religious freedom, a commission on international religious freedom, and an advisor on such matters to the national Security Council. The major flaw in the act is the lack of teeth.[326]

Title IV of the act outlines presidential actions available to promote religious freedom and if necessary to punish countries that engage in or tolerate violations. Unfortunately, taking action against violators is left to the discretion of the president, and in the case of President Obama, he seldom if ever uses the act to advance religious freedom anywhere in the world.

A future president should use the act to punish violators, and the 114th Congress prepared language to strengthen the act. Congressman Chris Smith (Republican, New Jersey) is leading the effort to amend the act to "advance religious freedom globally through enhanced diplomacy, training, counterterrorism, and foreign assistance efforts, and through stronger and more flexible political responses to religious freedom violations and violent extremism worldwide." Christians should encourage their congressional delegations to support a tougher IRFA.

Once amended, the IRFA won't go far enough, according to some of the nation's leading Christian aid leaders, however. Franklin Graham with Samaritan's Purse said we must adjust our attitude toward some of the worst violators of religious freedom like Saudi Arabia and Iran.

Graham said, "The Saudis are supposedly our friends [but] they are friends who kill all Christians and they destroy all Christian churches." General Boykin would pull out all stops on the Saudis because of their anti-Christian persecution: Use economic penalties, trade agreements, and leverage foreign military sales.

Tom Farr, who worked for years on religious freedom inside the State Department, said the only way to get Middle Eastern governments to protect Christians is to use "an interest based approach." State must use "not just carrots and sticks," Farr explained, but demonstrate to the Middle East regimes that "to have religious freedom is to have a stable democracy, sustained economic growth and security." He believes such arguments might entice countries like Egypt to "opt for stable democracy," which begins by granting full equality to Egypt's large Coptic Christian population.

Fourth, another approach Christians ought to advocate is the creation of a Leahy-like law for religious freedom. There are two laws on the books named after Vermont Senator Patrick Leahy that "prohibit the use of state funds for assistance or defense funds for any training, equipment, or other assistance to a foreign security force unit where there is credible information that such unit or individual in the unit has committed gross human rights violations."

Christians should call for similar language in a new law or as an adjutant to IRFA for use with countries that commit "gross religious freedom violations" like Saudi Arabia. Under such a provision, no U.S. department could engage in favorable action of any kind with a nation found to commit "gross religions freedom violations" and only modify those restrictions as the violator nation changes its treatment of religious freedom.[327]

Fifth, the State Department should modify its immigration policy to rescue more Christians facing genocide. The Obama administration currently restricts Middle East immigration to mostly Muslims facing government-sponsored threats like Syria. Such policy may well mean America is also importing an anti-Christian mindset, which will further erode chances of the "Never Submit" campaign plan and increase home-grown terrorism.

Franklin Graham recommends a very different approach. For national security reasons, he would stop all "Muslims from coming in [to the U.S.] while there is a war." He believes Europe should do the same out of concern for regional safety. Graham would issue visas for Christians facing genocide to emigrate.

Christians in the war-torn parts of the Middle East have no place to go. The Muslims can relocate to other Muslim countries, but not the Christians. American Christians should pressure the government to stop the flow of Muslims and open the floodgates to Middle East Christians with no place to flee.

Finally, encourage Muslim leaders who oppose extremists and embrace democratic views. Tom Farr, the former State Department official who serves today as the director of the Religious Freedom Project at Georgetown University, said the U.S. needs to help courageous leaders like Egyptian President Abdel Fattah el-Sisi, who called on Islamic clerics to do some self-examination.

President el-Sisi spoke to a gathering of Islamic leaders in January 2015 to encourage a religious revolution in the Islamic Middle East. "I say and repeat, again, that we are in need of a religious revolution," el-Sisi said. "You imams are responsible before Allah. The entire world is waiting on you. The entire world is waiting for your word…because the Islamic world is being torn, it is being destroyed, it is being lost. And it is being lost by our own hands."[328]

He continued:

We need a revolution of the self, a revolution of consciousness and ethics to rebuild the Egyptian person—a person that our country will need in the near future.

It's inconceivable that the thinking that we hold most sacred should cause the entire Islamic world to be a source of anxiety, danger, killing and destruction for the rest of the world. Impossible that this thinking—and I am not saying the religion—I am saying this thinking.

This is antagonizing the entire world. It's antagonizing the entire world! Does this mean that 1.6 billion people (Muslims) should want to kill the rest of the world's inhabitants—that is 7 billion—so that they themselves may live? Impossible![329]

President el-Sisi is one of the few Middle East leaders waking up to the need for radical transformation. He and the few other like-minded regional leaders such as Jordan's King Abdullah II ought to be encouraged, which will require the West to come alongside such leaders.

How can we encourage such a transformation? It is likely the private-sector American Christians will have to step up to the plate. What follows is an example of just that—although perhaps it was a decade too soon.

Back in 2007 and 2008, Bill Gertz, a reporter with the *Washington Times* and editor of the *Washington Free Beacon*, and this author approached the Bush administration at the undersecretary of defense and state level to advocate an approach that would encourage efforts to counter Islamist extremism through a religious reformation in the Middle East. Then Undersecretary of State Karen Hughes was receptive to our recommendations, but she didn't want to take the lead. However, then Undersecretary of Defense Douglas Feith dismissed our ideas as naïve. Of course, while the Bush administration toughened homeland security and fought wars in the Middle East, it arguably did nothing helpful to attack the underlying problem with Islam.

In a nutshell, we told Hughes and Feith that "the key to countering Islamist extremism lies in developing and implementing an ideological solution. This could involve nothing less than a religious reformation." We recommended that both government and the private sector have roles in the strategy to defeat Islamic extremism. People of faith must take the lead, however. Then we advocated the creation of a network of centers for nonviolent faith to "protect the good guys [like el-Sisi and Abdullah], and stop the others."

Those briefings took place just as U.S. forces began the surge into Iraq's Anbar Province to halt Islamic extremism. We told the secretaries at the time that "whatever the answer, a long-term program is needed to provide a theological and practical counter to Islamist extremism." Then we recommended waging an ideological, or ideas-based, war against Islamist extremism.

Now, almost a decade later, the problem we identified to the Bush administration officials is much worse, yet our government seems totally clueless about a solution. It is past time for Christian Americans to engage the political processes (again) by offering recommendations and demanding solutions, especially as Christians are dying at the hands of Islamists.

CALL TO ACTION AT THE DEFENSE DEPARTMENT

Christians should insist that the Defense Department take on three critical missions. It must rid itself of bankrupt political correctness in order to appropriately focus on the correct enemy. It must defeat ISIS and

ISIS' franchises, and it must help secure Middle East Christians facing grave danger before it is too late.

First, the Defense Department needs to be scrubbed clean of political correctness so it can properly identify the enemy—Islamists. Thanks to both Presidents Bush and Obama, the Pentagon refuses to identify Islamists as the enemy, Muslims who rigidly follow their religion's ideology accompanied by violence. Rather, the military brass under orders pretends the enemy is Islam's hijackers. Both presidents have repeatedly asserted, "Islam is a religion of peace." No, Islamists aren't hijackers; they are just orthodox followers of Islamic teachings.

Failure to properly identify the enemy impacts virtually every decision the Pentagon makes about the conduct of the global war with Islamic terrorists. Perhaps if the political correctness is removed under future leadership, then steel-trap military minds can get down to the business of focusing on the real enemy to help stop the Christian genocide in the Middle East as well as a host of other threats against America.

The 2008 case of U.S. Army Reserve Major Stephen Coughlin best illustrates how political correctness and a strong pro-Islam bent at the Defense Department endanger America's national security.

On January 3, 2008, Major Coughlin, a part time soldier, was serving as a civilian contractor with the Pentagon's Joint Staff J2 (intelligence) when his company told him that his contract would not be renewed because he had become too "politically hot." Reportedly, Mr. Hesham Islam, the senior advisor for international affairs to then deputy secretary of defense Gordon England, asked Coughlin to "soften his message" regarding his research for the J2 on Islamic doctrine. Coughlin refused, and then Islam was reportedly heard referring to Coughlin as a "Christian zealot with a poison pen."[330] That was shortly before Coughlin lost his job.

The Coughlin-Islam story broke into the national news, prompting the Foundation for Defense of Democracies (FDD) to further research the matter. That led to their publication of an article, "Questions for the Pentagon: Who Is Hesham Islam?" That article indicates that Hesham Islam was England's point man for the Pentagon's outreach programs to

Muslim groups such as the Islamic Society of North America, or ISNA. Both Islam and England attended ISNA conventions and hosted ISNA delegations at the Pentagon.[331]

Steve Emerson, executive director of the Investigative Project on Terrorism, tracks Islamic extremist networks. He described Hesham Islam as "an Islamist with a pro-Muslim Brotherhood bent who has brought in groups to the Pentagon who have been unindicted co-conspirators."[332]

ISNA, according to FDD, was named by the Department of Justice as a member of the U.S. Muslim Brotherhood and an unindicted coconspirator in the 2008 case of the Holy Land Foundation that allegedly provided millions of dollars to Hamas, the Palestinian terrorist group.

This author met with Major Coughlin in early 2008 as the issue of Coughlin's firing was swirling in the press. Coughlin reviewed his research with this author, which appeared to be faithful to the Islamic scriptures, and his analysis reflected great objectivity, as expected from a lawyer. It was evident then and now to this author that Mr. Islam's "soften" directive to Coughlin was totally political and ran contrary to the nation's best security interests.

Perhaps Coughlin's best work on the threat posed by Islamic teachings is his thesis that was submitted to the National Defense Intelligence College in July 2007, "To Our Great Detriment: Ignoring What Extremists Say about Jihad." The thesis abstract (below) demonstrates how dangerous political correctness at the Pentagon has come to threaten our national security, especially when it comes to Islam.

In comments made at the National Defense University on 1 December 2005, Chairman of the Joint Chiefs of Staff General Peter Pace explained to his audience the importance of "understand[ing] the nature of the enemy" if we hope to defeat jihadi extremists. Comparing our situation today, with that faced by an earlier generation who had to deal with the reality of the Nazi threat, General Pace suggested a simple solution to complying with his injunction: "read what our enemies have said. Remember Hitler.... He said in writing exactly what his plan was that we collectively ignored to our great detriment (emphasis added)." Just as we ignored Hitler's articulation of his strategic doctrine in Mein Kampf, so too are we on the verge of suffering a similar fate today, if we fail to seriously assess the extremist threat based on jihadi strategic doctrine.

To address this challenge, I pose three fundamental questions:

- Why have we failed to do a doctrine-based threat assessment?
- What is the doctrinal basis of the jihadi threat?
- How can we come to understand the jihadi threat?

From these three questions, the thesis concludes that Islamic law forms the doctrinal basis of the jihadi threat that can only be understood through an unconstrained review of the Islamic law of jihad. The failure to undertake a doctrine-based assessment of the enemy reflects a decision not to do so. Accepting assurances from moderate Muslims that Islam had nothing to do with the events of 11 September 2001, President Bush made policy statements holding Islam harmless for the actions done by "extremists" in Islam's name. To accommodate, threat analysis was replaced by an analytical process that focuses almost exclusively on the war's imputed underlying causes. For those questions relating to Islam, the approach has been to defer to moderates and cultural experts for the answers we rely on to make WOT (War on Terror) related decisions. Because only the war's underlying causes are the ones deemed relevant, the enemy's stated doctrine is dismissed as irrelevant. In the WOT, however, the enemy unambiguously states that he fights jihad in furtherance of Islamic causes. Denial of an Islamic basis to a war that the enemy says is grounded in Islamic doctrines of jihad reflects the acceptance of enormous risk.

As it turns out, the jihadis are able to find a doctrinal basis for their notions of jihad in Islamic law. A review of Islamic law from modern treatments to the classical authorities reveals an interlocking, overlapping, seamless web of Islamic law on jihad that is uncommonly unified and consistent in **defining jihad as warfare against non-Muslims to establish the religion**. (emphasis added) This legal definition of jihad remains consistent through the 1400 year span that incorporates the contributions of the authorities relied on in the thesis.

Because our inability to understand the enemy stems from a decision not to know him, this thesis recommends the return to a threat analysis process as the methodology to analyze the enemy's stated doctrine. Because the enemy in the WOT states Islam as its doctrine, this means an unconstrained analysis of the Islamic law of jihad as found in the authoritative writings of recognized Islamic authorities. When this is done, we will quickly realize what we have ignored "to our great detriment."[333]

Coughlin's story illustrates how political correctness undermines our national security willfully ignoring Islam as the source of Islamist doctrine. This fact isn't lost on experienced hands who deal with Middle Eastern crises.

An American with extensive experience in the region said he has "no confidence in our government or military to know what's best" to do in the Middle East because "the U.S. lacks discernment." General Boykin said the U.S. is "not taking [the threat] seriously." But many Americans involved in relief operations in the Middle East interviewed for this book agreed on one thing: Our military must destroy ISIS.

Second, President Obama promised: "We will degrade, and ultimately destroy, ISIL [ISIS] through a comprehensive and sustained counter-terrorism strategy."[334] However, as General Boykin said, "We aren't doing enough."

Obama's strategy is to recruit regional partners to do the fighting while the U.S. supports with intelligence, logistics, and conducts air strikes. However, those so-called regional partners aren't stepping up to contain and defeat ISIS. That leads the outsider to ask: Can ISIS be defeated without U.S. boots on the ground?

It is noteworthy that Egyptian President el-Sisi answered that question: "It is understood that for the U.S. military to carry out their [anti-ISIS] mission, they need boots on the ground. This is one important aspect of how the mission can be successful."[335] However, there is no sign that Obama intends to commit sufficient U.S. forces to defeat ISIS, and neither are the regional powers (other than Iraq and Iran) showing any sign of stepping into the fight with ground troops. The implication is that ISIS will continue to conquer territory and kill more innocents.

Third, Christians must insist that the U.S. military secure Middle East Christians threatened by ISIS by helping to create enclaves and arm them to defend themselves. These issues were addressed in the previous chapter; however, the U.S. military ought to take the lead in both efforts and not wait for others. American Christians must pressure the government to lead.

General Boykin supports creating special enclaves guarded by multinational forces and arming Christians. "I would want someone to give me the opportunity to defend myself and my family" if threatened by extremists, Boykin explained. He would also provide Christian militia with intelligence and advisors, something only the group Sons of Liberty International is doing in the Nineveh Plain.

ENGAGE POLITICAL CAMPAIGNS

Politicians are most vulnerable to public interests when running for office. That is why Christians must work to influence political candidates regarding the issue of genocide in the Middle East.

First, Christians should provide political candidates with fact sheets about the issue. Those fact sheets must summarize the elements of genocide and point out America's treaty obligations vis-à-vis the 1948 convention. There must also be a fact sheet outlining the conditions now seen in the Middle East demonstrating the evidence of genocide and another must address actions the U.S. should take such as that outlined earlier in this chapter.

Second, Christians must insist that every political candidate for national office complete a survey on the issue and then Christians must publish those results. Here are some questions to consider for the survey.

1. What role does Islam play in our war with ISIS?
2. The Bush and Obama administrations referred to Islam as a "religion of peace." However, terror groups like ISIS and al-Qaeda take their fighting doctrine from Islam. Are we at war with Islam? Explain your answer.
3. The Middle East is very hostile to Christians. Many have been killed and hundreds of thousands fled their homes because of hostile action. Further, countries like Saudi Arabia do not allow Christians to practice their faith openly and other countries treat Christians as second-class citizens. What would you do to improve life for Christians in the Middle East?
4. Do you believe Christians in the Middle East face genocide? If so, what would you do to stop that genocide?
5. Do you favor a Leahy-like law that would prohibit the U.S. government from taking any favorable action with a foreign government found to persecute or allow the persecution of Christians?

Encourage Christians to use the survey responses to further engage the candidates and then to decide which candidates best satisfy the voter's interests. Widely circulate the survey results to inform voters about candidate positions regarding Christian genocide.

Third, Christians should insist that candidate platforms address genocide and the unacceptable persecution and discrimination against Christians in Middle East countries. Those platforms must outline specific actions the candidates will fulfill if elected, as well as who the candidates will appoint to oversee the execution of those platform promises.

CONCLUSION

American Christians have a moral obligation to participate in a "Never Submit" campaign that engages their government and politicians seeking national office in order to help save fellow believers in the Middle East and coincidentally help bring America back from the brink of moral self-destruction. This is not an option for those faithful to God's Word. What remains is to establish such a campaign under prominent leadership to include current and former Christian government and military leaders, well known religious leaders (such as Franklin Graham), and former residents of Muslim dominated countries who are Christians and can clearly articulate the facts of the genocide and the tenets of Islam.

CHAPTER 15

INDIVIDUALS, CHURCHES, AND COMMUNITIES

Vaccinating Against Failure in Middle East

A mericans must wake up to the fact that the fight with Islamists threatens their communities, and will only get worse if not properly and soon thoroughly countered. Therefore, besides those actions outlined in the previous three chapters, this chapter recommends that Christians and their neighbors take off the gloves of political correctness and put their hearts and minds in full gear. The most important future fight against Islam may be at the local level.

Islamist attacks have already come to America in the form of the 9/11 attacks on the Twin Towers, the Boston Marathon, Fort Hood, and other lesser publicized actions. Mosques are popping up across the nation—more than three thousand now—and demands for sharia law are heard in our largest cities. The threat is real, it is burgeoning, and it will not disappear on its own.

It is time for Christians, local churches, and their communities to aid in the defeat of the Islamist threat against Christians abroad before it comes any further to our neighborhoods. Simultaneously, we need to vaccinate American communities against Islamization, anticipating that

Middle East style atrocities and genocide of Christians could eventually happen here as well.

The perception that Islamic terrorism is growing for America is widespread, according to national polling. Americans are more concerned today than at any time in the last few years about the Islamic extremist threat to our homeland and, as a result, are willing to support committing U.S. ground troops once again to fight the terrorist enemy in the Middle East before it gets worse and perhaps comes here.

Specifically, an April 2015 CNN/ORC poll found that 68 percent of Americans say ISIS is a very serious threat, compared with just 39 percent who say so about Iran and 18 percent for China.[336] Other surveys by the *Washington Post* and *ABC News* show public support for air strikes against ISIS rose from 45 percent in June 2014 to 77 percent in February 2015.[337] Meanwhile, *CBS News* polling found support for committing ground troops grew from 39 percent in September 2014 to 57 percent in February 2015.[338]

Public polls also indicate rising concern about the possibility of terrorist attacks in America. Gallup finds that the segment of Americans who express a "great deal of concern" about the possibility of a terrorist attack on the U.S. has increased twelve points, from 39 percent to 51 percent since February 2014. Pew Center polling shows a sharp rise between July 2011 and September 2014 in the level of U.S. public concern about Islamic extremism around the world. In July 2011, 37 percent of respondents were "very concerned"; in September 2014, 62 percent were.[339]

The increasing concern fuels the willingness to spend more on national security. For the first time since 2002, Gallup found in February 2015 that a plurality of Americans (34 percent) feel the U.S. is spending too little on national defense.[340] During the past year, the proportion saying we spend too little grew by six points (from 28 percent to 34 percent), while the portion saying we spend too much declined from 37 percent to 32 percent. Today, the country is more polarized on the spending issue than at any time since 1981.

What explains the growing concern and support for overseas military action? William Galston of Brookings Institution offers a straightforward explanation for the increasing anxiety: "The widespread sense that chaos is overcoming order around the world in ways that directly threaten the American people appears to be reshaping public sentiment in the direction of a more muscular foreign and defense policy than the Obama administration has pursued up to now."[341]

The sense of widespread chaos is moving some politicians to make rather courageous declarations unheard of until now. One of the best examples was a frontal attack on Islam as an agent of extremism by a British political leader, which earned the inevitable negative response from the left.

In March 2015, British Home Secretary Theresa May unveiled a series of proposals aimed at combating Islamic extremism "in all its forms." May's proposals reflect a declaration of war against Islamists and provides a clear agenda of important actions which warrant a hearing in America.[342]

The home secretary called for many tough measures to curb the growing Islamic threat: Ban Islamic hate preachers, shut down extremist mosques, review whether sharia courts in England and Wales are compatible with British values, crack down on Islamic extremism in British prisons, monitor how police are responding to so-called Islamic honor crimes, and change the citizenship law to ensure that successful applicants respect British values.

Secretary May defined extremism in her hard-hitting speech on March 23, 2015. It is "the vocal or active opposition to fundamental British values, including democracy, the rule of law, individual liberty and the mutual respect and tolerance of different faiths and beliefs."

Then she singled out Islamic extremism for its radical behavior:

There is increasing evidence that a small but significant number of people living in Britain—almost all of whom are British citizens—reject our values. We have seen the Trojan Horse plot to take over state schools in Birmingham. Some concerns about religious supplementary schools. Widespread allegations of corruption, cronyism, extremism, homophobia and anti-Semitism in Tower Hamlets. Hate speakers invited to speak at British colleges and universities. Segregation by gender allowed at universities and even endorsed by Universities UK [a lobbying group representing British universities]. Charities and the generosity of the giving public abused by extremists. Examples of sharia law being used to discriminate against women. Thousands of "honor" crimes committed every year. And hundreds of British citizens who have traveled to fight in Syria and Iraq.

It's clear from these examples that extremism can take many forms. It can be ideological, or it can be driven by social and cultural norms that are contrary to British values and quite simply unacceptable. We have been clear all along that the Government's counter-extremism strategy must seek to defeat extremism in all its forms, but it's obvious from the evidence that the most serious and widespread form of extremism we need to confront is Islamist extremism.

Islamist extremists believe in a clash of civilizations. They promote a fundamental incompatibility between Islamic and Western values, an inevitable divide between "them and us." They demand a caliphate, or a new Islamic state, governed by a harsh interpretation of Sharia law. They utterly reject British and Western values, including democracy, the rule of law, and equality between citizens, regardless of their gender, ethnicity, religion or sexuality. They believe that it's impossible to be a good Muslim and a good British citizen. And they dismiss anybody who disagrees with them—including other Muslims—as "kafirs," or non-believers.

Extremism is not something that can just be ignored. It cannot be wished away. It must be tackled head on. Because where extremism takes root the consequences are clear. Women's rights are eroded. There is discrimination on the basis of race and sexuality. There is no longer equal access to the labor market, to the law, or to wider society. Communities become segregated and cut off from one another. Intolerance, hatred and bigotry become normalized. Trust is replaced by fear, reciprocity by envy, and solidarity by division.

But tackling extremism is also important because of its link to terrorism. Not all extremism leads to violence and not all extremists are violent, but there is without doubt a thread that binds the kind of extremism that promotes hatred and a sense of superiority over others to the actions of those who want to impose their beliefs on us through violence.

I know there are some people who disagree with me. They say what I describe as Islamist extremism is simply social conservatism. But if anybody else discriminated against women, denounced people on the basis of their religious beliefs, rejected the democratic process, attacked people on the basis of their sexuality, or gave a nod and a wink in favor of violence and terrorism, we wouldn't hesitate to challenge them or—if the law was broken—call for their prosecution and punishment.

The game is up. We will no longer tolerate your behavior. We will expose your hateful beliefs for what they are. Where you seek to spread hate, we will disrupt you. Where you break the law, we will prosecute you. Where you seek to divide us, we will stand united. And together, we will defeat you.

Predictably, May's strategy drew considerable opposition from the inevitable naysayers. Unfortunately, a similar strategy outlined by former Prime Minister Tony Blair in August 2005 was defeated. That strategy came in the wake of the London bombings that killed fifty-two and injured seven hundred. Like May, Blair at that time vowed to show that the "rules of the game are changing" for Islamic terrorists. But that plan died due to infighting within the Labour government and alleged threats to human rights laws.

May's strategy was hailed by Haras Rafig, the managing director of the Quilliam Foundation, a counter-extremism think tank. Rafig said in an interview with *Newsweek* magazine:

> For the lifetime of this coalition government we have had no published strategy on tackling the ideas and ideology behind non-violent extremism. We are still having the same conversations. We are still talking about Sharia law, still talking about learning more, still talking about tackling non-violent extremism, why aren't we doing it?[343]

May's speech is reminiscent of World War II, when a clear and present danger was presented by Winston Churchill among others to his fellow countrymen, but rejected. That rejection almost cost Great Britain total loss and inevitable subjugation to the Nazi regime.

America's problems with Islamists may not be as pronounced as those facing the British. However, the threats to our homeland are rapidly emerging and our political leaders with a few exceptions lack the backbone demonstrated by home minister May to say, much less do, what is necessary to arrest the problem.

It is time for America to not only learn from May, but to form a coalition to lead the Western world away from imminent cataclysmic events.

In the meantime, anxiety grows as our so-called leaders play golf.

That's why a groundswell of action must start at the community level with a massive vaccination campaign. Much like health service professionals call for mass vaccinations when a population faces an infectious disease like polio or smallpox, clear-eyed Americans must see the threat of Islamic extremism coming like an infectious disease to every community.

Below is a list of vaccination targets to protect American communities. Ask yourself whether or not your community is doing enough in each of the following areas, and if not, then take action.

VACCINATE CITIZENS FROM
MISINFORMATION AND IGNORANCE

Christian pastors must inform and call their congregations to action. Former Congressman Frank Wolf, a champion for the persecuted, said the American "church is apathetic" and "silent" about the situation in the Middle East.[344] Wolf cited Ecclesiastes 4:1 to emphasize his view of the American church:

> So I returned, and considered all the oppressions that are done under the sun: and behold the tears of such as were oppressed, and they had no comforter; and on the side of their oppressors there was power; but they had no comforter.

"The church totally ignores the issue of Christian persecution," General Boykin said in agreement with Congressman Wolf.[345] Open Door's Curry was less blunt: "Many pastors have yet to fully realize the impact of persecution and the potential threat to the West."[346]

Faith McDonnell, director, Religious Liberty Program with the Institute on Religion and Democracy, is more nuanced. She said Christians in the U.S. don't know enough about the crisis because "the Western churches have their own agenda,…[and] they ignore the biblical mandate to speak out and support Christians being persecuted."[347]

McDonnell continued: "So many are not familiar enough with the tenets of Islam and they don't know how to approach the subject without sounding like Islamphobes." She suggested that some pastors may in fact avoid speaking out about Islam for fear of being arrested.

Pastors need to be bold like Dallas pastor, Robert Jeffress. The pastor told *Fox News'* Bill O'Reilly, "You have to tell the truth, Bill. And the truth is, Islam is a false religion built on a false book written by a false prophet."[348]

Jeffress boldly told O'Reilly: "Fact: Mohammed, the founder of

Islam, was a man of violence who committed all kinds of atrocities, including ordering six hundred Jews to be beheaded," he argued. "When these [Islamic] terrorists engage in these acts, they are simply following the example of their spiritual leader."

Lawyer Travis Weber, director of the Center for Religious Liberty at the Family Research Council, agrees pastors need to call attention to the persecution. However, he argues that the issue gets too little attention from pastors because there is too little reporting on the issue by the mainstream press. He offered that Christians can access information about the persecution on many websites.[349]

The consensus among Christian leaders interviewed is that pastors need to speak out—and soon. Farr, a Catholic, admits that not enough pastors are speaking out. Nina Shea with the Hudson Institute agreed. She said not enough pastors are talking about the issue. Perhaps, according to Farr, they are under pressure to conform to the culture's dismissive message.[350]

Whatever the reason, too many pastors and church leaders remain silent. What's not in dispute is the fact that the crisis is real and getting worse. Further, there is plenty of material on the issue. McDonnell called on all Christian leaders "to be innocent as doves and as wise as a serpent regarding what Islam is and what it is doing and wise about how they speak about it from the pulpit." But they must speak and now!

General Boykin agrees. He explained that Islam illustrates Isaiah 5:20: "Woe unto them that call evil good, and good evil; that put darkness for light, and light for darkness." "It is time for pastors to talk about the realities of evil and Islam by terrorists is pure evil," Boykin said. Pastors who fail to inform their people results in Christians being "ill prepared to recognize evil and deal with it."

It follows that once Christians are aware of the evil, then they must warn those within their social circles about the threat. That is how to vaccinate our communities with information against Islam.

VACCINATE AGAINST A
CRIPPLING MUSLIM HIJRA

More Muslims are immigrating into the U.S. than even Congress knows about, and with them come potentially significant challenges for local communities. We need to stop Muslim immigration as long as the war with Islam continues and simultaneously increase the immigration of persecuted Christians.

In April 2015, Congressman Trey Gowdy (Republican, South Carolina), chairman of the House Judiciary Subcommittee on Immigration and Border Security, sent a letter demanding the Department of State halt the resettlement of refugees in the city of Spartanburg in his district. Gowdy objected to the "lack of notice, information and consultation afforded to me and my constituents," and then posed questions such as, "Do any of the refugees to be resettled in the Spartanburg area have criminal convictions?"[351]

The necessity for more oversight of the refugee process is an emergency that warrants the immediate attention of every community, especially when considering Muslim immigration, which is a form of jihad called *hijra* that dates back to the time of Muhammad.

I charge you with five of what Allah has charged me with: to assemble,

to listen, to obey, to immigrate and to wage Jihad for the sake of Allah

—Quote from Hadith (five "charges" for Muslims)[352]

Hijra means "migration" and is an Islamic organizational strategy that has the goal of jihad by nonviolent means—also known as "civilization jihad" or "Islamization." Migration is a religious obligation, according to Sam Solomon and E. Al Maqdisi in their book, *Modern Day Trojan Horse: The Islamic Doctrine of Immigration.*[353]

Geert Wilders, a Dutch politician, endorsed *Trojan Horse,* stating: Muslims in the West are bringing about the "gradual and incremental transformation of our societies and legal systems, or what it terms 'Islamisation' of our democratic societies by the vast growing numbers of Muslim immigrants who are importing Islam into our Western way of life."

Hijra is just as threatening to the West as violent jihad. Solomon and Maqdisi wrote:

> One can see that the threat from Islam doesn't just come in the form of Islamic terrorism by suicide bombers trying to wreak havoc in our cities. More often, it comes in the form of gradual and incremental transformation of our societies and legal systems, or what is termed "Islamisation" of our democratic societies by the vast growing numbers of Muslim immigrants who are importing Islam into our Western way of life.

The U.S. is a prime hijra target, as evidenced by the Muslim immigration flow. A 2012 U.N. report indicates the U.S. tops the list of countries that accepted refugees with 50,097. But the real number of immigrating Muslims is much higher, perhaps as the Pew Forum on Religion and Public Life reports, one million legal immigrants a year enter the U.S. and at least one hundred thousand are Muslims.[354]

The size of the total Muslim population in the U.S. is not well understood either. Pew Research pegs that group at 2.75 million; most (1.7 million) have arrived at American shores since 1992. The radical Council on American Islamic Relations (CAIR) says the U.S. Muslim population is really closer to seven million, which could be more accurate than Pew's estimate given CAIR's keen interest in the topic. Both Pew and CAIR will agree the U.S Muslim population grew significantly over the past twenty years and it is expected to grow even more in the future in part due to high immigration, but also due to the 2.5-children-per-Muslim-woman fertility rate compared to an average of 1.9 children for American women.[355]

An issue of considerable concern given the growing Muslim population is the number of American Muslims that support Islamic extremism. An August 2011 Pew study, "Muslim Americans: No Signs of Growth in Alienation or Support for Extremism," asked Muslim respondents this question: "How much support for extremism is there among Muslim Americans?" Pew found that 21 percent answered a "great deal/ fair amount." Extrapolate that across the 2.7 to 7 million Muslims in America, and that's somewhere between 567,000 and 1,470,000 who support extremism. No wonder those same respondents said they were very or somewhat concerned that there could be a possible rise in Islamic extremism in America.

The numbers associated with the growing American hijra are serious, and they mean something especially important to jihadists behind what the Muslim Brotherhood calls its "civilization jihad." In perhaps the most blatant and overt documentation of Islamic intentions, the Brotherhood's 1991 strategic plan, the Explanatory Memorandum on the General Strategic Goal of the Group in North America, declares its goal to "destroy the Western civilization from within." It intends to accomplish that goal, as the Dutchman Wilders said, through "gradual and incremental transformation of our societies" vis-à-vis changing the demographics, legal systems, and governments of the infidel states. Unfortunately, almost no politician or citizen has ever heard of the memorandum, yet here one can plainly see the smoking gun.

What can concerned Americans do? Ann Corcoran, the author of a monograph, "Refugee Resettlement and the Hijra to America," provides a long list of things to do, beginning with gathering more information and then challenging the U.S. government's Refugee Admissions Program to control the influx of costly and culturally unsuitable refugees.[356]

The immigration problem, based on Congressman Gowdy's comments above, is out of control. It's time to reverse Muslim migration. Does any community really want to blindly increase the number of people inside America who favor Islamic extremism?

VACCINATE LOCAL MUSLIMS FROM EXTREMISM

There are at least two possible ways to vaccinate local Muslims against extremism: Lead them to salvation through Jesus Christ or help them reform their faith to reject extremism.

Christians are morally obligated to reach out to Muslims in the name of Christ. McDonnell indicated that "befriending Muslims is the first step." Franklin Graham agrees that "God loves Muslims and Christ died for Muslims," and "Yes, we should reach out to Muslims."

Tom Doyle has considerable experience working with Muslims both in the Middle East and in America. He points out that 60 percent of self-identified Muslims don't practice Islam. "Muslims are open" to the gospel, Doyle said, but Satan has created a "logjam" to "keep Christians from reaching out to Muslims." The "logjam" is keeping "Christians in fear of and hating Muslims." But Doyle says that's an unbiblical view. In fact, the Bible calls on Christians more than three hundred times not to fear. Rather, we are to love our enemies."[357]

Georges Houssney grew up in Tripoli, Lebanon, where he developed "a deep love for Muslims." Today he directs Horizons International, a Muslim evangelism ministry.

Houssney documented the views of hundreds of Muslim converts over a number of years. His findings are rather revealing about the Muslim's receptivity to Christianity. Houssney uses ten questions with multiple choice answers to demonstrate Muslim convert views.[358]

The people who responded to this survey represented a good cross-section of Muslim society:

1. Before I became a Christian, I was:
   - 40% were moderate.
   - 40% had been nominal Muslims.
   - 20% were self-described fanatic Muslims before their conversion. All of them said fear dominated their relationship with God.

2. As a Muslim, did you feel that your relationship with God was based on fear, love, or duty/doing what is required?
  - 75% said it was based on fear.
  - 40% included duty as a basis of their relationship with God.
  - 5% said that as Muslims they felt that they had been worshiping God rather than duty.
  - Not one single respondent said that their relationship with God had been based on love when they were Muslim.

3. What characteristic of God means most to you now?
  - 75% of the respondents mentioned the love of God.
  - 25% mentioned God's forgiveness.

4. "What was the major factor in drawing you to Christ?
  - 85% of respondents cited the love of Christians as one major factor.
  - 60% cited it as the exclusive factor.
  - 30 % cited disappointment with Islam.
  - 25% noted that there were other reasons not listed leading to their conversion.
  - 25% experienced dreams and visions, most of Jesus but some various dreams.
  - 15% mentioned the Christian concept of God.
  - 5% cited the Bible as the sole factor in their conversion.

5. "What was the main change in your life after becoming a Christian?"
  - 40% were attracted to the reality of having a personal relationship with God.
  - 30% were drawn to the love of God and his fatherly nature.
  - 25% of the responses talked about relief from fear.

Some of the comments added were:
  - Free at last.

- My mind has been transformed by Christ.
- Smile, love, tolerance.
- Joy and happiness.
- Hope.
- My life! Everything! I am a different being!
- 180° = total change.

6. What was your view of Islam before your conversion?
- 55% described it as a cultural system (65% of the formerly secular Muslims checked this.)
- 55% described it as a religion.
- 35% described Islam as a political system.
- 20% indicated that all three aspects, political, cultural, and religious.
- 75% of the formerly fanatic Muslims described Islam as primarily a religious system.
- 65% of the formerly nominal Muslims described it as by-and-large cultural.

The formerly moderate Muslims were fairly evenly divided on that issue:
- 25% saw it as political.
- 20% saw it as cultural.
- 30% saw it as religious.

7. "Do you think that the God of the Bible is an entirely different God than the Allah of Islam?"
- 65% wrote that the two are entirely different.
- 10% wrote that they are not entirely different.
- 25% wrote that God of the Bible and the Quran are both different and similar.

8. After becoming a Christian, did you feel that you were worshipping the same God?
   - 90% wrote that they feel that they are worshipping a different God.
   - 5% wrote both "yes" and "no".
   - 5% wrote that they felt they are now worshipping the same God.

9. Did you have any dreams or visions?
   - 60% responded that they had experienced a dream or vision or both.
   - 15% did not respond to this question.

10. What characteristic of God means most to you now?
    - 75% wrote "Love of God."
    - 15% wrote "grace."
    - 15% wrote "forgiveness."
    - 5% did not answer.

What the results of Houssney's survey tell us matches what others said about Muslim receptivity to the gospel. A Muslim's conversion to Christ is driven by Jesus' love and the love of His people. That conclusion should compel every church in America to reach out to Muslims in their communities, and that especially includes recent immigrants from the horrid battlefields of the Middle East.

Traumatized immigrants need friends. What better opportunity do Christians have than to introduce Muslim immigrants to America by offering them kindness, physical help relocating, and help in adjusting to the American culture? Eventually, that friendship will earn the privilege of sharing the gospel with the Muslim friend.

It is important for Christians to learn how to lead a Muslim to Christ. They need to understand some important points about Islam and their suspicions about Christians. Those suspicions must be conquered.

Here is a warning Christian Soldiers Ministries provides would-be Christian witnesses to Muslims.

> We need to remember, when seeking to witness to Muslims, that we are working in an atmosphere poisoned by the memories of these and more recent (e.g., the U.S.'s two invasions of Lebanon) Muslim casualties. It is only by the grace of God that we have as much opportunity as we do to work with Muslims. If we exhibit any form of cultural superiority, religious triumphalism, or selective amnesia concerning the sins of the West, perceived as Christian, we only make matters worse. More to the point, the denigration of Islam as a religion or slurs against its founder, Muhammad, will not be tolerated. Working with Muslims calls for an especially sensitive approach.[359]

It is best for Christians and their churches to prepare for a ministry to Muslims by learning from groups that help Christians and internationals with Muslim evangelism. For example, Horizons International (http://engagingislam.org) will come to your church to set up such an outreach.

Another very important approach to vaccinating the Muslim community from extremism is to encourage reformation. Indeed this is a controversial approach.

Can Islam be reformed? Amir Taheri, a columnist and author of eleven books on Islam, dismissed the idea. "The sad fact is that Islam cannot be reformed, if only because it lacks a recognized authority capable of proposing, let alone imposing reform," Taheri wrote. He bases that conclusion on personal experience dating back to the 1970s.[360]

Taheri covered as a reporter an eight-Muslim-country effort led by Tunku Abdul-Rahman, a former Malaysian prime minister, to propose "mild, non-theological reforms." But, according to Taheri, "The whole exercise collapsed after a few meetings, because no one knew how to propose reforms, let alone find an authority to impose them."

He argues that reforming Islam today is harder than ever. It is a correct opinion that the bulk of Islamic energies are political, not theological. Taheri explains that the West faces today a "war waged by a part of Islam against the democratic world." He suggests that perhaps the only way for the West to deal with modern Islam and win "is to mobilize the resources of its nation-states for facing the challenge on all fronts—political, economic, and cultural and, when needed, military.

"Once the Western democracies have admitted to themselves that this is a war," Taheri said, "they would be in a position to seek allies in the Muslim world by posing the only question that really matters in a state of war: Are you with us or against us?" But because the West can't agree on "a common analysis of the situation," that failure "enables opportunist Muslim powers to hedge their bets by helping or at least tolerating the terrorists under the banner of Islam."

Ayaan Hirsi Ali, the author of three books on Islam, outlines the case for Islamic reform in a *Wall Street Journal* article. But first she dispels the politically correct notion repeated by Western politicians like Obama that somehow violent acts committed in the name of Islam can be divorced from the religion. Her message is simple: "Islam is not a religion of peace."[361]

Hirsi Ali states the "fundamental problem is that the majority of otherwise peaceful and law-abiding Muslims are unwilling to acknowledge, much less to repudiate, the theological warrant for intolerance and violence embedded in their own religious texts." She rejects the notion that ISIS and other extremists haven't just "hijacked" Islam because they cite the very same religious texts used by all Muslims.

"Instead of letting Islam off the hook with bland clichés about the religion of peace, we in the West need to challenge and debate the very substance of Islamic thought and practice. We need to hold Islam accountable for the acts," Hirsi Ali insists.

The Muslim world, according to Hirsi Ali, is divided into two camps: Medina Muslims and Mecca Muslims. The Medina Muslims favor the forcible imposition of sharia as their religious duty, and they condone violence. This group refers to Christians (and Jews) as "pigs and monkeys," and they believe Islam prescribes death for apostasy, stoning for adultery, and hanging for homosexuality. The violence-prone Medina Muslims make up perhaps 3 percent of the world's 1.6 billion believers, or forty-eight million people.

The Mecca Muslims—the vast majority of all Muslims—are loyal to their religion but are not inclined to violence. They focus on religious observance.

Next, Hirsi Ali points out an important fact about the Muslim community for those interested in seeing reform. She explains the Mecca and Medina worldviews of Islam engage in a daily struggle to be faithful to their particular view. Many Muslims withdraw into self-governing enclaves, which is widely evident in Europe and a growing phenomenon in America like in Dearborn, Michigan. This so-called cocooning allows the Muslim immigrants to wall off outside influences to protect their children from the non-Muslim community.

There is only one viable strategy for reforming Islam: containing the threat posed by the Medina Muslims, according to Hirsi Ali. The Medina and Mecca Muslims must do two things: First, "identify and repudiate those parts of Muhammad's legacy that summon Muslims to intolerance and war, and second, persuade the great majority of believers…to accept this change."

However, Hirsi Ali identified five precepts central to Islam that makes it resistant to reform. She contends reform must render these five areas harmless.

1. Muhammad's semi-divine status, along with the literalist reading of the Quran.
   Muhammad should not be seen as infallible, let alone as a source of divine writ. He should be seen as a historical figure who united the Arab tribes in a pre-modern context that cannot be replicated in the 21st century. And although Islam maintains that the Quran is the literal word of Allah,

it is, in historical reality, a book that was shaped by human hands. Large parts of the Quran simply reflect the tribal values of the seventh-century Arabian context from which it emerged. The Quran's eternal spiritual values must be separated from the cultural accidents of the place and time of its birth.

2. The supremacy of life after death.
The appeal of martyrdom will fade only when Muslims assign a greater value to the rewards of this life than to those promised in the hereafter.

3. Sharia, the vast body of religious legislation.
Muslims should learn to put the dynamic, evolving laws made by human beings above those aspects of Sharia that are violent, intolerant or anachronistic.

4. The right of individual Muslims to enforce Islamic law.
There is no room in the modern world for religious police, vigilantes and politically empowered clerics.

5. The imperative to wage jihad, or holy war.
Islam must become a true religion of peace, which means rejecting the imposition of religion by the sword.

Only Muslims can reform their faith, but certainly the West and local communities in America working closely with them can help. Hirsi Ali agrees. "We in the West have an enormous stake in how the struggle over Islam plays out. We cannot remain on the sidelines, as though the outcome has nothing to do with us."

Unfortunately, those Christians most familiar working with Muslims and Muslim converts to Christianity like Georges Houssney agree with Amir Taheri not Ayaan Hirsi Ali. "Realistically," Houssney, with many decades of working with Muslims in the Middle East, said, "You can't reform Islam. The Koran is clear and it can't change. You can't reinterpret the Koran to promote a more moderate version."

VACCINATE PUBLIC SCHOOLS
FROM ISLAMIC PROSELYTIZING

The restrictions on separation between church and state evidently don't universally apply when it comes to Islamic proselytizing in American schools. In fact, across the U.S., many taxpayer-funded schools, while excluding any reference to Christianity, are waging a propaganda war that extols Islam under the guise of multiculturalism.

Parents of school-age children must be the vanguard in the fight to expose Islamic propaganda creeping into public schools. That propaganda will feed the emergence and sympathy for Islamists down the road. Consider:

- A Colorado high school principal allows students to recite the Pledge of Allegiance in Arabic—"one nation under Allah."[362] Something similar happened in April 2015 at Pine Bush High School, Middletown, New York, when the Pledge of Allegiance was read in Arabic over the school public address system.[363]
- Non-Muslim Michigan high school girls wore hijabs (a veil that covers the head and chest worn by Muslim women) to a class to "explore religion and identity."[364]
- Islam is uncritically presented in textbooks without mention of Islam's violent history.
- Massachusetts middle school students took a field trip to the Islamic Society of Boston Cultural Center—the Saudi-funded mosque where the Boston marathon jihad murderers Tamerlan and Dzhokhar Tsarnaev attended. The students were separated by gender and then asked to join adult Muslims in prayer.[365]

- A father who objected to the characterization of Islam as a peaceful religion in his daughter's history class was issued a restraining order. The former U.S. Marine Corps father said: "If [students] can't practice Christianity in school, they should not be allowed to practice Islam in school."[366]
- A Florida high school uses a state-approved world history book that has a thirty-six-page chapter on Islam, but no chapters on Christianity or Judaism, according to State Rep. Ritch Workman. The representative said the authors of the chapter "make a very obvious attempt not to insult Islam by reshaping history." He cites the text, which describes Muhammad taking over Medina as "people happily accepted Islam as their way of life," but disregards that "tens of thousands of Jews and non-believers were massacred by [Muhammad's] armies."[367]

Pro-Islam propaganda like the above seeps into public schools through multiple routes: textbooks, teacher training, outside speakers, and special types of public schools.

A textbook-monitoring organization showed in a 2008 study that public school textbooks "present an incomplete and confected view of Islam that misrepresents its foundations and challenges to international security." For example, a middle school text, *HistoryAlive! The Medieval World and Beyond* provides examples of Islamic jihad without mentioning war, conquest, or subjugation: "Muslims should fulfill jihad with the heart, tongue, and hand. Muslims use the heart in their struggle to resist evil. The tongue may convince others to take up worthy causes, such as funding medical research. Hands may perform good works and correct wrongs."[368]

Plainly, distortions about Islam in American textbooks are not unusual. The American Textbook Council reports that "Islamic organizations, willing to sow misinformation, are active in curriculum politics. These activists are eager to expunge any critical thought about Islam from textbooks and all public discourse. They are succeeding, assisted by partisan scholars and associations."[369]

Pro-Islam teacher training is an issue as well. A National Review Online article investigated Islamist influence over K–12 teacher training at colleges and universities. Clearly, Saudi money has immense influence over America's Middle East studies thanks to Title VI of the Higher Education Act.[370]

Federally funded Middle East studies are required by Title VI, which entails designing lesson plans on the Middle East for America's K–12 teachers. These lessons are included in American K–12 curriculum. Meanwhile, the Saudis fund organizations that design Saudi-friendly, English-language K–12 curricula that are strategically passed to "outreach coordinators" at taxpayer-subsidized universities.

A Jewish Telegraphic Agency investigative report states:

Saudi Arabia is paying to influence the teaching of American public schoolchildren. And the U.S. taxpayer is an unwitting accomplice.... Often bypassing school boards and nudging aside approved curricula…these materials praise and sometimes promote Islam, but criticize Judaism and Christianity.[371]

Sandra Stotsky, a former senior associate commissioner of the Massachusetts Department of Education, wrote in her book, *The Stealth Curriculum: Manipulating America's History Teachers*, "Most of these materials have been prepared and/or funded by Islamic sources here and abroad, and are distributed or sold directly to schools or individual teachers, thereby bypassing public scrutiny." She also writes that after the 9/11 attacks on America, "the Saudi government had sent U.S. schools thousands of packages of educational materials that traced most problems in the Middle East to the doorstep of Western colonialism."[372]

There are also publically funded charter schools that are blatant about promoting Islam. The public charter school in Inver Grove Heights, Minnesota, Tarek ibn Ziyad Academy (TIZA), is named after General Tarek ibn Ziyad, the Berber general who entered Gibraltar in AD 711 on behalf of the Umayyad Caliphate, which then ruled Spain.

The school adjoins the Muslim American Society and requires girls to wear headscarves. Arabic is mandatory, and prayer times and Islamic holidays are observed.[373]

TIZA shares a facility with the Muslim American Society (MAS) of Minnesota, which offers classes to students. MAS "is the de facto arm of the Muslim Brotherhood in the U.S.," said Steven Emerson, director of the Investigative Project on Terrorism. "The agenda of the MAS is to… impose Islamic law in the U.S., to undermine U.S. counterterrorism policy."[374]

How can parents vaccinate their children from public school-based Islamic proselytizing? Determine how to influence the selection of textbooks, teacher training, and curricula. Further, the taxpayer should not permit charter schools like TIZA to be co-located with MAS, much less allow MAS to promote its Islamic agenda on the public dime.

VACCINATE COMMUNITIES AGAINST ISLAMIC EXTREMIST GROUPS

Many Islamic groups operating in the U.S. engage in political action, but are identified as religious organizations. Communities need to monitor these groups to ensure that they are engaged in legal actions that don't promote extremism.

The Clarion Project hosts a website (www.clarionproject.org) that identifies 108 Islamic groups found in twenty-nine states. The largest and best known group is the Council on American Islamic Relations (CAIR). Consider some facts about CAIR that make it a concern.

CAIR is "America's largest Islamic civil liberties group" that grew out of the Islamic Association for Palestine, a group associated with Hamas, a Palestinian terrorist group, according to the U.S. State Department.[375]

In 2007, the U.S. Justice Department labeled CAIR an unindicted co-conspirator in the trial of the Holy Land Foundation for financing Hamas. CAIR, according to court records, was listed among "individuals/

entities who are/were members of the U.S. Muslim Brotherhood's Palestine Committee and/or its organizations."

In November 2014, CAIR was officially designated a terrorist organization by the United Arab Emirates along with the Muslim Brotherhood, al Qaida, al Nusra, and Boko Haram.[376]

A U.S. Muslim Brotherhood memorandum was entered into evidence during the Holy Land Foundation trial. The memorandum describes the Brotherhood's role as engaging in a "Civilization-Jihadist Process." It states:

> The Ikhwan [Muslim Brotherhood] must understand that their work in America is a kind of grand Jihad in eliminating and destroying the Western civilization from within and "sabotaging" its miserable house by their hands and the hands of the believers so that it is eliminated and God's religion is made victorious over all other religions.

CAIR's key players have radical associations. Nihad Awad, CAIR's executive director, said, "I am in support of the Hamas movement more than the PLO [Palestinian Liberation Organization]."

Ibrahim Hooper, CAIR's spokesman, said in 2003 that sharia law would replace the U.S. Constitution if Muslims became the majority.

CAIR and other Muslim Brotherhood entities embrace a strategy called "gradualism." Muslim Brotherhood spiritual leader Youself Qaradawi stated, "Gradualism in applying Sharia is a wise requirement to follow." "Gradualism" consists of five phases:

1. The "secret establishment of leadership."
2. "Gradual appearance on the public scene." Phase 2 calls for "infiltrating various sectors of government," "gaining religious institutions," "gaining public support and sympathy" and "establishing a shadow government."

3. The "escalation phase" focuses on "utilizing mass media." The document says that this stage is "currently in progress."
4. "Open confrontation with the government through...political pressure" and "training on the use of weapons domestically." The document says that there are "noticeable activities in this regard."
5. The final phase: "Seizing power to establish their Islamic Nation under which all parties and Islamic groups are united."

The term "Islamophobia" is in part attributable to CAIR and its Muslim Brotherhood partners. Abdur Rahman Muhammad, a former member, described a secret meeting in which the decision was made to use the term as a political weapon. "This loathsome term is nothing more than a thought-terminating cliché conceived in the bowels of Muslim think tanks for the purpose of beating down critics," Muhammad said.

CAIR also took aim at another offensive term, "Islamist," a reference used to support the imposition of sharia law as a governmental system. CAIR said it is "currently used in almost exclusively pejorative context." The Associated Press gave in, discarding the use of "Islamist" to describe Islamic extremists.

Georges Houssney, the executive director for Horizons International, is a Lebanese Christian who frequently travels to that country where he works with Syrian refugees. Houssney said CAIR works closely with many other like-minded Islamic organizations that try to influence the American education system, recruit mayoral candidates, and members of Congress by supporting their campaigns financially. "When they get more Islamic influence they will shoot for the White House," Houssney said. "Then if a Muslim gains the White House he will use executive orders like Obama to change everything to be Muslim friendly" and more than likely turn Christians into second-class citizens.[377]

VACCINATE COMMUNITIES FROM SHARIA LAW

Political Islam aims to replace American constitutional law, which would be catastrophic for non-Muslims, women, and the American way of life.

Islamic groups like CAIR and all Muslim Brotherhood associated entities intend to impose sharia law on American communities. That's a key aim of the Muslim Brotherhood dating back to founder Hassan al-Banna, who said: "It is in the nature of Islam to dominate, not to be dominated, to impose its law on all nations and to extend its power to the entire planet."[378]

Sharia law deals with a broad range of issues: crime, politics, economics, and personal matters to include sex and even social etiquette. For Muslims, sharia is considered the infallible law of god and is used as a significant source of legislation in most Muslim countries.

Sharia derives from two primary sources: the Koran and the Sunnah. Where sharia enjoys official status, it is interpreted by Islamic judges and local imams.

Most countries do not recognize sharia, but there are exceptions even in the West. In Britain, the Arbitration Act of 1996 allows sharia family law to be used to resolve certain civil disputes—but not without controversy.

A report by Baroness Caroline Cox claims that "Muslim women across Britain are being systematically oppressed, abused and discriminated against by sharia law courts that treat women as second-class citizens." That report, "A Parallel World: Confronting the Abuse of Many Muslim Women in Britain Today," warns against the proliferation of Islamic tribunals that undermine the fundamental principle that there must be equality for all citizens under one law of the land.[379]

The baroness' report claims that Muslims use the Arbitration Act to make legally binding decisions, which is evidence of "jurisdiction creep." The so-called sharia courts are adjudicating matters outside the arbitration framework, such as criminal cases involving domestic violence.

The British experience with "sharia courts" should be a warning to Americans. No jurisdiction in the U.S. should allow sharia to trump local laws or, for that matter, gain even the slightest foothold. Like Franklin Graham said, "This is the U.S.A. and we have a [C]onstitution. Sharia law is not parallel to Judeo-Christian law."

Article VI of the U.S. Constitution is clear:

This Constitution, and the laws of the United States which shall be made in pursuance thereof; and all treaties made, or which shall be made, under the authority of the United States, shall be the supreme law of the land; and the judges in every state shall be bound thereby, anything in the Constitution or laws of any State to the contrary notwithstanding.

Sharia law is the practical implementation of the Islamic ideology, which is totally incompatible with American law as evidenced by Article VI. Graham agrees, stating, "We are a land of free people. Sharia keeps people enslaved. Those who want Sharia…can go back to the countries they came from."

Unfortunately, sharia law courts are already in some American communities. Irving, Texas, Mayor Beth Van Duyne found out just how tough it is to ban sharia once it gets started.

Dallas, Texas, has a functioning sharia tribunal that became the proverbial camel's nose under the tent for Van Duyne's effort to ban a similar tribunal in Irving. Mayor Van Duyne wrote an op-ed in the *Dallas Morning News*: "It is true that I was alarmed by this development [a functioning sharia tribunal in Dallas] since Sharia law is clerically based and there is no evidence that this 'court' (as it was called initially) aligns its determinations with American laws." Further, she wrote, "Nor is there any procedural guarantee that constitutional rights are protected in this setting.[380]

Americans should learn the errors of the British system and take prudent, measured actions to educate, inform and secure the rights of women in our nation.

My repeated commitment to uphold the primacy of American law and constitutional protections for Texans, including and especially immigrant women, has been characterized as something like a hate campaign.

Predictably, Van Duyne's efforts to uphold constitutional rights drew outrage from the Muslim community, which has long-term ambitions to replace all American laws with sharia.

"It is baffling to comprehend the amount of controversy generated by my support as mayor of Irving for a state law that simply asks family law judges to uphold American fundamental constitutional rights when deciding a case that involves a conflicting foreign law," she wrote.

The mayor pointed out the sharia tribunal's decisions are binding, according to Texas law. "Currently, Texas courts allow parties to subject themselves to foreign laws rather than state laws in family law matters (see the case *Jabri vs. Qaddura* from 2003). It states, 'Once the party establishes the claim within the arbitration agreement, the trial court must compel arbitration and stay its own proceedings,'" she pointed out.

"In other words, as much as we have heard that these tribunals are 'nonbinding,' the fact is they are enforceable in Texas courts even when foreign law is the foundation. Also of note, Texas has the third most Sharia law cases in the country."

Mayor Van Duyne warned those who attack her: "Those who have worked to demean my intent and demonize my actions may not care about protecting these women, but that will not deter me from standing for them and their rights on American soil."

American communities had better wake up to the threat posed by Islamists seeking to install sharia law at the local and national levels, thus trumping American constitutional law and imposing Islam on the American way of life. Sharia is like an aggressive form of cancer that cannot be cured—only slowed from time to time, and ultimately deadly. The good news is that there is a preventative a vaccination, Article

VI, which says the U.S. Constitution is "the supreme law of the land." Sharia "law" should have no place in America.

VACCINATE YOUTH FROM ISLAMIC TERRORISM

American communities must take action to vaccinate their youth from the influence of Islam. Otherwise, more young Americans will join ISIS and others will turn their anger on soft targets here at home.

On May 6, 2015, FBI Director James Comey delivered a dramatic assessment of the domestic threat posed by ISIS: There are "hundreds, maybe thousands" of people from across America receiving recruitment overtures from the terrorist group or directives to attack.[381]

Director Comey said ISIS is leveraging social media through Twitter and other platforms pushing young Americans to launch assaults. "It's like the devil sitting on their shoulders, saying 'kill, kill, kill,'" Comey said.

ISIS' social media recruiting strategy is the most aggressive and sophisticated by any terrorist organization since 9/11, resulting in Americans heading overseas to fight alongside the Islamists and others turning their anger on targets here at home.

There are already an estimated 180 Americans fighting for ISIS in Iraq and Syria, according to the Department of Homeland Security.[382] Many are just like Hasan Edmonds, who was stopped before boarding an airplane on March 25, 2015, on his way to join ISIS.

FBI special agents arrested the twenty-two-year-old Edmonds at Chicago Midway International Airport moments before he was to board an airplane bound for Egypt, where he intended to join ISIS. He is charged with conspiring to provide material support for a terrorist organization—himself.[383]

The Edmonds case illustrates the developing American jihadist trend. The FBI's criminal complaint indicates that Edmonds, who maintained a Facebook account under the name "Hasan Rasheed," received a friend request from an informant who identified with a pro-ISIS view and a suggestion that he was an ISIS member living abroad.

Hasan divulged to his Facebook "friend" that he was in the process of raising travel funds to join ISIS in Syria. Facebook contacts continued for two months, and there was a face-to-face meeting with a presumed ISIS member as well.

The complaint indicates Edmonds' main goal for emigrating to ISIS' caliphate in Syria would be to, in time, return to carry out attacks in America such as the January 7, 2015, attack at the Paris offices of the satirical magazine *Charlie Hebdo*.

Clearly, Edmonds never made it out of the country to join ISIS. Stratfor, a Texas-based intelligence service, reported that "those who have traveled overseas to fight with jihadist groups or have conducted domestic grassroots attacks shows that they are similar to the people the FBI catches in sting operations" like the one that caught Edmonds.

Abdirahman Sheik Mohamud, twenty-three, wasn't caught in an FBI sting and in fact he traveled to Syria to join ISIS, where he trained with weapons and explosives, hand-to-hand combat, and breaking into houses. After his training, an Islamist cleric instructed Mohamud to return to America and commit an act of mass destruction.[384]

Fortunately, Mohamud was nabbed by federal authorities in Ohio because he committed "an act of mass destruction." According to unnamed authorities in a *USA Today* article, Mohamud is "one of several anti-American terrorist hopefuls who came to the U.S. with a murderous mission."

The U.S. government monitored several "private conversations" between Mohamud and his brother, Abdifatah Aden, regarding Mohamud's terror-seeking plans. Aden had already joined al-Qaeda's Syrian affiliate Jabhat al-Nusra Front.

Mohamud, a naturalized U.S. citizen, traveled to Syria in April 2014. His indictment states that Mohamud planned to kill Americans, particularly soldiers and police officers. He also allegedly discussed traveling to a Texas military post to "kill three or four American soldiers execution style."

The British have a similar problem. An estimated seven hundred British jihadists are in Syria and Iraq fighting for ISIS or al-Nusra Front.

Shiraz Maher, a senior research fellow at the International Center for the Study of Radicalization, King's College London, said the center monitors some seven hundred of the twenty thousand foreign fighters with ISIS from ninety countries around the world. The center estimates there are four thousand Westerners with ISIS and Nusra Front.[385]

Maher outlined the profile of the typical Western jihadist now with ISIS or the al-Nusra Front. "The average British fighter is male, in his early 20s and of South Asian ethnic origin," he began. Then he continued:

> He usually has some university education and some association with activist groups. Over and over again, we have seen that radicalization is not necessarily driven by social deprivation or poverty.... Other than those who go for humanitarian reasons, some of the foreign fighters are students of martyrdom; they want to die as soon as possible and go directly to paradise. We've seen four British suicide bombers thus far among the thirty-eight Britons who have been killed. Then there are the adventure seekers—those who think this will enhance their masculinity, the gang members and the petty criminals too; and then, of course, the die-hard radicals, who began by burning the American flag and who then advanced to wanting to kill Americans—or their partners—under any circumstance.[386]

Mohammed Emwazi, the famous British Jihadi John, the ruthless executioner of Western journalists and aid workers that appears in ISIS videos, has a common background, according to Maher. He is the son of a comfortable middle-class family and earned a degree in computer programming.

In the U.S., Minneapolis-St. Paul is an Islamist recruiting mecca for overseas groups. Most of the recruits from the twin cities tend to come from the large Somali Muslim community.[387]

In the past, many Twin Cities Somalis went overseas to join the al-Qaeda-linked group, al-Shabaab; terrorists from that group attacked the Kenyan Garissa University College on April 7, 2015, killing 148 Christian students.[388]

Al-Shabaab is losing recruits to ISIS, according to Bob Fletcher, with the Center for Somalia History Studies. "And the reason is that ISIS controls land, they control cities," Fletcher explained. ISIS is attractive because it offers the "opportunity to build something, to build a new society, and that is very, very exciting for a lot of kids."[389]

"The recruiters get a hold of these young people, they mentor them, they assess them, they identify them," Abdirizak Bihi, with the Minneapolis-based Somali Advocacy Center. Most disturbing is the fact that ISIS is successfully recruiting some of the best and brightest students.

"The idea has always been that ISIS and even al-Shabaab targets those [high school drop-out] kids. But we later came to find out that even an 'A' student in universities and colleges are also vulnerable to this powerful propaganda machine," Omar Jamal, a Twin City Somali community activist, said. "And it has been very successful—kids are responding to it."

According to Jamal, radical Islamic ideology is a powerful recruitment tool for ISIS—and the Islamic State's success breeds attraction.

"ISIS thus far has succeeded in putting up an image where they are righting the wrongs and respecting the Muslim world—that they're bringing respect back," Jamal told CBN News reporter. "And it's working for them."

American communities must vaccinate their youth from the influence of Islamists. Otherwise, more young Americans will join ISIS and others will turn their anger on targets here at home.

VACCINATE OUR PRISONS FROM ISLAMIC EXTREMISM

There are three physical venues best suited for Islamic radicalization: radicalized mosques, education establishments, and prisons. A 2008 Rand Corporation report states "imprisonment may increase a prisoner's susceptibility to adopting new and radicalized ideas or beliefs."[390]

The Rand report indicates that a prisoner's susceptibility to radicalized ideas is referred to as a "cognitive opening." The report suggests that similarities between the "psychological experiences that make young Muslims susceptible to radicalization and the psychological impact of imprisonment on individuals in general." Thus, incarcerating young Muslims may well compound their vulnerability to radicalization.[391]

Prison can have a similar impact on other populations, which may explain why some seek solace in religion and thus experience a vulnerability to extremist views. That perspective may explain why in part American prisons are a ripe breeding ground for Islamic extremists, especially among the African-American inmate population.

"Some 135,000 inmates [in American prisons] convert to Islam annually, and almost all of these converts are African Americans," states a report by discoverthenetworks.org.[392] It is noteworthy that a report by the Center for Islamic Pluralism asserts: "African American correctional inmates are particular targets for exploitation by Islamists because of their pre-existing hostility to America and its justice system."[393]

The Saudi Arabian government is a significant player in this religious revolution within America's prison population. Specifically, the Saudi government ships tens of thousands of Korans to U.S. prisons annually via the National Islamic Prison Foundation, which underwrites a "Prison Outreach." That outreach seeks to convert American inmates to Islam, facilitated by many Saudi-funded chaplains working in American prisons that push Saudi Arabia's version of Islam, Wahhabism.[394] "[Wahhabism] generally refers to a movement that seeks to purify the

Islamic religion of any innovations or practices that deviate from the seventh-century teachings of the Prophet Muhammad."[395]

Islam expert Stephen Schwartz wrote in the *Weekly Standard* that "radical Muslim chaplains…acting in coordination to impose an extremist agenda…have gained a monopoly over Islamic religious activities in American state, federal and city prisons and jails."[396] Schwartz explained that radical Saudi chaplains use humiliation, discrimination, and even physical threats.

"Imagine," Schwartz wrote, "each prison Islamic community as a little Saudi kingdom behind prison walls, without the amenities. They have effectively induced American authorities to establish a form of 'state Islam'" in correctional systems, according to Schwartz.[397]

Robert Spenser, director of Jihad Watch, wrote that "the principal organization that approved Muslim chaplains for U.S. prisons was the Islamic Society of North America (ISNA). Despite continuing to enjoy a reputation as a moderate Muslim group, ISNA was in 2007 named an unindicted co-conspirator in a terrorism case involving funding of the jihadist group Hamas." ISNA is closely aligned with the Muslim Brotherhood, which is engaged in a "grand jihad in eliminating and destroying Western civilization from within."[398]

A 2003 *Wall Street Journal* article confirmed the Wahhabi influence among blacks in American prisons. The article quotes a New York Wahhabi imam, Warith Deen Uman, who until the year 2000 helped run New York's Islamic prison program. "The U.S. risks further terrorism attacks because it oppresses Muslims around the world. 'Without justice, there will be warfare, and it can come to this country, too,' Uman said. The natural candidates to help press such an attack, in his view: African-Americans who embraced Islam in prison."[399]

For twenty years, Imam Umar helped run New York's Islamic prison program, recruiting and training dozens of chaplains. The Saudi government helped by sending him to Saudi Arabia, where he learned and then brought back that country's Wahhabi form of Islam.[400]

"Even Muslims who say they are against terrorism secretly admire and applaud" the 9/11 hijackers, Imam Umar wrote in his unpublished memoir. He explained that the Koran does not condemn terrorism against oppressors of Muslims. "This is the sort of teaching they don't want in prison," the imam said. "But this is what I'm doing."[401]

The Saudi government makes prison Dawah, proselytizing of Islam, a priority. Evidently, the Islamic Affairs Department of the Saudi embassy in Washington is the hub for proselytizing material shipped to American prisons, and the Saudi government pays for prison chaplains to travel to Saudi Arabia for worship and study during the Hajj, the pilgrimage to Mecca Muslims must make at least once in their lives.

Saudi Arabia's prison proselytizing program is very successful, as evidenced by the radicalism played out by prison "graduates" on American streets.[402]

In 2005, Bush administration officials busted a terrorist plot to attack non-Muslims at military and Jewish sites in Los Angeles on the fourth anniversary of 9/11. The plot was devised by militant Muslim converts of Jam'iyyat Ul-Islam Is-Saheeh (Arabic for "Assembly of Authentic Islam") who had sworn allegiance to violent jihad while incarcerated at California's New Folsom State Prison.

Convicted terror conspirator Jose Padilla converted to Islam during a stint in a Florida jail and reportedly joined forces with terrorist recruiters after his release.

Aqil Collins, a self-confessed jihadist-turned-FBI informant, converted to Islam while doing time in a California juvenile detention center. At a terrorist camp in Afghanistan, he went on to train with one of the men accused of kidnapping and beheading *Wall Street Journal* reporter Daniel Pearl.

In an East Texas prison, inmates were recruited with a half-hour videotape featuring the anti-Semitic rants of California-based Imam Muhammad Abdullah, who claims that the 9/11 terrorist attacks were actually carried out by the Israeli and U.S. governments.

Federal corrections officials told congressional investigators during the Bush administration "that convicted terrorists from the 1993 World

Trade Center bombing were put into their prisons' general population, where they radicalized inmates and told them that terrorism was part of Islam."

Patrick Sookhdeo, a Muslim convert to Christianity and author of *Islam: The Challenge to the Church*, warns that Islam, "alone among world faiths, has very clear-cut aims for reorganizing society to conform to its teaching. Because of this, Muslim minorities are impacting their host societies in the West in a way which no other faith is doing" and that includes inside American prisons.[403]

American prison officials must guard against the spread of radical Islam, which teaches violence and hatred for non-Muslims. Radical imam chaplains who encourage terrorism have no place working with inmates, and government prison authorities should send Saudi Arabia's prison radicalizers packing.

CONCLUSION

Americans must wake up to the fact that the Christian genocide in the Middle East, if not stopped, will ultimately threaten their communities. Even if Islamists don't succeed in clearing out the Middle East of Christians, they will continue to wage their war against the West—and based on the above material, their radical influence is already here making headway toward their goal of Islamizing America.

EPILOGUE

slamists are at war with all non-Muslims, fueled by their fundamentalist interpretation of the Koran and their prophet's radical hadiths. There are ample clues their war will grow, not just because Christians are facing genocide in the Middle East, but because the Islamists' ranks are swelling and the non-Muslim world stupidly and silently refuses to confront Islamists—extremist Muslims given to violence—as the enemy.

This volume outlines Islam's radical agenda and the Muslim-promoted conditions that encourage Christian genocide. Former Muslims describe in this volume the Islamic threat to the non-Muslim world in simple, irrefutable terms backed by evidence of extremist Islamic behavior, their radical thinking, cultural psychology that rejects social integration and eschatology.

Islamic eschatological—end-times—views, coupled with their prophet's take-no-prisoner teachings, motivates extremist groups like ISIS now rampaging across large swaths of Africa, the Middle East, and Central Asia. ISIS' influence is growing, even in the West, where it enjoys considerable success thanks to the extremists' siren-like use of sophisticated social media to lure vulnerable youth. Young people flock from as many as ninety countries to ISIS-hosted jihadist training camps for ideological indoctrination and to learn killing skills before their terrorist mentors send the newly minted Islamic terrorists home poised to savage their communities on call.

Meanwhile, the vast majority of the so-called moderate global Muslim population is rapidly growing past 1.6 billion strong, and they, too, must share the blame for Christian genocide and the gratuitous violence in the Middle East because they have failed to reform Islam's savage minority, which numbers in the tens of millions. Instead, so-called moderates turn a complacent eye to extremist atrocities, and so do Islamic governments—especially those in the Middle East that sanction many of the conditions that contribute to Christian genocide.[404]

Worse, expect that once the Islamists cleanse the Middle East of Christians, they will turn their war to Israel and other global regions where they have already done plenty of groundwork through aggressive immigration and seeding Islamic insidiousness in communities, schools, mosques, and prisons, and in local governments through sharia tribunals.

What can be done? This volume proposes a "Never Submit"-like campaign that provides a detailed, global effort involving far more than government action. Local communities, churches, strong leaders, and individual Christians must confront the Islamic threat head on, both in the Middle East and at home.

Victory won't be easy or fast but the alternatives are stark. Either the non-Islamic world accepts the radical goals espoused by groups like ISIS, or collectively it harnesses the recommended "Never Submit" campaign proposals to defeat Islam's violence and barbaric influence.

Of course, there are clues that as Islam's war intensifies, the fight will be taken out of our hands. Bible prophecy provides ample reason to believe the clash of civilizations now front and center may well portend the long-anticipated end times. But until that time, we must do our part; defend the faith and our civilization against the violence and hatred promoted by Islam's evil.

In conclusion, consider the words of Rabbi Jonathan Cahn, who addressed a United Nations conference entitled, "The Persecution of Christians Globally: A Threat to International Peace and Security." The entire text of the speech is at Appendix 2.

Rabbi Cahn's April 2015 speech reminded the audience that it was seventy years earlier when the concentration camps of the Third Reich were liberated. "In their liberation, the allies forced the nearby townsfolk to walk through the camps to face the unimaginable depths of horror that Nazism had led to," Rabbi Cahn said.[405]

"But when they walked through those camps in the spring of 1945 they were forced to not only to confront the evil of Hitler and the evil of Nazism—but the evil of their own. For in the end, it was their guilt that was the critical and decisive factor. Without their silent complicity, without their sin of omission and self-interest, the mass murder of six million Jewish men, women and children, could never have taken place."

Rabbi Cahn juxtaposes the silent complicity of the Germans in the face of evil Nazism with the genocide facing Christians today:

And now, after almost two thousand years, some of the most ancient Christian communities, from the Copts of Egypt, to the Nestorians and Assyrian believers of Syria, to the Chaldean and Assyrian believers of Iraq are in danger of extermination, geno cide. As the evil of ISIS and its allies sweeps across the Middle East, an ancient civilization is being annihilated, its people perishing, crucified, decapitated and buried alive in their ancestral soil.

Then the Rabbi soberly warns:

It is written that on the Day of Judgment, we will be either upheld or condemned by the good or bad we did or did not do to God, to Messiah. And when we ask Him, "When was it that did we do good to You?" Or "When was it that we sinned against You?" He will answer, "When you did it to the least of these my brothers, you did it to Me."

Therefore, if we refuse to get involved and help these, the least of His brothers, what are we doing? We are refusing to help the Messiah. If we turn a deaf ear to their cries, we are turning a deaf ear to the cries of the Messiah.

Rabbi Cahn left the audience with a plea:

Do not go down in the annals of history and in the judgment of God as the bystander who saw the evil but did nothing to stop it.… Do not be guilty of another holocaust.… Open up your heart and your life and do whatever you have to do to save them. Messiah is screaming! Messiah is being buried alive! Messiah is being beheaded. Messiah is being crucified…again! Save Him! Save the Messiah! Deliver those who are being delivered to death! For God's sake…do the right thing!

PROPHECY 101

Racing To the End Times

Prophecy 101 is a brief overview of biblical prophecy for those not familiar. It is not all inclusive, but provides sufficient detail for the reader to understand that God has had a plan from the beginning of time that is still being fulfilled and will culminate at a specific future point in time known only to God.

Prophecy is recorded in the first chapter of the first book of the Bible, Genesis, and is included in every one of the sixty-six books, culminating with the final words of Christ in the last chapter of the final book, Revelation. There are 1,239 prophecies in the Old Testament and 578 prophecies in the New Testament for a total of 1,817. These prophecies are contained in 8,352 of the Bible's verses, or 26.8 percent of the total text.[406]

Approximately half of all Bible prophecies have been fulfilled exactly (some to the very day and hour) as prophesied hundreds and thousands of years prior. We can be assured that those yet unfulfilled will also occur exactly as God has planned. Thus we have a map to understand where we are in God's plan today.

What seems clear from this vantage point is that God's plan will soon be brought to conclusion. In the context of this book, prophecy allows us to understand the current Christian catastrophe in the Middle East as another clue leading to the end times, as well as an indication of the horrible times ahead.

FROM HERE TO ETERNITY

The following is a general outline of future history in a general as it will occur according to God's prophetic plan outlined in the Bible. It is not all inclusive; volumes are written on each subject and eschatologists vary in their interpretations and arrangements of the sequence. With those caveats, based on prophetic Scriptures, these major prophecies events will occur and give context to the remainder of this Appendix.

The Rapture and Resurrection

There is coming a moment in time when Christ will be told by the Father to go call His children into heaven. This is what the premillennial, pretribulation adherent of biblical eschatology believes will be the Rapture (see 1 Corinthians 15:51–55 and 1 Thessalonians 4:13–18). Christians (all truly born-again believers) will be instantaneously changed into immortal beings, or, if they have already died, they will be resurrected to immortal life. These will be instantly in the presence of Jesus, who will then take them to heaven, where He has prepared dwelling places for them since His ascension (read John 14:1–3).

The Rapture is a sign-less, imminent event. There are no specific signs mentioned in prophecy that indicate the timing of it and therefore it could happen at any time after Christ sat at the right hand of God in heaven following His resurrection. Christ commanded Christians to watch the world around them in order to discern when the time is approaching, but the exact time and day will remain a mystery until that moment.

On the other hand, Christ gave numerous prophecies concerning the tribulation period and His second coming. We know from Scripture that Christ will return to earth accompanied by the raptured Christians at the Battle of Armageddon. Therefore, evidence that the Tribulation is near means the Rapture of the saints is even closer.

Judgment and Rewards for Christians

The raptured Christians will stand before Christ in judgment to receive certain "crowns" which are rewards for the works they have done in Christ's service while they were still alive after they received salvation by accepting Christ as their Savior. Their unproductive works are said to be burned up, indicating that they were not done for Christ.

The raptured Christians are not judged for their sins because Christ already paid their debt on the cross. They received their salvation and were raptured based on their faith in Christ. Those who did much for Christ will receive much in rewards while those who did little or nothing will receive few or no rewards, although they will be with Christ for eternity in glory.

Old Testament believers will not go to the Father (heaven) in the Rapture and resurrection with the church, but will do so at the end of the Tribulation period.

Celebration

When the believers receive their crowns of reward, they will take part in the Marriage Supper of the Lamb. This is the celebration of Christ's Bride, His church (believers who have been resurrected and raptured), joining Him for eternity (heaven). At that point they lay their crown rewards at Christ's feet in submission and recognition that they could only perform their earthly works because it was Christ working through them and nothing on their own.

Armageddon

Jesus will return with His Bride to earth at the point that all armies are gathered at Armageddon in the area of Megiddo, also called the Plains of Esdraelon (or Jezreel, an area in present-day north-central Israel). These armies will have come to fight to the death and take over all of Israel and Jerusalem, in defiance of God. Israel and Jerusalem are God's touchstone to humanity in geographical terms.

They will have been brought to this great killing field by God, Himself, because they have tried to take over this Holy Land—and, in effect, the whole world—in order to establish themselves above the throne of God. The human rebels have, through governments and regimes, "divided" God's land, which He covenanted to give to Abraham, Isaac, and Jacob's progeny, the Jews. For doing this to His land, God has brought them to this great killing field (read Joel 3:2).

It is Satan, Lucifer the fallen angel, who has influenced the earthly rebels to defy God for millennia. His top minion, the Antichrist (the first beast mentioned in Revelation 13), will be the chief leader of the military forces who have come to wage man's final war, Armageddon.

Just as this great, horrific conflict is about to end all life on earth (read Matthew 24:21), Jesus Christ, followed by His Church Age saints (Christians) riding on heavenly, white steeds, breaks through the boiling, black clouds above Megiddo and speaks to the armies gathered to try to stop Him (Jesus) from returning to earth (Revelation 19:11).

When Jesus speaks, all of the armies gathered near Megiddo literally explode. The blood pools to the height of that measured from the ground to a horse's bridle rein. Blood flows for hundreds of miles because of the millions who have died on the Plains of Esdraleon. The great birds of carrion feast on the flesh of dead kings, captains, and others, the prophecy says.

Following Armageddon, Jesus has angels seize the Antichrist and his chief henchman, the False Prophet. The two are thrown into the

Lake of Fire and then Satan is bound by a single, heavenly angel who casts Satan into the bottomless pit, where he will remain for one thousand years.

Judgment for the Survivors

All peoples who are still alive after the carnage at Armageddon are gathered outside Jerusalem (eighty-five miles to the south) for the judgment of the nations. This is called the "sheep and goats judgment." Those who are believers are on Christ's right hand. Unbelievers among the nations are on His left hand. The lost (unbelievers) are cast into what is termed "outer darkness." The believers go into the Millennial Kingdom—the thousand-year kingdom that will be ruled by Jesus Christ. Believers enter the Millennial Kingdom in their mortal bodies, but will have long life and repopulate the earth. When they die, they will be resurrected in their immortal bodies to serve with those already in heaven.

Old Testament Saints Resurrected

At some point after Christ returns to earth, the Old Testament saints are resurrected to life to be citizens of heaven and children of God forever. These are the people who died before Christ, but believed in God and are said to be righteous in God's eyes. Abraham is a prime example.

The Millennial Kingdom

Church Age saints, the Bride of Christ, will reign with Christ in their supernatural bodies, the change having taken place earlier when the Rapture occurred. These saints will commute between the heavenly city, the New Jerusalem, which hovers above planet earth itself, and earth. Peace will reign and Christ will be physically present ruling on earth from Jerusalem.

Satan Released and Rebels

At the end of Christ's thousand-year reign, Satan is let out of the bottomless pit. He immediately rallies a huge army from among those who are alive (in their mortal bodies on the earth) but have refused to follow Christ. This vast army rages toward Jerusalem to take it over, but Christ instantly destroys them. Satan is then cast in the Lake of Fire, where he will spend eternity in suffering, joining the Antichrist and False Prophet who have already been for a thousand years.

Final Judgment

When the Millennial Kingdom comes to a close, the unbelievers from all of history will be resurrected and stand before Christ in what the Bible calls the "Great White Throne judgment." They will be judged according to their works while they were alive. But no one can be saved through their works alone and all will be thrown into the Lake of Fire for eternity.

Eternity Arrives

Following the Great White Throne judgment, God completely remakes the heavens and the earth, and eternity replaces time that had been created for mankind's history. All the saved enter the eternal state.

DISTRESS AND PERPLEXITY

Bible prophecy's most detailed descriptions of the end-times come from the very tongue of Jesus. He responds to His disciples' question about the wind-up of history.

> And as he sat upon the mount of Olives, the disciples came unto
> him privately, saying, Tell us, when shall these things be? and

what shall be the sign of thy coming, and of the end of the world? (Matthew 24:3)

That question continues to echo today while issues and events raise anxieties and fears of what the future might hold.

Just prior to his statement in Matthew 24:3, Jesus told His disciples that the beautiful temple in Jerusalem they could see on the horizon from their place on the Mount of Olives would be totally destroyed. There would not be one stone left upon another. A couple disciples, tradition tells us, lived to see Jesus' words fulfilled when in AD 70 the Roman General Titus, on orders from his father, Emperor Vespasian, put down the Jewish insurrection. The Romans, despite Titus' order to spare the temple, burned the grand edifice and then tore it down stone by stone to steal the gold and jewels from the rubble.

The disciples then asked Jesus when this destruction would happen, and about the end of the world. Jesus explained how things will be when human history comes to its end, covering not only the geophysical and astrophysical conditions, but also the socioeconomic characteristics of the very end of days. Jesus told them:

> And there shall be signs in the sun, and in the moon, and in the stars; and upon the earth **distress of nations, with perplexity;** the sea and the waves roaring;
>
> Men's hearts failing them for fear, and for looking after those things which are coming on the earth: for the powers of heaven shall be shaken. (Luke 21:25–26, emphasis added)

Keep in mind Jesus was speaking about His second coming here, which we explained would happen after the Rapture and after the Tribulation. Jesus' answer is only relevant to those alive at the time of the Tribulation, not for the church, which by then will be raptured, gone to heaven. Nevertheless, there are clues in Christ's answer as to how close we are to those end times.

IS THIS THE TIME OF
DISTRESS AND PERPLEXITY?

We are indeed as Jesus described in Luke 21at a time of "distress of nations, with perplexity." Certainly distress and perplexity will continue to increase and reach its height during the Tribulation, but the trend has already started. This is one of the key signs Jesus said will mark the time as the "end of the world" approaches.

Jesus said in response to His disciples' questions:

> So likewise ye, when ye shall see all these things, know that it is near, even at the doors. Verily I say unto you, This generation shall not pass, till all these things be fulfilled. (Matthew 24:33–34)

It is the opinion of many eschatologists that the Matthew 24:33–34 generation is alive today. There are various interpretations as to what constitutes the time span of a generation, but suffice it to say that if we are the last generation, there is little time remaining before the world will be in the Tribulation period. But, once again, this is a mystery that only God can explain.

Proof that this present world system might be nearing the end is evident daily, even hourly and minute by minute as we watch one catastrophe after another reported in the news.

Sadly, according to prophecy, there must come much horrendous conflict in this fallen world before the light of eternity breaks through the black, boiling clouds that we now see rumbling above a planet ripe for judgment. Specifically to the point, the genocidal madness perpetrated by militant, fanatic Islam serves as a clarion call of warning and the blood of Christians suggests events are building-up to the end.

STAGE SETTING AND CONVERGENCE

There is a temptation to look at the Tribulation period prophecies, especially in Revelation, and conclude that many of them are already underway: famine, earthquakes, wars, and rumors of wars (some eschatologists claim that a better translation of this phrase is "terrorisms"). But, the events described in Revelation are those of the Tribulation period that today's Christians will not witness, since they will already be with Christ in heaven, having been raptured.

However, the increase in the frequency and intensity of these events today is often termed as "stage setting." In other words, we are getting a preview of what will happen in the Tribulation period although it will be many times worse. To the watchful Christian, this stage setting is a warning requiring an alarm to be sounded.

Recently students of prophecy wrote about the convergence of signs. That is, in the past we have seen certain individual signs like earthquakes increase in frequency and power. War and famine have always been with us in certain parts of the world. But now we see what many claim is a new phenomenon: All the individual signs are occurring with greater frequency and power at the same time. In other words, the signs of the end times are simultaneously converging on planet earth with a synergistic effect.

The following is evidence of the "new phenomenon" of signs of the end times.

ECONOMIC DISTRESS AND PERPLEXITY

The global economic situation is a significant sign. Economists who don't have their heads in the proverbial sand must wonder: "How long can the instability in worldwide monetary matters continue before there is total collapse, bringing on global depression, or worse?" To put it in biblically prophetic terms, there is growing "distress with perplexity" in today's financial markets.

Many of the economic pressures that led to the 2007–2008 financial crisis and collapse are present today, and are building hourly. The most frequently given analogy is to that of a constantly growing bubble that is bound to pop at some point. But when?

That question or similar questions are constantly heard echoing through the talking-head financial programs and are seen in text on the blogs of the Internet. At the same time, a calm demeanor is maintained by those presenting financial news and prognostication through mainstream news venues. There is at the very least a severe disconnect between the mainstream and sub-communication strata when it comes to whether the nation and world face critical circumstances in the arena of economy.

More frequently, there is an advisory mantra from the economic gurus to buy gold and silver as a hedge against coming monetary financial disaster. Others advise storing great quantities of food, water, and other essentials of life in order to survive some period when there are no services and lawlessness abounds.

Global monetary governing institutions such as the International Monetary Fund and controlling bodies such as the Federal Reserve System have used most everything in their fiscal bag of tricks to stave off financial collapse. We've heard the term "kick the can down the road" ad nauseum. Unprecedented interest rate gyrations have been utilized to prevent rampaging inflation that, because of unbridled printing of currencies, would otherwise decimate national economies like in the case of the Weimar Republic in the Germany of pre-Hitler days.

Still, the national debt of the United States, at more than $18 trillion as of this writing, continues to grow exponentially. Every nation in Europe and in the more industrialized nations faces similar economic gloom and doom, even if their burden of debt is less from nation to nation. All are in the red, with little hope of solution to pull them out of their debt abyss.

Again, while this generation is not in that most horrific time of Tribulation, it can see a foreshadowing of just what Jesus was predicting. Austerity measures brought about by governments within the European Union such as Greece have caused rioting, as the welfare state of the socialist governments can't keep up with the funding needed to pay those who are not wage earners.

One needs only to look to Greece recently to understand that the stage might be about to be set for that time in the future predicted to be the worst in history—the time when the "seas" of peoples will be roaring.

The election of a young, charismatic, leftist leader Alexis Tsipras to prime minister of Greece points out how such rebellion against austerity measures can bring to power a leader who promises peace and prosperity. This is similar to the circumstances that brought a young Adolf Hitler to power and a warning to America that such measures (welfare cuts for example) could cause our "seas" to roar, even revolt.

DEADLY DISTRESS AND PERPLEXITY

Distress and perplexity have different meanings for different societal structures and individuals within the cultures involved. For regions such as Sudan and others in like circumstances, not knowing where the next bit of food might be found is certainly the most severe form of both distress and perplexity.

We have all seen the stark videos of the children of those regions, their stomachs distended, their emaciated bodies almost lifeless, and their eyes wide in the throes of starvation. This is distress at its worst. Famine comes at the end of not dealing adequately with this direst of the human condition.

Too often, starvation is the result of genocide by omission. It is genocide nonetheless, and as heinous as any inflicted by ISIS or other beastly horde.

Governments of countries where starvation is rampant are often ruled by dictators who hoard to themselves, their cronies, and their military the foods and other stuffs vital to supporting the lives of the hapless people. No matter how much aid pours in from donor nations around the world, the plight of the people in these areas never changes.

As a matter of fact, reports from nations where starvation is rampant tell that the problem is spreading, not lessening, in scope and severity; and this, despite continuing and even increased efforts by governments and nongovernmental organizations to feed the hungry.

The Bible foretells a coming time when starvation will far surpass any such time in history.

> And when he had opened the third seal, I heard the third beast say, Come and see. And I beheld, and lo a black horse; and he that sat on him had a pair of balances in his hand.
>
> And I heard a voice in the midst of the four beasts say, A measure of wheat for a penny, and three measures of barley for a penny; and see thou hurt not the oil and the wine.
>
> And when he had opened the fourth seal, I heard the voice of the fourth beast say, Come and see.
>
> And I looked, and behold a pale horse: and his name that sat on him was Death, and Hell followed with him. And power was given unto them over the fourth part of the earth, to kill with sword, and with hunger, and with death, and with the beasts of the earth. (Revelation 6:5–8)

For the dying, diseased people who have no hope of rescue, the prophecy might as well be describing their situation today.

GEOPOLITICAL ERUPTION

Bible prophecy presents, in relatively specific terms, how world issues and events will be in alignment and converging while the end times unfold. This is true in socioeconomic matters, as seen thus far. The foretelling of things to come involving those of geopolitical import is profoundly more illuminating. Here is a look at the most observable prophetic stage-setting that looks to be relevant to the present hour.

Daniel the prophet was given a stunning look into the future. Daniel, as a young man chosen by Nebuchadnezzar to be one of the king's counselors, interpreted a dream the Babylonian monarch had one night as he lay in troubled sleep. The dream was of a metallic statue of a man made of gold, silver, brass, and iron. The image's feet and toes were of iron mixed with clay. The various metallic portions of the image's human form represented, most students of Bible prophecy agree, four succeeding world kingdoms that would come on the earth throughout human history.

These kingdoms have been identified as Babylon, Medo-Persia, Greece, and Rome. Daniel was told to prophesy that a fifth empire would be the final world government. The fifth was represented by the feet and toes that were made of iron mixed with clay.

History has proven that the first four empires have come on the world scene and either been overthrown, or, in the case of Rome, simply declined to the point that it went out of existence as an empire. Most prophecy scholars hold that the final kingdom is yet to come—the one represented by the two feet and ten toes which will be the "Revived Roman Empire."

THE GLOBALISTS' DREAM

Today, internationalists—the global power brokers—have their own dream. They call for a New World Order, as it has been termed for decades going back to the 1940s when the phrase was coined by author H. G. Wells. There is an incessant call for national sovereignty to give way so that the world can come together as one.

Dr. Henry Kissinger, perhaps the best known such globalist thinker, said at the outset of Barack Obama's election to the U.S. presidency that Obama was primed to create a New World Order. He further told PBS interviewer Charlie Rose in 2014:

> There is a need for a new world order... I think that at the end of this [Obama] administration, with all its turmoil, and at the beginning of the next, we might actually witness the creation of a new order—because people looking in the abyss, even in the Islamic world, have to conclude that at some point, ordered expectations must return under a different system.[407]

Developments within Europe, where resided the heart of the ancient Roman Empire, cause many, including this writer, to believe that the final form of world government, as prophesied by Daniel, is taking shape today. From the Club of Rome that first met in 1957 to the present European Union that serves as prototype for ten world economic trading blocs that are in the making, the feet and toes of Nebuchadnezzar's metallic dream-vision seem in the process of fulfillment.

The New World Order is nothing more than the call for a one-world government with a one-world currency. All that remains is for a leader to step forward and lead the way. One is coming soon.

SUPER LEADER WITH A SOLUTION

A civilization-shuddering moment is coming. The massive bubble that is building, which includes uncontrollable, unbridled financial dynamics, as briefly touched upon above, will explode, and the results will instantly bring about cultural and societal catastrophe. The "distress and perplexity" prophesied by Jesus Christ will suddenly cause the seas of humanity to roar in protestation never seen before on the planet.

It will be crisis beyond all that has ever been. There will be an outcry for governments to provide answers that will restore sanity to a world gone mad with worry over the hardships that are suddenly crushing in on humanity. But, from where will answers come? Leaders of every stripe have been unable to even rein in a modicum of financial troubles. Can there be expected *hope and change* that will truly restore life that is anywhere near what it was before the world-rending crash?

Bible prophecy foretells that the answer will be forthcoming from a leader to whom all the world will look for salvation from their problems. That man will one day be worshiped as their god.

Daniel was given a glimpse of the man who will be at the head of this return to Babel when the world once again tries to come together as a single entity in rebellion against God. We looked at that coming "beast" earlier. He will bring Israel and its enemies—as well as much of the world—together in supposed peace. But, it will be a deadly peace (Daniel 8:25).

The man will be a Roman prince, according to Daniel's foretelling:

And after threescore and two weeks shall Messiah be cut off, but not for himself: and the people of the prince that shall come shall destroy the city and the sanctuary; and the end thereof shall be with a flood, and unto the end of the war desolations are determined.

And he shall confirm the covenant with many for one week: and in the midst of the week he shall cause the sacrifice and the oblation to cease, and for the overspreading of abominations he shall make it desolate, even until the consummation, and that determined shall be poured upon the desolate. (Daniel 9:26–27)

The system Daniel envisioned is likely to be a system of electronic funds transfer of some description that will eliminate cash worldwide. Additionally, this solution to the world's economic situation will likely include a redistribution of wealth that is all in electronic currency units.

And he causeth all, both small and great, rich and poor, free and bond, to receive a mark in their right hand, or in their foreheads:

And that no man might buy or sell, save he that had the mark, or the name of the beast, or the number of his name.

Here is wisdom. Let him that hath understanding count the number of the beast: for it is the number of a man; and his number is six hundred threescore and six. (Revelation 13:16–18)

Who is this prince that is to come? Is he the one man who can solve the world's economic problems around whom the entire world will rally? Is he the genius who will control all the wealth on the planet? He is better known as the Antichrist; the man who will be indwelt by Satan himself.

COMING WARS IN PROPHECY

The climactic battle of the age will take place at Armageddon at the end of the Tribulation period when Christ returns to the earth and slays the world armies surrounding Jerusalem and initiates the Millennial Kingdom. Prophecy points to numerous military actions that are yet future; major books and articles cover each of them. Here we will mention just four prophecies that have at least one element in common: They all involve Israel and the surrounding Islamic nations that will likely impact the Christians in the area, if there are any left at that point.

GOG OF MAGOG

The prophet Ezekiel foretold that a massive gathering of peoples will, when the end times are in view, come down from the north of Jerusalem to take plunder from Israel. He was told to give very specific regions that would comprise this force. The list is stunning in terms of things we observe taking place in that part of the world at this very moment.

One of today's best-known prophecy scholars wrote:

Students of Bible prophecy have long expected a Russian military move in the Middle East. Early in the twentieth century, Dr. [Harry A.] Ironside wrote: "In the last days, the final head of the Russian people will look with covetous eyes upon the great developments in the land of Palestine. They will determine that Russia must have her part of the wealth there produced. Consequently, we have the picture of a vast army, augmented by warriors from Persia, Cush, Phut, marching down toward Palestine." (Jack Van Impe, www.jvim.com/newsletter/pastissues/2010/20101025.html)

Russia is determined by many scholars to be the chief culprit in the predicted invasion. First consider Ezekiel's prophecy:

And the word of the Lord came unto me, saying,
Son of man, set thy face against Gog, the land of Magog, the chief prince of Meshech and Tubal, and prophesy against him,
And say, Thus saith the Lord God; Behold, I am against thee, O Gog, the chief prince of Meshech and Tubal:
And I will turn thee back, and put hooks into thy jaws, and I will bring thee forth, and all thine army, horses and horsemen, all of them clothed with all sorts of armour, even a great company with bucklers and shields, all of them handling swords:
Persia, Ethiopia, and Libya with them; all of them with shield and helmet: Gomer, and all his bands: and many people with thee. (Ezekiel 38:1–6)

How can one determine from this description, strangely put to most readers today, that it can be interpreted to show a Russian-led coalition?

Be assured—the belief that Russia will lead such a force, and that hordes from certain modern regions to the north of Israel will join the leader called "Gog" is a reliable interpretation.

Today's hourly news brings word of how closely Russia and Iran (a major part of ancient Persia) are interacting. One of the most dominant Russian leaders ever, President Vladimir Putin, has arisen to threaten regions that were under the chains of the former Soviet Union, such as Ukraine. Turkey has turned from being a secular-run state to one under an increasingly dominant Islamist regime. Turkey, too, is aligning closely with Russia in these days that look to be very much the end times.

Ezekiel prophesied that God, Himself, will put "hooks in the jaws" of the leader of Russia. The bait will be, again according to the Ezekiel 38–39 prophecy, economic in nature. The Russians and others of the coalition will attack toward the mountains of Israel to "take great spoil," as the King James Version Bible translation has it.

Recently, Russia has come under tremendous economic pressure, receiving sanctions by America and the Western alliance because of its bellicose threatening of Ukraine and others. The ruble fell precipitously against the U.S. dollar because the cost per barrel of oil fell tremendously when Saudi cut petroleum prices. Putin needs funds, as Russia's exports of oil and gas are its chief sources of national income.

Since the oil price pressures were brought to bear on Russia, Putin has reached out to China to make deals that will perhaps bring economic pressures upon the United States. With China holding huge amounts of dollars in U.S. Treasury bonds, the Sino-Russian (along with other countries) alliance might well succeed.

At any rate, a Russian leader, according to Ezekiel, will one day look to his south to realize there is great spoil to feed his greed for power to fund his military ambitions.

All of this is strong indication that these are times very near the end of this Age of Grace.

PSALM 83

This brief Psalm, which many believe is also a prophecy, describes a coalition of all the Islamic countries that share a border with Israel. They have formed a military alliance with one goal:

> Come, and let us cut them [Israel] off from being a nation, that the name of Israel may be remembered no more. (Psalm 83:4)

That perfect coalition where they are all of one accord is not totally in place today, but given their relationship and cooperation in the past Arab—Israeli wars, such a group could come together virtually overnight. Hamas, Hezbollah, and other terrorist groups are today rearming and digging assault tunnels toward and likely under their borders with Israel. There seems little question that their intent is to kill all the Jews and Christians in Israel.

It is fascinating to discover that all the nations that will attack Israel under Russian leadership (Gog of Magog noted above) are listed in Ezekiel's prophecy in chapters 38–39. All of the nations are Islamic, but none of them has a common border with Israel. Looking at a map, one can see that the nations listed in Psalm 83, all Islamic, form an immediate inner circle with Israel in the middle while the nations in Ezekiel's prophecy for an outer ring.

All attack routes from the outer ring must pass through the inner ring, but why are the lists different? Based on the writings of other prophets, many experts have concluded that the war of Psalm 83 precedes Ezekiel 38–39. Therefore, the absence of the names of the Psalm 83 nations in Ezekiel's coalition list is because they have already been defeated and Israel has occupied some of the vast territories.

As pointed out previously, there is enormous oil wealth in those lands that would be occupied, and an economic collapse in Russia could easily account for a desire to conquer the rich reserves that Israel controls.

ISAIAH 17

The burden against Damascus. Behold, Damascus will cease from being a city, and it will be a ruinous heap. (Isaiah 17:1)

Damascus Syria is said to be the oldest continuously occupied city in the world. The prophecy goes on to indicate that the Israelis are responsible for the destruction and it occurs overnight. Many speculate that the city cannot be destroyed in one night by conventional means; rather, nuclear weapons would have to be involved.

It takes little imagination to understand how Syria would become an Israeli target today given Syria's actions in the region. Perhaps Damascus is destroyed as a result of the Psalm 83 war, since Syria is a member of the attacking coalition. Or the destruction could come from some other confrontation. In any case, the demise of Damascus will be an earth-shattering event.

JEREMIAH 49

Elam is the subject of destruction of Jeremiah's prophecy.

For I will cause Elam to be dismayed before their enemies and before those who seek their life. I will bring disaster upon them, My fierce anger, says the Lord; And I will send the sword after them until I have consumed them. (Jeremiah 49:37)

Elam is part of Iran today, located on the western side of Iran along the Persian Gulf. It is of significance because it includes the city of Bush-ehr, which is the location of a large nuclear reactor built by Russia.

The prophecy indicates that God is fiercely angry with Iran/Elam. It seems likely that God is fiercely angry with Iran's constant calls for the extermination of Israel, their support of terrorist organizations that are carrying out military actions against Israel, Iran's funding of terrorist organizations carrying out Christian genocide, and Iran's torture and murder of Christian pastors. Destruction will come upon Iran/Elam from military action by more than one country. There are also indications that God supernaturally acts in the destruction and perhaps both supernatural and man's military action are involved. In any case, there will be a worldwide dispersion of the area residents in the aftermath. Perhaps nuclear fallout will drive the people into exile.

Again, little imagination is required to see the circumstances under which Iran would be attacked are evident in the daily media.

SUMMARY

These four prophecies (Ezekiel 38, Psalm 83, Isaiah 17 and Jeremiah 49) involve Israel's Islamic neighbors and are yet to be fulfilled. World events point to a soon fulfillment of all four, any one of which would be a world-changing event. There is no clear evidence whether there is a fixed sequence for the prophecies to occur or whether they could all be part of one event that takes time to move from one to the other. As Christians we must be watching all the possibilities all the time.

As a final note, the outcome of Ezekiel's prophecy deserves special attention. The other three prophecies appear to be the result of military action, the Israeli Defense Forces as THE major if not sole player. However, the IDF apparently does not play a role in the victory foretold by Ezekiel, for it is God Himself who brings about the destruction of the attackers through supernatural events. God tells us why:

> Thus I will magnify Myself and sanctify Myself and I will be known in the eyes of many nations. Then they shall know that I am the Lord. (Ezekiel 38:2)

This event will spell the end of Islam because many nations will reject Allah when they see for the last time that their god is powerless—in fact, does not exist. God will Himself destroy Islam as well as its inventor, Satan.

CONCLUSION

The final books of the Bible were written hundreds of years before Muhammad and his followers brought Islam to the world. The Bible does not contain any direct prophecies concerning the current genocide of Christians in the Middle East at the hands of Muslims. However, there are references to the persecution of Christians in general. John 16:2 was a warning Jesus Christ gave his disciples: "The time is coming that whoever kills you will think that he offers God service."

Most of the disciples were martyred just as He prophesied. However, that verse could also be taken as a general warning for Christians down through the Church Age, and that is in fact what we see in the Middle East, Africa, and China today.

In Revelation 13:15 and 20:4, we see that during the Tribulation, perhaps millions will be martyred when they become believers and refuse the demands of the Antichrist to accept the mark of the beast. Beheading is given as one method of killing. (This does not imply that Muslims are involved although beheading is a favored method of killing Christians today. Beheading has been a favorite method of execution down through the ages by many nations.)

While there is no direct reference to Islam, the obvious conclusion is that Christians are prophesied to suffer and die for their faith throughout the Church Age and on into the Tribulation.

THE CRIES OF THE MESSIAH

by Rabbi Jonathan Cahn

t is April, 2015. Seventy years ago, this spring, the concentration camps of the Third Reich were liberated. In their liberation, the allies forced the nearby townsfolk to walk through the camps to face the unimaginable depths of horror that Nazism had led to.

But for most of those who lived in those towns by the camps and, for that matter, throughout Germany, it was not unexpected. It was well-known that the Jews were being hunted down and taken in cattle cars to concentration camps where horror and likely death awaited them. They knew it, but did nothing to stop it. They themselves weren't in danger. Why should they have risked their comfort, their safety, their well-being for those who *were?*

But when they walked through those camps in the spring of 1945 they were forced to not only to confront the evil of Hitler and the evil of Nazism—but the evil of their own. For in the end, it was their guilt that was the critical and decisive factor. Without their silent complicity, without their sin of omission and self-interest, the mass murder of six million Jewish men, women and children, could never have taken place.

In 1964, in the city in which this gathering has convened, a young woman named Kitty Genovese was approaching her apartment door when she was attacked by a man wielding a knife. The young woman was brutalized over the course of approximately one half-hour. At least 12 people heard her screams or saw parts of the attack during those 30 minutes. But the majority did nothing to help her.

Some weren't sure what the screams outside their closed windows were. But they never bothered to find out. It was cold outside and they were comfortable inside the warmth of their apartments. One neighbor, who actually saw the attack pondered whether he should even bother to ask another neighbor to call the police. His explanation, "I didn't want to get involved." As a result of the bystanders of this city, the life of Kitty Genovese was violently snuffed outside her apartment door.

And now as we meet in the city of the bystanders of that crime, another crime is taking place outside our closed windows. Seventy years after the bystanders of Nazi Germany walked through the death camps of the holocaust, another stream of victims are being led to their deaths.

Again it involves a satanic evil of hatred, violence, and sadistic cruelty. And again it involves an innocent people marked for destruction—the followers of Jesus, known throughout the world as "Christians," those who are taught, when struck, to turn the other cheek, when cursed, to bless, and when persecuted, to forgive those who oppress them. These constitute, by far, the most persecuted religious group on earth, oppressed, afflicted, hunted down and killed—men, women and children—the sacrificial lambs of the modern world.

We meet in the world's most revered gathering place of nations. And as kings, leaders, ambassadors and delegates convene here to discuss international issues, within the borders of over 60 of those nations, Christians are being persecuted by their own governments or by those in whose midst they live—from North Korea, to Iran, to Afghanistan, to Syria, Nigeria, Iraq, Pakistan, Vietnam and Indonesia, and many, many more. In North Korea, Christians are imprisoned, sent to labor camps, tortured, and killed, for the crime of owning a Bible. In Nigeria entire

Christian village populations have been massacred. In Orissa India, 70,000 Christians have been forced to flee their homes. In Syria, 80,000 Christians have been quote "cleansed" from their homes. In Indonesia, Muslims have put 10,000 Christians to death.

And now, after almost 2,000 years, some of the most ancient Christian communities, from the Copts of Egypt, to the Nestorians and Assyrian believers of Syria, to the Chaldean and Assyrian believers of Iraq are in danger of extermination, genocide. As the evil of ISIS and its allies sweeps across the Middle East, an ancient civilization is being annihilated, its people perishing, crucified, decapitated and buried alive in their ancestral soil. The Vicar of Baghdad recounted this year how Isis ordered four Christian children to renounce Jesus and follow Muhammad. "No," they said, "We love Yeshua…He has always been with us." These were the last words the children ever spoke on this earth as Isis beheaded them.

We hear the accounts of the early Christians being led into Roman arenas to be torn apart by wild beasts. And we ponder how savage and barbaric those days were. We wonder what we would have done had we been there. If we had lived in those days and could have saved the lives of the innocent, would we have saved them?

But the truth is we *do* live in those days. More Christians have been persecuted, brutalized and killed in the modern age, than in any other. Every year, tens of thousands of Christians are dehumanized, tortured or killed, and over 100 million Christians live under the darkness of persecution. It is the modern age that holds the most savage and barbaric of days. And what are we doing as Christians are being led away to be devoured?

This very body, the United Nations, adopted the Universal Declaration of Human Rights which declares that everyone has the right to "manifest his religion or belief in teaching, practice, worship, and observance."

In the World Summit Outcome Document of September 2005, paragraph 139, the United Nations declared that the international community has the responsibility to protect populations from genocide, ethnic cleansing, and crimes against humanity. So the question must be asked, "Where are all the resolutions?" "Where are all the troops?" "Where are all the actions taken to protect the most persecuted people on earth?" "And where's the universal outcry?" It's a strange and immoral silence, the same strange and immoral silence that allowed 6 million Jews to be delivered to their deaths.

We must not repeat the mistake of the last century. Evil never stays put. The same darkness that destroyed 6 million Jewish lives would end up destroying over 60 million lives throughout the world. The evil that first warred against the Jewish people was a harbinger of what would soon overcome the earth.

In the days when coal miners were dying of black lung disease, an answer was found in the caged canary. The canary was brought deep into the mines. If it grew sick and died, it would be the sign and the alarm that the air inside the mine was toxic. What happened to the caged canary was a harbinger of danger.

The persecuted Christian is the caged canary of the modern world. The Christian is the first target of evil, and so the sign and the alarm of a toxic evil in the world and a growing danger. And if we don't deal with that evil when it targets others on distant shores, we will surely deal with it when it targets us on our own shores.

No civilization can call itself *moral* if it fails to defend its most defenseless against that which seeks to devour them. No nation can call itself *good* if it sits back and does nothing of effect as the forces of evil murder the innocent. And no people can call themselves "*Christian*" if they watch passively on the sidelines as those who share the name of Messiah are oppressed and killed for their faith.

If our faith consists of how comfortable and prosperous God can make us in this world, as we deafen our ears to the cries of those who are in this world neither comfortable nor prosperous, our brothers and sisters imprisoned and tortured for their faith, how can we bear the name

"Christian?" On the Day of Judgment we will be asked, "Why did you do nothing to save them?" And what will our answer be?

It is written in the book of Hebrews, "Remember those who are in chains as in chains with them." So as we sit on our couches in front of our television sets in our air-conditioned homes, are we remembering our brothers who sit on the stone floors of prison camps as they suffer for their faith? They would say to us now, "Do not forget us in our suffering." "Remember us." "Remember us as our enemies come to take our lives." "Do not forget that we once lived and that we once gave our lives for our faith and His namesake."

We cannot forget them. We must remember them. And we must help them.

What would you do if in your neighborhood, a band of criminals had taken over the house next door and were holding your neighbors hostage? What if every day, they oppressed them, humiliated them, beat them, abused them, tortured them and began planning their deaths, father, mother and children?

What if through your windows at night you could hear their muted screams for help, but did nothing? You didn't try to save them yourself. You didn't tell your other neighbors and gather them together to help. You didn't even bother to call the police. In the end, how would you be judged? The answer is unavoidable: You would be judged as guilty, as immoral; you would be judged as evil.

And what if they didn't live next door, but down the block. What if they lived a town away, a nation away, or an ocean away? Would it make any difference? Does geography in any way alter or lessen the charge and requirement of morality? It does not. So if men, women and children, across the world are now being held captive, beaten, tortured and put in danger of death, and we know about it, if we hear their distant screams, but choose to do nothing, then how will we, in the end, be judged? We will be judged likewise as guilty and immoral. We will be judged as evil.

It is written that on the Day of Judgment, we will be either upheld or condemned by the good or bad we did or did not do to God, to Messiah. And when we ask Him, "When was it that did we do good to You?" Or "When was it that we sinned against You?" He will answer, "When you did it to the least of these my brothers, you did it to Me."

Therefore, if we refuse to get involved and help these, the least of His brothers, what are we doing? We are refusing to help the Messiah. If we turn a deaf ear to their cries, we are turning a deaf ear to the cries of the Messiah.

And on that day, He will say to us, "When my village was burned down in Nigeria, why did you do nothing to help Me? When I was imprisoned inside a labor camp in North Korea, why did you forgot Me? When Isis came to kill my family, why did you not help us? And when I was tortured, when I was beheaded, when I was buried alive, when I was crucified, why did you ignore my cries for your help? Why did you let Me perish? Now depart from me, for I never knew you."

When that day comes, let it not be said of us that we heard the cries of God and did nothing to help Him. In the time it takes us to hold this session more people will be brutalized, more lives snuffed out. If it was your family about to be destroyed, if it was your life about to be taken, if it was your little child about to be beheaded, and others could have helped but chose not to, what would you think? Then let us do the only right and moral thing we can do. As it is written in the Scriptures: "Deliver those who are being delivered to death."

Do not go down in the annals of history and in the judgment of God as the bystander who saw the evil but did nothing to stop it, who heard the screams of the Kitty Genoveses of this world but chose to let them die outside your door, who watched the cattle cars deliver the innocent to their deaths but chose to stay silent. Do not be guilty of another holocaust.

Open up your windows and hear their cries. Open up your doors and step outside your dwelling. Open up your heart and your life and do whatever you have to do to save them. Messiah is screaming! Messiah is being buried alive! Messiah is being beheaded. Messiah is being crucified…again! Save Him! Save the Messiah! Deliver those who are being delivered to death! For God's sake…do the right thing! Thank you.

⸺

Rabbi Jonathan Cahn, the senior rabbi at the Beth Israel Worship Center in Wayne, New Jersey, gave the preceding speech to a United Nations conference entitled, "The Persecution of Christians Globally: A Threat to International Peace and Security." Cahn is the author of *The Harbinger* and *The Mystery of the Shemitah*.

NOTES

1. Quoted from an email by Charmaine Hedding, Shai Fund, April 28, 2015.
2. Islamic State of Iraq and Syria (ISIS), Islamic State of Iraq and ash-Sham (ISIS), also known as Islamic State of Iraq and the Levant (ISIL), or simply Islamic State. This volume will reference the Islamic State of Iraq and Syria or ISIS as the Islamic extremist rebel group controlling territory in Iraq and Syria with affiliates elsewhere, Libya, Nigeria, and Afghanistan.
3. Raymond Ibrahim, "Christian Slaughter," *Gatestone Institute*, February 1, 2015, http://www.gatestoneinstitute.org/5169/christmas-slaughter-muslim-persecution.
4. Holocaust History Terminology, Holocaust History Glossary, http://www.jchb.org/neveragain/materials-for-educators/holocaust-history-terminology/.
5. "State Department: Christian Presence in Middle East Becoming 'Shadow of Is Former Self'," *Fox News*, July 28, 2014, http://www.foxnews.com/politics/2014/07/28/state-department-christian-presence-in-middle-east-becoming-shadow-its-former/.
6. Ibid.
7. "A speech by the Prince of Wales at an Advent reception for Christians from the Middle East, Official Website of the British Monarchy,

December 17, 2013, http://www.princeofwales.gov.uk/media/
speeches/speech-the-prince-of-wales-advent-reception-christians-
the-middle-east.

8. "Archbishop Fears for Christians in Middle East," BBC, December 9,
   2011, http://www.bbc.com/news/uk-16111973.

9. "Ex-Lebanon Leader: Christians Target of Genocide," CBS
   News, January 3, 2011, http://www.cbsnews.com/news/
   ex-lebanon-leader-christians-target-of-genocide/.

10. Andrew Katz, "Pope Francis: 'No Middle East Without Christians',"
    Time, November 21, 2013, http://world.time.com/2013/11/21/
    pope-francis-no-middle-east-without-christians/.

11. Kevin Liptak, "Obama: We Are Not at War with Islam," CNN,
    February 18, 2015, http://www.cnn.com/2015/02/17/politics/
    isis-obama-extremism-summit/.

12. Micah Zenko, "Countering ISIS: The Pentagon Wants Perpetual
    Warfare," *Newsweek*, February 1, 2015, http://www.newsweek.
    com/countering-isis-pentagon-wants-perpetual-warfare-303440.

13. Samuel Huntington, "The Clash of Civilization," *Foreign Affairs*,
    September 1993, http://www.bintjbeil.com/articles/en/d_
    huntington.html.

14. Jonathan Fox, "Are Middle East Conflicts More Religious?," *Middle
    East Quarterly*, Fall 2001, http://www.stevendroper.com/religion.pdf.

15. "Obama's speech in Cairo," *New York Times*, June 4, 2009,
    http://www.nytimes.com/2009/06/04/us/politics/04obama.text.
    html?pagewanted=all&_r=0.

16. Ibid.

17. "Nina Shea Explains How American Christians Can Stand Up
    for Their Persecuted Brethren Overseas," *National Review*, August
    1, 2013, http://www.nationalreview.com/article/354874/
    killing-christians-interview.

18. B. Christopher Agee, "'The Storm Is Coming': Franklin
    Graham Shares Grim Prediction after ISIS Kills 21 Christians,"
    Western Journalism, February 17, 2015, http://www.

westernjournalism.com/storm-coming-franklin-graham-shares-grim-prediction-isis-kills-21-christians/#zK6xUKywIo7t vMy4.99.

19. Francis A. Chullikatt, "Religious Freedom the First Freedom on Which Democratic Societies Are Built," testimony before the U.S. House of Representatives Committee on Foreign Affairs, February 10, 2015, http://docs.house.gov/meetings/FA/FA16/20140211/101747/HHRG-113-FA16-20140211-SD002.pdf.

20. Peggy Noonan, "The Genocide of Mideastern Christians," *The Wall Street Journal*, September 12, 2014, http://www.wsj.com/articles/the-genocide-of-mideastern-christians-1410474449.

21. Todd M. Johnson and Gina A. Zurlo, "Ongoing Exodus: Tracking the Emigration of Christians from the Middle East," *Harvard Journal of Middle Eastern Politics and Policy*, Vol. III, 2013-2014, http://www.gordonconwell.edu/resources/documents/JMEPP-JohnsonaandZurlo.pdf.

22. "Christian Migrants," Pew Research Center, March 8, 2012, http://www.pewforum.org/2012/03/08/religious-migration-christian-migrants/.

23. "Over 110,000 Iraqis Have Entered the US Since the End of the Bush Administration," Refugee Resettlement Watch, February 4, 2015, https://refugeeresettlementwatch.wordpress.com/2015/02/04/over-110000-iraqis-have-entered-the-us-since-the-end-of-the-bush-administration/.

24. "In Troubled Mideast Where Christian Populations Are Shrinking, Pope Calls for Interfaith Dialogue," *Jerusalem Post*, November 28, 2014, http://www.jpost.com/Middle-East/In-troubled-Mideast-where-Christian-populations-are-shrinking-Pope-calls-for-interfaith-dialogue-383125.

25. "Periodic Update: United Nations High Commissioner for Human Rights," Independent International Commission of Inquiry on the Syrian Arab Republic, December 20, 2012, http://www.ohchr.org/Documents/Countries/SY/ColSyriaDecember2012.pdf.

26. "Genocide Alert: The Arab Republic of Egypt," Christian Solidarity International, May 2013, http://csi-usa.org/documents/Egypt%20 Genocide%20Alert.pdf.

27. Bruce Wallace, "Amid Instability In Egypt, Coptic Christians Flee To U.S.," *All Things Considered*, NPR, January 4, 2013, http://www.npr.org/2013/01/04/168609672/ amid-instability-in-egypt-coptic-christians-flee-to-u-s.

28. Former Congressman Frank Wolf: Looming Genocide for Iraq's Minorities, Religious Freedom Coalition, February 20, 2015, http://www.religiousfreedomcoalition.org/2015/02/20/former-congressman-frank-wolf-looming-genocide-for-iraqs-minorities/.

29. Rupert Shortt, "The Middle East Is Red with the Blood of Christians," *The Telegraph* (London), February 16, 2015, http://www.telegraph.co.uk/news/worldnews/islamic-state/11416779/ The-Middle-East-is-red-with-the-blood-of-Christians.html.

30. NR interview with Nina Shea, "Killing Christians," *National Review*, August 1, 2013, http://www.nationalreview.com/article/354874/ killing-christians-interview.

31. "World Watch List," Open Doors USA, https://www. opendoorsusa.org/christian-persecution/world-watch-list/.

32. Raymond Ibrahim, "Egyptian Bishop: Security Services Complicit in Anti-Christian Violence, Middle East Forum," May 4, 2015, http:// www.meforum.org/5218/agathon-state-complicity.

33. Ibid.

34. "Violent Attacks Against Religious Minorities in the Islamic Middle East Since January 1, 2010," https://www.google. com/fusiontables/DataSource?docid=1qLvUnVwGzy-oshh5M8kJgDXQel-ohCQ7RhdcHUQ#rows:id=1.

35. Janelle P., "Prayer for a Christian Mother Held by ISIS for Months," Open Door USA, May 7, 2015, https://www. opendoorsusa.org/christian-persecution/stories/tag-blog-post/ prayer-for-a-christian-woman-held-by-isis-for-months/.

36. "Middle Eastern Christians Battered," Jerusalem Center for Public

Affairs, May 22, 2014, http://jcpa.org/article/middle-eastern-christians-battered/#sthash.Ab7iazEh.dpuf.

37. Ibid.

38. Ibid.

39. Ibid.

40. Ibid.

41. "Violent Attacks Against Religious Minorities in the Islamic Middle East Since January 1, 2010," https://www.google.com/fusiontables/DataSource?docid=1qLvUnVwGzy-oshh5M8kJgDXQel-ohCQ7RhdcHUQ#rows:id=1.

42. Ishaan Tharoorn, "Islamic State burned a woman alive for not engaging in an 'extreme' sex act, U.N. official says", *Washington Post*, May 22, 2015, http://www.washingtonpost.com/blogs/worldviews/wp/2015/05/22/islamic-state-burned-a-woman-alive-for-not-engaging-in-an-extreme-sex-act-u-n-official-says/?tid=pm_world_pop_b.

43. Bernard Lewis, "Islam and the West: A Conversation with Bernard Lewis," Catholic Education Resource Center, *The Pew Forum on Religion & Public Life*, April 27, 2006. Hay-Adams Hotel Washington, DC), http://www.catholiceducation.org/en/culture/catholic-contributions/islam-and-the-west-a-conversation-with-bernard-lewis.html.

44. Bill Warner, editor, *The Islamic Trilogy*, Vol. 2, *The Political Traditions of Mohammed, The Hadith for the Unbelievers* (Center for the Study of Political Islam, 2006) p. X.

45. Ibid.

46. Ibid.

47. Bill Warner, *Sharia Law for the Non-Muslim* (Center for the Study of Political Islam, 2010) Chapter 5.

48. Bill Warner, *The Islamic Doctrine of Christians and Jews* (Center for the Study of Political Islam, 2010) p. 4.

49. Koran 40:35(as cited in Warner, *The Islamic Trilogy*, Vol. 2, *The Political Traditions of Mohammed, The Hadith for the Unbelievers*).

50. Sahih Bukhari, Vol. 5, book 58, No. 148 (as cited in Warner, *The Islamic Trilogy,* Vol, 2, *The Political Traditions of Mohammed, The Hadith for the Unbelievers*).

51. Ishaq, 125 (as quoted in Warner, *The Islamic Doctrine of Christians and Jews*).

52. Koran 47:4 (as cited in Warner, *The Islamic Trilogy,* Vol, 2, *The Political Traditions of Mohammed, The Hadith for the Unbelievers*).

53. Koran 6:25 (as cited in Warner, The Islamic Trilogy, Vol. 2, *The Political Traditions of Mohammed, The Hadith for the Unbelievers*).

54. Koran 86:15 (as cited in Warner, *The Islamic Trilogy*, Vol. 2, *The Political Traditions of Mohammed, The Hadith for the Unbelievers*).

55. Koran 8:12 (as cited in Warner, *The Islamic Trilogy,* Vol. 2, *The Political Traditions of Mohammed, The Hadith for the Unbelievers*).

56. Koran 9:29 (as cited in Warner, *The Islamic Trilogy*, Vol. 2, *The Political Traditions of Mohammed, The Hadith for the Unbelievers*).

57. Koran 3:28 (as cited in Warner, *The Islamic Trilogy*, Vol. 2, *The Political Traditions of Mohammed, The Hadith for the Unbelievers*).

58. Bill Warner, editor, "The Political Traditions of Mohammed," *The Islamic Trilogy*, Vol. 2 (The Center for the Study of Political Islam, 2006) p. 4.

59. Ibid., p. 72.

60. Ibid, p. 51.

61. Ibid, p. 53.

62. Ibid.

63. "Hajj Fact Sheet," U.S. Passports & International Travel, Bureau of Consular Affairs, U.S. Department of State, http://travel.state.gov/content/passports/english/go/Hajj.html#.

64. From Mecca To Jerusalem: Muslims & Their Feelings, A Jew with a View, not dated, https://ajewwithaview.wordpress.com/tag/kafirs/.

65. "Punishment for Non-Muslims for Entering Makkah and Madina," Life in Saudi Arabia, not dated, http://life-in-saudiarabia.blogspot.com/2014/10/punishment-for-non-muslims-for-entering.html#. VUaok_lVhBc.

66. Sahih Bukhari, Vol. 2, book 23, No. 483 (as cited in Warner, *The Islamic Trilogy*, Vol. 2, *The Political Traditions of Mohammed, The Hadith for the Unbelievers*).

67. Sahih Bukhari, Vol. 9, book 89, No. 271 (as cited in Warner, *The Islamic Trilogy*, Vol. 2, *The Political Traditions of Mohammed, The Hadith for the Unbelievers*).

68. Bill Warner, *The Islamic Doctrine of Christians and Jews*, (Center for the Study of Political Islam, 2010) p. 72.

69. Ishaq, 404 (as cited in Warner, *An Abridged Koran The Reconstructed Historical Koran*) .

70. Ishaq, 407–8 (as cited in Warner, *An Abridged Koran The Reconstructed Historical Koran*) .

71. Ishaq, 409 (as cited in Warner, *An Abridged Koran The Reconstructed Historical Koran*).

72. Sahih Bukhari, Book 3, Nos. 48 & 850 (as cited in Warner, *The Islamic Trilogy*, Vol. 2, *The Political Traditions of Mohammed, The Hadith for the Unbelievers*).

73. Koran 2:191.

74. Koran 2:216.

75. Koran 4:89.

76. Koran 9:36.

77. Sahih Bukhari, Vol.2, book 23, No. 483.

78. "Jihad: Jihad According to the Shafi'I School," Study of Islam, Movement of Belgium Former Muslims, not dated, http://www.exmuslim.org/jihad-according-to-the-shafii-school.html.

79. Koran 4:95.

80. Koran 9:29.

81. Sahih Bukhari, Vol. 1, book 2, No. 28.

82. Bill Warner, editor, "The Political Traditions of Mohammed," *The Islamic Trilogy* Vol. 2, (The Center for the Study of Political Islam, 2006) p. 88.

83. Sahih Bukhari, Vol. 6, book 60, No. 139.

84. Sahih Bukhari, Vol. 7, book 62, No. 137.

85. Sahih Muslim, Book 8, No. 3432 (as cited in Warner, *The Islamic Trilogy*, Vol. 2, *The Political Traditions of Mohammed, The Hadith for the Unbelievers*).

86. Bernard Lewis, *Islam and the West: A Conversation with Bernard Lewis*, Catholic Education Resource Center (*The Pew Forum on Religion & Public Life*, April 27, 2006, Hay-Adams Hotel Washington, DC), http://www.catholiceducation.org/en/culture/catholic-contributions/islam-and-the-west-a-conversation-with-bernard-lewis.html.

87. The five permanent members of the U.N. Security Council are: China, Russia, France, the United Kingdom, and the United States.

88. Jordan Schachtel, "Defecting Iranian Journalist: U.S. at Nuclear Talks 'to Speak on Iran's Behalf'," *BreitBart* London, March 28, 2015, http://www.breitbart.com/national-security/2015/03/28/defecting-iranian-journalist-u-s-at-nuclear-talks-to-speak-on-irans-behalf/.

89. Ibid.

90. "The World's Muslims: Religion, Politics and Society," Pew Research Center, April 30, 2013, http://www.pewforum.org/2013/04/30/the-worlds-muslims-religion-politics-society-overview/.

91. Muslim Publics Share Concerns about Extremist Groups, Pew Research Center, September 10, 2013, http://www.pewglobal.org/2013/09/10/muslim-publics-share-concerns-about-extremist-groups/.

92. Ibid.

93. "Today's Middle East: Pressures & Challenges," Zogby Research Services LLC., November 2014, http://b.3cdn.net/aai/a6466ad6476c08d752_bum6b4j6l.pdf.

94. Thomas Lifson, "Former Muslim Sounding the Alarm," *American Thinker*, November 13, 2014, http://www.americanthinker.com/blog/2014/11/former_muslim_sounding_the_alarm.html#ixzz3SZZ7nKhk.

95. "History of the Muslim Brotherhood in Egypt,"

Wikipedia, http://en.wikipedia.org/wiki/
    History_of_the_Muslim_Brotherhood_in_Egypt.

96. Erick Stakelbeck, "Ex-Muslim Speaks Out about 'The
    Koran Dilemma'," *CBN News*, May 11, 2012, http://
    www.cbn.com/cbnnews/us/2011/september/
    ex-muslim-speaks-out-about-the-koran-dilemma/.

97. Ibid.

98. Paula Bolyard, "Former Muslim Tells Obama How It
    Really Is With Islam and ISIL," *PJ Media*, September
    4, 2014, http://pjmedia.com/tatler/2014/09/04/
    former-muslim-tells-obama-how-it-really-is-with-islam-and-isil/.

99. Kevin Liptak, "Obama: We Are Not at War with Islam," CNN,
    February 18, 2015, http://www.cnn.com/2015/02/17/politics/
    isis-obama-extremism-summit/.

100. "Mark Gabriel," Islam Expert Answers Challenges, not dated, http://
    www.bibleprobe.com/MarkGarbriel-Introduction.htm.

101. "Surah," Wikipedia, http://en.wikipedia.org/wiki/Surah.

102. Surah 49:10, *Muhsin Khan* (as cited in http://www.bibleprobe.
    com/MarkGarbriel-Introduction.htm).

103. Ibn Hisham, *The Life of Muhammad*, 3rd ed., pt. 6, Vol. 3 (Beirut,
    Lebanon: Dar-al-Jil, 1998), p. 8 (as cited in http://www.bibleprobe.
    com/MarkGarbriel-Introduction.htm).

104. Muhammad Sameel 'Abd al-Haqq, "The Doctrine of an-Nasikh
    wa'l Mansukh: Abrogation in the Qur'an and the Idea of a Hijacked
    Religion," Part 2, *Everything Islam*, June 27, 2011, https://
    everythingislam.wordpress.com/2011/06/27/the-doctrine-of-an-
    nasikh-wa%E2%80%99l-mansukh-abrogation-in-the-quran-
    and-the-idea-of-a-hijacked-religion-part-2-muhammad-sameel-
    %E2%80%98abd-al-haqq-definitions-of-abrogation-an-nasikh/.
    Note: "The Arabic words *nasikh* and *mansukh* are both derived
    from the same root word *nasakha* which carries meanings such as 'to
    abolish', 'to replace', 'to withdraw' and 'to abrogate'. The word *nasikh*
    (an active participle) means 'the abrogating', while *mansukh* (passive)

means 'the abrogated'. In the technical language of the *'ulama* these terms refer specifically to certain parts of the Qur'anic revelation, which have been 'abrogated' by others. According to the jurists who support and elaborate a doctrine of abrogation within the *Qur'an*, the *Qur'an* itself refers to it and it is not a later development of the *'ulama*, developed following the generation of the *Tabi'in*: "None of Our revelations do We abrogate or cause it to be forgotten, but We substitute something better or similar: knowest thou that God has power over all things? [*Qur'an* 2: 106]."

105. Thomas Madden, "The Abuse of Christianity's Holy Wars," *National Review*, November 2, 2001, http://www.nationalreview. com/article/220747/crusade-propaganda-thomas-f-madden.

106. Ryan Muro, "Blaming the Crusades for Jihad," Daily Mailer, *FrontPage*, September 23, 2013, http://www.frontpagemag. com/2013/ryan-mauro/blaming-the-crusades-for-jihad-2/.

107. Ibid.

108. Timothy Furnish, "How the Media Misconstrue Jihad and the Crusades," Center for History and News, July 6, 2008, http://www. churchinhistory.org/pages/crusades/timothy.htm.

109. James Hitchcock, "The Crusades and Their Critics," Catholic Education Resource Center (Reprint, James Hitchcock, "The Crusades and Their Critics,"*Catholic Dossier* 8 no. 1 (January–February 2002), http://www.catholiceducation.org/en/culture/ history/the-crusades-and-their-critics.html.

110. "Allah as Moon-god," Wikipedia, http://en.wikipedia.org/wiki/ Allah_as_Moon-god.

111. Jan Willem van der Hoeven, "The Main Reason for the Present Middle East Conflict: ISLAM and not 'The Territories'," International Christian Zionist Center, 2000, as cited in http://www. eretzyisroel.org/~jkatz/mainreason.html , p.45.

112. "Church of the Holy Sepulchre," 2015, http://www. churchoftheholysepulchre.net/.

113. Thomas Madden, "The Real History of the Crusades," Catholic

Education Resource Center (Reprint Thomas F. Madden. "The Real History of the Crusades," *Crisis* 20, No. 4 (April 2002) Cited in http://www.catholiceducation.org/en/controversy/the-crusades/the-real-history-of-the-crusades.html.

114. Lawrence Duggan, "Indulgence," *Encyclopedia Britannica*, http://www.britannica.com/EBchecked/topic/286800/indulgence.

115. Thomas Madden, "The Real History of the Crusades," Catholic Education Resource Center (Reprint Thomas F. Madden, "The Real History of the Crusades,"*Crisis* 20, No. 4 (April 2002) Cited in http://www.catholiceducation.org/en/controversy/the-crusades/the-real-history-of-the-crusades.html.

116. Jonathan Simon Christopher Riley-Smith, *The Crusades Christianity and Islam* (Columbia University Press, 2008), https://books.google.com/books?id=7KzNAQ9tCOsC&pg=PT44&lpg=PT44&dq=jonathan+riley-smith+and+%E2%80%9Chad+to+persuade+their+listeners+to+commit+themselves%22&source=bl&ots=RF9VojvZSp&sig=UmlU75qdZSkZNMo-KtsJZ0j4L54&hl=en&sa=X&ei=wBjvVLzKEMO7ggTO8oPgDg&ved=0CCUQ6AEwAQ#v=onepage&q=jonathan%20riley-smith%20and%20%E2%80%9Chad%20to%20persuade%20their%20listeners%20to%20commit%20themselves%22&f=false.

117. Fred Cazel, "Financing the Crusades," in *A History of the Crusades*, ed. Kenneth Setton, Vol. 6 (Madison, WI: University of Wisconsin Press, 1989) 117.

118. http://www.crisismagazine.com/2012/crash-course-on-the-crusades [cites: Thomas Madden, *New Concise History of the Crusades*, (New York, NY: Rowan & Littlefield Publishers, Inc., 2005), 148. and Quoted in Regine Pernoud, *The Crusaders – the Struggle for the Holy Land*, trans. Enid Grant, (San Francisco, CA: Ignatius Press, 2003) 23.

119. http://www.crisismagazine.com/2012/crash-course-on-the-crusades [Cites: France, *Victory in the East: A Military History of the First Crusade* (Cambridge: Cambridge University Press, 1994), 142].

120. Jan Willem van der Hoeven, "The Main Reason for the Present Middle East Conflict: ISLAM and not 'The Territories'," International Christian Zionist Center, 2000, http://www. eretzyisroel.org/~jkatz/mainreason.html.

121. Remarks by the President at National Prayer Breakfast, Washington, D.C., February 5, 2015, https:// www.whitehouse.gov/the-press-office/2015/02/05/ remarks-president-national-prayer-breakfast.

122. Steve Weidenkopf, "Crash Course on the Crusades," *Crisis Magazine*, July 24, 2012, http://www.crisismagazine.com/2012/ crash-course-on-the-crusades.

123. Samuel Huntington, "The Clash of Civilizations," *Foreign Affairs*, Summer 1993, http://www.foreignaffairs.com/articles/48950/ samuel-p-huntington/the-clash-of-civilizations.

124. Jonathan Fox, "Are Middle East Conflicts More Religious?," *Middle East Quarterly*, Fall 2001, http://www.meforum.org/135/ are-middle-east-conflicts-more-religious.

125. "Text: Obama's Speech in Cairo," *New York Times*, June 4, 2009, http://www.nytimes.com/2009/06/04/us/politics/04obama.text. html?pagewanted=all&_r=0.

126. "Armenian Genocide," United Human Rights Council, not dated http://www.unitedhumanrights.org/genocide/armenian_ genocide.htm.

127. As cited in Leo Hohmann, "Will History Repeat Itself? Lessons From The Armenian Genocide," April 24, 2015, http://www.prophecynewswatch.com/2015/April24/243. html#OiMPcHXDsf3duG3V.99.

128. Ibid.

129. "Armenian Genocide," United Human Rights Council, not dated, http://www.unitedhumanrights.org/genocide/armenian_ genocide.htm.

130. Ibid.

131. William Schabas, "Convention on the Prevention and Punishment

of the Crime of Genocide," Audio Visual Library of International Law, United Nations, not dated, http://legal.un.org/avl/ha/cppcg/cppcg.html.

132. "CSI letter to President Barack Obama," Christian Solidarity International, November 30, 2011, http://csi-usa.org/Obama_Letter.html.

133. David Suissa, "The Silent Killing of Christians," *Jewish Journal,* July 31, 2013, http://www.jewishjournal.com/david_suissa/article/the_silent_killing_of_christians.

134. Michael Synder, "Why Is Obama So Silent aout the Vicious Persecution of Christians All Over the Globe?," April 24, 2015, Prophecynewswatch.com,http://www.prophecynewswatch.com/2015/April24/242.html#dhIOm7v0ZCqQHcRO.99.

135. "GENOCIDE ALERT: Defend Middle East Christians & Other Religious Minorities!," Christian Solidarity International, not dated, http://csi-usa.org/persecution.html.

136. "Egypt," 2013 Annual Report, United States Commission on International Religious Freedom, http://www.uscirf.gov/countries/egypt, p. 50.

137. "Al-Azhar University," Wikipedia, http://en.wikipedia.org/wiki/Al-Azhar_University.

138. Jonathan Fox, "Religious Discrimination against Religious Minorities in Middle Eastern Muslim States," Civil Wars, Vol. 15, No. 4, December 18, 2013, HTTP://DX.DOI.ORG/10.1080/13698249.2013.853413.

139. Hilal Khashan, "Arab Uprisings May Doom Middle East Christians," *Middle East Quarterly*, Vol. 21, No. 4, Fall 2014, http://www.meforum.org/4801/arab-uprisings-may-doom-middle-east-christians.

140. Ibid.

141. Raymond Ibrahim, "Christmas Slaughter: Muslim Persecution of Christians," Gatestone Institute, February 1, 2015, http://www.gatestoneinstitute.org/5169/

christmas-slaughter-muslim-persecution.

142. "Iran Sentences American Pastor Saeed Abedini
to 8 Years in Prison," *Fox News*, January 27, 2013,
http://www.foxnews.com/world/2013/01/27/
iran-sentences-american-pastor-saeed-abedini-to-8-years-in-prison/.

143. Benjamin Weinthal, "Irans Regime Targets Evangelical Christians as
National Security Threat," *Fox News,* March 21, 2014, http://www.
foxnews.com/world/2014/03/21/irans-regime-targets-evangelical-
christians-as-national-security-threat/.

144. "Witness Statement of Davood Irani," Iran Human Rights
Documentation Center (IHRDC), March 2, 2014, http://
www.iranhrdc.org/english/english/publications/witness-
testimony/1000000520-witness-statement-of-davood-irani.
html?print.

145. "Elam's Mission," http://www.elam.com/page/elams-mission.

146. "Discrimination and Intolerance in Iran's Textbooks," Freedom
House, not dated, https://freedomhouse.org/report/special-reports/
discrimination-and-intolerance-irans-textbooks.

147. Ten Years on Saudi Arabia's Textbooks Still Promote Religious
Violence, The Hudson Institute's Center for Religious Freedom,
2011, http://www.hudson.org/content/researchattachments/
attachment/931/sauditextbooks2011final.pdf.

148. "Friday Sermons in Saudi Mosques: Review and Analysis," Special
Report No.10, MEMRI, September 26, 2002, http://www.memri.
org/report/en/0/0/0/0/0/0/736.htm.

149. "Arab Media Reactions to Paris Terror Attacks—Part I: Arab Papers,
Columnists Claim West Is Now Paying the Price for Supporting
Terror," Special Dispatch No. 5937, MEMRI, January 19, 2015,
http://www.memri.org/report/en/0/0/0/0/0/0/8384.htm.

150. "Discrimination against Religious Minorities in IRAN,"
International Federation of Human Rights, Paris, France, August
2003, https://www.fidh.org/IMG/pdf/ir0108a.pdf.

151. "Egypt," 2013 Annual Report, United States Commission on

International Religious Freedom, http://www.uscirf.gov/sites/default/files/resources/2013%20USCIRF%20Annual%20Report%20(2).pdf, P. 54.

152. "Egypt," 2013 Annual Report, United States Commission on International Religious Freedom, http://www.uscirf.gov/sites/default/files/resources/2013%20USCIRF%20Annual%20Report%20(2).pdf, P. 51.

153. "Kuwait," 2013 Annual Report, United States Commission on International Religious Freedom, http://www.uscirf.gov/sites/default/files/resources/2013%20USCIRF%20Annual%20Report%20(2).pdf, p. 298.

154. Salim Mansur, "Death by Lashing: Saudi Arabia," June 11, 2015, http://www.gatestoneinstitute.org/5949/badawi-lashing-saudi-arabia.

155. "Contemporary Islamist Ideology Authorizing Genocidal Murder," Special Report No. 25, MEMRI, January 27, 2004, http://www.memri.org/report/en/0/0/0/0/0/0/1049.htm.

156. Contemporary Islamist Ideology Authorizing Genocidal Murder," MEMRI, Special Report No. 25, January 27, 2004, http://www.mcmri.org/report/en/0/0/0/0/0/0/1049.htm.

157. "Iran," 2013 Annual Report, United States Commission on International Religious Freedom, http://www.uscirf.gov/sites/default/files/resources/2013%20USCIRF%20Annual%20Report%20(2).pdf, p. 71.

158. "Iran," 2013 Annual Report, United States Commission on International Religious Freedom, http://www.uscirf.gov/sites/default/files/resources/2013%20USCIRF%20Annual%20Report%20(2).pdf, P. 76.

159. Eric Chen, "Chaldean Christian leader: ISIS 'Systematically Beheading' Children in Iraq," The Gospel Herald World, August 6, 2014, http://www.gospelherald.com/articles/52128/20140806/chaldean-christian-leader-isis-systematically-beheading-children-in-iraq.htm.

160. Global Militarization Index 2013: Rearmament in the Middle

East and Asia, November 6, 2013, http://m.reliefweb.int/report/613790/world/global-militarization-index-2013-rearmament-in-the-middle-east-and-asia.

161. "Saudi Deputy Minister Of Religious Affairs: 'Pakistan's Atomic Bomb Belongs to The World Of Islam'; Yemen's Houthi Rebels and Their Patrons Dream of Occupying Mecca And Medina," MEMRI, Special Dispatch No. 6066, June 5, 2015, http://memri.convio.net/site/R?i=0MakYzxuXdNHJv1S_h6HMA.

162. Reza Aslan, "The Christian Exodus," *Foreign Affairs*, September 11, 2013, http://www.foreignaffairs.com/articles/139917/reza-aslan/the-christian-exodus.

163. Anthony Cordesman, "The Underlying Causes of Stability and Unrest in the Middle East and North Africa: An Analytic Survey," August 21, 2013, http://csis.org/publication/underlying-causes-stability-and-unrest-middle-east-and-north-africa-analytic-survey-0.

164. John Alterman, "Religious Radicalism after the Arab Uprisings," CSIS, December 15, 2014, http://csis.org/publication/introduction-changing-geopolitical-landscape-0.

165. Ibid, p.1.

166. Ibid, p.2.

167. "Saudi Preacher Proves that the Earth Is Immobile," Why Evolution Is True, https://whyevolutionistrue.wordpress.com/2015/02/17/saudi-preacher-proves-that-the-earth-is-immobile/.

168. Anthony Cordesman, "The Underlying Causes of Stability and Unrest in the Middle East and North Africa: An Analytic Survey," August 21, 2013, http://csis.org/publication/underlying-causes-stability-and-unrest-middle-east-and-north-africa-analytic-survey-0.

169. Ibid.

170. Ibid.

171. "Fertility rate, total (births per woman)," The World Bank, http://data.worldbank.org/indicator/SP.DYN.TFRT.IN.

172. John McLaughlin, "The Great Powers in the Middle East," March 6, 2015, http://csis.org/publication/great-powers-new-middle-east.

173. "Golf," http://obamagolfcounter.com/.

174. Stoyan Zaimov, "Franklin Graham Says Obama's 'Sympathy to Islam' Will Lead to Christian and Jewish Persecution in America," *Christian Post*, March 3, 2015, http://www.christianpost.com/ news/franklin-graham-says-obamas-sympathy-to-islam-will-lead-to-christian-and-jewish-persecution-in-america-135010/#lveederpOp1vFubI.99.

175. Ibid.

176. Joseph Loconte, "Barack Obama's Toothless and Feckless Foreign Policy," *Observer*, August 13, 2014, http://observer.com/2014/08/ barack-obamas-toothless-and-feckless-foreign-policy/.

177. Jared Malsin, "Christians Mourn their Relatives Beheaded by ISIS," *Time*, February 23, 2015, http://time.com/3718470/ isis-copts-egypt/.

178. Harriet Alexander, "John Kerry and Bashar al-Assad dined in Damascus," *The Telegraph*, September 3, 2013, http://www. telegraph.co.uk/news/worldnews/middleeast/syria/10283045/ John-Kerry-and-Bashar-al-Assad-dined-in-Damascus.html.

179. Patrick Goodenough, "Syrian President Assad Regarded As a 'Reformer,' Clinton Says," *CNS News*, March 28, 2011, http://www.cnsnews.com/news/article/ syrian-president-assad-regarded-reformer-clinton-says.

180. Victor Davis Hanson, Five Military East Blunders, *National Review*, February 17, 2015, http://www.nationalreview.com/article/398698/ five-middle-east-blunders-victor-davis-hanson.

181. Barack Obama, "My Plan for Iraq," *New York Times*, July 14, 2008, http://www.nytimes.com/2008/07/14/opinion/14obama. html?_r=0.

182. Christopher Coughlin and Andrea Strickler, "Case Study: Skilled Procurement Ring Charged in Illegally Obtaining Goods for Iran," Institute for Science and International Security, May 5, 2015, http:// www.isis-online.org/uploads/isis-reports/documents/Skilled_ Procurement_Ring_Faratel_5May2015.pdf.

183. "Obama's Failed Nuclear Policy and Khamenei's Duplicity," FRONTPAGE MAG, February 17, 2015, http://www.frontpagemag.com/2015/majid-rafizadeh/obamas-failed-nuclear-policy-and-khameneis-duplicity/.

184. Bonnie Goodman, "US-Israel Crisis Reactions: Obama Official Calls Netanyahu Coward, Chickensh*t," *Examiner*, October 29, 2014, http://www.examiner.com/article/us-israel-crisis-reactions-obama-official-calls-netanyahu-coward-chickenshit.

185. Yann Le Guernigou, "Sarkozy Tells Obama Netanyahu Is a 'Liar'," *Reuters*, November 8, 2011, http://www.reuters.com/article/2011/11/08/us-mideast-netanyahu-sarkozy-idUSTRE7A720120111108.

186. "Alexandra Jaffe, "GOP Trgets Obama for Kosher Deli 'Random' Comments," CNN, February 11, 2015, http://www.cnn.com/2015/02/11/politics/obama-kosher-deli-random-comments/.

187. Gavriel Fiske, "Israel Said Willing to Give up 90% of West Bank," *The Times of Israel*, February 6, 2014, http://www.timesofisrael.com/israel-reportedly-ready-to-give-up-90-of-the-west-bank/.

188. Barack Obama, "Peace Is the Only Path to True Security for Israel and the Palestinians," *Haaretz*, July 8, 2014, http://www.haaretz.com/news/diplomacy-defense/israel-peace-conference/1.603324.

189. Joby Warrick, "In Yemen, Clinton Urges Social Reform," *The Washington Post*, January 12, 2011, http://www.washingtonpost.com/wp-dyn/content/article/2011/01/11/AR2011011107142.html.

190. Ted Cruz, "ICYMI: Sen. Cruz Op-Ed in *The Washington Times*: Yemen's Collapse Demonstrates Obama's Foreign Policy Failures," January 26, 2015, http://www.cruz.senate.gov/?p=press_release&id=2119.

191. Ibid.

192. "Yemen Crisis: Saudi Arabia 'Repels Houthi Border Attack'," *BBC*, May 1, 2015, http://www.bbc.com/news/world-middleMore%20than%201.

193. "Official Yemen News Agency Says Sanaa, Iran Sign Areement to

Open Direct Flight Routes," *Associated Press,* February 28, 2015, http://www.foxnews.com/world/2015/02/28/official-yemen-news-agency-says-sanaa-iran-sign-agreement-to-open-direct-flight/.

194. "Obama: Egypt's transition must begin now," *Associated Press*, February 2, 2011, http://www.ynetnews.com/articles/0,7340,L-4022658,00.html.

195. "Center Report Reveals Radical Islamist Views and Agenda of Senior State Department Official Huma Abedin's Mother," Center for Security Policy, July 22, 2012, http://www.centerforsecuritypolicy.org/2012/07/22/ties-that-bind/.

196. Adam Entous, Julian E. Barnes and Jay Solomon, "U.S. Pressure on Mubarak Opens a Rift With Arab Allies," *Wall Street Journal*, February 4, 2011, http://www.wsj.com/articles/SB10001424052748 70437610457612261082864 8254.

197. "Factbox: Egyptians Want More Islam in Politics: Poll," *Reuters*, February 2, 2011, http://www.reuters.com/article/2011/02/02/us-egypt-islam-poll-idUSTRE7116ND20110202.

198. Robert Tait, "Muslim Brotherhood: Radical Islamists Or Reluctant Democrats?," *Radio Liberty*, January 31, 2011, http://www.rferl.org/content/muslim_brotherhood_feature/2293237.html.

199. Barry Rubin, "The Region: The Declaration of War that Went Unnoticed," *Jerusalem Post*, October 10, 2010, http://www.jpost.com/Opinion/Columnists/The-Region-The-declaration-of-war-that-went-unnoticed.

200. An Overview of the Egyptian Muslim Brotherhood's Stance on U.S. and Jihad; Translation of Its Draft Political Platform, Special Dispatch No. 3556, MEMRI, February 3, 2011, http://consp77.tumblr.com/post/3090882820/an-overview-of-the-egyptian-muslim-brotherhoods.

201. Ibid.

202. Ibid.

203. Fiona McCallum, "Christian political participation in the Arab

world," Islam and Christian–Muslim Relations, Vol. 23, Issue 1, 2012, http://www.tandfonline.com/doi/abs/10.1080/09596410.2011.634593#.VQyRzY7F_ic.

204. "Council of Representatives of Iraq," Wikipedia, http://en.wikipedia.org/wiki/Council_of_Representatives_of_Iraq.

205. "Michel Aflaq," *New World Encyclopedia*, http://www.newworldencyclopedia.org/entry/Michel_Aflaq.

206. Christa Case Bryant, "What the Middle East Would Be Like without Christians," *Christian Science Monitor*, December 22, 2013, http://www.csmonitor.com/World/Middle-East/2013/1222/What-the-Middle-East-would-be-like-without-Christians.

207. "Assyrian Bishop on Why Christianity Is Vital to the Middle East," *Assyrian International News Agency*, September 13, 2014, http://aina.org/news/20140913003159.htm.

208. "What Is a 'Christian Culture?,'" The Twelve Tribes, quote from C.S. Lewis, *Mere Christianity*, cited in http://twelvetribes.org/articles/christian-culture.

209. "The Future of Christians in the Middle East: A View from the Holy Land," *Thinking Faith*, February 9, 2015, http://www.thinkingfaith.org/articles/future-christians-middle-east-view-holy-land#_edn3.

210. "Catholic Church and Health Care," Wikipedia, http://en.wikipedia.org/wiki/Catholic_Church_and_health_care.

211. "Catholic Church, Unresolved Issues," Wikipedia, http://en.wikipedia.org/wiki/Wikipedia:Catholic_Church/Unresolved_issues.

212. Christa Case Bryant, "What the Middle East would be like without Christians," *Christian Science Monitor*, December 22, 2013, http://www.csmonitor.com/World/Middle-East/2013/1222/What-the-Middle-East-would-be-like-without-Christians.

213. Ibid.

214. Francis J. Beckwith, "The Christian Citizen," Christian Research Institute, no date, http://www.equip.org/article/

the-christian-citizen/#christian-books-2.

215. "Collaboration," Holocaust Encyclopedia, U.S. Holocaust Memorial Museum, http://www.ushmm.org/wlc/en/article. php?ModuleId=10005466.

216. "New Order (Nazism)," Wikipedia, http://en.wikipedia.org/wiki/ New_Order_(Nazism).

217. "Germany: Establishment of the Nazi Dictatorship," Holocaust Encyclopedia, U.S. Holocaust Memorial Museum, http://www. ushmm.org/wlc/en/article.php?ModuleId=10005204.

218. "Heinrich Himmler," Holocaust Encyclopedia, U.S. Holocaust Memorial Museum, http://www.ushmm.org/wlc/en/article. php?ModuleId=10007407.

219. "Nazism and Occultism," Wikipedia, http://en.wikipedia.org/wiki/ Nazism_and_occultism.

220. "The Influence of the Occult on the 1939 German Expedition to Tibet," Tibet Talk, December 24, 2009, https://tibettalk.wordpress. com/2009/12/24/the-influence-of-the-occult-on-the-1939-german-expedition-to-tibet/.

221. "Heinrich Himmler," Holocaust Encyclopedia, U.S. Holocaust Memorial Museum, http://www.ushmm.org/wlc/en/article. php?ModuleId=10007407.

222. "World Watch List," Open Doors USA, https://www. opendoorsusa.org/christian-persecution/world-watch-list/.

223. "North Korea," "World Watch List," Open Doors USA, http:// www.opendoorsuk.org/persecution/worldwatch/north_korea. php.

224. Ibid.

225. "Final Solution," Holocaust Encyclopedia, U.S. Holocaust Memorial Museum, http://www.ushmm.org/wlc/en/article. php?ModuleId=10007328.

226. "Collaboration," Holocaust Encyclopedia, U.S. Holocaust Memorial Museum, http://www.ushmm.org/wlc/en/article. php?ModuleId=10005466.

227. "Persecution of Christians Reached Historic Levels in 2014. Will 2015 Be Worse?," *Religion News Service*, January 7, 2015, http://www.religionnews.com/2015/01/07/persecution-christians-reached-historic-levels-2014-will-2015-worse/.

228. Ibid.

229. "Antisemitism," Holocaust Encyclopedia, U.S. Holocaust Memorial Museum, http://www.ushmm.org/wlc/en/article.php?ModuleId=10005175.

230. "Middle Easterners See Religious and Ethnic Hatred as Top Global Threat," Pew Research Center, October 16, 2014, http://www.pewglobal.org/2014/10/16/middle-easterners-see-religious-and-ethnic-hatred-as-top-global-threat/.

231. Ibid.

232. Ibid.

233. "Nearly 150 Dead in Al-Shabaab School Attack, Kenyan Officials Say," *Fox News*, April 2, 2015, http://www.foxnews.com/world/2015/04/02/garissa-attack-kenya/.

234. "The United States and the Holocaust," Holocaust Encyclopedia, U.S. Holocaust Memorial Museum, http://www.ushmm.org/wlc/en/article.php?ModuleId=10005182.

235. Ibid.

236. "Never Again: Heeding the Warning Signs," Holocaust Encyclopedia, U.S. Holocaust Memorial Museum, http://www.ushmm.org/remember/days-of-remembrance/past-days-of-remembrance/2013-days-of-remembrance/2013-theme.

237. "Kristallnacht," Holocaust Encyclopedia, U.S. Holocaust Memorial Museum, http://www.ushmm.org/research/research-in-collections/search-the-collections/bibliography/kristallnacht.

238. "Apathy and Responsibility: The American Response to the Holocaust," Renaissance the Poet (blog), https://renaissancethepoet.wordpress.com/2015/02/06/apathy-and-responsibility-the-american-response-to-the-holocaust/.

239. Freda Kirchwey, "While the Jews Die," *Nation*, March 13, 1943. *American Views the Holocaust 1933-1945: A Brief Documentary History*, Edit. Robert H. Abzug (Boston: Bedford/St. Martin's, 1999), 152–155.

240. Telephonic interview with Matthew VanDyke, Founder, Sons of Liberty International, April 1, 2015.

241. "No More Christians in Mideast within 2 Years," *WorldNetDaily*, March 29, 2015, http://www.wnd.com/2015/03/no-more-christians-in-mideast-within-2-years/#zHdCQ96wuUMP2le0.99.

242. David Francis, "Obama Slaps Europe for Failing to Integrate Muslims," *Foreign Policy*, January 16, 2015, http://foreignpolicy.com/2015/01/16/obama-slaps-europe-for-failing-to-integrate-muslims/.

243. Ibid.

244. "Law Enforcement Warning Sent about American Youth," ISIS, March 5, 2015, *CBS* 6 TV, http://wtvr.com/2015/03/05/law-enforcement-warning-sent-about-american-youth-isis/.

245. Texas Cartoon Attack Exemplifies the Grassroots Threat, *STRATFOR*, May 4, 2015, https://www.stratfor.com/analysis/texas-cartoon-attack-exemplifies-grassroots-threat.

246. "ISIS Claim Responsibility for Shooting at Texas Muhammad Cartoon Contest," *Fox News*, May 5, 2015, http://www.foxnews.com/world/2015/05/05/isis-claim-responsibility-for-shooting-at-texas-muhammad-cartoon-contest/.

247. "Deceiving the Public," Holocaust Encyclopedia, U.S. Holocaust Memorial Museum, http://www.ushmm.org/wlc/en/article.php?ModuleId=10007822.

248. Ibid.

249. Michael Chapman, "Rev. Graham: Obama, Holder Pushing a 'New Morality That Does Not Include God'—'An Anti-Christ Movement'," *CNS News*, March 11, 2015, http://cnsnews.com/news/article/michael-w-chapman/rev-graham-obama-holder-

pushing-new-morality-does-not-include-god.

250. Telephonic interview with former Congressman Frank Wolf, March 31, 2015.

251. "Britain's War on Christianity: America's Future Fight?," *CBN News*, September 17, 2013, http://www.cbn.com/cbnnews/world/2009/July/Britains-War-on-Christianity-Americas-Future-Fight/?Print=true.

252. John Hawkins, "7 Examples of Discrimination against Christians in America," *Townhall*, September 17, 2013, http://townhall.com/columnists/johnhawkins/2013/09/17/7-examples-of-discrimination-against-christians-in-america-n1701966/page/full.

253. "72 Virgins," http://wikiislam.net/wiki/72_Virgins. "It was reported in the hadeeth of al-Miqdaam ibn Ma'di Karb that the Prophet (peace and blessings of Allaah be upon him) said: 'The martyr (shaheed) has seven blessings from Allaah: he is forgiven from the moment his blood is first shed; he will be shown his place in Paradise; he will be spared the trial of the grave; and he will be secure on the Day of the Greatest Terror (the Day of Judgement); there will be placed on his head a crown of dignity, one ruby of which is better than this world and all that is in it; he will be married to seventy-two of al-hoor al-'iyn; and he will be permitted to intercede for seventy of his relatives.' According to another report, the martyr has six blessings from Allaah. According to other reports (the number is) six, or nine, or ten—Narrated by al-Tirmidhi, who said it is a *hasan hadeeth*. Also narrated by Ibn Maajah in al-Sunan, by Ahmad, by 'Abd al-Razzaaq in al-Musannaf, by al-Tabaraani in al-Kabeer, and by Sa'eed ibn Mansoor in al-Sunan."

254. Arie W. Kruglanski et al, "Terrorism—A (Self) Love Story: Redirecting the Significance Quest Can End Violence," *American Psychologist*, Vol. 68, No. 7, October 2013, 559-575, http://www.google.com/url?sa=t&rct=j&q=&esrc=s&frm=1&source=

web&cd=1&ved=0CB4QFjAA&url=http%3A%21%2Fwww.
researchgate.net%2Fprofile%2FJocelyn_Belanger%2Fpublicatio
n%2F257837729_Terrorism-A_%2528self%2529_love_story_
Redirecting_the_significance_quest_can_end_violence%2Flinks%2F0
0463527fe1a79161c000000.pdf&ei=2LRDVbPbGoHcgwTAzYG4A
w&usg=AFQjCNE2UWQdkSeqeQIBvaQOZ4Y3172NVQ&bvm=
bv.92189499,d.eXY.

255. Neal Horsley, "How Las Vegas Fueled the 9/11 Bombers," *Christian
    Gallery News Service*, July 4, 2004, http://www.christiangallery.com/
    LeavingLasVegas.htm.

256. Kasra Naji, *Ahmadinejad: The Secret History of Iran's Radical Leader*
    (Los Angeles: University of California Press, 2008), 144.

257. Iranian Ayatollah Khamenei https://twitter.com/khamenei_ir/
    status/22815824658.

258. Greg Tepper, "Israel a 'cancerous tumor' and Middle East's
    biggest problem, Iranian supreme leader, says'," *The Times
    of Israel*, August 19, 2012, http://www.timesofisrael.com/
    khamenei-israeli-a-malignant-zionist-tumor/#!.

259. Walter McKenzie, "Understanding Taqiyya—Islamic Principle of
    Lying for the Sake of Allah," Islam Watch, April 30, 2007, http://
    www.islam-watch.org/Warner/Taqiyya-Islamic-Principle-Lying-for-
    Allah.htm.

260. Joel C. Rosenberg's Blog, https://flashtrafficblog.wordpress.
    com/2015/02/23/what-does-isis-want-to-usher-in-the-end-of-days-
    heres-the-short-version-must-read-article-in-the-atlantic/2/23/2015.

261. Graeme Wood, "What ISIS Really Wants," *The Atlantic*, March
    2015, http://www.theatlantic.com/features/archive/2015/02/
    what-isis-really-wants/384980/.

262. Bill Warner, editor, *The Islamic Trilogy*, Vol. 2, *The Political Traditions
    of Mohammed, The Hadith for the Unbelievers*, (Center for the Study
    of Political Islam, 2006) p. X.

263. Sahih-Muslim Hadith, Vol. 41, Chap. 9, Hadith 6924, per Abu
    Huraira from Quran/ Hadith study site: The Only Quran.

264. "Why Islamic State Chose Town of Dabiq for Propaganda," *BBC*, November 17, 2014, http://www.bbc.com/news/world-middle-east-30083303.

265. Graeme Wood, "What ISIS Really Wants," *The Atlantic*, March 2015, http://www.theatlantic.com/features/archive/2015/02/what-isis-really-wants/384980/.

266. David Reagan, "What Are the End-Time Prophecies of Islam?," Information from: Lamb & Lion Ministries, not dated, http://www.lamblion.com/articles/articles_islam2.php.

267. "Doctrine for the Armed Forces of the United States," Joint Publication 1, U.S. Department of Defense, March 25, 2013, p. I-11, http://www.dtic.mil/doctrine/new_pubs/jp1.pdf.

268. "The Meaning of Islam," http://www.barghouti.com/islam/meaning.html.

269. William Wilberforce (1759 - 1833), *BBC*, http://www.bbc.co.uk/history/historic_figures/wilberforce_william.shtml.

270. Ibid.

271. "William Wilberforce (1759–1833): The Politician, The Abolition Project," http://abolition.e2bn.org/people_24.html.

272. William Wilberforce (1759–1833), *BBC*, http://www.bbc.co.uk/history/historic_figures/wilberforce_william.shtml.

273. Dietrich Bonhoeffer, Christian History, August 8, 2008, http://www.christianitytoday.com/global/printer.html?/ch/131christians/martyrs/bonhoeffer.html.

274. Ibid.

275. Dietrich Bonhoeffer, Jewish Virtual Library, https://www.jewishvirtuallibrary.org/jsource/biography/Bonhoeffer.html.

276. "Dietrich Bonhoeffer Biography," Biography Online, http://www.biographyonline.net/spiritual/dietrich-bonhoeffer.html.

277. Dietrich Bonhoeffer, *Ethics, Touchstone Books*, http://www.amazon.com/Ethics-Dietrich-Bonhoeffer/dp/068481501X.

278. Ibid.

279. Martin Luther King Jr., Letter from Birmingham Jail, August 1963, http://www.uscrossier.org/pullias/wp-content/uploads/2012/06/king.pdf.

280. Ibid.

281. Interview conducted with "anonymous" on April 8, 2015.

282. Sun Tzu, Brainyquote, http://www.brainyquote.com/quotes/authors/s/sun_tzu.html#0QPMCEi7bWUztwld.99.

283. Dylan Stableford, "Dzhokhar Tsarnaev's Mother: 'My Sons Are Innocent'," *Yahoo News*, April 9, 2015, http://news.yahoo.com/tsarnaev-mother-statement-guilty-verdict-boston-marathon-bombing-trial-172613856.html.

284. Nicolai Sennls, "Muslims and Westerners: The Psychological Differences," New English Review, May 2010, http://www.newenglishreview.org/Nicolai_Sennels/Muslims_and_Westerners%3A__The_Psychological_Differences/.

285. Email response received from Nicolai Sennels [nicolaisennels@gmail.com] on April 11, 2015.

286. From *Silenced* by Paul Marshall and Nina Shea, p.xvii, as cited in http://www.religiousfreedomcoalition.org/2013/02/07/Is-violence-a-sign-of-islams-strength-or-its-weakness/.

287. "Logistics Quotations," WWW Virtual Library: Logistics, http://www.logisticsworld.com/logistics/quotations.htm.

288. Cal Thomas, Helping Iraqi Christians, Tribune Content Agency, LLC, October 27, 2014, http://calthomas.com/columns/helping-iraqi-christians.

289. "Middle East," Refugees International, http://refugeesinternational.org/where-we-work/middle-east.

290. Ibid.

291. The Plight of Christians in the Middle East, Center for American Progress, March 12, 2015, https://www.americanprogress.org/events/2015/03/06/108083/the-plight-of-christians-in-the-middle-east/.

292. "Middle East," UNHCR, April 2015, http://www.unhcr. org/5461e6068.html.

293. Jonah 1, NIV, https://www.biblegateway.com/ passage/?search=Jonah+1.

294. "Counterinsurgency," Field Manual 3-24, U.S. Army, December 15, 2006, http://usacac.army.mil/cac2/Repository/Materials/ COIN-FM3-24.pdf.

295. Nour Malas, "Iraq's Christians Take Up Arms to Fight Islamic State," *Wall Street Journal*, February 3, 2015, http://www.wsj.com/articles/ iraqs-christians-take-up-arms-to-fight-islamic-state-1423017266.

296. Senior staff member for the U.S. House of Representatives Armed Services Committee via email on May 7, 2015.

297. Missy Ryan, "Obama Administration Seeks to Alter Bill That Has Caused Fror in Iraq," *The WashingtonPost*, May 6, 2015, http://www. washingtonpost.com/world/national-security/obama-administration- seeks-to-alter-bill-that-has-caused-furor-in-iraq/2015/05/06/ db8c71c4-f404-11e4-84a6-6d7c67c50db0_story.html.

298. Ibid.

299. "UK Urged to Provide Syrian Christians with Arms," *Middle East Monitor*, March 12, 2015, https://www.middleeastmonitor.com/ news/middle-east/17476-uk-urged-to-provide-syrian-christians- with-arms.

300. "Christians Arm as Middle East Perils Mount,"*Fox News*, September 5, 2014, http://www.foxnews.com/world/2014/09/05/ christians-arm-as-middle-east-perils-mount/.

301. Strategic Communications, Cyberspace & Information Operations Study Center, Air University Library, http://www.au.af.mil/info-ops/ strategic.htm.

302. "Information Operations," Joint Publication 3-13, Joint Staff, U.S. Department of Defense, November 20, 2014, http://www.dtic.mil/ doctrine/new_pubs/jp3_13.pdf.

303. Interview with Tom Doyle via telephone on March 25, 2015.

304. Muslim 'refugees' throw Christians overboard in Mediterranean crossing, Refugee Settlement Watch, April 17, 2015, https://refugeeresettlementwatch.wordpress.com/category/christian-refugees/.

305. "Documents required to obtain a visa," Holocaust Encyclopedia, U.S. Holocaust Memorial Museum, http://www.ushmm.org/wlc/en/article.php?ModuleId=10007456.

306. The Religious Affiliation of U.S. Immigrants: Majority Christian, Rising Share of Other Faiths, Pew Research Center, May 17, 2013, http://www.pewforum.org/2013/05/17/the-religious-affiliation-of-us-immigrants/#affiliation.

307. "What Was the Underground Railroad?", Maryland Public Television, 2015, http://pathways.thinkport.org/about/about1.cfm.

308. "The Citizen in de Tocqueville's America," Constitutional Rights Foundation, not dated, http://www.crf-usa.org/election-central/de-tocqueville-america.html.

309. Ibid.

310. Alexis De Tocqueville, *Democracy in America*, Edited by Eduardo Nolla, Translated from the French by James Schleifer, Liberty Fund Inc., Indianapolis, Indiana, http://classiques.uqac.ca/classiques/De_tocqueville_alexis/democracy_in_america_historical_critical_ed/democracy_in_america_vol_2.pdf, p. 572.

311. "The Citizen in de Tocqueville's America," Constitutional Rights Foundation, http://www.crf-usa.org/election-central/de-tocqueville-america.html.

312. Alexis De Tocqueville, *Democracy in America*, Edited by Eduardo Nolla, Translated for the French by James Schleifer, Liberty Fund Inc., Indianapolis, Indiana, http://classiques.uqac.ca/classiques/De_tocqueville_alexis/democracy_in_america_historical_critical_ed/democracy_in_america_vol_2.pdf.

313. Ibid., p. 467.

314. "Alexis de Tocqueville," Liberal International, http://www.liberal-

international.org/editorial.asp?ia_id=681.

315. "A Knock at Midnight," Martin Luther King Jr. and the Global Freedom Struggle, June 11, 1967, http://mlk-kpp01. stanford.edu/index.php/encyclopedia/documentsentry/ doc_a_knock_at_midnight/.

316. Richard Doster, "Politics: Why Christians Must Be Involved," byFaith, November 4, 2014, http://byfaithonline.com/ politics-why-christians-must-be-involved-2/.

317. Ibid.

318. Michael Chapman, "Vatican Chief Justice: Obama's Policies 'Progressively More Hostile Toward Christian Civilization'," *CNS News*, March 21, 2014, http:// www.cnsnews.com/news/article/michael-w-chapman/ vatican-chief-justice-obama-s-policies-progressively-more-hostile.

319. Interview with LTG Boykin via telephone, April 14, 2015.

320. Foreign Military Sales Act of 1968, Pub.L. 90–629, 82 Stat.1320-2, enacted October 22, 1968.

321. "Convention on the Prevention and Punishment of the Crime of Genocide," Adopted by the General Assembly of the United Nations, December 9, 1948, https://treaties.un.org/doc/ Publication/UNTS/Volume%2078/volume-78-I-1021-English. pdf.

322. Ibid.

323. Emily Backes, "On This Day: U.S. Fully Adopts Genocide Convention," Enough, November 4, 2010, http://www. enoughproject.org/blogs/day-us-ratifies-genocide-convention.

324. "Text Of Clinton's Rwanda Speech," *CBS News*, March 25, 1998, http://www.cbsnews.com/news/text-of-clintons-rwanda-speech/.

325. "Read Draft ISIS War Authorization Bill," *The Hill*, February 11, 2015, http://thehill.com/policy/ defense/232435-read-draft-isis-war-authorization-legislation.

326. The International Religious Freedom Act of 1998, 150th Congress, http://www.state.gov/documents/organization/2297.pdf.

327. State Department law—Section 620M of the Foreign Assistance Act of 1961 (22 U.S.C. § 2378d), last amended by section 7034(l) of Public Law 113-76; Defense Department law - 10 U.S.C. § 2249e, as added by section 1204 of Public Law 113-291; see also section 8059 of Public Law 113-235.

328. Dana Ford, Salma Abdelaziz and Ian Le, "Egypt's President Calls for a 'Religious revolution'," *CNN*, January 6, 2015, http://www.cnn.com/2015/01/06/africa/egypt-president-speech/.

329. Ibid.

330. Robert Spenser, "The Implications of the Dismissal of Stephen Coughlin," Joint Staff, Pentagon, Jihad Watch, January 12, 2008, http://www.jihadwatch.org/2008/01/the-implications-of-the-dismissal-of-stephen-coughlin-joint-staff-pentagon.

331. "Questions for the Pentagon: Who is Hesham Islam?," Foundation for Defense of Democracies, April 30, 2015, http://www.defenddemocracy.org/media-hit/questions-for-the-pentagon-who-is-hesham-islam/

332. Ibid.

333. Stephen Collins Coughlin, "To Our Great Detriment": Ignoring What Extremists Say About Jihad, thesis, Abstract National Defense Intelligence College, July 2007.

334. "President Obama: 'We Will Degrade and Ultimately Destroy ISIL'," The White House Blog, September 10, 2014, https://www.whitehouse.gov/blog/2014/09/10/president-obama-we-will-degrade-and-ultimately-destroy-isil.

335. Lally Weymouth, "Egyptian President Abdel Fatah al-Sissi, Who Talks to Netanyahu 'a lot,' Says His Country Is in Danger of Collapse," *Washington Post*, March 12, 2015, http://www.washingtonpost.com/opinions/egypts-president-says-he-talks-to-netanyahu-a-lot/2015/03/12/770ef928-c827-11e4-aa1a-86135599fb0f_story.html.

336. Jennifer Agiesta, "*CNN*/ORC poll: ISIS a bigger threat than Iran, Russia," *CNN*, April 22, 2015, http://www.cnn.com/2015/04/22/politics/cnn-orc-poll-isis-iran-russia/index.html.

337. "Broad Backing for Air Strikes on ISIS; Less for US Forces as Advisers in Iraq," ABC News, October 1, 2014, http://abcnews. go.com/blogs/politics/2014/10/broad-backing-for-air-strikes-on-isis-less-for-u-s-forces-as-advisers-in-iraq/.

338. Growing Concerns about ISIS, *CBS News* Poll, February 19, 2015, http://www.realclearpolitics.com/docs/2015/CBS_021915.pdf.

339. "Growing Concern about Rise of Islamic Extremism at Home and Abroad," Pew Research Center, September 10, 2014, http://www. people-press.org/2014/09/10/growing-concern-about-rise-of-islamic-extremism-at-home-and-abroad/.

340. Justin McCarthy, Americans Split on Defense Spending, Gallup, February 20, 2015, http://www.gallup.com/poll/181628/americans-split-defense-spending.aspx.

341. William Galston, "The American People to its Leaders: Ground Troops against ISIS and a Stronger National defense," Brookings, February 20, 2015, http://www.brookings.edu/blogs/fixgov/posts/2015/02/20-isis-national-defense-galston.

342. Soeren Kern, "British Home Secretary to Islamic Extremists: 'The Game is Up'," Gatestone Institute, April 2, 2015, http://www. gatestoneinstitute.org/5479/britain-islamic-extremists.

343. Luke Hurst, "'The Game Is Up' for Extremists in Britain, Says Home Secretary," *Newsweek*, March 23, 2015, http://www.newsweek.com/game-extremists-britain-says-home-secretary-316071.

344. Frank Wolf telephonic interview March 31, 2015.

345. William Boykin telephonic interview April 14, 2015.

346. David Curry telephonic interview April 9, 2015.

347. Faith McDonnell telephonic interview April 20, 2015.

348. Autaro Garcia, "Fox Contributor Pastor Robert Jeffress tells O'Reilly: 'Islam Is a False Religion'," *Rawstory*, October 24, 2014, http://www. rawstory.com/2014/10/fox-contributor-pastor-robert-jeffress-tells-oreilly-islam-is-a-false-religion/.

349. Travis Weber telephonic interview April 16, 2015.

350. Thomas Farr telephonic interview April 8, 2015.

351. "Muslim Colonization Of America: The Hijra And The Hijacking Of America's Refugee Resettlement Program," Religious Freedom Coalition, April 22, 2015, http://www.religiousfreedomcoalition. org/2015/04/22/muslim-colonization-of-america-the-hijra-and-the-hijacking-of-americas-refugee-resettlement-program/.

352. Sam Solomon and E Al Maqdisi, *Modern Day Trojan Horse: The Islamic Doctrine of Immigration* (Charlottesville, VA: ANM Publishers), 10.

353. As cited in "Refugee Resettlement and the Hijra to America," published by the Center for Security Policy Press, http://www. centerforsecuritypolicy.org/wp-content/uploads/2015/04/ Refugee_Resettlement_Hijra.pdf.

354. "The Religious Affiliation of U.S. Immigrants: Majority Christian, Rising Share of Other Faiths," Pew Research Center, May 17, 2013, http://www.pewforum.org/2013/05/1// the-religious-affiliation-of-us-immigrants/#affiliation.

355. "Fertility Rate, total (births per woman)," The World Bank, http:// data.worldbank.org/indicator/SP.DYN.TFRT.IN.

356. Anne Corcoran, "Refugee Resettlement and the Hijra to America," monograph published by Center for Security Policy, April 20, 2015, http://www.centerforsecuritypolicy.org/2015/04/20/ refugee-resettlement-and-the-hijra-to-america/.

357. Tom Doyle interview via telephone March 25, 2015.

358. Georges Houssney, "Factors leading to conversion of Muslims to Christ," Biblical Missiology, April 8, 2013, http://biblicalmissiology. org/2013/04/08/factors-leading-to-conversion-of-muslims-to-christ/.

359. "Witnessing to Muslims," Christian Soldiers Ministries was granted permission to post this article by the Christian Research Institute, CRI, P.O. Box 7000, Rancho Santa Margarita, CA 92688, http:// www.cbn.com/spirituallife/onlinediscipleship/understandingislam/ Witnessing_to_Muslims.aspx.

360. Amir Taheri, "France, the West and the Islamist Challenge,"

Gatestone Institute, April 7, 201, http://www.gatestoneinstitute.
org/5511/france-the-west-and-the-islamist-challenge.

361. Ayaan Hirsi Ali, "Why Islam Needs Reform," *Wall
Street Journal*, March 20, 2015, http://www.wsj.com/
articles/a-reformation-for-islam-1426859626.

362. Pamela Geller, "Colorado High School Students Say Pledge
In Arabic: 'One Nation Under Allah'," http://pamelageller.
com/2014/04/colorado-high-school-students-say-pledge-arabic-
one-nation-allah.html/.

363. "Arabic version of Pledge of Allegiance at Pine Bush High School
Ignites Furor," *Times-Herald Record*, March 18, 2015, http://www.
recordonline.com/article/20150318/NEWS/150319327.

364. Pamella Geller, "'One Nation Under Allah': The Islamization
of American Public Schools," *Breitbar*, April 29, 2014,
http://www.breitbart.com/big-government/2014/04/29/
the-islamization-of-american-public-schools/.

365. Ibid.

366. Anne Steele, "Why a Marine Dad Was Banned from His Daughter's
School for Objecting to Islam Essay," *Christian Science Monitor*,
October 30, 2014, http://www.csmonitor.com/USA/USA-
Update/2014/1030/Why-a-Marine-dad-was-banned-from-his-
daughter-s-school-for-objecting-to-Islam-essay.

367. Todd Starnes, "Does High School Textbook Have Islamic Bias?,"
Fox News, July 29, 2013, http://radio.foxnews.com/toddstarnes/top-
stories/does-high-school-textbook-have-islamic-bias.html.

368. Pamella Geller, "'One Nation Under Allah': The Islamization
of American Public Schools," *Breitbar*, April 29, 2014,
http://www.breitbart.com/big-government/2014/04/29/
the-islamization-of-american-public-schools/.

369. Ibid.

370. Stanley Kurtz, "Saudi in the Classroom," *National Review*, July
25, 2007, http://www.nationalreview.com/article/221607/
saudi-classroom-stanley-kurtz.

371. Adapted from ""Saudi in the Classroom," by Stanley Kurtz (July 25, 2007) and cited in "Saudi and Arab Influence on American Education," discoverthenetworks.org, http://www.discoverthenetworks.org/viewSubCategory.asp?id=213.

372. Ibid.

373. "A Citizen's Guide to Islamist Curricula in Our Public Schools," Stop the Madrassa, https://stopthemadrassa.wordpress.com/about/a-citizen%E2%80%99s-guide-to-islamist-curricula-in-our-public-schools/.

374. Joseph Abrams, "Group That Funded Rep. Ellison's Pilgrimage to Mecca Called a Front for Extremism," *Fox News*, January 8, 2009, http://www.foxnews.com/politics/2009/01/08/group-funded-rep-ellisons-pilgrimage-mecca-called-extremism/.

375. "Special Report: The Council on American Islamic Relations," The Clarion Project, http://www.clarionproject.org/sites/default/files/CAIR Council-on-American-Islamic-Relations-factsheet.pdf.

376. Chuck Ross, "United Arab Emirates Designates Two American Muslim Groups As Terrorist Orgs," *The Daily Calling*, November 15, 2014, http://dailycaller.com/2014/11/15/united-arab-emirates-designates-two-american-muslim-groups-as-terrorist-orgs/.

377. Georges Houssney interviewed by telephone on April 23, 2015.

378. "The Muslim Brotherhood," The Investigative Project on Terrorism, http://www.investigativeproject.org/profile/173.

379. Soeren Kern, "UK: Sharia Courts Abusing Muslim Women," Gatestone Institute, April 8, 2015, http://www.gatestoneinstitute.org/5512/sharia-courts-muslim-women.

380. Tim Brown, "Texas Mayor Blasts Islamists' Sharia Law Controversy: I Will Not Be Deterred," Sons of Liberty Media, April 17, 2015, http://sonsoflibertymedia.com/2015/04/texas-mayor-blasts-islamists-sharia-law-controversy-i-will-not-be-deterred/.

381. Kevin Johnson, "FBI Director Says Islamic State Influence Growing in US," *USA Today*, May 7, 2015, http://www.usatoday.com/story/news/nation/2015/05/07/isis-attacks-us/70945534/.

382. Leslie Stahl, Homeland Security, *60 Minutes*, *CBS News*, April 5, 2015, http://www.cbsnews.com/news/ homeland-security-jeh-johnson-60-minutes-lesley-stahl/.

383. "Recent Arrests Confirm Jihadist Trends," STRATFOR, April 2, 2015, https://www.stratfor.com/weekly/ recent-arrests-confirm-jihadist-trends.

384. John Bacon, "Ohio Man Accused of Planning U.S. Terror Strike," *USA Today*, April 16, 2015, http:// www.usatoday.com/story/news/nation/2015/04/16/ ohio-indicted-islamic-state-terrorism/25879443/.

385. Mary Anne Weaver, "Her Majesty's Jihadists," *The New York Times Magazine*, April 19, 2015, http://www.nytimes.com/2015/04/19/ magazine/her-majestys-jihadists.html?ref=world&_r=1.

386. Ibid.

387. Erick Stakelbech, "Radicalized: ISIS Propaganda Attracting American Youth," *CBN News*, December 16, 2014, http://www.cbn.com/cbnnews/us/2014/December/ Radicalized-ISIS-Propaganda-Attracting-American-Youth/.

388. Duncan Mirri, "Kenyan University Students March to Demand Security after Garissa," *Reuters*, April 7, 2015, http://www.reuters.com/article/2015/04/07/ us-kenya-security-idUSKBN0MY1HF20150407.

389. Erick Stakelbeck, "Radicalized: ISIS Propaganda Attracting American Youth," *Christian Broadcasting Network*, not dated, http://www1. cbn.com/radicalized-isis-propaganda-attracting-american-youth.

390. Greg Hannah, Lindsay Clutterbuck, Jennifer Rubin, "Radicalization or Rehabilitation," RAND Corporation Technical Report, 2008, http://www.rand.org/content/dam/rand/pubs/technical_ reports/2008/RAND_TR571.pdf, p.x.

391. Ibid. , p.x.

392. "Radical Islam and U.S./European Prisons," discoverthenetworks. org, Adapted, in part, from "The Jihadi Virus in Our Jails," by Michelle Malkin (May 22, 2009); and "Jailhouse

Jihad," by Robert Spencer (May 28, 2009), http://www. discoverthenetworks.org/viewSubCategory.asp?id=104.

393. "Black America, Prisons and Radical Islam," Center for Islamic Pluralism, September 2008, http://www.islamicpluralism.org/ documents/black-america-prisons-radical-islam.pdf, p.7.

394. "Radical Islam and U.S./European Prisons," discoverthenetworks. org, Adapted, in part, from "The Jihadi Virus in Our Jails," by Michelle Malkin (May 22, 2009); and "Jailhouse Jihad," by Robert Spencer (May 28, 2009). http://www. discoverthenetworks.org/viewSubCategory.asp?id=104.

395. "Black America, Prisons and Radical Islam," Center for Islamic Pluralism, September 2008, http://www.islamicpluralism.org/ documents/black-america-prisons-radical-islam.pdf.

396. Jessica Vrazilek, "Islam in the Big House," *Weekly Standard*, April 24, 2006, http://www.cbsnews.com/news/islam-in-the-big-house/.

397. Ibid.

398. Robert Spenser, Jailhouse Jihad, discoverthenetworks.org, May 28, 2009, http://www.discoverthenetworks.org/Articles/Jailhouse%20 Jihad2.html.

399. Paul Barrett, "How a Muslim Chaplain Spread Extremism to an Inmate Flock," *Wall Street Journal*, February 5, 2003, http://www. wsj.com/articles/SB104439509371468I453.

400. Ibid.

401. Ibid.

402. "Radical Islam and U.S./European Prisons," discoverthenetworks. org, Adapted, in part, from "The Jihadi Virus in Our Jails," by Michelle Malkin (May 22, 2009); and "Jailhouse Jihad," by Robert Spencer (May 28, 2009), http://www. discoverthenetworks.org/viewSubCategory.asp?id=104.

403. Mark Earley, "A Little Saudi Kingdom behind Prison Walls," Breakpoint.org, August 17, 2006, http://www.breakpoint.org/ commentaries/5402-a-little-saudi-kingdom-behind-prison-walls.

404. "World's Muslim population more widespread than you might think," Pew Research Center, June 7, 2013,

http://www.pewresearch.org/fact-tank/2013/06/07/
worlds-muslim-population-more-widespread-than-you-might-think/.

405. Jonathan Cahn, "Rabbi Jonathan Cahn Addresses United Nations About Christian 'Holocaust'," *Charisma News*, April 17, 2015, http://www.charismanews.com/world/49251-rabbi-jonathan-cahn-addresses-united-nations-about-christian-holocaust.

406. Wayne Jackson, "How Many Prophecies Are in the Bible?," http://webcache.googleusercontent.com/search?q=cache:zIUPFzNysP8J:https://www.christiancourier.com/articles/318-how-many-prophecies-are-in-the-bible&hl=en&gl=us&strip=1.